MX 0709772 7

AF443381

Global News Production

Lisbeth Clausen

Global News Production

Copenhagen Business School Press
2003

Global News Production

© Copenhagen Business School Press
Printed in Denmark
1. edition 2003

ISBN 87-630-0110-1

Site	MIDDLESEX UNIVERSITY LIBRARY
TP	
Accession No.	0709772
Class No.	070.4332 CLA
Special Collection	✓

Distribution

Scandinavia
Djoef/DBK, Siljangade 2-8, P.O. Box 1731
DK-2300 Copenhagen S, Denmark
Phone: +45 3269 7788, fax: +45 3269 7789

North America
Copenhagen Business School Press
Books International Inc.
P.O. Box 605
Herndon, VA 20172-0605, USA
Phone: +1 703 661 1500, fax: +1 703 661 1501

Rest of the World
Marston Book Services, P.O. Box 269
Abingdon, Oxfordshire, OX14 4YN, UK
Phone: +44 (0) 1235 465500, fax: +44 (0) 1235 465555
E-mail Direct Customers: direct.order@marston.co.uk
E-mail Booksellers: trade.order@marston.co.uk

All rights reserved. No part of this publication may be reproduced or used in any form or by any means – graphic, electronic or mechanical including photocopying, recording, taping or information storage or retrieval systems – without permission in writing from Copenhagen Business School Press at www.cbspress.dk

Preface and acknowledgements

I first became interested in studying social processes in international news communication when I was working with national TV production crews in Japan. As the manager of the Danish Garden at the International Exposition in Osaka in 1991, I had the opportunity to participate in numerous TV programs and I became particularly fascinated with the work processes of the news production crews who under great time pressure were able to collect information, take pictures, make interviews and present stories from the Exposition on air as national news that same evening.

As part of the "International News Flow in the 1990s" research project at Copenhagen University in 1995, I again became interested in studying the production processes behind news output. Watching and coding hours of international news programs for statistical purposes made me curious about the production processes. I wanted to learn more about how international stories are combined through visuals and texts and I was particularly interested in exploring how foreign correspondents who work under time pressure are able to communicate complex political and economic stories to their home audiences. Hence the focus of the study became the communication strategies and decision-making processes in global news production.

I was a research fellow at Keio University, from May 1996 through November 1997, and worked for one and a half-year to set up and complete the research project. I made observation at the Public Service Station NHK and the commercial station TV Asahi and visited the newsrooms of the commercial stations TBS, FUJI, and NTV. The observations in the newsrooms and numerous informal interviews with news producers became the basis for my understanding of their work-processes. The informal interviews and information gathered through observations were formalised through tape-recorded interviews towards the end of my stay. The in-depth interviews with executive managers, producers, anchors, foreign correspondents and scriptwriters amounted to more than 40 and form the basic material for this book. The research set-up is described in Appendix Four.

In the following I would like to pay tribute to the many individuals who have contributed to the set-up and follow-through of this project. Without their professional and personal help, feedback and inspiration this book would not have been possible.

The book is a rewriting of my Ph. D. Dissertation: *The 'Domestication' of International News. A study of Japanese TV Production.* In the rewriting I have incorporated advice from the Ph.D. Assessment Committee members Peter Kjær, Simon Cottle and Charles Tackney whom I thank for their thorough assessment. An article which summarises the main findings of the research entitled "Localising the Global. 'Domestication' Processes in the Production of International News" is forthcoming in *Media, Culture and Society* by Sage Publications.

I thank the Danish Research Council for financing the research and Sam K. Steffensen for 'headhunting' me to the project at the Department of Intercultural Communication and Management at Copenhagen Business School. I am grateful to my colleagues and Head of Department, Sven Bislev who provided exceptionally good working conditions. I thank the administrative staff for their support at all times.

I would like to pay tribute to my academic advisor Stig Hjarvard for the initial inspiration to do newsroom studies, for helping me tighten up my arguments, and for involving me in the *Global Media Cultures* project at Copenhagen University. I thank

Peter Wad for encouragement throughout and Brian Moeran for detailed comments on early drafts of chapters.

I thank Ito Youichi whose introductions enabled the newsroom studies and interviews in Japan and who included me in the *International News Flow Studies* at Keio University as a Research Fellow. I thank my Keio seminar students and members of the team for translating and contributing to the initial analyses of the News Flow material.

I am grateful to Mr. Hattori and Ms. Hara at the NHK Broadcasting Culture Research Institute for their helpful advice on doing research in Japan and for their valuable introductions to executive staff at the national broadcast stations and prominent media personalities. I thank the honorary members of the Japan National Press Club, Asahi journalist Matsuyama Yukio and specialist on broadcast media, Omori Yukio, for their insights.

I am indebted to the executive managers of international political news production who contributed with information about the state of affairs in current news production in Japan: Bruce Dunning at CBS, Hiramoto Kazuo at TBS, Oto Hiroshi at Fuji TV, Mayama Yuichi and Morishige Kyousuke at NTV.

At NHK, I am grateful to Ohnuki Yasuo for the initial introduction and support of the project and Wada Ikuo for granting observation 'ad libitum' in the international newsroom. I also thank the staff from foreign correspondents, editors to scriptwriters for their participation in interviews and willingness to explain their work during the months of observation. They include Mr Morohoshi, Mr Wada, Ms Komiyama, Mr Sunohara, Mr Yanigizawa, Mr Hayashi, Mr Matsudate, Mr Tanaka, Mr Ikeda, Mr Matsuyama, Mr Tajima, Mr On, Mr Yamamoto, Mr Tsukamoto, Mr Koide, Mr Murada, Mr Tabata and Mr Maeda (from NHK International Radio).

From TV Asahi, I thank the Chairman, Ito Kunio, for his encouragement. I thank Suenoby Yoshimasa and Watanabe Kojiro for their full support, for elaborate talks about news production and for introducing me to anchors, political commentators and international production staff including Mr Wada, Ms Komiya, Ms Hanamura, Mr Oki, Mr Nagai, Ms Asamoto, Mr Hayashi, Mr Kawanishi, Mr Watanabe and Mr Zoppetti for interviews on several occasions.

I thank Chris Paterson for including me in the Ethnographic Production Research panel at the IAMCR conference in Leipzig in July 1999 and Pamela Shoemaker for her comments and ideas on this occasion. I thank the Media and Global Culture panel at the Nordicom Conference in August 1999 for comments on an early draft of the methodological chapter. And I thank Ellis S. Krauss for his advice while in Japan and Ingunn Hagen and Nigel Holden for helpful comments on Chapter Three concerning sense-making and sense-giving in news production. I appreciated the advice of Simon Cottle on Chapter Two concerning News Production Studies.

I am indebted to the following people for their assistance. Natsuko Holden for making excellent transcriptions and translations of the Japanese interviews. Her advice in linguistic matters is also appreciated. Linda Schaberg for her comments on Chapter Four and Eight concerning gender in News Production and her encouragement of the project throughout. Maribel Blasco for proof-reading the dissertation. Jesper Jensen for IT support including audio-visual manoeuvring and conversions from Japanese to European standards. Mette Mørk for repro-work. Birgit Støvring for library assistance. And Anne Marie Søderberg and Inger Berg Møller for excellent mentoring.

Finally, I thank my mother for commuting to Tokyo and to Copenhagen to assist our family, my husband Knud Munk for daily encouragement and continuous support. I kiss

Sofia and Amanda who were born in the process of writing and to whom I owe much inspiration - and time.

Copenhagen, January 2003.
Lisbeth Clausen

Contents

List of figures

Chapter One

'Global' news

Introduction

Modernisation and cultural globalisation theories almost ritually refer to the 'globalisation of media' as an evident factor in the globalisation process (Giddens, 1991b; Robertson, 1992; Beck, 1997; Lash and Urry, 1994).

Paraphrasing Giddens, the sense today of inhabiting one world is in large part a result of the international scope of media communication. TV news programmes provide a mosaic of international images. A world information order – an international system of the production, distribution and consumption of informational goods – has come into being (Giddens, 1989: 548).

The fact that we are presented with world events and historical handshakes may give viewers a sense of inhabiting one world. In this way, McLuhan's vision from the 1960s of a "global village" has come true. However, the present study argues that while the communication of news may include homogenising elements global events are *also* mediated according to different national, organisational and professional strategies and McLuhan's idea of a 'global village' in this perspective is more appropriately termed 'global villages'. The plural form implies that global audiences are increasingly stratified by media content which is specifically geared towards national interests.

Although we may experience single incidents and world events together with the rest of the world on some occasions, the common experience is still sporadic and indirect. As argued by Lash and Urry (1994) in "Economies of Signs and Spaces", people are bombarded with cultural artefacts or 'signifiers' and increasingly become incapable of attaching 'signified' or meanings to them. In other words, the perception skills and cognitive capacity of the individual viewer do not develop according to the international institutions of mass media and politics. Audiences do not regularly receive the same information, nor do they build up an identical stock of world knowledge. The study in this respect presents evidence to the statement by Thompson that although images of certain events may be presented worldwide there is similarly a process in which "International images are interpreted differently in different social and cultural contexts" (Thompson, 1995: 11) by news producers and audiences alike. In other words the 'homogenisation' of world audiences through mass media is met with different 'cultural filters' or 'gate-keeping' mechanisms.

This book is a study of these 'cultural filters' and 'gate-keeping' mechanisms in international news production. With specific focus on Japan, it investigates the strategies national producers use to assign meanings to signs and symbols before they are disseminated through the broadcasting media. It is written with the notion that there is no "global" news, as theorised by some media scholars, by demonstrating that international stories, through production practices, are 'domesticated' and geared towards local audiences for cultural and political reasons (Gurevitch, Levy and Roeh, 1991). 'Domestication'[1] as elaborated below is understood as a process of *framing*:

---

[1] To make sure, 'domestication' refers to a process of making information fit in a frame of reference for audiences within nation state boundaries. It is not as a starting point intended to connote an understanding of the national or nationalism as a political counter measure to globalisation in order to protect cultural identity as described in the following. "Excessive inflows of information and cultural products from foreign countries can endanger cultural identity. Every nation, like every individual, has contradictory desires. They want to learn from and imitate others, but at the same time they want to be different from others. Just as every individual wants to create and maintain his or her individuality, every nation wants to create and maintain its cultural identity. Then a sense of cultural identity usually includes the sense of continuity and pride or self-esteem. Therefore, although no nation would oppose inflows of foreign cultures and information per se, it would like to keep it under a certain level or under its control" (Ito,

recognising, defining, selecting and organising information as news for audiences and actors in a certain national context.

In order to describe the meeting between global events and national news broadcasting, I propose to investigate the strategies used by national producers to assign meaning to international events by analysing the production and presentation of specific news considered 'global' in the "Co-operative Study of Foreign News and International News Flow in the 1990s"[2] (henceforth referred to as the International News Flow Study). The events in focus are The Nato invention in Bosnia, the UN Women's conference in Beijing and the French Nuclear Tests Mururoa in 1995.

The study is based on interviews with 40 media experts and news producers at the major Japanese broadcast stations, and newsroom observation mainly at the public station, NHK, and the commercial station, TV Asahi, in 1997. The interviews include managers, editors, foreign correspondents, news desk personnel, scriptwriters, producers and anchorpersons in order to follow the considerations in news production in its different stages of negotiation from the planning until the finished product. I describe the strategies and decision-making processes involved in producing the above news.

The factors that influence international news production are studied at four contextual levels. I explore the global influences of the international news agencies through business affiliation with Japanese national broadcasters, the national media environment and extra-media factors, the public service and commercial organisational factors and, finally, the professional news values and individual expertise of the journalist that influence his or her considerations in the interactive process of making international news.

In this chapter, I will describe the international news environment and conditions for global news mediation. Some media scholars argue that news is 'global' and news information is becoming increasingly homogenised due to the influence by the international news agencies. I shall return to these below. Many studies however oppose the homogenisation theory and argue for a differentiated [1] view on global communication, which involves elements of heterogenisation:[1] Against this backdrop, I will introduce the notion of 'domestication' and argue that news communication may lead to both homogenisation and diversification of world images. In other words while it may be true that 'global images' are distributes world-wide through 'transnational formats' they are also given local meaning through production practices. I will discuss the role of international news in society and list the international and domestic actors and factors that directly or indirectly influence the practices of news producers in the newsrooms. I will hence argue that the ability to *frame* is important in the communication of complex international information. In conclusion, I will present the challenges in international news production in Japan that are comparable with the challenges of importance in the dual broadcast systems of Europe.

1990: 441). In this view, the 'domestication' process thus may work instinctively or through socialisation within news workers to protect national identity. Strategies to protect national identity were not apparent in the Japanese newsrooms. Although audience appeal was the central concern, news producers were concerned that information mediation should following professional guidelines and less with national identity protection. 'Domestication' thus merely refers to processes of making information comprehensible to national audiences.

[2] The project "Coorporate study of Foreign News and International News Flow in the 1990s" is co-ordinated by Professor Robert Stevenson of the University of North Carolina and Professor Annabelle Sreberny-Mohammadi at Leichester University. A description of the project and a list of participants is available from the project web site: http//sunsite.unc.edu/newsflow/

Global processes of homogenisation

The homogenisation of products has been referred to in business studies as Mac Donaldisation and Cocacolanisation, inferring a homogenisation of consumer goods world-wide. Similar notions of homogenisation are proposed in 'global' news studies.

According to the US media scholar Chris Paterson, the international news agencies (described below) are largely responsibility for the 'homogenisation' of international news. The causes of this homogenisation or highly standardised television news agency agenda are due to the following factors: The similarity of extra-media factors that influence news production at the agencies, the similarity of news production routines among agencies, and competitive pressure to duplicate coverage by other agencies. Finally, Paterson argues that a universal focus on standard frames or themes in news coverage cause a homogenisation of international news. (Paterson, 1998). He describes the strategies of the news agencies as follows:

> The international news agencies go to great length, and take great pride in their ability, to provide a 'balanced', 'objective' view of the world in their news feeds. They generally admit, however, that their news feeds concentrate upon news of the industrialised world, but insist that the reason is that these countries established them and (mostly) pay for them. They also historically claim to provide 'raw' pictures and sounds, which enable broadcasters to construct their own international news stories (Paterson, 1998:84).

According to Paterson, the claim of balance and objectivity has historically served the agencies in the promotion of their product and their growth. In his view, the national broadcasters tend to rely too heavily on international news material supplied by the agencies. Broadcasters, despite evidence to the contrary (Hjarvard, 1995a, Malik, 1992[3]), continue to downplay the significance of the agencies. National broadcasters argue that the agencies only provide supplementary illustration to stories sometimes derisively called 'video wallpaper', but in reality according to Paterson *'agency material often constitutes the bulk of a story, including the 'spin' of the story*[4]' (Paterson, 1998: 85. my emphasis).

Against this, the present study found that in more than 3 hours of broadcasting (from the International News Flow Study see appendix 1) the material used by the national broadcasters was a mix of their own footage, visuals from the Japanese pool arrangement and agency material. In most presentations, agency material was edited and integrated as supplementary illustrations often mixed with on location materials from their own correspondents. Only two stories by national broadcasters (NHK and TV-Asahi) relied substantially on agency visuals. One piece of news, concerning the Nato bombings in Bosnia as an example, (which may be characterised as 'foreign news

---

[3] Malik, in a news agenda survey, demonstrates a world-wide congruence in international television coverage and warns that the power of the exchange systems and the TV news agencies is much greater than the public really feel or know. (1992:37-41).

[4] Paterson's analysis of the Finnish State Broadcaster, *YLE*, shows that most of *YLE*'s 2 minute and 26 second story about the rioting in Tahiti (News Flow material from 7th of September 1995) contains footage from Reuters Television. Large proportions of the story, including fully 30 second's worth at the start, is the edited visual text provided by Reuters. *YLE* is allowing the news agency to tell the story in its own edit of its own pictures, rather than extensively re-editing agency material or adding images from other sources. The *YLE* narrative is therefore substantially dictated by the visual text created by Reuters.

abroad as compared to foreign news at home) came close to being 'global' as much agency material was used. However, it was covered by the public service station and the commercial station on separate days as very short 'straight' news (See appendix 1) with differing visual material and story angles.[5] Another event (the second day of the UN Women's conference) featured the speech by Hillary R. Clinton, which was televised world-wide (see appendix 2 for visuals in Danish and Japanese coverage). Similar visuals were used extensively,[6] however, the stories were reported within a national framework of reference.

'Global' news stories according to Paterson may be defined as consisting of agency material as well as the agency 'spin' on stories. This direct use of agency material was not apparent in the Japanese news stories and the homogenisation effect therefore was not evident.

Many new commercial stations around the world have been designed from the outset to rely heavily on the agencies (see Helland, 1993). And some public service stations may use agency material extensively for financial reasons. However, in the Japanese case, the set up for international news production with correspondents and stringers world wide is elaborate, which enhances the possibility of covering events with Japanese held cameras and thus 'domesticating' news events.

It deserves mention that the international news agencies as information 'wholesalers' and 'agents of globalisation' as referred to by Paterson did have considerable influence on agenda setting in Japan. Three big agencies were thriving in the free-market system, namely AFP (France), AP (APTV, US) and Reuters (Reuters Television, USA) (Oliver Boyd-Barrett 1998: 16). These agencies were used frequently by Japanese national broadcasters (during the research period in 1997) as described in the empirical chapters.

---

[5] Related to Keesing's Record of World Events, in which Bosnia Herzegovina ranked first in September 1995, this news received little coverage in Japan (2.6). The newsworthy countries of Spain, Colombia, India and Taiwan were nearly invisible in Japan's news coverage, as was Europe (1%). Countries that were found less newsworthy in the comprehensive Keesing's "universe of events" namely Southeast Asia and East Asia, were found newsworthy in Japan. (Cooper-Chen, 1998a). The findings of Cooper in earlier comparative studies (1992) likewise show a different mix in foreign news coverage.

[6] It is not possible to determine whether these visuals are agency, pool arrangement or own pictures.

Processes of differentiation[7]

Volkmer (1999) in a study of CNN International, CNNI (The Turner Broadcasting System, Inc), argues for a more differentiated view in studies of globalisation processes in order to reveal new and specific structures. In her study, she finds that audio-visual communication strategies tend not to 'homogenise' the globe but work with strategies of diversification. As one example, the global market is segmented into markets for continental and regional programmes by exercising differentiated models of global journalism and of global market strategics The global operations are diversified in other economically effective ways such as time-slot placement of 'carrier' programmes, which are re-broadcast on national channels, and special-interest programmes. Finally, there is a strategy to produce news programs and engagement in news patterns of international co-operation. MTV likewise employs strategies of diversification. Euronews, a five-language satellite-transmitted news channel begun in 1994 available to millions, has on a smaller scale, had problems with unified news programs because of the different languages and political agendas of the European countries.

Supporting the notion of diversification, Parker in 'The Myth of Global News' (1994) points to the difficulties of one-world broadcasting in a multinational, multicultural political scene and argues against the notion of 'global' news.

Universal and particular elements in international news communication

Against the above, the present project views globalisation through news communication as a dialectic process including elements that may lead to *both* homogenisation and differentiation. The aim of the project is to explore and exemplify these processes.

It is also assumed that media play a major role in the global mediation of concepts and visual impressions and further that news increases the awareness and interconnectedness of social and political information across borders. In this sense, consciousness precedes the experienced and lived lives of most people or 'global audiences', which supports the notion of Giddens (1991: 187) that 'Although everyone lives a local life, phenomenological worlds for the most part are truly global'. The present project is concerned with the phenomenological world or 'global consciousness' (Robertson, 1992), affected by the proliferation of visuals and concepts through international news. In other words, the increased availability and penetration of media and access to information interconnect countries not only economically and politically

---

[7] A third tenet in the theorisation of globalisation processes (of which the first two are homogenisation and heterogenisation) is that of 'hybridisation', which according to Friedman (1994), is the cultural corollary of economic globalisation. Friedman questions whether there is more mixing of cultures today than earlier and, if so, he suggests that it may have to do with a particular reading of the world situation by sophisticated 'cosmopolitans'. 'Hybridisation' he argues is an attempt to define the cultural state of the world by upper and middle class Westerners who are consumers of cultural objects and images. Intellectuals from these groups engage in the rhetoric of the flowing and mixing of culture, something which, according to Friedman, is only surprising if one expected to find a prior ordered and highly classified world. The problem is that cultural products may well seem mixed to outsiders, but if one looks closely there may be little evidence of cultural hybridisation in the activities and discourses of actual groups of people. In the view of Friedman, *it is merely a trivial truism to state that cultures are hybrid and mixed, which then denies operational significance to the term 'hybridisation'*. Rather, according to Friedman, we need to focus *on how cultures are experienced.* The latter inspires the present project. From the perspective of the national news producers, international news was not perceived as *hybrid* forms. International news was not compared to CNN international news. Rather it was perceived as *Japanese international news.*

but also *psychologically*. As a matter of fact, the development in technology and the infrastructures of news distribution enable news access in any corner of the world. This makes development of the national cultural identity of any country rely more than ever on its knowledge about other cultures. And news plays an important role in the maintenance of a national cultural identity.

The constant inflows of information and the visibility of other cultures create a cultural and social reflexivity, which makes each cultural choice a conscious effort. News producers at the national broadcast stations, who work in the space between the global and the national, have included a *reflexive* hunch into their strategy for selection and production of international stories. The Janus-faced ability of both knowing international affairs *and* knowing the receiving audience is essential in the framing of international news information and an important element in the process of 'domesticating' news information, as elaborated upon below. The project thus investigates the strategies of news producers in professional interaction as *consumers* of international political information and *makers* of the political discourse in their society.

As argued above, the process of globalisation is as much a psychological phenomenon as it is an economic or political reality. Owing to the dynamic flows of media images, texts, sounds and graphics across countries, globalisation entails both an increased awareness of other cultures often in competition with one's local culture and much more immediate experience of the world as a whole. It is assumed in this project that news, as an institutionalised form of political communication and a conventional media genre, is both affected by globalisation trends and is itself an agent of these. This dialectic and dynamic approach to processes of globalisation has the following implication, as described by Robertson: 'Globalisation as a concept refers both to the compression of the world and the intensification of consciousness of the world as a whole' (1992:8). Robertson further argues that a characteristic of the 20th century is our participation in a twofold process of the '*interpenetration of the universalisation of particularism and the particularisation of universalism* (Robertson, 1992:1000. Original italics). The present study contributes with empirical support for this statement.

Figure 1:
Homogenisation and diversification through international news communication

Perspective	Universal	Particular
International news distribution infrastructure	'Global' concepts and policies	'Domestic' framing
National production strategies	'Domestication' of international news	'Global' news

The technological development and the distribution of news through international news agencies, as illustrated in the display, enable the diffusion of events globally while enhancing the inter-penetration of universal (in this specific case United Nations) concepts and policies. Meanwhile, as argued in the present text, processes of particularisation (highlighting familiar elements) are enhanced in the mediation of international information. The theories of 'global' news distribution and its consequential 'homogenisation of world cognition' thus are turned on their head. International news events as exemplified in this study are framed according to particular frameworks of interpretation shared by national audiences (or audience segments).

The fact that international events are presented within frames of interpretation of local audiences in each national country makes 'global' news *particular* to each country. UN concepts and political policies are, while mediated globally, 'domesticated' and made particular through news production. In other words, it is claimed in this text, as displayed in figure 1, that *news 'domestication' is a universal phenomenon and that 'global' news is particular to each country.* The argument is supported by the findings in this study that national broadcasters do not mediate the materials of the international agencies in unedited form nor do they follow the agenda of the international agencies blindly. On the contrary, national broadcasters select and produce news according to the political and economic participation of their country in the global community which results in differing news output worldwide. An empirical statement by a public service international news editor in Japan sums up the argument: "'Global' news in Japan is not like 'global' news anywhere" (NHK Chief Desk, interview July 17th, 1997).

In sum, audio-visual images of world events are conveyed through international news imprints on 'global' audiences. These news imprints, however, it is argued, are sporadic and do not lead to 'cognitive homogenisation' of world audiences. News is framed and interpreted differently in different national settings according to national frameworks of interpretation that may include differing factors and actors at the global, the national, the organisational and the professional levels of influence on news production and consumption.

As an additional observation supporting the view of diversification at the macro level, it became apparent in the interviews with news producers in Japan that the strategies for news coverage in the future focus on a 'return to Asia'. According to executive management at the five national broadcast stations, efforts were made to strengthen the coverage of Asian events. Regional strategies included moving staff back from Europe to Asia. As stated by an executive news manager, 'the past fifty years have been devoted to the West, the next 50 will be devoted to Asia'. It may be concluded in a 'global' news perspective that international news coverage and allocation of resources in the second largest economic power in the world follow strategies of regionalisation.

News 'Domestication'

As described above international news communication includes both 'universal' as well as 'particular' features. The universal characteristics refer to global formats and genre conventions as described below, while the particular characteristics refer to socio-cultural themes, actors and communication strategies in national media institutions. The process of selecting particular elements and adapting global information into a local framework is referred to in this project as 'domestication'.

The notion of 'domestication' is inspired by the research of Gurevitch et al. who found that:

> Media maintain both global and culturally specific orientations - such as by casting far-away events in frameworks that render these events comprehensible, appealing and 'relevant' to domestic audiences; and second, by constructing the

meanings of these events in ways that are compatible with the culture and the 'dominant ideology' of societies they serve. (Gurevitch, Levy and Roeh, 1991b: 207).

Based on their study of news production and audience reception in several European countries Gurevitch et al. concluded that in order to be judged newsworthy, an event has to be anchored 'in a narrative framework that is already familiar to and recognisable by newsmen as well as by audiences' (Gurevitch, Levy and Roeh, 1991: 207).

'Domestication' in this project similarly refers to audience appeals and efforts to shape news into frames of reference and ways of perceiving international events that are similar for news workers and audiences in the same national culture.

Further, the present study shows how the process of localisation or 'domestication' occurs at different levels in the production process a) At the global level media institutions serve as mediators between the international and the national through dissemination of international information into their economic political environment b) at the national level competing news institutions provide and process information according to legal rules and political system of their country c) at the organisational level information is negotiated against house norms and particular production strategies in each media institution and finally d) at the professional level individual producers, anchors, correspondents negotiate and 'bring information home' before it is communicated to the public at large.

The process of 'bringing information home' ('domestication') thus occurs at many levels in the production process. It is ingrained in the professional strategies of news producers in their effort to target news output to their *local* audiences as exemplified throughout this book.

It deserves notice that while the notion of 'domestication' in the study of Gurevitch et al. serves as a counter-conceptualisation to the notion of globalisation, the present study views the process of 'domestication' as an inevitable part of the globalisation process.

International News Flow

The news programs studied in the present project are based on material from the 'Corporate study of Foreign News and International News Flow in the 1990s' hence referred to as the 'News Flow Study' (Stevenson, 1995).

The first International News Flow study was conducted in 1978. Its findings led to a call for a redefinition of news, which was predominantly flowing from the Northern to the Southern Hemisphere. The debate became known as the New World Information and Communication Order (NWICO). The study was funded by UNESCO and covered 29 countries (Sreberny-Mohammadi et al. 1985). The findings reconfirmed and brought together the findings of many previous studies. One of these was the prominence of *regionalism.* Every national system devoted most attention to events happening within and to actors belonging to its immediate geographical region. Secondly, it was found that *politics* dominated international news reporting everywhere. 'Hard' news was presented by two political categories, namely political international and domestic news, followed by military, defence and economics, which accounted for the main stories. Finally, it was found that *political figures* dominated, comprising 25 to 60 per cent of all actors in international news; few other categories of actors received significant mention. Not surprisingly, the United States and Western Europe came out in the study as the consistent newsmakers in all parts of the world. It deserves mentioning that international news would focus on spectacular singular happenings, drawing attention for a short intense period of time, and that news from the developing world would focus on trouble and that overall news from this area overall was scarce[8].

A critique of the first study was made by Kaarle Nordenstreng (1985) one of the main architects of the study, who asserted that the topical approach represented a blind positivism. Nordenstreng called for the use of a delicate methodological instrument that would get at the qualitative sphere of image building, instead of just employing conventional categories of content analysis such as topics/types of news, countries/regions, etc.

> An understanding of foreign countries as reflected in news coverage requires a much more delicate methodology than the simple counting of how much attention is devoted to such categories (in topical terms) as politics, natural catastrophes, etc.... the fact that certain aspects of reality lend themselves to convenient measurement does not mean that those aspects are necessarily most essential to our understanding of reality (p. 634)

Proposals for the study of *meaning* rather than a merely topical approach to news came from a number of directions. This was incorporated in the qualitative part of the second study and served as inspiration for the present project. I shall return to this below.

The "Corporate study of Foreign News and International News Flow in the 1990s" was a follow-up study with participation by approximately forty countries, and it is currently still in progress. The goal of the study was to map the emerging global news geography, both in terms of the major suppliers of news, the geographic and cultural maps that news coverage represents, and the discourses and images of "otherness" that define "foreign" news. One of the concerns of the study, in a period of challenge to the sovereignty of the nation-state, was to examine how much news about the "foreign" is actually located at home[9] (Stevenson, 1995:1). The present study found Japanese international news to contain a high degree of local appropriation (See appendix 1: The local appropriation of 3 'global news).

The International News Flow Study team in Japan[10] employed a quantitative approach and provided statistical material for comparative analysis[11] (Ito 1998, 1996a;

---

[8] It has become clear that the international media environment was far more complex than that suggested by the 'cultural imperialism' model. The depictions of a hegemonic media system leading the global media appeared right in the realities of the 1970s, but is now a bygone era. (Sreberny-Mohammadhi, 1996: 180). The conventional categories of 'imbalances' and 'expansion' do not suffice to explain the global communication flow. New parameters of global communication revealing the parallelism of 'universal' and 'particular' elements, which involve global modes as well as local modes of communication, are needed. I will return to this below.

[9] Hjarvard (1995b) makes a critique of international television news flow studies in what he terms their 'mid-life crises'. He points to the shortcomings of the macro level analysis and the general propositions that have emerged from these studies based on the general idea that the more data (number of newspapers, TV channels, countries, weeks taken into account) the better. Hjarvard calls instead for a middle range analysis in the perspective of *interaction* that stresses the inter-relatedness between social actors and between different factors in the news *process*. His critique is well stated, however, the resources needed in international corporate studies as well as the challenges of access to newsrooms world wide makes the practical implementation of his proposal a challenge.

[10] The Japan team contributed 3,339 coded news stories from print and broadcast sources to the project's data base, which to date includes more than 48.000 news reports from 44 countries. The sample period included two weeks in 1995: September 3-9 (planned to coincide with the Fourth UN Conference on

16

Cooper-Chen 1998, 1996). The present project (in a study of 'meaning' construction) employed a qualitative approach[12]. (Clausen 2001). Although not quantifiable, it may provide complementary findings through detailed analysis of a few pieces of news and systematic accounts of the global, national, organisational and professional factors and actors that influence production practices and the final output of news.

The "international news flow" studies assume a linear notion of news flow among nations which does not take the interpenetrating and overlapping influences in the local production context into account. The present study of production processes suggests a contextual model which takes global, national, *and* organisational and professional conditions into account. It is found that each level influences the production of 'global' news in important ways.

A qualitative approach to international news flow studies further provides insights into the dynamics of globalisation processes which the one-way news flow studies implying a linear notion of 'news flows' from the 'centre' (North and West) to the periphery do not explain.

International news agencies

As mentioned above, the international news agencies are strong actors of globalisation in their function as international news wholesalers. As noted by some scholars and confirmed in the present project, the international news agencies have great influence in international newsrooms. Their strong agenda-setting function, however, does not necessarily lead to the 'homogenisation' of international information flows.

The leading Western agencies of the 1990s were generally acknowledged to be Agence France-Presse (AFP), Associated Press (AP), and Reuters. Two of these organisations, AP and Reuters (formerly Visnews), were involved in services both of print news for newspapers and audio-visual news (APTV and Reuters Television) for broadcasters. Because of the importance of television news, and for the agencies as suppliers of it, it is also necessary to add World Television News (WTN) to the list of major agencies. WTN was the successor of UPITN (Owned by the American agency, UPI, and the British television news station, ITN, it was owned by Capital Cities Corporation which, in turn, was taken over by Disney in 1996. WTN was bought by Reuters TV in 1998 a year after the interview survey of this project. Although these agencies are 'global' in the scope of their activities, they each retain significant associations with particular nations, namely France (AFP), the United States (AP) and

---

Women) and September 17-23. (Cooper-Chen, 1998a). The news flow data "is neither comprehensive nor random, and the capacity to generalise from the data may be limited" (Campell and Stevenson 1997:4, cf. Cooper-Chen, 1998a).

[11] Ito found trade to be the most important determinant, and added the presence of a news agency and log of population to important determinants of foreign coverage (Ito, 1998). Ann Cooper Chen's analysis of intrinsic and extrinsic factors influencing Japan's foreign coverage showed that the majority of international news was 'foreign news abroad' (58.3) with no Japanese involvement. Foreign news abroad with Japanese involvement covered 23.0%. The main actors in international news in the three national papers and two major news broadcasters, NHK and CBS, were state/nation officials. The dominant topics were found to be international economic/trade (18.9%), international politics (18.1%) and defence/conflict (12.2%). The main nation mentioned in stories was the US (19.3%), then France (8.5) and China (6.7). The second nation mentioned was the US (9.3%), then France (6.9) and China (6.7).

[12] The quantitative part of the International News Flow Studies is headed by Robert Stevenson, and the qualitative part of the project by Annabelle Screberny. The latter includes detailed analysis of news from the UN Conference on Women in Beijing (Stevenson, 1995). The findings of these qualitative studies are not included in the present project but may be used in future comparative research.

the United Kingdom (Reuters)(Boyd-Barrett, 1998). The three agencies were found to be the most important in the observation period in 1997.

The agencies of the Soviet Union (Tass now Itar-Tass) and China (Xinhau) are non-commercial news agencies with a function as departments of governments. These sources continue to be influential globally for information about Russia and China, but not as sources of news about other countries. This is similar to the situation of the Japanese national news agencies, Jiji Press and Kyodo News Service. They are not included in the international news services but remain national. The major reason for Kyodo's inability to compete with Anglo-Saxon and French international news agencies despite its scale and financial strength is language. In order for Kyodo to sell news reports in foreign markets, reports have to be translated into English or French. This is costly and, more importantly, delays distribution, which is fatal in the news agency business. This lack of an international market for Japanese language news is the largest reason for Kyodo's inability to become a genuine international news agency. In the case of major international news agencies, more than 20 per cent of their total revenue comes from sales to foreign mass media. But in the case of Kyodo, the sales to foreign mass media account for only a few percent. Kyodo does distribute news (mostly on Japan) to foreign mass media in English. This service, however, loses money for Kyodo (Ito, 1990).

The above news agencies, the international broadcasters CNNI and BBC NEWS SERVICE International, and the American national broadcasters, NBC, CBC, ABC, NewsCorp, among others, have established extensive linkages with national and local broadcasting systems, private and public, throughout the world for news feeds, specialised information services and video footage. At the same time, they represent a high exchange-based co-operative system and yet also a hierarchically organised global network dominated by U.S. and European-based organisations (Paterson, 1996, 1998).

The analysis in Chapter Six and Chapter Seven shows how agency stories influence the daily production of news at all levels from foreign correspondent on location to Tokyo 'gatekeepers'. The analysis shows how newsrooms rely on the Japanese news agencies scripts for translations of events and, even more importantly, it shows how the Japanese public service and five commercial stations' affiliation with CNN, BBC NEWS SERVICE, NBC, CBS and ABC, respectively, influences news production.

'Global' images, transnational formats and local meaning

In light of the above, it is not an overstatement to say that our lives as media users are saturated with global images. In one hour of television viewing (of zapping from one channel to the next) we are likely to be confronted with more visual impressions from around the world than years of images in an everyday life without media. This scenario is well described by Fiske:

> Post-modern culture is a fragmented culture, the fragments come together for the occasion and are not organised into stable coherent groupings by an external principle. Television is particularly suited to the culture of the fragment, for its continuous 'flow'... (Fiske, 1997b: 56).

Fiske notes that reality does not exist in objectivity, but is a product of *discourse* (Fiske: 1997b: 54) and of *discursive practices* as argued in the present project. There is a reality which differs from its photographic image or, more precisely, the reality of visuals are subjective slices of event as seen by someone and chosen from a multi-dimensional situation.] Being brought up with several hours of television viewing a day we often encounter experiences through television before we encounter the 'real' event. Our impressions of places, people and events are experienced through television first and stored in memory impressions. Impressions and experiences are mediated. They are aestheticised and imprinted as experience dis-embedded from the real life situation. This service from what you may call the 'audiovisual supermarket' is addictive because the stimuli are fast- moving and their presentations are increasingly *produced* to be easily consumable for the viewer (see Chapter 6).

As an example of such experiences, the images from the UN conference in Beijing vary widely in their relationship to what 'really' happened. The studio anchor, the reporter on the spot, pictures of the scenery, file footage, pictures of Hillary Clinton as she leaves Washington for Beijing, commentary by an 'expert' and participants in the event, computer graphics and props. All of these components brought together confuse the possible relationships between an event and its representation and their conventionality suggests that they are not representing a unique event so much as reproducing familiar images.

These 'post-modern' images according to Fiske, escape referentiality and ideology and the textual discipline exerted by organising concepts such as genre, medium or time. The post-modern sensibility does not experience this 'bricolage' of apparently unrelated images as in any way cacophonous or contradictory' (Fiske, 1997b: 56), for postmodernism he argues the crucial part of the play of images is the *sensuality of their surfaces*. This, in the case of international news, is taking the argument too far. Although aesthetic (emotive and sensual) elements of appeal are included also in news as I elaborate in the following chapter, international news (with empirical support in news at two networks in Japan) is still information intensive and strongly anchored in a national framework.

The continuous flow of images in the fragmented life of post-modernity as described above generates the ability to *frame* information so that it may be understood within the given context of the moment of occurrence paramount. Framing becomes a central tool for communication in information society. Framing, however, in the understanding of this project, implies an organisation of experience after logics of coherence, which both follow conventional ways of communicative expressions and have an 'ideological' spin. In this sense, the images of news presentations still follow the rationalities of meaning construction embedded in the production process.

The visuals or 'raw materials' disseminated through the international news exchange systems and the television news agencies are regarded by some as 'open' to meaning construction. 'Openness' implies that these visuals are not yet constrained by certain interpretations because they are not yet given text and background for interpretation; alternatively, multiple decodings for their meanings are still possible for the news producers. [It deserves mention that the 'raw' visual materials are not entirely 'open' as they have already been processed according to professional agency criteria.] However, as illustrated in the Japanese example, above, the materials leave room for editing and choice of visuals that fit the story line and 'spin' of local producers.

The visual materials from the agencies are sent primarily in the form of 'raw materials' that is unedited footage, including only 'natural sound'. The task of editing and framing these materials remains in the hands of news editors in the national broadcasting organisations. Thus, while the same visual materials might be used in different countries, they are edited, narrated and structured thematically by news producers who have a national audience in mind. According to Gurevitch et al.:

> News stories should be examined as related, in the same way as documented historical facts and incidents, to one or another myth or super-story or cultural theme, as these appear in different cultures. The meaning of a concrete news story is always produced in the public space of culture, and in the framework of a relevant family of stories, already familiar to the members. (Gurevitch et al., 1991b: 207)

The comparative analysis of the UN conference on Women in two national contexts is intended to do just that. It exemplifies how events are produced in the public spaces of culture within frameworks familiar to their members. (See Chapter Four).

However, although it is argued in the present project that the frames of interpretation are *local*, technological development combined with the commodification of news has made its marks on the aesthetic form of news. Even the news genre that has hitherto attempted to tell the 'truth' in a factual manner incorporates aesthetics and narrative forms in visuals and texts that appeal to and stimulate senses and cognition.

In order to sum up the discussion concerning 'globalisation effects' the notion of 'transnational formats' as proposed by McQuail needs mentioning. Much television and other media content has been effectively internationalised in terms of genre or format, even when it is locally produced. Typical of such 'international format's are quizzes, games shows, many soap operas, telenovellas and other dramatic fiction genres, the news itself, sporting events, chat shows, etc. (McQuail, 1992). To support this notion, formats in the present study of 'global' news in Denmark and Japan were found to be similar in many respects; however, content and aesthetic effects differed according to national, organisational and professional factors – in short, news is 'domesticated'.

News in society[13]

What is the role of news and how do information trends influence the work of news producers? Although the following assessment of the role of news and its implications on news production is based on Western observations it is equally applicable to Japan as an industrialised country and world leader in the strong economic triad with the EU and the United States.

A characteristic of today's society as an effect of technological development and the explosion of multimedia, is its suffusion and saturation with news information. News is part of the every day lives of most people. It penetrates our living places, our work spaces and can be accessed in almost every imaginable social space. News takes many

---

[13] Comprehensive analysis of present society has provided different concepts in order to capture its essential characteristics: (Beck, 1992) 'Disorganised Capitalism', (Lash and Urry, 1989) 'High Modernism' (Giddens, 1991). 'Postmodernity' (Fiske, 1997) and 'New(s) Times' (Cottle, 1999). Contributions from these works are used to explain the complexities and dynamics of processes of 'globalisation' and the role of media or more specifically political news in this process. 'Information society' (*Johoka Shakai*) was coined by the Japanese scholar *Umesao Tatakao* in 1962 (See Ito Youichi, 1991, 2000a for an account of the diffusion of the term outside Japan). The term embraces many of the characteristics of the above notions about society and, with an emphasis on information processing in this study of news production, it is applied and used throughout the book.

forms. It is delivered in different factuality genres, across mainstream and minority outlet and different mediums, and is distributed by a combination of traditional print and broadcasting means, as well as new on-line technologies, which enable 24-hour, 'real-time' communication capabilities (cf. Cottle, 1999a). News and visuals stretch and representationally bind our sense of interconnectedness with the global and the local, and with each other (Giddens,[14] 1991a; Tomlinson, 1994; Thompson, 1995).

The importance paid to information and the access to mass audiences through broadcast news has made it become a resource and opportunity for commercial and political promotion and public relations. The state, corporate institutions and even new social movements, for example, have their professional media spokespersons skilled in the strategies of media and much emphasis and reliance is put on media 'spin doctors'. News in a sense helps constitute the ritual of public life and political performance (Carey, 1989; Dayan and Katz, 1992) and is often consumed ritualistically in private spaces and domestic milieu where everyday routines may be structured around certain programmes (Morley 1986, Lull, 1988).

The logic of commerce, the commodification and the entertainment-driven nature of the cultural industries can all, according to its critics, lead to processes of news debasement and a 'refeudalisation' of the media as a 'pseudo-public sphere' (Habermas, 1989b). 'Packaged' news or 'newszak' (Franklin, 1997) 'news magazine', 'infotainment' and 'tabloidisation' are some of the characteristics of news connected to the *marketisation* trend, which has led the media to treat contemporary audiences as consumer cultures (Featherstone, 1991). The 'infotainment' and 'news magazine' style of the Japanese commercial broadcast, including subjective opinions of the anchors and commentators has led to a differentiation of styles between commercial broadcasters and public service stations between a 'news' and 'views' style of production.

News in the Japanese newsrooms was perceived both as 'public information' and 'popular culture'. The overlapping and contradictory strategies in the newsrooms as a result of the two approaches to news is elaborated in Chapter Four.

Audiences and 'global consciousness'

What are the effects of globalisation trends and media use from the perspective of ordinary viewers. This section explores the conditions for news communication and the perceptions of international news?

Against sociological views that the power and penetration of television furthers trends of isolation and standardisation, and that audiences get less and less informed the more they watch, reception studies show that people trim and skim information satisfactorily for their own everyday use as political citizens.

Ulrich Beck (1997) criticises the creation of global media networks because they at once create isolation and open up across the boundaries of countries and experts for a long-distance morality. This puts the individual in the position of having to take a continual stand *vis-a-vis* world events and the catastrophes and risks of society (Beck, 1997). People, in the view of Beck, meet around the world at the village greens of the

---

[14] The process of globalisation involves 'the intensification of world-wide social relations which bind distant localities in such a way that local happenings are shaped by events occurring many miles away and vice versa' (Giddens, 1990a: 64). This 'time-space distinction' (ibid) helps to create complex relations between local involvement and interaction across distance. In this stretching process of relations according to Giddens, there are numerous modes of connection and interaction across time and space.

21

television where they consume news. They are at once insignificant and yet sharing terrible scenes from civil wars. While governments (still) operate within the structure of nation states, biography is already being opened to the world society. This continual excessive demand on audiences causes the opposite reaction, namely no listening, simplifying, and apathy (cf. Beck: 137). More than a decade later, Bourdieu attacks the field of journalism (1998a). Bourdieu argues that journalists fill valuable time with nothing or almost nothing of relevance. Broadcast media have a *de facto* monopoly as the main source of information of a majority of citizens and therefore influence what is on the mind of many. The focus on the spectacular and dramatic as an effect of the commercial logic and the hunt for *scoops* does not keep citizens informed of their political duties. (Bourdieu, 1998a: 18-19).

Against these rather gloomy sociological views, audience research studies are divided in two. Some studies show that, in fact, technological development has made information comprehension more difficult (Dahlgren, 1992: 202). Within the empirical and cognitive psychological traditions, there has emerged a rather large and troublesome body of international literature showing that viewers often have emotional and cognitive difficulty relating to and comprehending television news information. Against this, research on news processing finds that people trim and skim political information sufficiently in order to manage their lives as informed citizens (Graber, 1984).

Although television news production styles have changed considerably with the multiplicity of discourses and rapidly-shifting segments (Hjarvard 1999), national television news as argued in this project still has its *raison d'etre* in its cultural anchoring and orientation. International reception studies confirm this proposition. The "News of the World: World cultures look at television" study found that viewers perceive news according to their social-cultural background. And that international news has one important function, 'namely to reconfirm a sense of security for ourselves, our family, our nation and the culture to which we belong' (Jensen, 1998:165). Importantly, in the light of the present study it was further found that the individual cases of reception and the news contents of the period studied implied a 'stepwise 'domestication' (Cohen et al. 1996) of the news from the viewer's perspective within a special cultural setting' (Jensen, 1998:179).

It serves notice that audience research shows that the dramatic developments in recent years in advanced information technologies does not alter the fact that, for the vast majority of citizens, television news broadcasts remain a prime source of information about the outside world (cf. Dahlgren, 1992: 202).

The following describes how audiences or extra-media actors (including politicians, NGO's, sponsors, interest groups, ordinary viewers) directly or indirectly influence news production or participate in news.

Political actors in news

News media essentially link together people and actors across vast areas of geographical space.[15] The actors in news are important carriers of international political discourse.

---

[15] Underlying these altered geographical spaces of social, communicative and cultural interaction are vast transformations in the global political economy of communication. A transnationalisation of media ownership and control: mergers and acquisitions (Barrett et al. 1998) is taking place. However, the structure of media ownership and control is increasingly becoming transnational, not 'global', as much of the acquisitions are still made within the US and Europe (ibid).

National leaders proclaim their intentions, while the diplomatic and international political community keep themselves informed through international news at the global as well as the local level. News media in this sense provide an important forum for the enactment of international as well as domestic politics.

As an example of (indirect) practices of communication, Volkmer (1999) describes how national leaders watch and turn to CNN for news information. The relationship between CNN and national governments is described as follows:

> I know that we have been used by governments in the past to get their point across because, my god, we are watched everywhere. We are watched in Cuba, we are watched in Moscow, we are watched in Libya. When Muammar Gadafi wants to get his point across, he picks up the phone and he calls CNN and says, 'Hey, I have got an interview. Would you like to interview me? I have got something, I want to tell you. I have a peace plan'. Yasser Arafat does the same type of thing. It was done with Saddam Hussein during the war. We had an interview… with him when nobody else [did]. So in that sense we are used to purvey a point of view but I don't think there is any official relationship with them (Volkmer, 1999:153. Interview with CNN staff).

Transnational communicative interactions are not limited to commercial concerns. The use of new communication technologies and the transnational flow of information also shapes politics and actions by non-governmental organisation (NGOs) and governments.[16]

The media play a central role in communication processes between micro and macro levels of interaction between social actors from different socio-economic and cultural contexts. News also helps to construct and affirm 'Imagined communities' (Anderson, 1983), and in so doing positions us in relation to 'others' and in relation to changing identities of self. Social theorists have noted how 'surveillance' is an integrated part in modern, bureaucratic societies. Thomson has argued that the media facilitate the 'historical transformation of visibility' in which social and political elites are now obliged to stage-manage public performances in front of the television audiences. The News media have become public arena or 'public spheres' (Habermas, 1989a) in which political contests are played out.

The socio-political actors involved in news are accompanies by professionals news mediators as described in the following sections.

News personalities

The consumer-orientation of news production, as observed in the Japanese newsrooms, has launched a new type of television personnel in order to accommodate the audience. These TV personalities work as a kind of cultural mediators[17] with the role of mediating between the expert information of television events and everyday lives of audiences. In the US, panellists take the role as intermediaries between the complex information presented in the program and the everyday life of the viewer. They debate and ask questions about political occurrences that the viewers may have asked. In France, a

---

[16] Public relations agencies of large organisations such as the UN, which currently has 3 departments (UNESCO TV, UNRWA TV and EPTV), and the European parliament Public relations Division produce programmes carried by CNN.
[17] 'Cultural Intermediaries' (Featherstone, 1991)

special category of TV performers, 'intellectuals' (*tottologo*) take this role. They commonly have a university degree but according to the French sociologist Bourdieu (1998b) their only expertise is trivialities. They comment and converse widely about any subject and their force is that they are always available, popular, quick-witted, eloquent and able to talk much and say nothing (Bourdieu, 1998b). In Japan, these television personalities are called special 'talents' (*tarento*). *Tarento* include actors, entertainers, foreigners who participate in various programs, including news, where they offer their commonsensical opinions and comments. Their only attribution at times is being different or cute (*kawai*) (see Kinsella 1997). News personalities also include newsreaders, commentators and casters. The latter are well-known and often powerful political figures in Japan, as elaborated upon in Chapter Five.

International news producers as mediators of complex information

Actors in news also include the news professionals such as foreign correspondents, editors, producers, scriptwriters, reporters, satellite operators and graphic designers. What kind of demands does 'news society' as described above put on international news producers, and what are their work conditions as mediators of 'global' information in national society?

In trying to disseminate information (that people want and need and should know), news producers both circulate and shape information. News production is interwoven with other parts of the social and news producers are active producers and composers of political discourse. Although many of the decisions made throughout the day are arbitrary and even though structural factors influence the work strategies of news producers, they have to be assertive and improve their expertise of knowledge and creativity in order to get assignments and on-air time for their stories.

It was found in the study of Japanese news rooms that international news managers see their role as twofold: First, as providers of information and commentary about international affairs including policy and diplomatic negotiation between nations to the domestic political and economic elite. Second, as mediators of international information to the nation at large, i.e. the general public. Although these journalistic aims require information-intensive coverage of economic and political news, there is awareness among news producers that the (cognitive) capacity of the general viewer does not render him or her capable of coping with high-level political interpretation. Rather, social and cultural issues with a human-interest story line, visuals of conflicts and disasters which have an instant emotional impact, are in demand. This pertains particularly to international news (which in cognitive terms require pre-established knowledge in order to make sense of its complexity) (the working procedures of individual news producers are elaborated in Chapters 5-7).

Initiatives were taken at the organisational level to develop human resources within the broadcasting companies in order to expand worldwide networks for information gathering and train local stringers abroad to select and produce stories with a Japanese perspective.

It was found that the political and ideological views of reporters, editors and publishers were strong because of the hitherto 'closed' system of hiring, in-company training and career advancement within the company. Headhunting was seen as a new way of accommodating the need for talented and competent staff in news production. The liberalisation of media ownership and advances in multimedia technology challenge the concept of national news broadcasting and creates an even greater demand for news producers to be experts in their field of knowledge while another requirement is being good performers. The trend follows a perceived market demand for news to be entertainment-oriented with news programs turning into 'wide-shows', 'infotainment' and 'news magazines'.

It was found in the newsroom that the production world events was undertaken through a dual system of sources namely own correspondents and international agencies. The Japanese international news corps is elaborate and covers every corner of the world. NHK and TV Asahi allocate enormous financial resources on international coverage, which makes it possible to develop stories independently of the agencies with Japanese-held cameras and on location, thus enhancing the degree of 'domestication'. Nevertheless, the structures and networking of international news agencies (mainly Western) and exclusive contracts between US broadcasters and NHK and the commercial stations, influence the work processes and final news output considerably.

In the outlook on the world from the perspective of Japanese international news producers, the US was the significant 'other' and most prominent actor in mind. US news maintained its importance while slightly in decline during the interviews in 1997. A focus on European news was shifting to a strong focus and investment in news from Asia.

The Japanese historical reference point, which was very much to the foreground in the minds of the present generation of media professionals, was the Second World War. The Japanese 'Peace Constitution' made after it lost the War under SCAP (the Supreme Commander of the Allied Forces) forms the basis for Japanese legal and political life. The legacy of the war constitution in present Japanese society is under debate. However, the war was still the national reference point of news framing, and two of the 'global' news stories described below were produced within this frame of reference.

As an important point in relation to the war, Japanese national agencies formed strong connections to the American networks after the war, and the following agreements of affiliation with mainly US and European national networks strongly influence Japanese media messages today.

Framing international news information

With the abundance of information that characterises present society, the essential tool of any communicator is the ability to *frame* (Fairhurst and Sarr, 1996). Newsmakers, as managers of complex information, have to be particularly good at determining the meaning of an event. They have to make sense of it, judge its character and significance and be able to mediate it *instantly*.

The process of *framing* based in this study on cognitive schemes models and scripts (Graber, 1984, Van Dijk 1988, Goffman 1986) serves to analyse how news producers select, collect and infuse personal experience and gained knowledge into their reportages. In order to communicate large amounts of complex international information, their challenge is to convey in simple terms the most relevant information in the few minutes or seconds allocated to their story 'on air'. Information processing also includes the negotiation with co-workers.

The concept of framing resembles the news producers own term to 'shape' information:

> When determining news value, the importance of news depends on the sense of closeness to the incident felt by the Japanese audience. This closeness or distance

can be cultural and physical and it can be emotional or factual. It is the role of the journalist to select information, which is close to the audience or to *shape* (*katachi ni suru*) it in order to give it a sense of closeness. This is primarily the role of the journalist. The journalist provides people with a window on the world and gives a perspective which makes what they see understandable (NHK, News desk. Interview September, 1997)

Shaping[18] thus is a term employed in the international newsrooms and conceptualised in the project as the notion of framing. The quote refers to a sense of closeness felt by Japanese audiences or alternatively it is a sense of closeness that can be *shaped* by news producers *qua* frameworks and textual compositions familiar to the audiences. This element of shaping, is included in the notion of 'domestication', which is an 'overarching' frame of reference to local culture in international news production.

The theories that appear to best explain the nature of journalistic work (discursive practices) at the micro level *and* news presentations or flows (strands) of discourses at the socio-cultural level are a combination of media and organisational studies of cognitive and discourse theory. Whereas schemes and cognitive frames illustrate the processes of knowledge accumulation in an 'inner world' (tacit), discourse(s) illustrate knowledge made accessible through language use in the 'outer world' (explicit). I have previously employed a cognitive approach to the study of audience reception of news (Clausen, 1997) and found it useful to explain how audiences 'receive' news. I will employ a more elaborate framework in the present approach in order to explain how news producers both 'receive' news information and further how they communicate it.

Priming (Fairhurst and Sarr, 1996) is a subcategory of framing involving the ability to prioritise information, simplifying it and presenting it appropriately for the occasion.

The concept of framing in this project explains the very process of news production and includes in the analysis the influence of all dimensions of the 'domestication' model. Embedded in this ability is the acquisition of an organisation's professional values, and in the case of international news knowledge about global affairs and how these may best be presented to national audiences. The concept of framing is based on the cognitive psychology notions of schemes and scripts and is used in this project to explain information processing.

The concept of framing has thus been found the most suitable analytical category to investigate the textual strategies in news production. The contextual factors influencing news production processes and news presentations are global, national, organisational and professional. The notions of framing and priming are elaborated upon in Chapter Three.

News broadcasting trends in Denmark and Japan

The development of news broadcasting in Japan and Denmark has a similar trajectory. The similarity in production output may be traced back to the similar backgrounds for business strategies of the dual broadcast systems in the two countries.

---

[18] Other expressions for making and producing news were *seisaku suru* and *kosei suru*. *Waku ni hameru*, is close to the term *framing*.

NHK is a non-profit public station, which relies on money from subscriber fees.[19] It is often compared to the BBC in England and the US public station, PBS. NHK has public obligations and strict standards for programming. The conventional NHK straight news presentation style was mimicked by the commercial stations, until the introduction of a new format by TV Asahi in October 1985.

Following the economic growth in the 1970s and 1980s, there was a great demand for more news. The conventional news presentation style was out of date for the younger generation. The commercial department at TV Asahi in cooperation with the TV production department brainstormed to develop a different style of program. The executive staff came up with a 'news magazine' style of interpretation based on audience demands at the time.

Three points were different in the new concept: It included commercials, and was easy to understand and broadcast in the evening prime time slot. Commercials were earlier connected to entertainment programs. In the new 'news magazine' commercials served as a division between news sections. The commercial networks and NHK had hitherto provided 10 to 20 minute programs, whereas *News Station* lasted 80 minutes. News was presented in an entertaining way and produced so that even Junior high school students were able to understand it. This became the trademark of *News Station*. The *News Station* innovators wanted to make a news entertainment version available, but still the assumption that people were informed at a certain level about political and economic news through newspapers. However, even themes such as economic and political news, were made entertaining and easy to understand through thorough introduction, use of props and commentary. No one believed that a news program could succeed but TV Asahi made a decision and the 'news magazine' went on the air. *News Station* became a very successful and high-rated news programme. While NHK continued its traditional production line many of the private stations were influenced by the presentation form of *News Station*.

Where Japan had had a dual system of public service and private stations since the end of World War Two, Denmark only had one public service channel, DR1, for 23 years until the monopoly was broken in October 1st 1988 when a second public service channel, TV2, made its debut. TV2 was partly financed by license fees and was therefore under the public service obligations prescribed by the government. In a declaration by the Ministry of Culture, TV2 was obliged to present 'factual' and 'impartial' programs, a wording which much resembles the Japanese legal stipulations discussed in the following chapter. TV2 was partly financed by commercials, and ideas from US commercial news programs were implemented in the new news program *Nyhederne*. (Despite it's public service obligations, TV2 is henceforth referred to as a commercial station). In order to keep news programs free of interference by sponsor interests, the Danish news, unlike the Japanese commercial stations, was not allowed to include commercials in the programs (only before and after). Some of these developments, however, resemble the strategies of the commercial station, TV Asahi. For instance, the new program was longer, 40 minutes, than audiences were previously accustomed to, and the news program included not only the traditional hard news themes but also lighter cultural and human-interest stories. A strategy of the commercial station was to break away from the 'speaking suit and ties' approach and include 'voices' of ordinary people in the news (Hjarvard, 1999:74-78). The intention behind

---

[19] The annual turnover of NHK is 2.1 trillion yen. In comparison, the turnover of all five private broadcasters is 600 billion yen. NHK ranks within the 10 richest broadcasters in the world along with its affiliate, ABC, which ranks higher.

this production strategy was that news information should not merely concern the lives of the powerful but should to a larger degree reflect the political consequences on the lives of ordinary people (a majority of viewers).

The strategy of the Danish commercial station was a bottom-up approach, and its mission was to make news relevant and close to the individual ordinary citizens. With surprising angles on news, it was to become a channel of the Danish citizens, not the authorities. The strategy of the commercial station affected the public station. The program concept of the early evening news program at DR1 was soon changed to include closeness, quick and live reporting, sharp angles, straight forwards and easily understandable informal language, energetic and dynamic narration, conscious use of real sound and experience-filled visuals. These changes in policy also had an effect on the later evening programs that were supposed to contain broad and in-depth coverage of the most important events of the day.

The bottom-up approach of the commercial Danish station resembles that of the Japanese TV Asahi. Politically, however, there was and still is a difference. Where the commercial stations both take the side of the ordinary citizens and represent the consequences of political and economic change from the point of view of ordinary people, the Japanese stations are more pronounced in their political views. The antiestablishment views of the commercial station, TV Asahi, and the pro-government points of views of the public service, NHK, are exemplified in the following analysis of news texts and in the production strategies analysed in Chapter Seven.

In the middle of the 1990s, as a consequence of news competition from the commercial station, TV2, the production strategies of the public service station, DR1, changed and also began to target viewers strategically in a more consumer-oriented approach. The formal symbols of authority, including the textual focus, the impersonal presentation form and the formal dress code was replaced with a stronger emphasis on the personal authority of the news presenters. The institutional trust was to be personalised through the studio host, and the host was attributed a central role through the emphasis on creating personal trust between host and audience. The professional roles of news personnel are elaborated below. It is noteworthy that while the popular approach of the commercial station was influencing production strategies at the Danish Public Service stations, this trend was less obvious in Japan. NHK's news production maintains the traditional values. Although the newsroom practices were showing competitive awareness, the traditional values and work procedures of NHK were maintained.

News in Japan

The omnipresence of the news media and its profound socio-political impact has inevitably made its role in society subject of discussion. Japan is no exception. As a leader in the information revolution with broad and sophisticated coverage, the penetration and influence of print and broadcast news range among the highest in the world. Meanwhile, the coverage of international news as measured by the number of reporters posted abroad may be more extensive than that of any nation on earth (Pharr, 1996; Cooper Chen, 1997)

Where the US news landscape may be characterised as an oligarchy with three dominant national networks (ABC, CBS and NBC), the European broadcasting system can be characterised as public service modelled after the BBC NEWS SERVICE news presentation style. In the 1980s, the state monopoly of the public stations in Europe was broken, introducing commercial stations in most countries. Japanese broadcasting has been a dual system of both public and private stations since the end of the Second World War when SCAP (The Supreme Commander of the Allied Forces) enforced the Japanese constitution, which also included rules for broadcasting.

The role of the Japanese media has been interpreted in various ways. The Dutch journalist Karel van Wolferen in his critical account of the Japanese system, names the Japanese media *servants* of the system (Wolferen, 1991) van Wolferen refers to what he terms 'pseudo' political debates in the media, which rest more on allusions of conspiracy than empirical facts. The 'conspiracy' allusions by Wolferen were not evident in the present analysis of newsroom practices and the 'pseudo' debates were not perceived as such by participating experts (see chapter 6). In the account by Krauss (1996), the Japanese media are portrayed as *servants* in the interests of the state in international diplomacy. Japanese officials see the press as an important ally in negotiations with the United States, particularly on trade issues. The Japanese officials defend their own position in bilateral negotiations by giving information and interpretations to the Japanese media.

The role of the media as intermediaries between political leaders was described above in a CNN case and confirms a perspective of *interaction* in news at various levels. The studies by Krauss are drawn upon for comparison of findings in the empirical chapters. The Korean scholar, Kim (1981), makes a thorough analysis of the relationship between the Japanese journalists and bureaucracy, also describing the Japanese media as *servants* of the system in a critical account. Interesting in relation to the analysis of the UN Conference on Women, which brings into focus the relationship with China, Kim, like the present study finds reservations on behalf of NHK to criticise China. The reason for the hesitance in both studies is twofold. One involves the diplomatic and political considerations as a pro government channel (or government mouth piece), another has to do with professional considerations. If comments are too critical permission to report from China may be endangered. Feldman (1993) and others describe the 'cosy relationship' between press club members and journalists as if this relationship is unique to Japan. US studies of news beats (Gans, 1980 and Tuchman, 1978, Gitlin, 1980) likewise describe a relationship of routinely privileged sources.

Comparative studies involving more countries may bring new insights into similarities in relationships between journalists and their sources which may not make the Japanese press club system stand out as unique. In the view of the noted Asahi journalist, Matsuyama Yukio, the Japanese press takes upon itself the role of the *fourth estate* or the role of *watchdog* (Matsuyama, 1993) in which media is an independent critical force on behalf of the public. The watchdog role is essentially how news producers preferred to define themselves and to see their own role. Nevertheless, some news producers particularly from anti-government media were quite aware and honest about the fact that making news was political (see Chapter Four) According to Matsuyama (1993), the Japanese press is very anti-establishment. The reason for this is the powerful and pro-conservative sentiment in Japan, including some press circles. In order to keep a better balance the press has to be progressive. This does not mean support for the opposition parties but rather that the liberal press castigates governmental shortcomings with great zeal. (Matsuyama, 1993: 8). The anti-establishment attitude dates back to the end of the Second World War, when even the liberal paper, Asahi, co-operated with the military government. As a reaction to this experience, it has become the instinct of newsmen, since the war not to curry favour with the government or with any part of the power-establishment (Matsuyama, 1993:6).

Susan Pharr, in an analysis of media and politics (1996), uses the metaphor of a *trickster* to describe the Japanese media as having a role involving all of the above. The media is outside the established order and functions as a mediator between that order and the realm of *chaos* (the unknown) and also the realm of *cosmos* (values and meaning). The media in this view ideally performs the role of evaluator of the established order, and is thus a critic and provider of alternative perceptions and meaning concerning the way the state and its opposition say things should be (Pharr, 1996). According to Pharr, the media in Japan like the media elsewhere takes all these positions at different times. The notion of trickster is based on the analysis of the role of the Japanese media from political scandals to shaping public opinion. The insights of some of these contributions are used for discussion of the political character and influence of politics on news production as explored in the present project (see chapter 6).

Finally, the relationship between the media, public and politics has been theorised by Youichi Ito (1996b, 1994) in order to explain the influence of mass media on the government's decision-making. In a tripolar model[20] including the government, the public and the media, Ito analyses the atmosphere (*kuuki*) and dynamics of influence between these three main constituents of collective political decision-making. The model is based on the assumption that mass media contents are basically heterogeneous in a pluralistic democracy, like Japan.

The divergent and overlapping views above presented the core of the media and its multifaceted role in society. The aim of the present study is not to determine the political role of the media in Japanese society, but to analyse as a starting point *how* the political climate influences production processes (see Chapter 6). The political environment was found to have great influence in spite of claims to the contrary. The 'commodification' of news was equally of concern in the international newsrooms. The pursuit of commercial interests was found to be in conflict with professional aims to provide political information as service in the public interest.

It deserves notice that while the Japanese dual broadcast system of one public service and several commercial stations in many ways resembles the European broadcast systems, much research on Japanese media and politics consists of comparative studies between the rather different systems of the US and Japan. The American political scientist, Ellis Krauss, addresses the problems of comparing such different systems by noting that the 'revisionist' approach (that he applies) inevitably finds media institutions in Japan and the United States *fundamentally different.* This problem, Krauss notes, is apparent in US reporting about Japan. Many institutions and practices that American reporters find "unique" about Japan resemble those found in Europe. However, as American-centred and bilateral relationship between the US and Japan dominate the perspective of reporters and editors of the American press and television, this understanding is rarely conveyed by the US media itself.[21] (Krauss, 1996: 268) According to Krauss, the problem with the revisionist view is that it may be giving a false impression of both nations: the former as a deviant and the latter as the norm.

---

[20] *Kuuki* is a kind of social pressure; therefore, it has a direction and intensity. It is similar to the "climate of opinion" in the "spiral of silence" (Noelle-Neumann, 1984). It makes people with minority opinions silent and creates a strong atmosphere of dominant opinion.

[21] See Reed (1993) about Japanese similarities to Europe and the artificiality of many U.S.-Japanese comparisons.

Frequently, it is the United States that is 'unique' and not Japan (ibid.). The problem in cognitive terms is that the general knowledge (mental scripts) and preconceptions of the researcher guides research questions and perceptions of the empirical field, thus reinforcing well-known stereotypes (see elaborate discussion about perceptions of Japanese uniqueness in chapter four).

The comparative analysis of news presentations (Chapter 4) and the analysis of production strategies between public service and commercial stations (Chapters 5-8) provide insights about Japanese news production from a European (Danish) perspective.

Does International news mean US news?

International studies on news flow and news content have provided material for concern about Western imperialism or hegemony[22] through the one-sided flow of information from West to East. Japanese news flow studies have lead to the findings that a vast number of international news items concern the United States.[23] In the view of some scholars and professionals, US news is excessive (Krauss 1996). The 'global' news event studied in this project was not a US event and it would therefore presumably contribute with a different aspect of the process of globalisation. Nevertheless, the Japanese coverage of the United Nation's Conference ended up focusing on US reactions for several reasons. Firstly, the US due to its world status and current problematic relationship to China was an inevitable political actor in news in Japan as anywhere in the world. Secondly, the Japanese historical past, its dependence on US guidance in political, economical and military matters was of importance in the choice of stories in the Japanese newsrooms. Finally, the Japanese affiliation with Western international news agencies and national broadcasters were important in the processes of choosing stories and angles as described in detail in the study of newsroom practices in Chapter 6.

The West-East or centre-periphery discussion, according to which the world capitalist system consists of 'centre', or rich exploiting countries and 'periphery', or poor exploited countries, looks different from Japan (Robertson, 1992). Japan has often, but perhaps short-sightedly, been considered to be a 'late entrant' to the 'world system,' a 'newcomer', which for relatively unexplored reasons has been able both to 'modernise' and in a certain way, 'become global'. This despite of Western, mainly American, complaints about its failure to participate fully in the international system.

Japan's modern history since its reopening to the world in 1868 after 250 years of isolation can be described in a simplified manner as a dynamic of 'de-Asianisation', 'Westernisation' and 'Japanisation'. The two famous slogans of late-nineteenth century Japan. '*Datsua Nyuo*' (escape from Asia, enter the West) and *Wakon Yosai* (Japan Spirit,

---

[22] As a sociological parallel, Tomlinson and others have pointed out that globalisation seems to be occupying the theoretical and explanatory ground that cultural and media imperialism has held (Featherstone, 1995; Tomlinson, 1991). Economically, globalisation is seen as the spread of capitalism as a system, of consumerism and commercialism as social ethics, and of the growing penetration and power of international corporations. Culturally, it is still seen by many as Westernisation, a variation on or updating of the idea of cultural imperialism and synchronisation (Tomlinson, 1991). The media imperialism and cultural synchronisation theories assumed a change in the power of media to affect cultures. Globalisation theorists seem to be reverting more to this mode of thinking seeing mass media as one recent wave in a very long series of cultural *interactions* on a global or nearly global level (Friedman, 1994)

[23] It was found in the quantitative assessment of the International News Flow Material that U.S. coverage supersedes the coverage of other countries (Ito, 1996a).

Western technology) illustrate these dynamics.[24] The analysis of international news strategies at the Public service and the commercial stations in Japan witnesses a strategic move back to Asia[25]. Although foreign correspondents and stringers were located around the world, foreign correspondents particularly at the commercial stations were moved back to Asia. (Chapter 5). This focus on geographical proximity and a growing emphasis on the coverage of regional affairs resemble the strategies in Europe to strengthen the coverage of EU politics and neighbouring country affairs.

International News Agenda

In most large cities in Japan CNN and BBC World News are available if you subscribe to a cable system. A multi-lingual channel system is incorporated and Japanese translation is available through the sub-voice channel. However, only a very small minority regularly watch CNN or the BBC. The difference in the way stories are 'framed' may be one of the reasons, but the more important reason is the difference in news items or news agenda and the priority given to those items. As described in the present study the differences in news agendas in Japanese and Danish television news programs were remarkable. Just as the agenda and priority to news stories differ from other countries (Cooper-Chen, 1992) the news list differs even between the stations in Japan (Miller, 1994). The fact that the agenda-setting and angle of stories differed was a result of differing public service and commercial production strategies as described in detail in Chapter 5).

Information balance

Before 1970 Japan was an information-importing country. After 1980, however, it has become an information-exporting country at least in news flows and mass culture. Information and cultural products from Japan increased not only in Asian countries but also in North America and Europe. News flows between the United States and Japan are still imbalanced in favour of the United States, but the news flows between Japan and major Western European countries such as the United Kingdom, France and West Germany are almost completely balanced in recent years. The trade of television programmes between the United States and Japan is almost balanced (9-7 in favour of the United States), and Japan exports three times more television programmes (a considerable amount are cartoons) to Western Europe than it imports from Western Europe (Ito, 1990) (the Japanese media system is described in Chapter Five).

Conclusion

This chapter has provided a description of the international news environment as a framework and introduction to the study of international news production and news output.

The focus of the book is to investigate the ways in which news producers shape or *frame* information by exploring the processes in which they make news, including the planning, decision- making and negotiation of individual and shared knowledge. The focal point of study is the *mental strategies* and *frames* of knowledge. Scripts and

---

[24] Mizuno (1997) divides the Japanese mentality into eight dominant features.

[25] Research on Japan in Asia's audio-visual markets describe similar observations (Iwabuchi, 1999).

models in cognitive theory are used to explain how news producers handle vast amounts of information and make this into news.

Against the notion that global news information leads to the standardisation of news and the homogenisation of the consciousness of world audiences through world-wide distribution and transmittance, I argue that news is 'domesticated' through production processes. Although events may be broadcast world-wide, the discursive practices of news producers involve degrees of subjective interpretation that influence each step of the production process. In other words, the frames of reference that news producers use to shape international information (visuals and text) are influences by multiple factors and actors at several levels of analysis. These levels, including the global, the national, the organisational and the professional level, are analysed systematically, and each analysis contributes with insights about globalisation (homogenisation) and 'domestication' (diversification) processes that impact final output.

The process of 'domestication',[26] it is argued, is a universal phenomenon, in news production as in individual information processing. At the macro level 'global' news like other information products is adapted and presented within frames of reference that make it suitable for *local* markets with imagined receivers or audiences in mind. At the micro level, the processes of framing and priming information (back-grounding, fore-grounding, selecting and rearranging) in news texts is an inevitable and necessary process in the 'transfer' of information from one framework to another. This processing of texts and visuals necessarily includes degrees of 'domestication'. The question then is not whether information is adapted but to which degree. The simple fact that news producers handle visuals and texts and that their own perception depends on mental processes that make information coherent through already existing knowledge (according to schema theory) inevitably causes information to be 'domesticated'.

The process of 'domestication' thus is an on-going issue throughout the book and each chapter serves to provide evidence of how news is adapted into the local and to what extent.

Much research has been done on production practices in Western newsrooms. Ethnographic studies of micro processes in newsrooms elsewhere are still scarce. The present project is a contribution with insights from Japanese international newsrooms. The following chapter is a discussion of orthodoxies, news trends and findings in Western newsroom studies in relation to observations in Japan.

Chapter overview

The book is divided into two: Part one (chapters 2-3) discusses news management in Japanese newsrooms in relation to findings in Western studies and elaborates on the notion of framing. Part two (chapters 4-7) is an analysis of news output and production processes at four levels namely the global, the national, the organisational and the professional.

---

[26] The notion that best captures the global similarity in institutional and management models is *isomorphism* as described in new institutional theory by Dimaggio and Powell (1991). The concept of institutional isomorphism explains the politics and rituals that pervade much modern organisational life, including modern mass media. Institutional models, however, are unlikely to be imported wholly into systems that are very different from the ones in which they originate. In other words, at the institutional level there is already a process of 'domestication' at work. The analysis of news production shows how information is shaped through institutional processes following international professional standards. News management models and production procedures are adapted to make standard news formats integrating elements familiar to local producers and consumers – in this case Japanese.

Chapter One, *'Globalisation and Localisation Processes in News Production*, outlines the notions of homogenisation and diversification in globalisation theories and introduces the idea of 'domestication'. The chapter presents a discussing about the role of news in society and the effect of news on our global consciousness. It presents the powerful international news agencies and discusses the role of news professionals and their work conditions as mediators of complex information. Finally, it presents the Japanese media system, which in many ways resembles the dual European media system with both public service and commercial news broadcasters.

Part I

Chapter Two, *Trends in Western and Japanese News Production,* discusses the observations in Japanese newsrooms in relation to findings in Western studies. The classic western studies in news production rest upon the assumption that news is made by bureaucratic routines in the spirit of professional objectivity, through a hierarchy of access to a forgotten audience. The classic studies further assume that news is public knowledge and that the routines of production lead to a rather homogenous outcome. Against this a 'second wave' of studies, including this project, support the notion that news production may be viewed as a cultural practice guided by subjective values (according to station strategies). The 'second wave' studies further assume that news output draws on cultural symbolism is produced with an imagined (very important) audience in mind in a popular cultural style and that the output is differentiated as a result of subjective communication practices. The chapter describes how production trends in the Japanese newsrooms resemble trends in Western newsrooms. It shows how the logic of the new economy in both parts of the world challenges the values in 'old-fashioned journalism'. In other words, rather than producing information with the intention of enlightening viewers, news producers treat news information as a cultural commodity and rather than addressing audiences like democratic citizens, they consider their viewers to be important consumers (of news and commercials).

Chapter Three, *Making Sense of International News*, describes theories used in this project to study the communication of complex information such as news. The concepts of framing and priming (based on models, scripts and schema from cognitive psychology) explain the communication and processing of information by news producers. The chapter is divided into three sections describing *textual framing* concerning visuals and language in news, *social framing* concerning interaction, emotions and senses and finally *contextual framing* concerning different factors of influence at the different levels of analysis from the global, the national, the organisational to the professional level. A 'domestication' model is presented in the final part of the chapter.

Part II

Chapter Four, *Global News Output in Denmark and Japan,* presents an analysis of 'global' news discourses (visuals and verbal accounts in news presentations). It is a qualitative analysis of the coverage of the UN Conference on Women in Beijing in 1995 as it was presented in Denmark and Japan. The dual broadcast systems in the two countries provide an exemplary case of news presentation first between countries in separate regions of the world, and secondly between public service and commercial organisational ways of handling news across cultures. The global, national and

34

professional *actors, discourses* and *communication strategies* are analysed in the two countries in order to describe similarities and differences in the process of framing 'global' political events for domestic audiences. The analysis of news presentations forms the basis for an analysis of influences on news production in the succeeding chapters.

Chapter Five, *The National Media Environment*, is based on interviews with media experts and national broadcasters at the five major stations in Japan concerning the influence of extra media factors on news production. First, the chapter brings a discussion about the debated broadcast law and the political nature of Japanese news. Second, it demonstrates how the structural affiliation between international news agencies and national Japanese broadcasters influences agenda setting processes. Third, it discusses the future challenges in news management where regionalisation (a return to Asia), technological advancement, headhunting and creative human resource activities were main concerns in the strategic planning by station executives. In conclusion, it is noted that station executives in times of growing competition from new and existing global and domestic channels, consider the culturally integrative character (the domestic perspective) of national news programs to be a competitive advantage.

Chapter Six, *Public Service and Commercial Organisational Factors*, explores the organisational flow of information and the communication processes in the Japanese public service station, NHK, and the commercial station, TV Asahi. The chapter describes the production processes of particular news programs namely the NHK *News Seven* and the TV Asahi *News Station* programs. It describes how the decision-making processes, the news values and the textual strategies differ at the two stations and consequently result in differing output. The chapter exemplifies how the economic foundation of the public service and commercial stations influence decision-making processes and how national politics influence the choice of themes and actors in news. It describes the organisation behind the 'news and views' presentation styles that characterises the public service and the commercial program respectively.

Chapter Seven, *Professional strategies*, presents the production of a specific piece of 'global' news: The UN Conference on Women. The account is based on interviews with news producers at the two stations and illustrates their challenges in discovering 'where and what is news' in the process of framing information at the conference. The chapter describes the planning, the negotiation between the field and the Tokyo office, the reporting on location and reflections about the final output. While Chapter Four provides an analysis of the news presentation, this chapter presents the individual considerations and negotiations in the choice and presentation of this particular piece of news. The criteria and production formula as found in the previous chapter differ at the public service and the commercial station. The chapter describes how these differences are reflected in the micro processes of news production at the two stations.

Chapter Eight, *(F)actors in international news production*, summarises and discusses the findings in each chapter. The factors and actors that influence the strategies of international news producers in their production practices are presented according to the global, the national, the organisational and the professional levels of analysis.

Part I

Chapter Two

Trends in Western and Japanese News Production

Given the importance of news media and news culture in today's society, ethnography is an efficient tool for delivering insights into the nature of news work and the dynamics of political and cultural information in news.

The 'classic' ethnographic studies have brought important insights into news production. The method of intensive and extensive newsroom observation has generated ethnographic insights into the cultural milieu and professional ideology of journalists. These studies, with a few exceptions, have hitherto mainly been done in Western newsrooms. Studies by the American political scientist Ellis S. Krauss (2000, 1996) are still among the few in-depth descriptions of Japanese newsrooms practices[27]. Against the more historical account of Krauss who provides an American perspective, the present study focuses on *processes* in news production and provides a European perspective on international news production in Japan.

Since the early ethnographic studies, economic, political and importantly technological change has led to a reconfiguration of news production and journalist practices which, as Cottle argues, calls for new theoretical assumptions and new avenues for ethnographic research (Cottle, 2000a). These global changes have equally influenced production practices in Japan, and the issues under discussion are equally applicable in the Japanese case. Changes in technology, mergers and acquisitions in media organisations, broadcast regulations and the marketisation of news were found to cause changes in some areas of news production practices in Japan while some professional issues remained the same.

This chapter discusses the observations in Japanese newsrooms in relation to findings in Western studies. The classic western studies in news production rest upon the assumption that news is made by bureaucratic routines in the spirit of professional objectivity, through a hierarchy of access to a forgotten audience. The classic studies further assume that news is public knowledge and that the routines of production lead to a rather homogenous outcome.

Against this a 'second wave' of studies, including this project, support the notion that news production may be viewed as a cultural practice guided by subjective values (according to station strategies). The 'second wave' studies further assume that news output draws on cultural symbolism is produced with an imagined (very important) audience in mind in a popular cultural style and that the output is differentiated as a result of subjective communication practices.

The chapter describes how production trends in the Japanese newsrooms resemble trends in Western newsrooms. It shows how the logic of the new economy in both parts of the world challenges the values in 'old-fashioned journalism'. In other words, rather than producing information with the intention of enlightening viewers, news producers treat news information as a cultural commodity and rather than addressing audiences like democratic citizens, they consider their viewers to be important consumers (of news and commercials).

'Classic' and 'second wave' studies in news production

The chapter layout is inspired by the communications scholar Simon Cottle's outline of research issues and findings in the 'classic' news production studies related to the more

---

[27] The studies by Krauss focus on the mutual coverage between Japan and the US as well as the relationship between NHK and the Japanese political system. The findings of Krauss's study are drawn upon in Chapter Five.

recent 'second wave' studies (2000a). The orthodoxies listed by Cottle provide a good platform for reviewing previous literature while discussing important issues in recent news production studies.

Cottle lists a number of questions which were also highly relevant in the observation of production processes and analysis of news output in Japan: The questions were concerning news and news production as: Bureaucratic routines or cultural practices? Professional 'objectivities' or new(s) epistemologies? Hierarchy of access or cultural symbolism? The forgotten or imagined audience? Public knowledge or popular culture? Homogenisation or differentiation?

Figure 2: Seven Orthodoxies in News Production Studies

From the orthodoxies of early vnewsroom studies towards new concepts
(Cottle, 2000a)

Bureaucratic routines - cultural practices
Professional 'objectivities' - new(s) epistemologies
Hierarchy of access - cultural symbolism
The forgotten audience - imagined audience
Public knowledge- popular culture
Homogenisation – differentiation
Selection – construction

A seventh orthodoxy is included in this chapter, which has been pertinent in news production studies, namely the question of whether news is selected or constructed? This epistemological question has divided and/or guided the framework of several production studies, including this one. In the following, these orthodoxies are discussed in turn and related to the approach and findings in Japan.

Bureaucratic routines or cultural practices?

The first orthodoxy concerns the notion of 'bureaucratic routine', which has been a central notion in the classic news production studies. 'Cultural practices' has gradually replaced the functionalist notion of routine.

The 'classic studies' including Warner, 1971; Epstein, 1973; Altheide, 1976; Tuchman 1973, 1978; Schlesinger, 1978; Golding and Elliott, 1979; Gans, 1980; Bantz et al. 1981, Soloski 1989 identify the importance of 'routine' in news production. In contrast to the early studies of news gatekeepers, with their tendency towards individualist, subjectivist and organisationally decontextualised explanations of news selection (White, 1950), the 'classic studies' in the following decades emphasised how news was an organisational and bureaucratic accomplishment. The view of routine I present below is a theoretical construct rather than an empirical reality. It has nevertheless influenced the analysis and description of previous news production.

Tuchman (1978) in her analysis of newsroom practices argues that the very essence of journalistic work is to 'routine the unexpected'. Routinisation, according to Tucman's study affects every level of production to the extent that 'news obfuscates social reality instead of revealing it. It confirms the legitimacy of the state by hiding the state's intimate involvement with, and support of, corporate capitalism' (1978:211).

Tuchman argues that news both draws upon and reproduces institutional structures. Through its arrangement of time and space as intertwined social phenomena, the news organisation disperses what she terms a 'news net'. By identifying centralised sources of information as legitimated social institutions, news organisations and news workers wed themselves to specific beats and bureaux. These sites of newsgathering are objectified as the legitimate and legitimating sources of information. Tuchman asserts that through what she terms 'naive empiricism' (1978: 210) "information is transformed into objective facts – facts as a normal, natural, taken-for-granted description and constitution of a state of affairs" (1978:211). In other words, through the sources identified with facts, newsmakers create and control controversy. The routine of news making is, as observed by Tuchman, generated through organisational structures which determine responsibilities and priorities among news workers.

Paraphrasing Tuchman, there are territorial, institutional, and topical chains of command, which require ongoing negotiations of responsibility and newsworthiness. Newsworthiness is a product of these negotiations intended to sort out strips of everyday occurrences as news. The negotiations legitimate the status quo i.e. the hierarchy among editors (1978:212). In Tuchman's study, which is concerned with the presentation of women's issues, she concludes that negotiations of newsworthiness are "a way to re-establish the supremacy of the territorial chain of command in news organisations, which incorporates 'political beats' and bureaux but excludes topical specialities such as women's news and sports. These sorts of news are thus rendered institutionally uninteresting". (1978: 210). In contrast, she continues, the topic of the territorial chain of command, stories about legitimated institutions, receive attention and so reify power. News work is embedded in a routine connection between news organisations and legitimated institutions. According to Tuchman, news workers and news organisations, faced with information dispersed by the 'news net', battle to impose a uniform rhythm of processing upon occurrences. News workers impose deadlines on defined stages of processing and so objectify a news rhythm. And, argues Tuchman, journalists draw on the way occurrences are thought to happen, in order to reproduce a state of affairs conductive to news processing (ibid). Using past experiences as guidelines for the present, they typify occurrences as news events. Events are routinely produced through what she calls 'the web of facticity' in which 'fact claims' are incorporated in the presentation form and the validation of information sought through a 'news net' of legitimate sources. (Tuchman, 1978 Chapter Four).

Upholding the status quo is also accomplished through the tendency to fit stories into prescribed angles, which is an important part of the routine. It is for routine purposes that journalists categorise events into five categories: soft news, hard news, spot news, developing news and continuing news[28] (Tuchman, 1978:211). Each news event is typified and developed according to standards that make this type of news appear factual. In other words, events are not inherently one category or the other but are selected, categorised and processed accordingly. Tuchman calls this routinised way of fitting stories into prescribed angles 'framing', a term is shall discuss in the following chapter. The prescribed angle in stories was already recognised by Galtung and Ruge (1965) who observed that "news are olds" which in their interpretation proves that rarely is anything 'new' in journalism; *only stories that fit highly prescribed patterns are reported.*

---

[28] The typifications provided by Tuchman (1978: 47-49) are also used in this book. In addition 'straight news', 'feature stories' and so-called 'specials' (5-15 minute 'documentaries') are used. Each type of news requires different procedures and journalistic considerations as described in the empirical chapters.

The notion of routine is also emphasised in the study by Schlesinger (1978). 'The news we receive on any given day is not as unpredictable as much journalistic mythology would have us believe. Rather, the doings of the world are tamed to meet the needs of a production system in many respects bureaucratically organised' (Schlesinger, 1978:47). According to Schlesinger, the routines of news production have definite consequences for the structuring of news. To delineate the main features of these routines 'goes some way towards providing a rational understanding of an important form of work' (ibid).

Finally, Fishman (1980) concludes that news workers 'do not invent new methods of reporting the world on every occasion they confront it. They employ methods that have been used in the past; they rely upon the standard operating procedures of their news organisation and of their profession' (Fishman: 14). Maintaining the notion of routine, Bantz, McCorkle, and Baade (1981: 385) compare television news operations to a 'news factory'. The reporters and photographers are nearly identical in terms of the production of a uniform product within a limited period of time. The 'news factory' system reduces a news worker's personal investment both in the segment he or she helps produce and in the entire newscast. This is the consequence of the interchangeability of news workers and the news workers' lack of control over the final product (p.382). 'Factory' is a strong metaphor in the description of production practices. It promotes the idea of routine and connotes a standardised product, which according to the present approach is rather deterministic.

In the line of arguments for news production as 'routine', time is described as a vital factor. The continuous effort to reach deadlines enhances the tendency to understand news production as routine. Limited time makes news producers choose the news items already at hand, whereas when more time is available they may follow up on stories which do not routinely come to the news organisation (Whitney, 1981). The expectations of immediacy in news reporting and the fact that more and more events are being transmitted instantaneously direct and 'live' (Schlesinger: 1978: 88) make concern about deadlines, a crucial feature of news production work. As noted by Schlesinger: 'If it is true that the clock is surely the crucial machine of an industrial civilisation then our looking at newsmen is simply a case of us the clock-conscious, watching the most clock conscious'[29] (Schlesinger, 1978: 84).

The bias towards immediacy, which in most studies is explained as a response to market conditions, is understood in the present study as a professional construction. The obsessive attitude towards time, as exemplified in on-location reporting 'here' and 'now' impressions, is upheld even in spite of many hours of time difference between the actual occurrence of the event in a far away country and its airing at home; news may, further, be edited on location and additional time taken to forward news packages. In the words of Schlesinger, the concern with time is a form of fetishism in which to have obsessions about time is to be professional. News production is so organised that its basic dynamic emphasises the perishability of stories. Where a story carries over from one day to the next, it is assumed that the audience will, after one day's exposure, be adequately familiar with the subject. It is always today's development, which occupies the foreground (ibid).

In conclusion, theories of 'routines' are well established. They are used not only to describe working processes in mass communication organisations but in all sorts of

---

[29] Schlesinger refers to two basic attitudes towards time. A 'humanistic time track' where individuals feel they have mastery or control over their activities. And 'a fatalistic time track' where the feeling is rather one of compulsion and obligation. (Schlesinger, 1978: 84).

organisations. Routines help explain the flow of work (of informational and material products). The notion of routines as a means to describe communication in organisations is productive in a sense because it provides a way to categorise and create regularity and manageability in a job that is inherently unmanageable. However, in the study of micro processes in Japanese newsrooms, the daily occurrences, the decision-making processes and the complex negotiations of information can hardly be described as 'routine'. As noted by Cottle (2000a), this explanatory reliance upon organisational routines as the 'prime mover' in news production tends towards a form of organisational functionalism and, in consequence, emphasises the determinacy of bureaucratic 'needs' over journalist agency.[30] This, according to Cottle, positions journalists as mere 'supports' or 'bearers' of the organisational system, rather than as active and thinking agents who purposefully produce news in and through their professional practices.[31] In agreement with Cottle, I find that a conceptual shift to 'practice', in contrast to 'routine' is necessary. The notion of 'practice' implies an understanding in this project of communication as a cultural practice or ritual (Carey, 1989). I shall return to this discussion below.

The notion of 'practices', however, is further replaced in this project with the notion of 'considerations' and 'strategies'. These notions imply nuanced forms of agency by including the intentions and emotions of news producers (strategy implies both influences of organisational structures as well as features of the individual news producer). Journalistic agency is understood in this project more as 'subjective' strategies in accordance with the early gate-keeping studies (White, 1950) and less with bureaucratic 'routines' as described in the 'classic studies' above. However, where the 1950's study of subjective biases relied on one newspaper editor, 'Mr. Gate', the present study is based on interviews and experiences of forty 'gate-keepers' or 'cultural mediators'. Where the subjective approach of the early gate-keeping studies involved decontextualised studies of professional biases, the present approach includes several *contextual* levels of influence on news production, namely the global, the national, the organisational and the professional.

Although news producers are, in fact, tied by all kinds of constraints they do have room for 'creativity'. The theoretical approach in this project assumes news producers

---

[30] The problem resembles the classic dilemma of structure and agency (which Giddens (1984) tries to overcome through *structuration* and Bourdieu (1984) through *habitus*, disposition, positions and position-taking. The Japanese have specifically linked 'inside' and 'outside' to meanings that specify "self" and "society". These multiple meanings are represented in paired sets of terms, which include *uchi* 'inside' versus *soto* 'outside'; *ura* 'in-back', what is kept hidden from others', versus *omote* 'in front', 'surface appearance' (Doi, 1986) and finally *giri-ninjo* referring to 'personal feeling' versus 'social obligations'. Doi points out that the meanings of each of these paired terms overlaps, so that aspects of self are at one pole, as *uchi, ninjoo, ura* and *honne*; while aspects of social life make the other pole, as *soto, omote, giri* and *tatemae*. Doi's observation is important, since it directly links aspects of self and society with degrees of in-sidedness and out-sidedness. These double sets of terms have been widely observed and discussed as occurring throughout Japanese society; for example, in political hierarchy (Ishida 1984); large enterprise organisation (Gerlach 1993; Hamabata 1990) health and illness (Ohnuki-Tierney 1984). The above indigenous terms have been used by numerous Japanese experts as organisational keys to various realms of society (Bachnik, 1994).

[31] The conceptualisation of 'practice', which Cottle borrows in part from Foucault, seeks to keep hold of the 'discursive' and the 'administrative' in the enactment and regulation of social processes. Here negative ideas of power, control and regulation as imposed from outside or from above, are broadened to include *a more discursive appreciation of the role of human agency and meanings within prevailing administrative procedures and 'regimes of truth'* (Cottle, 1999, my emphasis). Practices and discourses can thereby be seen as productive and facilitative, *as well as* repressive or imposed. The question of power is outside the realm of the project.

to be knowing and active individuals. Knowing and purposeful news producers were plentiful in the Japanese newsrooms, hence this more subjective approach to journalism proved to be applicable to Japanese news production, as exemplified in the empirical Chapters (4-7).

It deserves notice that although the present study opposes theoretical and practical notions of 'routine' as the main explanatory category of news production, the obsession with 'time' as described above, the exercise of legitimising information and the *strategies* of making news factual as described in the 'classic studies' and elaborated upon below were equally pervasive in the Japanese newsrooms.

Professional objectivity or new(s) epistemologies?

The second orthodoxy suggested by Cottle is the journalistic claim of a shared professional ideology of 'objectivity'.

The aim of objective reporting is incorporated in professional considerations through ways of legitimising sources and through technicalities whereby information is made to appear factual. Although these technicalities were incorporated in the Japanese professional strategies, the final news presentations differed, especially regarding political 'spins'. The professional ideology of objectivity was the norm and seemingly infused every step of the production processes in the newsrooms, however, the outcome

Figure 3: News Criteria (Wilkens, Lesley 1981: 18)

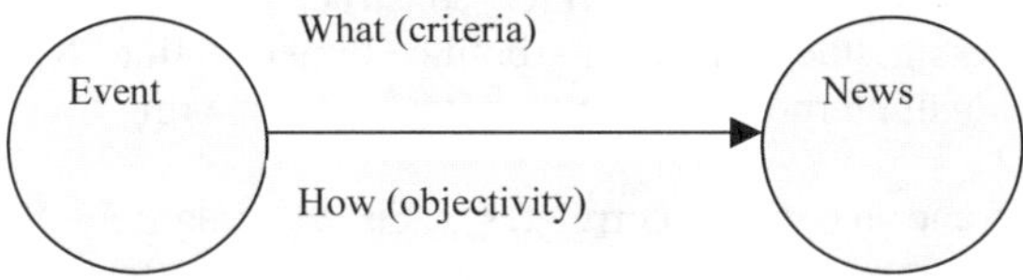

of this claim differed according to organisational and individual interpretations of the ideal. Closely connected to the criteria of 'objectivity' is the notion of 'newsworthiness'. These two notions are incorporated into the journalist's 'sense of news'. In the following these notions will be discussed based on the contributions of various scholars. Finally, I present the criteria for news production at the international agencies (Paterson 1998), which resemble the criteria most commonly expressed in the Japanese newsrooms.

There are two questions which confront the journalist when a story is selected from the multitude of events, which occur in the world. The first is that of *objectivity:* namely, how accurately does such a selection reflect the real world? News is a natural category of events, which as a professional norm must be reported as objectively as possible. The second concerns news values: what is selected? What are the *criteria* of newsworthiness? Why are certain events headlined and others omitted altogether?

Scholars of the 'classic' news production studies agree that 'objectivity' is the most important professional norm. (Gans, 1980, Soloski 1989, Tuchman, 1972). 'Objectivity' is manufactured through textual claims of facticity as well as the use of legitimate sources of information. It is also agreed by these scholars that a consequence of the claim of objectivity is that authoritative sources of the social and political elite are routinely sought out. Gans describes how 'beat' reporters gather information from federal agencies. They are in return granted access to the news media. This relationship of mutual obligations between journalists and their sources both facilitates and complicates their work (Gans, 1980:132). "Although journalists do not set out to report the news so that the existing politico-economic system is maintained, their professional norms end up producing stories that implicitly support the existing order" (Soloski 1989:225). This 'strategic ritual' of legitimising sources and verifying information, Tuchman argues, can be theorised as a pragmatic response to the philosophical elusiveness of 'objectivity', as well as to the difficulties of reporting on contending social interests and their conflictual interpretative claims.

According to Cottle (2000a), the collective notion of objectivity in the first wave of news ethnography was due to the focus on high profile, mainstream national news outlets. These prestigious journalist outlets demand high standards of objectivity to maintain their position. However, as he rightly notes these studies are not representative of all news forms, and the orthodoxy of 'objectivity' cannot be assumed to represent a generalised journalistic commitment. Even within prestigious news outlets such as the BBC, it has been found that journalists and investigative reporters are fully aware of the philosophical difficulties attached to notions of objectivity, as well as the pragmatic conventions deployed in news presentation, which construct a semblance of 'balance' and 'impartiality'. The present study of Japan's public service station, NHK, supports these findings. The individual interpretations and strategies for making 'objective' news differed.

Ideas of 'objectivity' and its many correlates such as 'balance', 'impartiality', 'fairness', 'truthfulness', 'factual accuracy', do not exhaust the epistemological claims of journalism in theory as well as in the empirical field. The broadcasting law in Japan includes 'impartiality' and 'fairness' in its directives, however these were interpreted very differently at the two stations (as exemplified in chapter seven).

Recent developments and debates sparked by the new 'public journalism' in the U.S. and forms of advocacy journalism elsewhere point to a complexity in the field of news production. This is a trend that may be ascribed first of all to influences at the global level. The influences of the new economy with technological development growing competition in informational products, competing news channels (400 in Japan, see appendix 8) results in an orientation to market demands rather than state regulations of news production. This means, in practice, that broadcasters are less committed to their public service function and more focused on making 'consumer products'. As a side effect of this consumer orientation are new 'aesthetic expressions' in news texts. These new expressions allow for compositions of information and commentary, visuals and texts in new forms, which appeal more strongly to the emotional experience of audiences. This trend allows room for new interpretations of the terms 'factual' and 'objective'.

In support of this proposed new trend, in a recent study of production practices in the Norwegian public service station (NRK) and a commercial station, ideas of 'integrity' and 'autonomy' and independence of special interests (including personal) were journalistic ideals. Where 'integrity' and 'autonomy' were seen as important concepts for new producers, 'credibility' was the most important ideal among the audience (Helland, 1993: 278-279). The ideology of 'objectivity' in the study by Helland was not found to be strong at either station, which I interpret as a move away from the classic notion. In its place, it was found that 'balance' and 'impartiality' had a stronger position in the public service station than in the commercial (ibid.:276). The notion of 'objectivity' will be reflected upon below.

News value

As noted by Hall (1973) 'news values' are among the most opaque structures of meaning in modern society. All 'true' journalists are supposed to possess it: few can or are willing to identify and define it. Journalists speak of 'the news' as if events select themselves. Further, they speak about which news stories are the 'most significant', and which 'news angles' are most salient as if they were divinely inspired. Yet of the millions of events which occur every day in the world, only a tiny proportion ever become visible as 'potential news stories': and of this proportion, only a small fraction are actually produced as the day's news in the news media. We appear to be dealing, then argues Schlesinger, with a 'deep structure' whose function as a selective device is not transparent even to those who professionally make the news. The 'deep structures' (which I refer to as schemata or event models in the following chapter), include values and dimensions that guide journalists in their selection of events. The types of news value vary greatly by study.[32]

It was found in the study of Gans that foreign news deals with the same kinds of people and activities as domestic news, but since it does so in fewer and shorter stories, it also brings the priorities in domestic news into sharper focus. It was further found that foreign news is generally treated with less detachment: explicit value judgements that would not be considered justifiable in domestic news appear in stories about the rest of the world, particularly in the US case from Communist countries. Thus, foreign news renders overt some of the values in domestic news production (Gans, 1980: 31). It was found in the present study that the study of foreign news production brought insight into foreign diplomacy and relations between Japan and other countries. International political discourses were more prominent than domestic political statements (in international news production, that is. Domestic news of scale was prioritised in all cases over international news). Or more precisely, international actors (Hillary R.

---

[32] It is generally agreed in production research that newsworthiness is multidimensional. Stempel (1962) distinguished six factors of newsworthiness: suspense-conflict, public affairs, human interest, timeliness, positive event, and controversy about politics and government. Buckalew (1969) found five dimensions of newsworthiness. Normality, significance, proximity, timeliness and visual availability. Golding (1981) found that news values were based on three sets of criteria:*The Audience.* Is this important to the audience or will it hold their attention? Is it of known interest, will it be understood, enjoyed, registered, perceived as relevant? *Accessibility- in two senses, prominence and ease of capture. Prominence*: to what extent is the event known to the news organisation, how obvious is it, has it made itself apparent? *Ease of capture*: How available to journalists is the event - is it physically accessible, manageable technically in a form amenable to journalism; is it ready prepared for easy coverage, will it require great resources to obtain? (3) *Fit.* Is the item consonant with the pragmatics of production routines? Is it commensurate with technical and organisational possibilities? Is it homologous with the exigencies and constraints in program making and the limitation of the medium? Does it make sense in terms of what is already known about the subject? These criteria very much resemble the cognitive approach of the present study, which is described in detail in the following chapter.

Clinton, for instance) were prominent and prioritised over domestic politicians and government spokesmen. The difference in value judgements between foreign and domestic news was not apparent in the Japanese study, rather the value in international news was expressed according to the political stance of the broadcaster, which was pro government at the public service station and anti-government at the commercial station. The Japanese public station (in a perceived role as a government spokeschannel) would criticise the US only as far as the international agencies were concerned but never more. The private station had no qualms in this matter, and engaged in open criticism through subjective presentation style. The criticism was mainly against the domestic government and China.

In a psychology of perception approach, Galtung and Ruge (1965) line up criteria for foreign news. [33] They argue that there are culture-bound factors influencing the transition from 'events' to 'news', and the four factors they deem important in the North-Western part of the world are:

> The more the event concerns elite nations, the more probable that it will become a news item.
> The more the event concerns elite people, the more probable that it will become a news item.
> The more the event can be seen in personal[34] terms, as due to the action of specific individuals, the more probable that it will become a news item.
> The more negative the event in its consequences, the more probable that it will become a news item[35] (Galtung and Ruge, 1965: 56).

In other words, the more the event concerns elite or centre people, the more probable that it will become a news item and there is some measure of ethnocentrism or cultural proximity operative. (Galtung and Ruge, 1965). The hypotheses of Galtung and Ruge have been influential in international news research. Although critical objections have been raised against their heuristic model of news criteria and the narrow methodology

---

[33] Galtung and Ruge's theory on news criteria is developed in a study of 'The Structure of foreign news: The presentation of the Congo, Cuba and Cyprus crises in four foreign newspapers', from 1965.

[34] Galtung and Ruge (1970) ask why news stories are so often 'personified'? Why do reporters write of persons and not structures, of individuals and not social forces? They cite a number of possible explanations, some of which are 'cultural'. There is cultural idealism – the Western view that individuals are masters of their own destiny responsible for their acts through the free will they exercise. There is the nature of story-telling itself, with the need in narrative to establish 'identification'. There is also what they call the 'frequency factor' – that people act during a time-span that fits the frequency of the news media (better than do the actions of 'structures' that are much harder to connect with specific events in a 24-hour cycle). An answer may be found in human consciousness as suggested by Schudson (1997). Further, the Danish scholar, Bent Fausing (1994), describes the urge to view ('skuelysten'; Fausing: 115) as a form of identification of self in relation to the opposite sex. Following the psychoanalysis of senses of Freud (1973), Fausing asserts that viewing has a memory of itself; it is one of the strongest forces of contact with the outer world. The curiosity for watching other people thereby identifying our-selves is developed in infancy (ibid). In sum then 'psycho-aesthetics' may be defined as a visual form of knowledge.

[35] The factors 'frequency', 'threshold', 'unambiguity', 'meaningfulness', 'consonance' 'unexpectedness', 'continuity', 'composition' are "culture free in the sense that we do not expect them to vary significantly with variations in human culture - they should not depend much on cultural parameters" (Galtung and Ruge p.68). The present analysis shows that just as there are no 'meaning-free' or 'raw' visuals, so there are no culture-free concepts. The very heart of cognitive theory as employed in the present project rests on the assumption that knowledge is acquired on top of previous knowledge, which is culture bound. Any information (concept) that is made discursive, therefore, has been through the hand (mind) of someone who is culturally bound somewhere.

46

employed (Hjarvard, 1995a), the theoretical points listed above concerning international newsworthiness are still applicable. The present study proved the centre and elite concern, the concentration on people and the ethnocentric and cultural proximity thesis to be valid. It deserves notice that the feeling of 'proximity' was not merely related to geographical distance but rather a calculated news production means of constructing a sense of closeness and familiarity between the viewers and event by drawing upon previous knowledge about the country in focus. Alternatively, a familiar situation or a recognisable story frame would be set up in order to create familiarity (See exemplification in chapter 6). A negative 'spin' in the reporting of the UN Conference was employed as an effective rhetorical means to make complex information coherent (See Chapter 4).

Another early observation in news production studies which was prominent in the present study was as pointed out by Grey (1966). In a study of a Supreme Court journalist, he noted that a journalist's decision about what should pass through the 'gate' depended on what other journalists were doing and saying. In other words, *journalists feel compelled to validate their own news sense by showing that others are interested in the same story.* Close attention to other journalists on location and to other media reports were standard procedures, as described in the present study. Besides validating own interpretations, an eye on other media was necessary due to fierce competition among media and the reluctance to let the competition get a 'scoop'. Staff in the newsrooms and journalists in the field were continuously watching the presentations of competing national channels and foreign national and international networks to be in tune with recent developments in their search for news angles on stories.

News values that sum up many of the above studies of domestic and international news production and resemble most of those mentioned in the *international* newsrooms of the present study have derived from research on the international news agencies (Paterson 1998: 93). The list includes *timeliness, proximity, consequence, human interest* (emotional value), *prominence, conflict* and, importantly, *visual quality*, and finally *topicality*. Timeliness was connected to judgements about whether a story was up to date in relation to Japanese recent media and political discourse. Proximity was, as mentioned above, the estimated sense of closeness felt by the Japanese audiences. Consequence in international news was judged as the relation of the news item to Japanese socio-political circumstances. The news mix in Japan differed from the rest of the world as described in the previous chapter, and the degree of 'domestication' was high (see quantitative and qualitative analysis of 3 'global' news stories in appendix 1). Human interest was a highly applicable news value in Japan especially at the commercial stations. The presentation of stories concerning the fate of individuals with an emotional appeal was considered successful reporting at the private stations. Prominence concerned how well known story actors were. Government officials or representatives of nations were prominent actors. Conflicts (from wars to political disagreements) was one of the most prominent values because critical situations often demarcated clear views of pros and cons which were easy to mediate as news. The visual quality was a major factor dictating news. Although the bulk of information is presented by professional newsreaders in still (static) positions visuals are paramount in the choice of news themes. *Topicality* (*topics* or *wadaisei* as they were termed in Japanese) was mainly mentioned in the commercial newsrooms. The value of topicality was more prominent in the 'infotainment' and 'tabloid' styles of broadcast news. *Topicality* (which included accidents, disasters and social stories) was an incorporated news value replacing political economic commentary at some commercial stations. This bore witness to the market orientation of news production, mentioned above. Topicality was not a theme at the public service station.

To sum up, the news values derived from production studies at the international news agencies as listed above (Paterson, 1998) resemble those expressed in the Japanese international newsrooms. The models of international news production, whether at the agencies or in international newsrooms, are similar. However, one important difference between their approaches is their audience considerations. Where, according to Paterson, the determining interest of the agency coverage is a few favoured Western broadcasters, namely the BBC, CNN and ABC (1998: 94), the Japanese broadcasters as demonstrated in the present study aim at a national audience guided by a different socio-political and economic agenda.

In sum, a range of news criteria was presented above. The notion of 'objectivity' was found to be a 'classic' journalistic news criterion, but the 'philosophical elusiveness' of the concept was reflected in today's newsrooms introducing new(s) epistemologies. The notion of 'objectivity' was interpreted and put into practice with variations from the prestigious public station, NHK, at one end to the commercial and gradually more 'populist' and 'tabloid' presentation forms of five commercial stations at the other end. The 'ideal', which was the notion of 'objective' reporting, was a virtue, however this basic journalistic criteria was often compromised in the 'real' situation of news production (See Chapter Five interviews with executive managers). The news production practices and considerations were greatly influenced by business and marketing decisions. Even at NHK, which was based on a licence fee and therefore not dependent on sponsorship, the market mechanisms and concern with viewer ratings were at work. The private stations at the other end of the spectrum made what they called 'instant news', which involved the production of informational products that, like instant food, were easily consumed and immediately digestible.

This emotional appeal of 'human interest' stories, rather than the appeal to rationality with statistical corroboration and political economic commentary is termed a 'subjectivist' epistemology (Cottle, 2000a: 25). The subjectivity can be constructed through a variety of textual means, including prominent use of visual, vernacular language and interviews designed to elicit emotive and experiential accounts. The 'subjectivist' epistemology and its variant forms are not necessarily confined to the populist appeals and excesses of tabloid output. According to Cottle, attention to mainstream, and even prestigious 'serious' news output, also reveals how elements of this subjectivist news epistemology are becoming textually inscribed across the range of news forms. The subjective approach was represented in the Japanese international news production in a variety of forms from 'news' to 'views' journalism. (See Chapter 4). Nevertheless, it deserves mention that the Japanese public service (NHK) and the commercial station (TV Asahi) were more 'objective' in their approach to international news coverage than their Danish counterparts (See news presentation Chapter Four and production practices chapter six).

Hierarchy of access or cultural symbolism?

The third orthodoxy suggested by Cottle is the question of access. The question of access to media coverage implies access to the symbolic environment of society. The notions do not exclude each other but are mutually dependent, as I shall argue below.

48

Access to mass media is important as it is a means of becoming part of the symbolic environment. Organisations are constituted in communication and exist not as activity systems but also as symbolic realities in interaction with the surrounding symbolic environment. A news organisation selects items from among the pool of stories available. If a news editor does not select a news story, it fails to become part of the symbolic environment (Bantz, 1990: 503). For the broadcasting station and the rest of the nation, this event never happened. Access to the symbolic environment is therefore vital for social actors.

The question of access, according to Cottle, combines the view of bureaucratic processes and the ideology of objectivity discussed above. The media, on the one hand use sources to legitimise their information and hierarchical access, and these routine connections to legitimate sources in return routinely privilege the voices of the socially powerful, and marginalise or even silence those of the institutionally non-aligned and powerless, as described by Gitlin (1980). It is generally agreed in news production studies that economically and politically powerful sources have more access to the media and, therefore, more opportunity to insert messages into media channels (Gans, 1980). Resource-poor groups may have to resort to deviant acts to attract media attention.

The existing social order is thus maintained through a hierarchical order of access to media. The police (Fishman, 1980) or government bureaucrats (Shoemaker & Reese, 1996) are among the privileged sources. In the Japanese case, the relationship with government and business officials through the press club system (Feldman, 1991) maintains the social structure and hierarchical order in the 'cosy' relationship between the political and economic elites and the press. The access of the powerful and their view is further assured by the capacity of resource-rich sources to produce 'pseudo-events' (Signal, 1973).

The notions of hierarchical access and the ideological hegemony of capitalism are expressed in their most extreme form by Edward Herman's and Noam Chomsky's *Manufacturing Consent* (1988). Herman and Chomsky offer a 'conspiracy' model of the mass media. They compare the American press with Pravda in the Soviet Union and argue that the propagandistic character of news is due to the fact that the news is produced by a concentrated industry of several dozen profit-making corporations. The industry depends on advertising for its profits and government officials for its sources. It is intimidated by right-wing pressure groups, and imbued with anti-communist ideology.[36] In the same line of argumentation, Bagdikian (1982) describes what he refers to as the most alarming developments in the mass media in the last twenty-five years. One is the impact of the US-controlled media run by big corporations, and the other development is the subtle but profound impact of mass advertising on the form and content of the advertising-subsidised media, newspapers, magazines and broadcasting, which privileges elites in the mass media. The orthodoxy of hierarchical access has been widely propagated in critical media studies.

The empirical analysis of newsroom practices shows that multiple interests are at work at different levels of decision-making processes within media organisations.

---

[36] As argued by Schudson (1997: 153), the cultural knowledge that constitutes 'news judgement' is too complex and too implicit to label simply 'ideology' or the 'common sense' of a hegemonic system. News judgement is not as unified, intentional and functional as these terms suggest. Its presuppositions are in some respects rooted much more deeply in human consciousness and can be found much more widely in human societies than capitalism or socialism of industrialism or any other particular system or social organisation and domination can account for.

Influences work top down and bottom up. News workers belong to different networks within the organisation and operate daily in different production units. The dictation by elites does not find empirical grounding in the study of micro processes. The notion of conspiracy[37] resembles that of routine, above. These notions reflect the conceptual frameworks employed in news production studies. Macro perspectives and middle-range analysis of empirical fields allow for such gross categorisations whereas closer investigation and 'thick' descriptions of micro processes provide more nuanced pictures. In other words, in close investigation of micro processes, multiple contextual influences emerge in which the notions of 'routine' and 'conspiracy' do not suffice.

As noted by Cottle critical studies tend to be less theoretically sensitive to, and empirically underplay, the ways in which cultural forms employed in news, such as 'story', 'narrative', 'ritual', 'performance', 'myth', can condition the way in which news producers position news actors symbolically. 'In these more textual ways then, news producers may play more of a hand in the 'emplotment' of news voices within news stories than is often acknowledged by sociological accounts of strategic source competition and news entry' (Cottle, 2000a:27). The 'emplotment' of 'voices' is investigated in the present study. It attends in detail to how the journalist's preconceived story ideas or 'frames' result in the pursuit of certain voices and commentary which elicit the expected statement. It was found that sources were actively selected to represent the particular interests of the news producers. The choice of 'voices' between the public service station and the commercial station differed greatly according to the political ethos of the station. Given the commercial station's commitment to adversarial journalism, it showed more 'creativity' in the strategic use of ordinary 'voices' than the public service station.

In sum, the present study of public service and commercial stations sheds lights on different aspects of the notion of 'hierarchical' access by analysing which and how 'voices' are represented in news. This process is found to involve multiple external and internal factors and actors at different hierarchical levels. The question of access is addressed in Chapter Six and Seven, where differing organisational factors as well as the motivation and expertise of individual news producers were found to influence the choice and staging of actors in news.

In the view of critical scholars, the organisational requirements of news combined with the professional ideology of 'objectivity' routinely privilege the voices of the powerful. It deserves mention that even though the Japanese commercial news presentations represented multiple 'voices' due to a production ethos of representing 'the people', political and social elites *did* dominate the screen (Chapter 4-7). Access and 'voices' were not arbitrary by any means. They were carefully chosen and their statements edited according to the storyline, which reflected the views of the broadcasting stations.

---

[37] The 'conspiracy theory' approach was initiated by Adorno and Horchheimer's analysis of the culture industry (1972), which occasioned a massive debate. The theory has been met with criticism especially in cultural studies where scholars like Morley (1986) and Ang (1985) as elaborated below have focussed on how audiences are active decoders and 'manipulators' rather than passive victims of media messages (TV). In the light of industry finance, the conspiracy theory is seen to be simplistic and making a gross generalisation of the 'culture industry'. In the study of a Japanese advertising agency, Moeran (1996) argues that if conspiracy means 'a ganging up of big business interest against the unprotected and innocent consumer, then the perceived conspiracy is between advertisers, agencies and media, on the one hand, against the general public (or 'masses'), on the other' (Moeran 1996: 194). This is possible when seen from a single viewpoint, however, argues Moeran, there is rarely, if ever, a single point where the interests of all concerned coincide.

As a final note, it is noteworthy that an implicit normative functionalism has been smuggled into many studies: the idea that the news media should serve society by informing the general population in ways that arm them for vigilant citizenship' (Schudson, 1997: 156). Schudson is sympathetic to the fact that the media should play a role and serve society in a democratic way, but he notes that historically it is not a good approximation of the role that the news media have played anywhere. The news media have always been a more important forum for communication among elites (and some elites more than others) than with the general population. In this perspective, the present study shows that the catering to audiences and markets, especially in the case of the commercial stations, requires more 'voices' of the people. Perceived market demands and the ensuing business gains set the agenda for themes of interest. The allocation of resources for certain themes at the commercial station was 'outside the institutional interest' of the public service station. The hierarchy and perceived importance in the symbolism of consumer society thus differs from the hierarchy of official elitist political symbolism.

The forgotten audience or the imagined audience?

The fourth orthodoxy concerns the 'forgotten audience', which is referred to in 'second wave' studies as the 'imagined audience'.

The lack of involvement of news audiences in processes of news production has been a repeated orthodoxy. Cottle refers to the study by Schlesinger, in which a chapter "The missing link: 'professionalism' and the audience' Schlesinger (1978) addresses the problem:

> The missing link refers to a structural lacuna between the producers and consumers of news. In fact the title to this chapter holds the key to its argument: that broadcast news is the outcome of standardised production routines; that these routines work themselves out within an organisational structure which has no adequate point of contact with the audience for broadcast news; and that there is, therefore, no sense in which one can talk of a communication taking place, which is truly alive to the needs of the news audience. (Schlesinger, 1978:106)

Although asserting that the 'missing link' between producers and audiences is now an orthodoxy in the field, Cottle (1993) reports that his own study of regional news programme production showed that newsroom staff had little knowledge of programme ratings and audience profiles, even though senior managers claimed that these were taken very seriously (Cottle, 1993). The audience according to Cottle was thus, in a sense, still 'forgotten'. Against these findings, Japanese news producers expressed varying degrees of awareness and knowledge about their audiences as elaborated further below.

In an early study of journalistic practices, Gieber (1963) distinguishes between two categories of journalists. The 'introjective' journalist takes on the values and feelings of the audience and is thus influenced by a perception of what the audience wants. The audiences values in this perspective are internalised and influence/change the cognitive system of the journalist. The 'projective' journalist assumes that the audience's values and feeling are similar to his or her own. Where projective news producers will follow their own personal judgements, introjective news producers will be sensitive to the concern of the audiences and therefore be more sensitive to perceptions about audience demands than to personal values and feelings. Both types of journalist were found in Japanese newsrooms (Chapters 6-7). The 'introjective' journalist who was sensitive to audience demands as well as the 'projective' type who imagines the audience to be interested in the same issue as himself were found at both Japanese stations in varying degrees. Audience considerations were described as included in production practices ranging from the choice of theme, perspective, and wording to information density. The description of audiences varied from very detailed demographic descriptions to overall impressions. The concern with market shares and audience ratings was found to influence the production and negotiation of news mainly at management level but rating were also mentioned as a concern by scriptwriters and trainees.

According to Cottle, 'mass audiences', by definition, have been unknowable to news producers as well as to news academics, notwithstanding the production of institutional audience research ratings or academic surveys (cf. Cottle 2000a:28). Large audiences in Cottle's view are always going to prove elusive as empirical, complexly-differentiated objects of inquiry, and research instruments, at best, are destined to produce blunt findings only (ibid.). An 'imagined audience', however, as studied by Cottle (1993) (and in the present project) "can reveal much of interest about the different constructions and appeals of different news forms as well as their selection and inflection of particular news stories". (Cottle, 2000a: 29)[38].

The concepts of 'mass audience' or 'mass society' are somewhat outdated in a national context and even more so in a global context (as pointed out in the *segmentation* market strategies of CNNI in the previous chapter). The restructuring of traditional patterns of 'togetherness' is moving towards 'individualisation' (Beck, 1997), a trend which also characterised developments in news marketing strategies. New concepts of diversity are found especially within the field of political communication in response to a 'growing social and political pluralism that corresponds to the diversity of the information environment' (Neuman, 1991: 38). In the US, the established networks of ABC, CBS NBC and PBS are decreasing their shares in a highly fragmented market. The original goal of domestic programming for government-regulated or public service broadcasters was social integration, political 'unification' through the use of a domestic 'news' framework. (Dahlgren, 1991). The concepts of unification are in decline, as observed in the fall of public-service-broadcasting market shares in Western and Southern European countries. The services are losing their 'cultural' function in many countries, and facing increasing competition from other national and international broadcasters. This trend includes the 'news' sector.

In the light of these structural changes, the present study found that the Japanese news producers did inscribe 'imagined audiences' into their particular news forms. As national news broadcasters, they continuously referred to the Japanese people as masses. Meanwhile, as noted above, top editors, news desk staff, script-writers and correspondents included viewer considerations in the processes of story-framing, choice of visuals, actors and verbal accounts. The considerations of audiences were included in the communication strategies at both the individual and group level of decision-making. Audience considerations were found to have a prominent place in the minds of the news producers.

In conclusion, interviews about the 'imagined audience' revealed a dimension of news differentiation in the selection and inflection of particular news stories. The

---

[38] The ethnographic approaches to audience reception studies are plentiful (see Jensen 1991 for an overview) revealing detailed insights about audiences viewing habits, gratification sought and information processing (See Clausen 1997 for a Japanese reception study).

'marketisation' of news was found to have considerable influence for the simple reason that audience popularity meant increases in market shares which attracted sponsors at the commercial stations and gave a competitive edge to the public service stations which was important for professional pride and reputation. It also attracted sponsors at the commercial stations and helped in budget negotiations at the public service station. Market ratings were circulated daily and mentioned at evaluation meetings. They appeared to be the *raison d'etre* of the investigated flagship news programs.

Public knowledge or popular culture?

The fifth orthodoxy presented by Cottle introduces two different views on news. Firstly, news may be understood as public knowledge, which represents the normative functionalistic perspective on news production which was prominent until the mid-1980s. Secondly, news may be seen as public culture, which reflects a cultural approach to news introduced in the 1980s cultural studies approach in audience reception studies.

Liberal as well as critical positions concerning news production, the latter defending the news media as public watchdog, organ of political opinion-formation, and facilitator of processes of democratic representation, have shared a rationalist approach to 'public opinion' based upon ideas of informal transmission. As observed by Cottle, today's news forms, which are seemingly trading on the terrain of popular culture, are anything but rational 'information conveyance'. Supporting this argument, Dahlgren (1992) argues that given the specific audio-visual structure of TV news and its production conventions, as well as the epistemic qualities of television, it is more instructive to treat TV news as a form of 'cultural discourse', rather than 'information'. As such, 'the daily recurrence and readily recognisable features of the programmes serve to link the viewer and his/her every day life to the larger world in a manner which is ritualistic, symbolic and ultimately mythic, rather than informational' (Dahlgren, 1992: 205). Meanings in this popular cultural approach arise in the interface between programmes and viewers and are *not* injected into the audience through a hyperdemic needle as suggested in the conception of the transmission model. Sociological approaches to news production and content analysis in particular have tended to approach news in terms of this 'transmission' model. I shall return to this model below.

From various points of departure, Altheide (1985), Meyrowitz, 1985 and Postman (1985) address the question of the historical specificity of the medium's *way of structuring our perceptions and knowledge of the world*. Their research suggests that television, as a medium, is not geared to conveying messages, though all of them would acknowledge that some messages and information certainly do get conveyed. Rather, these studies suggest that *the real significance of television lies elsewhere, within the more fundamental domain of the organisation of collective perception*. For these authors, television is the key to understanding a historical transformation currently underway in the very manner in which we collectively produce meaning, or literally 'how sense is made' (Dahlgren 1992:205). The study of meaning and sense-making are objectives of the present project, which is why the *organisation of meaning of events and the collective and individual perception in this meaning creation process* are important. The project is concerned with the way in which news producers frame arbitrary slices or cuts from the stream of ongoing activity (Goffman 1986: 10) and make this into meaningful news. In the study of communication in production processes as communication in news presentations, an analysis of 'aesthetic' effects becomes important.

Altheide and Snow (1979) pointed out a few decades earlier, that the logic of media formats has been so taken for granted by both communicator and receiver that it has been overlooked as an important factor in understanding media. The study of media formats and its 'aesthetic' forms as strategies of communication are important in order to describe television news as an institutionalised genre (Helland, 1993)[39]. New as an institutionalised genre communicates events, as demonstrated in this project, *as both public knowledge and popular culture.*

As pointed out by Hjarvard (1999), the differentiation between news as public knowledge or as popular culture is based on an epistemological view. The understanding that news is knowledge and communicated in a process of 'transmission' is favoured in a positivist or empirical philosophical tradition, while the understanding that news is public culture and communicated as ritual, is favoured in a philosophy of social construction.

Figure 4: Two Approaches to News Communication: Transmission and Ritual. (Hjarvard, 1999: 25).

Transmission	Ritual
Mediation of information	Social/symbolic construction
Objective reflection Fact	Subjective interpretation Fiction
Rationality Empirical documentation	Emotion Ideology
Referential function Content	Aesthetic function Form

This study introduces a more interpretative and social constructivist approach to communication, which I shall discuss below.

The use of 'aesthetics' in the present research implies a unique interplay between visuals and texts that characterises the presentation *form* of news in the social construction perspective. News as it is understood is communicated according to genre conventions which are known and expected by news producers and audiences alike. The production of news reports from 'new journalism' and 'live' reports, to talk show journalism and 'infotainment' use 'aesthetic' effects and appeals in their visual and

---

[39] Helland (1993: 60) lists four different dimensions of genre relevant for the analysis of media texts. *The aesthetic dimension,* which may be defined in terms of conventions that allow for a certain expression. *The ritual dimension* which are systems of orientations, expectations and convention, which in a way establish a mode of communication between the addresser and the addressee (Jensen, 1986). *The cultural institutional dimension,* where the genre of news is analysed as text in specific social and historical contexts. More specifically, news is understood as a social construction of form, in the sense that it grows out of a particular socio-economic formation and serves a number of crucial functions for that formation. In abstract terms, Jensen argues that we may label news as a *social institution,* whose task it is to make information publicly available. (p. 31). 'Social institutions' may be defined as "the cement of social life. They provide the basic living arrangements that human beings work out in their interaction with one another and by means of which continuity is achieved across the generations". Giddens (1989:381). *The ideological dimension* is an understanding that news is moulded by market forces and by political interest and through legislative measures. This understanding is contrary to theories of news as neutral and objective. The perspective of ideology sees the news genre as an instrument of control over the symbolic environment, or as and important institution contributing to the struggle of defining the social (ibid: 62).

verbal expressions. News, even the 'short news' and 'straight news' have incorporated forms and expressions that guide aesthetic impressions. Some journalistic forms are connected with high degrees of authenticity and legitimacy. Authority is, among other effects, a result of conventional aesthetic forms. A non-narrative factual form is often considered more 'true' than a narrative form, which mixes information, interpretations and attitudes (p.27). Thus, aesthetic application, as pointed out by Hjarvard, is not only used in the construction of social and symbolic artefacts it is also applied in the mediation of information such as news presentations.

The notion of 'aesthetics' is employed in the present project to describe communicative forms in news. In theoretical terms, news is perceived through cognitive and affective stimuli. 'Aesthetic' expressions are perceived through a 'synergy' of senses involved in the cognitive process of meaning creation which cannot merely be explained as computerised 'information processing' as suggested by top-down cognitive approaches and the transmission model.

In conclusion, the theoretical framework of the present study combines the understanding of news as 'public knowledge' *and* 'popular culture'. The distinction between the two was, however, expressed in the newsrooms. There was a perceived gap between the perception of news as 'public knowledge' and 'popular culture', which was connected to the problem of 'business reals' and 'professional ideals' as discussed above. The 'business reals' refer to the competitive market orientation in news production, which was inevitable at the commercial stations; and the 'professional ideals', the traditional journalistic norm, which were practised at the public service station. Executive news producers at all five stations and newsroom observation at the public service and the commercial stations revealed that the market orientation and entertainment focus were gradually winning terrain over the traditional model of 'objective' journalism.

In a global perspective, the marketisation of news has influenced news production world-wide. The European break with the public service monopoly and the new competition of commercial station news programs has changed news programs and communication forms from being perceived as public knowledge to communication forms that may be recognised as public culture. In Japan, where the dual broadcast system already existed, the new influences led the commercial stations to break with the public service style of news transmission. The introduction of 'news magazine' style programmes in the 1980s, which were funded by commercials broke, with the public service tradition and incorporated aesthetic expressive forms from other public cultural domains.

Homogenisation or differentiation?

The sixth orthodoxy discussed by Cottle concerns the homogenisation or differentiation (heterogenisation) of news products and production procedures. The issue is discussed in a global perspective in the previous chapter, where I put forward the hypothesis that international news is 'domesticated'. The newsroom observations in Japan point to a *differentiated* view of news production in a global context. The production procedures at the public service and commercial stations differed greatly according to national, organisation and professional contextual traits. Although news formats may be similar world-wide, the content differed according to the influences of factors and actors at these contextual levels.

The view of homogenisation is, according to Cottle, based on theorisation of news as organisationally disposed, as a matter of bureaucratic routine and shared professional ideology. These theories point towards news homogenisation, standardisation of form, and ideological conservatism. In the 1970s and 1980s this model tended to apply to the prevailing critical theories, and neo-Marxist theories of ideological reproduction in particular.

The new perspectives on globalisation in news production studies differ from these. As suggested by Cottle: "Today theory has moved on and there is generally an increased recotnition by most media academics of the more dynamic and contested nature of public discourses as well as the textual complexities involved in the representational play of power. 'Discourse', 'hegemony', 'public sphere' are today's key concepts in the arsenal of news researchers and each, in its variant interpretations, often signals this more fluid, less certain, more politically contingent, less ideologically closed, state of affairs. Even political economy perspectives point to economic trends that need not always, further trends of global media conglomeration and consequently news homogenisation" (Cottle, 2000a: 31). In support of the differentiation theory, Volkmer in 'News in the Global Sphere' (1999) describes the new developments towards the transnationalisation of news programming as *fragmented*, *diversified* and *segmented*. (See introductory chapter).

The present study thus argues for a *differentiated* view on news and news production. Nevertheless, as Cottle (2000a) suggests, the news field is subject to powerful countervailing forces of homogenisation, which make political economy perspectives as relevant as ever in the interrogation and explanation of dynamics in the marketplace and in commercial conglomeration.

Selection or construction?

As a final and seventh orthodoxy (which is not included in the list by Cottle, I introduce in short the discussion of 'social realism' and 'social construction'. Without getting into a sustained discussion on the epistemology and ontology of social constructivism it should be noted that the project is inscribed in the interpretative, social constructivist tradition as elaborated upon in the following chapter.

Similar to the distinction between 'public knowledge' and 'popular culture' dichotomies described above, previous studies of news production can be divided into two main bodies of research, one using the perspective of 'transmission' and the other using the perspective of 'construction'. In the transmission perspective, news is conceptualised as a linear flow of information and the producers may be 'gatekeepers' (White, 1950) selecting or rejecting incoming information. In the construction perspective news is a social artefact and news producers may be 'cultural intermediaries' (Featherstone, 1992) framing and reorganising international information for domestic audiences, thus instigating cultural change and/or reproducing the status quo through the (re)construction of cultural identity.

As discussed above, researchers using the perspective of construction view news as a social artefact. Social conventions and practices, specific values, and the allocation of material resources work together to produce a given outcome: news. The social institution is the primary unit of analysis; the form, content and volume of news are all a product of the social practices of the news institutions. Researchers employing the perspective of selection traditionally focus on the news event. World events are the unit of analysis that determines the structure of foreign news. The social institutions (journalism, press, etc.) play a secondary, intermediate role as 'selector' or gatekeeper; they perform functions like selection, rejection, re-editing. As found in the discussion of orthodoxies, above, the production of news is not solely a matter of one or the other. The conceptual framework of the present study integrates the two perspectives, which allows news to be defined as both 'public information' as well as 'public culture'.

In the project, I occasionally use the notions 'gate-keeper' and 'gate-keeping'. In this use I adhere to the original use of the metaphor by the social psychologist, Kurt Lewin (1947), who studied 'social change' by analysing the American people's food patterns. In this use I refer to the psychological processes of the gate-keepers and the forces and (f)actors that affect his or her considerations in the production of international news. The *subjective* view applied in the present project is inspired by the early gate-keeping studies in news production as initiated by White (1950), in which news producers were acknowledged to exercise personal bias in their choices of news items. However, where the early studies were less concerned with organisational and wider social influence on news production, this study systematically analyses the influence of extra media factors.

The Strategic Dilemmas in Public Service and Commercial Broadcasting

Drawing upon the outline by Cottle, the present chapter has discussed six (seven) orthodoxies of the classic ethnographic studies, which are relevant for the present study and place it within the 'second wave' of ethnographic news production studies.

In summary, this study 'destructures' the functionalist approach to news production, which relies on bureaucratic routines. It gives credit to journalistic agency and the ability of journalists to purposefully produce news as active thinking agents. A cognitive approach (as elaborated in the following chapter) views news producers as empowered individuals who engage in decision-making processes and consciously and purposefully produce news. The notion of 'routines', which connotes deterministic bureaucratic constraints, is replaced with the notion of 'strategies', in which structural factors may be regarded as *resources* for action as opposed to *constraints*.

The present project deals with access to news media, not as a possibility for a hierarchy of powerful elites engaged in hegemonic and ideological 'conspiracy', but as a public forum or a universe of cultural symbolism which features 'voices' selected and incorporated by news producers according to national, organisational and professional factors. The project investigates the 'imagined audience' as professionally inscribed working considerations (deep structure) and as important (f)actors implied in news production, not least because of the market orientation and awareness of viewer ratings.

The study bridges between the notions of 'public knowledge' and 'popular culture' at the theoretical level through a cognitive framework and provides empirical evidence of a tendency in Japan as well as in Europe for news producers to integrate information and entertainment ('infotainment'). In other words, news producers increasingly prioritise emotional aspects of news events over political and economic commentary, which has traditionally characterised 'objective' news reporting. The latter is gradually becoming a mythical notion in newsrooms in Japan although it is still the professional norm. In a concern for ratings and commercial success, public (although to a less extent) and private broadcasters negotiate their commitment to the journalistic ideal of 'objectivity'. The recent more subjective journalistic styles are strongly guided by global commercialisation and liberal economic trends.

Finally, arguing against theories of global homogenisation, the study provides an empirical case of differentiated (domesticated) international news production and output.

The orthodoxies derived from Western news production studies provided a platform for discussing the approach and findings in Japanese newsrooms. Where the discussions in the present chapter included many different aspects and trends affecting contemporary news production, the following chapter presents a theoretical and analytical framework which enables a more narrow and systematic analysis of global, national, organisational and professional influences on micro- processes in international news production.

Chapter Three

Making sense of international news

The essential tool of the manager of meaning is the ability to frame. To determine the meaning of a subject is to make sense of it, to judge its character and significance. To hold the frame of a subject is to choose one particular meaning (or set of meanings) over another. When we share our frames with others (the processes of framing), we manage meaning because we assert that our interpretations should be taken as real over other possible interpretations (Fairhurst and Sarr, 1996:3).

Priming and framing in news communication

In trying to disseminate information (that people want and need and should know), news producers both circulate and shape information. News production is interwoven with other parts of the social as described in previous chapters. In the process of making visuals and texts into news journalists choose particular combinations of information and meanings over others. News producers handle political and social information and in the process of framing news event they manage meaning and the interpretations of events over others. In this perspective they are powerful actors in the creation of social knowledge. The present chapter establishes a theoretical framework that encompasses and explains the interconnectedness between macro flows of information in society through news information and professional strategies in micro processes in the construction of news output.

The process of 'domestication', it is argued, is a *universal* phenomenon. At the macro level, 'global' news like other informational products is adapted and presented within frames of reference of *local* national audiences. News is produced with imagined receivers or audiences in mind. At the micro level (of collective interaction), the framing of information (back-grounding, fore-grounding, selecting and rearranging), which is an inevitable and a necessary process in the 'transfer' of information from one framework to another, includes degrees of 'domestication' according to shared organisational rules. The question then is not whether information is adapted but to which degree. The very fact that news producers handle visuals and texts and that their own perception depends on mental processes that make information coherent through already existing knowledge (according to schema theory) inevitably causes information to be 'domesticated'.

The chapter is divided into three parts presenting the *textual* the *social* and the *contextual* framing of information. Textual framing refers to the strategies and conventions for presenting events and assembling verbal and visual expressions in news presentations. The social framing refers to models for action and emotional behaviour in social interaction (in news presentations and in interaction with colleagues) and finally the contextual framing refers to the influences of actors and factors on news production at the global, national, organisational and professional level. In conclusion a model is presented that summarises the different levels of analysis in the study of the 'domestication' of news events.

An interdisciplinary approach

The theoretical framework is a synthesis of ideas of scholars from different disciplines. 'Frames', 'scripts' and 'models' from cognitive theory are employed as used by the American political scientist, Graber (1984); the Dutch linguist, van Dijk (1991); and the American sociologist, Goffman (1986). The 'domestication' model, which is used as an analytical model for the empirical chapters, shows the influence of factors and actors in news production at four contextual levels: global, national, organisational and professional. The model is mainly inspired by American researchers on media effect, Shoemaker and Reese (1996), who include a hierarchy of contextual levels from the ideological, extra media, the organisational, routines and the individual level. It is also inspired by the English discourse Analyst Norman Fairclough who emphasise the importance of the contextual level of production/consumption and the socio-cultural level of influence on media texts. These notions of contextual levels are implemented in the present model.

Before commencing with the theoretical framework, the following is a short presentation of previous research in media studies that employs the notion of frame. The presentation is not exhaustive but merely serves to exemplify uses of 'frame'. Most of the studies implicitly assume communication to be a linear model of transmission (see discussion in the previous chapter) and take their point of departure in a theoretical hypothesis. Against this, the present study takes a more interpretative constructivist approach with its point of departure in the empirical field and subsequently applies a theoretical framework. I will argue for the advantages and disadvantages of these approaches below.

Related research

In news content

Research on recurrent frames in news content either focuses on frames in relation to *specific issues* or on more *generic frames* transcending specific issues (see De Vreese 2001 for an overview). Neuman, Just and Crigler (1992) have identified 'human impact' 'powerlessness', 'economic' and 'moral' values, and 'conflict' in frames in US news. These resemble the news values of journalists as discussed in the previous chapter. De Vreese (1999), in a study of the introduction of the European coin into the common market, investigated the prevalence of an 'economic consequences' news frame in news texts as well as the impact of this frame on readers' thoughts. De Vreese found that within the economic consequence frames the media were overly technical in their coverage and the respondents were evaluative and interpretative in their reception. Another study in the effects tradition, by Iyengar (1991), made a distinction between *episodic* and *thematic* news frames, in which episodic news frames emphasised special events and specific features of persons and issues, while thematic frames emphasised general and abstract aspects. Iyengar found that in US broadcast news there was an increasing focus on episodic news formats in which political issues were presented one by one in a specific perspective, rather than in an overall and general perspective. Consequently, audiences formed a fragmented and concrete picture of their surroundings rather than a general and comprehensive understanding. These studies contribute with insights about *what* and *how* news is presented and with what 'effect'. By taking their point of departure in a theoretical hypothesis, they concentrate on the investigation of predetermined categories and are less sensitive to the dynamics and contextual aspects of the empirical field.

Against this backdrop, the present project takes it points of departure in the empirical field. The theoretical framework is later assembled to best explain and reflect the patterns emerging in the field. Often, as in the present project, a combination of theories from different disciplines is required in order to describe these dynamics.

In news production

The concept of frame has been employed as a key idea in ethnographic news production studies (Tuchman, 1978; Gitlin, 1980; Fishman, 1980). Gitlin (1980) argues that through routines and professional conventions journalists 'naturalise' the social world. 'Frames' are defined by Gitlin as 'principles of selection, emphasis and presentations

composed of little tacit theories about what exists, what happens and what matters'
(1980: 6). Tuchman (1972) the author of "Making News, the Social Construction of
Reality" although not explicitly cognitive in her approach, employs the notion of frame
in her study of newsroom practices as well as in studies of news presentations. "Frame
analysis may help in the study of the principles of organisation that underlie the
selection and definition of news events" (Tuchman 1972). Tuchman is, like the present
project, inspired by Goffman's notion of 'frame' defined as "principles of organisation
which govern events" (Goffman, 1986:10). The implicit rules that govern the 'setting'
the 'context' or the 'frame' of face-to-face interaction by "defining the situation", shape
the meanings generated within it (Goffman, 1986). I will return to this below.

The ethnomethodological and interactionist studies by Goffman and Tuchman have
been criticised for concentrating on the 'frame' of the situation suggesting that face-to-
face interaction could be fully understood as a self-contained unit of analysis without
recourse to matters outside its frame. The present analysis, although observing
interaction as a method of triangulation (verification of interview statements), is
interested in exploring and explaining the considerations and *mental processes* behind
decision-making. It is concerned with the influences on news production practices from
the point of view of the news producers in particular situations, but also from the
perspective of executive managers and media experts who provide a socio-political
view of external influences on news production practices.

In the study of frames in "American and Japanese Political Discourse" Hiroko Furo
divides the concept of frame into two categories: frame as an interactive frame and
schema as a structured expectation. (2000: 320). She concludes that "the American
politicians and Japanese politicians have different interactive frames resulting from their
different expectations in political discourse" and that "These different schemas can
trigger miscommunication in cross-cultural communication between American and
Japanese politicians" (2000: 336). The conclusions are based on the study of U.S.
politicians turn-taking in a television program in the U.S. and Japanese politicians turn-
taking in a television program in Japan. The cross-cultural comparison thus is based on
observations on interactive frames and schema of expectation in each culture
respectively rather than observations on frames of interaction and expectation between
the two cultures. Against this backdrop, the present study similarly explores frames of
interaction in television news in Japan and Denmark respectively. Additionally this
study explores the cultural and professional schemes of expectation behind news
production through interviews with news producers.

In audience research

Cognitive approaches have been employed and developed in audience research (see
Höijer *et al.* 1998). Cognition as an explanatory framework for information processing
in US audiences has been employed by Graber (1984). The frame perspective has been
conceptualised as 'super-themes' explaining how world audiences watch and make
sense of international political news in different cultural settings (Jensen, 1998).
Whereas the effect studies, mentioned above assume a linear model of communication
from sender to receiver, audience reception studies as employed in the present project,
take a more interpretative, contextually sensitive approach. This will be discussed
further below.

The present project is an analysis of the framing processes in international news
production with reference to global, national, organisational and profession influences.

Framing in a cognitive perspective

Cognitive theory is used to explain sense-making and communication within a large number of academic disciplines. Apart from its home in psychology, cognitive theory can be seen to influence anthropology, linguistics, sociology, organisational studies and film theory. It may not be a coincidence that one of the 1995 Nobel prizes was awarded to Robert E. Lucas for an economic theory which *emphasises people's expectations, which is one of the key concepts of cognitive theory* (cf. Höijer 1998), my emphasis). Cognitive theory and the use of *frame* as an analytical concept has been developed and is well established in mass communication research, especially in the areas of content analysis, audience reception and news production as outline above. Cognitive theory is employed in this project to explain the shared expectations and strategies of actors in news communication. I will return to the notion of strategies below.

The concept of *framing* is based on 'schemata' from cognitive psychology. Framing concerns meaning construction and is used throughout the thesis as an analytical category with two aims: firstly, the concept of framing makes it possible to explain *how meaning is constructed within news texts, in processes of news production, and socio-culturally*. The strength of cognitive theory is its ability to explain meaning-creating processes by individuals and in communicative events. In this particular project cognitive theory is particularly suited to make a theoretical framework which explains information processing regardless of national culture and thereby escapes the Japanese conventional Japanese ways of categorising management and interpersonal communication.

The concept of framing is used to explain 'domestication' processes in two ways: At the micro level it explains the psychological processes of news producers who accept information and processed this in relation to individual pre-existing schemes before mediated visuals and text through professional schemata and scripts for what news should look like. At the macro level the concept of framing explains how national media institutions 'domesticate' news according to professional models for which information is presumed suited for national audiences.

In sum frame theory is applied in the present project as it accomplishes these important areas:

Frame theory provides a framework which explains meaning production in media texts and in social practices as individual *and* as socially shared knowledge - inner scripts of individuals (models in the mind) and outer world scripts (models in the world)

It helps explain how news events can be particular kinds of *cultural* models, and can be related explicitly to other cultural phenomena – thus news items must be considered an informational as well as a cultural product.

It provides scripts and models for professional interaction

It provides models for emotions and senses.

It may be conceptualised as context sensitive and functions by integrating dichotomies of macro and micro levels, thus providing a framework to explain human experience and the processing of social information.

Again, the chapter is concerned with *textual*, *social* and *contextual* framing. The notion of 'schemes' and 'schemata' are used interchangeably as the plural forms of schema.

Cultural imprints on information processing

The following section explains how information is processes and 'domesticated' or 'taken home' by the individual. The main point in this section on information processing theory is that information is perceived, related and incorporated into existing schemes or frames of knowledge in memory.

The explanation of information processing is inspired by the political scientist, Dorris Graber. In *Processing the News* (1984) she examines the ways in which people seek out, understand, and utilise political information presented in news. She employs *schema theory*, "an integrative and particularly context-sensitive extension of social psychological analysis" (Graber, 1984:26), to chart the patterns of recognition and the retention upheld in news audiences. Schema theory is applied in this project to explain how news producers process, recognise, retain and retrieve information.

The theory behind Graber's cognitive approach is based on the detailed description of information processing given in the 11-stage model. (Appendix 3). It may be summarised as involving the following steps:

First there is the message reception. Next, the integration process starts with a series of questions to determine whether and how the new information relates to stored concepts, and whether it is worth processing. Such questions would include: Does it cover a topic about which the receiver already has information? Is it a familiar or predictable consequence of familiar knowledge? Does it make sense in the light of past experience? Or does it convincingly contradict past experience? Is it worth considering? Is it redundant?

If the answers to such questions indicate that the information is both worthwhile and reasonably well related to established thought schemes readily brought to mind, it is integrated into them. If, however, the answers do **not** indicate this, the information or its source may be discredited and rejected. Alternatively the new information may alter or replace the previous schema that has been called into question. In order to summarise the information processing, schemes perform four major functions. (1) They determine what information will be noticed, processed, and stored so that it becomes available for retrieval from memory. (2) They help individuals organise and evaluate new information so that it fits into their established perceptions, thereby making it unnecessary to construct new concepts whenever familiar information is presented. (3) Schemes make it possible for people to go beyond the immediate information presented to them and fill in missing information, thereby allowing them to make sense (inferences) from abbreviated communications. (4) Finally, *schemes help people solve problems because they contain information about likely scenarios* (referred to below as social scripts and models) and ways to cope with them (Graber, 1984: 24 my emphasis). In this way, schemes explain the evaluation, storage and retrieval of information and are thus a strategic tool for problem solving and social action. It is noteworthy, as stated by Graber, that emotions are important when accepting or storing information (Ibid: 172). The incorporation of an affective dimension in cognition according to Graber helps to delineate the difference in previous research between emotion and information. The notion of emotions is elaborated upon in a section below.

Cognitive psychologists have described schemas as pyramidal structures "hierarchically organised with more abstract or general information at the top and

64

categories of more specific information nested within the general categories" (Graber, 1984: 23). More simply, this means that most schemas contain conceptions of general patterns, along with a limited repertoire of prototypical examples to illustrate them. The general patterns are usually common sense models of life situations that individuals have either experienced personally or encountered vicariously. They may be embedded in an overarching ideological conception that helps structure the subordinate levels of the schema, or they may exist side by side with only casual connections (Graber, 1984: 23).

Importantly for the 'domestication argument', schema acquisition bears the imprint of the particular culture in which learning take place. Thus, children raised in the same culture learn the schemes common to their culture and the processing strategies that lead to them. The cultural imprint is deepened further throughout life because information sources usually reflect general cultural or sub-cultural values. Ultimately, the schema system is an *"enormous brain-filling, painfully learned store of principles, doctrine, dogma, premises, values, theories, prejudices, habits, codes, defences and the like developed and passed on by people, who share common experiences and processing rules"* (Graber, 1984: 148. my emphasis). The schema system thus explains 'domestication' as the conceptual pillars of information in individuals. Cultural schemes, according to Graber, are imprinted in the early years of childhood and more than a decade before professional training begins. This essentially explains the 'domestication' hypothesis. Cultural schemes are developed and form the cognitive bases for perception of the world. News impressions and knowledge acquisition are based on these schemes.

Schemes that are culture bound include ideas about the appropriate time and place for an event to occur and ideas about the minutiae of behaviour expected from the participants. They encompass ideas about the causes of what is good and what is evil, and ways of coping with the everyday questions of life. They also include ideas about the purpose of life and broad norms of behaviour to be followed by people in a variety of social roles; be it singly or in a group. They may learn which dimensions of a given situation are worth noting and which can be safely ignored. *"There is a culturally given metaphysics, an ethics, an epistemology, and a value scheme"* (Graber, 1984: 149, my emphasis). The national culture is thus included in basic cultural schemes that again influence information acquisition through life and in the professional lives of for instance news producers as studied in this project. Cultural schemes in this framework may be defined as information about appropriate behaviour in given situations. Inferences about other cultures may be made and news information stored. However, the opposite tendency is also a likely scenario. Early acquisition and hardening of schemes may explain why people carry social consciousness norms throughout life. To quote Lippmann (1922) an American political scientist:

> "For the most part, we do not first see, and then define, *we define first and then see.* In the great blooming, buzzing confusion of the outer world, we pick out what our culture has already defined for us, and we tend to perceive that which we have picked out in the form stereotyped for us by our culture" (Lippmann, 1922: 81. My emphasis).

Most people, in cognitive terms, rely primarily upon culturally provided explanations because they lack the interest, and often the capacity, to break out of the cultural norms and think independently. They also lack the stimulus unless they are directly confronted with different cultures. On the whole, according to Graber "people tend to be conventional and conformist" (Graber, 1984:150). This, of course, may be said about news producers to some extend. However, interest[40] as seen below is a main motivator for acquiring new knowledge and interest may lead to independent thinking and change of perceptions.

Some cognitive psychologists have viewed schemes only in cognitive terms (as 'factual' information without taking emotions into consideration), but Graber argues that schemes also contain memories of feelings and evaluations about the concepts in question (Graber, 1984:180). The picture that emerges from Graber's survey is one of a people (the Americans) who deal with a potentially overwhelming flow of information more successfully than one might think. They trim, skim and simplify, but for the most part people get enough news to function effectively in their particular socio-political location. Moreover, they are capable of *taking news items that lack background and positioning them in contexts that are both cumulatively and personally meaningful.* While general understanding more than factual detail is most effectively retained through this process, Graber argues that over time, general understanding is enough to create a relatively well-informed public, which is central to the functioning of a democratic political system.[41] 'Information overload' and the notion of 'noise' in communication theories is similarly a work condition that news producers cope with.

In short, Graber's study shows that the schema concept is applicable when studying political thinking and understanding through news. It presents evidence that the schemes used for political thinking possess those characteristics that cognitive psychologists have described for schemes dealing with simpler types of knowledge. The schema concept is appropriate for studying the process of dealing with information about international political events as news.

Important in this section were the basic conceptual schemes with cultural imprints which explain early encounters with information as important because the way information is stored takes its point of departure in knowledge that is already there. The definition of information and meaning construction depend on pre-existing schemes. Culture in this view is a form of knowledge. The following concerns *meaning construction* as it is understood in schema theory and implemented in this project.

---

[40] Education is a vital factor in developing schemes (Graber, 1984:196). Similar research in international news reception studies supports this finding (Jensen, 1991; Pittelkow, 1985). Graber's study further demonstrates that "experience is the best teacher" (Graber, 1984:195) i.e. those who have experience in political matters and those whose thinking abilities have been developed through higher education have more sophisticated schemes than people who do not have such experience. However, experience does not automatically produce greater learning and sophistication if interest and motivation is lacking. Overall, Graber's survey shows that intelligence (knowledge structures) and experience are stronger predictors of sophistication than higher education in itself (Graber, 1984:195). The specialisation of international journalists and the practical dimension of their vocation thus provide excellent conditions for knowledge acquisition.

[41] Graber's study however, lends further support to a troublesome finding of mass media research; namely that the knowledge-rich tend to get richer while the knowledge-poor stay poor (Graber, 1984:210; See also Jensen, 1991; and Pittelkow, 1985). Reception analysis in Japan showed that people who did not read daily newspapers or watch television news regularly had no schemes of knowledge and no inference mechanisms to make sense of news programs (Clausen, 1997). Discourses in other words have will not resonate with audiences who are not equipped for 'decoding' them. The problem at large is one of educational policy (Masterman, 1985), not the production of news.

Textual framing

Schema theory may be used to analyse any text and specifically to analyse news presentations. The analysis of texts involves the analysis of *meaning*[42] or semantics. Text semantics formulate the interpretative rules for words, sentences, paragraphs, or whole discourse[43]s. An important semantic concept used to describe meaning is that of proposition, which may be roughly defined as 'the conceptual meaning structure of a clause' (van Dijk, 1977). According to van Dijk one of the important concepts studied in text semantics is the *local coherence* of the text: How are the subsequent propositions in the text bound together? A condition of such textual local coherence is that the propositions refer to facts that are related by, for instance, time, cause, and consequence. A key property of discourse is that it is not only locally but also globally coherent. Apart from the meaningful relations between continuous sentences, a text also has an overall semantic unity. This *global coherence* is described by what we intuitively know as themes, topics or *frames*. Topics, conceptually, summarise the text, and specify its most important information. In theoretical terms, such topics can be described as semantic macro-propositions, that is, as propositions derived from sequences of propositions in the text. This derivation is obtained by deploying such macro-rules as selection, abstraction, and other operations that reduce complex information to a readily absorbed form. The hierarchical set of topics or macro-propositions forms the thematic or topical structure of the text. Language users employ such *macro-structures* to understand a text globally, and then to summarise it. By convention in news discourse, the top of this macro-structure is expressed in the headline and lead paragraph.

People need tremendous amounts of world knowledge to derive such macro-propositions (topics). In international news production, deriving such macro-propositions, which is essentially the exercise of framing and the challenge of news production, includes decisions about *what to* and *how to* present information. For news producers with many years of professional expertise and experience abroad, it was a

---

[42] 'Meaning' Dahlgren defines as the process of *making sense of the world*. It has to do with creating a general coherence in our lives, of establishing an order on which to anchor our existence. Also, it has to do with integrating into our world-view the continuous stream of new phenomena we encounter. For each of us, the production of meaning can have a dimension which is very private and even idiosyncratic - we all have our own sphere of what he refers to as 'personal knowledge'. Yet, the foundations of meaning are largely social. Collective interaction, inter-subjectivity and cultural patterns are the basis for much of the sense making we do in everyday life. TV news programmes, as ell as other mass media, play a central role in the production and maintenance (and even subversion) of meaning (Dahlgren, 1992: 203).
Besides the conception that TV news texts have moved from being treated as essentially closed to *polysemic*, offering an array of possible readings; the 'reader' or viewer has graduated from being passive to active in terms of creating his/her own meaning. Meaning is also situational. Context and its appropriate discourse play a large role in structuring and delimiting meaning (Dahlgren, 1992:207).
Meaning has also been conceptualised by Berger and Luckman, who use conceptual schemes to explain the interpretation of experience, not to one another but to a type of experience that is either stored in subjective knowledge or taken from a social store of knowledge: "....meaning is constituted in human consciousness: in the consciousness of the individual who is individuated in a body and who has been socialised as a person" (Berger and Luckman, 1995:10).
[43] The notion of 'discourse' is the legacy of the textual analysis in humanistic research. The assuption behind the concept is that languae is the primary medium of interchange between humans and reality in processes of perception, cognition and action. The present employs the concept of discourse to refer to the use of language and semiotic systems of meaning in social contexts. Through language, events becomes social, intersubjective and accessible for analysis.

continuous dilemma to try to present happenings in the depth they deserved. Although aware of the professional guidelines and the time limitations in news production, the news producers felt at best that presentations were superficial.

The coherence in news, Van Dijk asserts, relies on a canonical form in news discourse. The constitutive categories of the news report generally reveal the conventions and rules of news as a genre. Topics in this view are organised by an abstract schema - superstructure - consisting of conventional categories. These specify the overall function of the topics in the text (van Dijk, 1980; cf van Dijk, 1991:114). Like stories or debates, news reports follow a hierarchical schema, consisting of such conventional categories as: headline and lead (together forming the summary); main events; context and history (together forming the background); verbal reactions; and comments. Typical of news stories is that these categories, as well as their global semantic content, are expressed discontinuously, as 'instalments', throughout the text. For each category, the most important information is expressed first, in a top-down strategy that assigns a 'relevance structure' to the text.

Van Dijk's news *schema* or superstructures refer here to written news. However, similar schema or superstructures have been found in other types of news report and used as explanatory categories and structural bases for meaning construction in news. (superstructures in news as a genre: Jensen (1986); schema theory and narration in television news[44]: Pittelkow (1985). The superstructure of news presentations was found to apply to Japanese written news reports (See Clausen and Thelle, 1994).

A difference found between Japan and other countries in its international news broadcast presentations was the 'newspaper style' production. There was an emphasis on coherence of the verbal message over the visual story. Further, Japanese audio-visual news presentations were supplemented with written headlines resembling the newspaper format of other Asian news producers in countries using Chinese Characters. An analysis of 'instalments' and the creation of global coherence through framing of visuals and texts is presented in Chapter Four.

The textual framing of news is a product of news production practices and mental strategies of news producers. The scripts and models for interaction in news are elaborated upon in the following.

Social framing

Our shared, social knowledge of scripts (described in detail below) of, for instance, eating out, travelling, etc. provides the so-called 'missing links' between the concepts and propositions in texts. In news communication we rely on shared information to make sense of visuals and texts. A text, to use an analogy, may be described as a

---

[44] Pittelkow (1985), studying the reception of Danish broadcast news describes how schema activation is vital for overall comprehension of the news. The news presentation is structured in a way that activates schemes relevant for coherence of the specific stories. The audience has certain expectations about the structure of news presentation, and these help organise and activate relevant schemes. Pittelkow defines schemes as complicated psychological patterns that "include unconscious as well as conscious imagination as well as biases and emotions" (Pittelkow, 1985:447, my translation). Schema-activation occurs in the reception process, and successful schema organisation is dependent upon the qualifications of the recipient. This knowledge of audience reception mechanisms is important in the understanding of how news producers arrange texts and visuals as 'instalments' to make coherence.

semantic 'iceberg' of which only the tip is actually expressed. The remaining information is, by presupposition, already known by the sender and receiver. This dependence on world knowledge and beliefs, in the view of van Dijk, can render coherence subjective, ideological or both. I will return to the ideological dimension below. 'World knowledge' may be implicit (tacit) or explicit as described below.

Discourse analysis of news is not confined to its textual structures. According to van Dijk, these structures express or signal various 'underlying' (implicit) meanings. The textual structures are assigned meanings by language users, or, to be precise, by their mental processes. A few theoretical concepts are necessary to explain which mental structures and processes are involved in both text reception, construction and meaning (re)production. In understanding a text, the meaning of the text itself is gradually and strategically constructed and represented in memory as a *text representation*. Language users possess unique, personal representations of the news events referred to by the text. This knowledge representation in memory is called a (situation or event) *model*. This model not only features the information expressed through the text representation; it also contains much other information about the event. Some of this presupposed or underlying information is derived from action *scripts*. Such scripts are, as also described by Graber, culturally shared, conventional knowledge representations about well-known and commonly known episodes of social life. In the terminology of van Dijk, *models* may feature individually and biographically unique information, while *scripts* are general and social.

Event models in memory according to Van Dijk not only feature knowledge, but also opinions or evaluative beliefs about events and their participants. The evaluative implications of a text may be explained by spelling them out in a description of the mental models of the journalist. If a news report is 'biased', this is usually because the mental model of the journalist embodies structures and opinions which favour a particular perspective on an event. It follows that critical analysis of the meaning of discourse (the approach taken by van Dijk) will often involve a tentative reproduction of these beliefs. If social cognition about different social groups and social events is similar (in van Dijk's case minorities; in the present study political actors and international events), then, van Dijk insists, they are being monitored by the same fundamental interpretation framework, i.e. by the same *ideology*. Ideology features the basic norms, values, and other principles geared towards realising the group's interest and goals, as well as towards the reproduction of and legitimisation of its standpoints. A main point in the research of van Dijk is to show the transition of ideology from journalist to reader. Against this backdrop, the present project assumes that audiences are active in meaning construction (Dahlgren 1992) and not passive receivers of ideological 'injections'.

In sum, *schemata, models* and *scripts* serve to explain knowledge (discourse) in society, in texts and in the minds of actors. The following is an elaboration of the scripted forms and models for action in social processes. It also elaborates on the distinction between *knowing what* (intellectual knowledge) and *knowing how* (practical knowledge).

Frames and multiple realities

Everyday activities consist of quickly changing frames (Goffman. 1986: 563). Ordinary and professional daily lives consist of a series of differently framed episodes. To each of these episodes we bring different attributes (collegial, business relation, familial) and adopt different kids of behaviour (formal, informal, ritual, professional) as we communicate with different kinds of people. Westerners and Japanese alike are aware (through mental scripts and models) of the ways in which each frame functions and accordingly adapt their social behaviour (Moeran, 1996: 268).

In order to investigate how 'strips' [45] ' of experience (Goffman, 1986:10) are organised in international news presentations, the *interaction* and role-playing of political (foreign and domestic) and professional actors (foreign correspondent and news presenters in the studio) are studied in the present project. A study of this role-play (Goffman, 1986) may bring insights into the conventional schemes and scripts about behaviour in news.

In "Frame Analysis" (Goffman 1986), cognitive schemes provide a basis for the conceptualisation of social behaviour. A frame, according to Goffman, is a "scheme of interpretation in which the particulars of the events and activities which we attend are organised and made sensible" (1986:10). We have been sensitised to the idea that the 'same' event is dependent on the framework from which it is perceived and thus many 'realities' may be simultaneously occurring among (and even within) participants in the same set of activities. The interest of Goffman is to reveal the details underlying the construction of meaning, both individually and in interaction. The frames within which meaning is constructed and social norms upheld in situations and contexts of face to-face-interaction are in focus. Goffman was less interested in the social structures surrounding these frames. Inspired by the social constructivist view of Schultz, Goffman attributed priority to people, not to the world.[46]

In other words, Goffman pays attention to the attribution of meaning as an inscription of body in the surrounding landscape. He refers to Schutz: "*And to the fact that our bodies always participate in the everyday world whatever our interest at the time, this participation implying a capacity to affect and be affected by the everyday world*". (Schutz, 1962: 342, cf Goffman, 1986: 5 my emphasis). So instead of saying that a sub-universe is generated in accordance with certain structural principles, Goffman states that it has a certain "cognitive style". Inspired by the multiple realities view of Schulz, Goffman speaks of provinces of meaning and not of sub-universes because "*it is the meaning of experience and not the ontological structure of the objects which constitute reality*". (ibid: 231, cf. Goffman, 1986:4, my emphasis) The perspective of Goffman, like Schultz, is situational. Meaning in this perspective is a concern for what one individual can be alive to at a particular moment. Goffman explains the notion of frame as follows: 'I assume that definitions of a situation are built up in accordance with principles of organisation, which govern events – at least social ones - and our subjective[47] involvement in them; frame is the word I use to refer to such

---

[45] 'Strip' Goffman (1986:10) refers to as any arbitrary slice or cut from the stream of ongoing activity, including sequences of happenings, real or fictive, as seen from the perspective of those subjectively involved in sustaining an interest in them. Linear presentation, in Goffman's view, constrains what is actually a circular affair. News presentations are a composition of arbitrary slices assembled in a linear progression of events from introduction, on-location pictures, expert and interview explanations and concluding remarks.

[46] 'For we will find that the world of everyday life, the common-sense world, has a paramount position among the various provinces of reality, since only within it does communication with our fellowmen become possible. But the common-sense world is from the outset a socio-cultural world, and the many questions connected with the inter-subjectivity of the symbolic relations originate within it, are determined by it, and find their solution within it'. (Schutz, 1962: 294, cf. Goffman 1986).

[47] The inevitability of subjectivity rests upon the involvement and life experience. Our personal trajectory consists of 'whole series of mental photographs' acquired throughout personal and professional social

of these basic elements' (Goffman: 1986:10-11). Frame analysis, in accordance with this notion of Goffman, is an investigation of such basic elements or 'strips' in the 'organisation of experience' (Goffman, 1986: 11). 'Strip' Goffman (1986:10) refers to as any arbitrary slice or cut from the stream of ongoing activity, including sequences of happenings, real or fictive, as seen from the perspective of those subjectively involved in sustaining an interest in them. Linear presentation, in Goffman's view, constrains what is actually a circular affair. News presentations in this view may be seen to be a circular affair in which arbitrary non-linear slices of reality are assembled into a story-line with a linear progression from introduction, on-location pictures, expert and interview explanations to concluding remarks.

Goffman(1986) introduces the notions of 'front stage' and 'back stage' which resemble the Japanese dichotomies of *honne* and *tatemae* the 'real intentions behind action' and the 'up front performance'. The underlying intensions behind performance and discursive actions are discussed in the section on strategy below.

In sum meaning as presented above meaning is assumed to be 'relational' and 'situational'. However, while the subjective involvement of news producers is the focus of investigation in the present project the surrounding organisations and socio-cultural environment is also taken into consideration in the analysis.

Frames in interaction

The ability to communicate the most suitable information in a given situation is described by Goffman as creating *memorable* moments

> ..it is rare in "natural" conversation that the best answer is provided on the spot, rare that witty repartee occurs, even though this will often be the aim. Indeed, when during informal talk a reply is provided that is as good as the one that could be later thought up, then a *memorable* event has occurred". (Goffman, 1986:501).

Gofmann's description concerns communication in face-to-face situations but may well be applied to mass mediated communication, which revolves around the creation of such 'memorable' events. A criterion for competent on-the-spot commentary in news is to make it "as good as the one that could be later thought up". The strategies and skills that enable such communication are investigated in the present study through the analytical categories of *framing* and *priming* which derive from cognitive psychology and refer to the 'conceptual schemes' and methods or cognitive models of expression (van Dijk 1988; Graber 1984). The famous Japanese news caster Kume Hiroshi at News Station is exceptionally good at creating 'memorable moment'. See elaboration in Chapter 7.

The aim is thus to investigate the textual strategies of news producers, i.e. the ways in which they shape or *frame* visuals and texts. The social strategies and processes of negotiation in news-making including the planning, decision-making and negotiation of individual and shared knowledge are investigated, and finally contextual dimensions concerning actors and factors at four analytical levels: the global, the national, the organisational and the professional.

---

experience (Bourdieu and Wacquant, 1992: 205). These experiences and mental photographs are idiosyncratic to the person involved.

With emphasis on the production of international news and processes in the interim of mediating international political information to national audiences, the theoretical framework helps to explain how journalists organise 'strips' of experience (Goffman, 1986:10) into text and visuals in news compositions. The term 'strips' refers to 'any arbitrary slice or cut from the stream of ongoing activity, including here sequences of hapenings, real or fictive, as seen from the perspective of those subjectively involved in sustaining an interest in them. Goffman, 1986:10). The 'organisation of experience' by this definition assumes that journalists may know intellectually and/or have experienced events in order to be able to mediate them.[48]

News in a perspective of *interaction* concerns social actors, while social actors participate in news. The framing of experiences in news production processes is thus twofold. News producers (foreign correspondents) transfer information and make sense of it *socially* through interaction[49] with colleagues, while it is their professional task to frame and organise 'strips' of experience *textually* in news presentations. The roles and identities in news presentations are set up following a scripted story line. Politicians, experts, ordinary citizens, spokesmen for organisational views, professional journalists play their roles according to prescribed rules. Foreign and domestic political actors behave and communicate according to expectations. The choreography of political events and 'photo opportunities' are carefully planned according to pre-existing scripts (imagined performance) by the actors. The historical handshakes and faces turned towards the cameras are carefully staged, resembling theatrical performances (Goffmann, 1986). Through the camera, actors are captured and moments made historical 'reality'. The news media itself resembles the memory of society through its audio-visual documents referred to again and again. Just like cognitive machinery, events are retrieved and replayed[50] thus reinforcing and priming certain incidents over others.

Emerging strategies

The models and scripts of the "cognitive machinery" are continuously negotiated. Each new frame in communicative acts is influenced multiple factors. The multiple factors of influence on decision-making processes pose challenges to information processing.

---

[48] In the classical discussion between empiricism and rationalism, advocators for empiricism hold that all knowledge is based on experience and the human mind is not equipped with a set of concepts in advance of experience. Advocators of rationalism believe that reason alone, without any reliance on experience, can reveal the nature of reality. The introduction of pragmatism in the middle of the 20th century was bridging between the two by suggesting that people might be able to know in both ways. The basic assumption of this project follows the latter approach to knowledge in believing that people are able to know both on the basis of experience *and* based on reason through intellectual exercise.

[49] What is crucial in ritual professional games is the sense of affirmation that exchange partners derive from successful encounters, the feeling of selfhood that are reinforced in the ritual game is the sense of affirmation that exchange partners derive from successful encounters.

[50] As sociologist Raymond Williams describes on a visit to the US in the 1970s, it was difficult for him to differentiate between commercials and movies. Williams was not familiar with US culture and rules of interaction, so he was not able to break the code of meaning in the fragmented strips of experiences shown on TV between commercials and TV dramas. The use of archive material in news and documentary likewise makes it difficult to differentiate between time and space. Historical events become uppermost in memory, others fade out just as it is illustrated in the model of discourse strands above. Life and death become virtual when dignitaries appear from the archives and time and again are displayed in "the flower of their youth". Although they may have died decades ago their appearance and personal frames occupy a vivid place in our memory. Television, in this sense, is as fragmented in time and space as memory.

Frames of interaction and meaning creation are as discussed above contextual and continuously changing. The notions of strategy or emerging strategies (Mintzberg, 1987) as used in this project reflect the conditions of change. The notion of strategy is used in this project to analysed decision-making processes. These processes may be intentional or based on emerging strategies as described in the following.

Mintzberg's (1987) five p's for strategy include *plan, ploy, pattern, position* and *perspective*. Strategy may be a plan, a sort of consciously intended course of action, a guideline to deal with a situation. A child may have a strategy to get over a fence, a company a strategy to gain market shares while the journalist has a strategy to make events into news. If plans can be attended they can also be realised. Strategy that encompasses the resulting behaviour of conscious intent may be defined as a pattern, a pattern in a stream of action. By this definition, strategy implies consistency in behaviour, whether or not intended. The study of practices, as in the present project, thus provides clues about the strategies behind 'consistent behaviour'. Mintzberg distinguishes between *intended* strategy and *realised* strategy and distinguishes between *deliberate* strategies and *emergent* strategies. In order to realise deliberate strategies precise intentions would have to stated in advanced and accepted by everyone in the company with no interference by market, political forces and so on. Likewise, a truly emergent strategy requires consistency in action without any hint of intention. Most strategies are placed on a continuum that exists between the two reflecting deliberate as well as emergent aspects. The fourth definition of strategy locates the organisation in the external environment, the fifth looks inside the organisation indeed inside the heads of the collective strategist, but in a broader view. Here strategy is a perspective, its content consisting not just of a chosen position, but of *an ingrained way of perceiving the world.* (my emphasis). A variety of concepts capture this notion; anthropologists refer to "culture" and sociologist to "ideology" military theorist to the "grand strategy" of armies, management theorist to "theory of the firm". The notion that best captures the collective intuition about how the world works, according to Mintzberg, may be the German "verstehen" or "weltanshauung" literally "worldview". The Japanese '*kuuki*', which literally means atmosphere, resembles this perspective of shared perceptions of the social. Mintzberg argues that by this latter definition strategy is a perspective shared by the members of an organisation, through their intentions and/or by their actions. The study of strategy formation thus become a study of the collective mind in order to understand how intentions diffuse through the organisation to become shared and how actions come to be exercised on a collective yet consistent basis. The shared values of news producers the study of 'news values and news criteria' and the collective strategies in making news in are studied in the present chapter and referred to as the production *formula*. The personal and individual strategies in dealing with this *formula* are studied in chapter six at the executive level, chapter seven at the organisational level and chapter eight at the professional (individual) level. Chapter Four provides an analysis of news presentations, which exemplifies the *realisation* and product of production strategies.

Priming and timing

Priming in a cognitive perspective relates to the explanation of information processing above and means to activate schemes. At the global level then priming may be understood as an activation of schemes at a larger level. For instance at the macro level media may bring issues to the attention of the public and thus activates certain schemes and set the agenda for political debate. At the micro level priming refers to the activation of schemes that make people concerned with certain issues. Fairhurst and Saar defines priming as follows:

Priming according to Fairhurst and Sarr (1996) is an important tool in communication and involves retrieving the information most appropriate for the situation. Priming is a way of preparing one's unconscious mind before thoughts are expressed through language. It is a necessary state of readiness that is critical for effective 'spontaneous' communication.

The definition by Fairhurst and Sarr involves the activation of mental schemes for expression through language. The use of language, as exemplified in the 'sense of news' described above, may be both unconscious and conscious. In the process of priming, certain schemes of information are activated above others according to professional and socio-cultural models and scripts. In communication in general and in news production in particular timing is an important factor.

The concern with time is paramount in news reporting; deadlines and limited time on air make news producers develop certain skills for prioritising information, choosing headlines, metaphors, narrative forms and roles and actors that audiences will recognise. The activity of priming and bringing certain information up front is already occurring in the initial negotiations between news producers in the field and the Tokyo office about the composition of visuals and text.

For the reporter on-site, and for the anchors and commentators the process of priming involves the mental preparation for the on-air presentations. The ability to priming is an 'art of communication' which particularly applies to the fleeting nature of broadcast news in which political reportage and interpretation has to seem spontaneous to be effective. Commentary on air is irrevocable which demands precision. Once a reporter has made his statements, time has passed. Often there is no time for carefully scripted speeches and information has to be framed in the immediacy of the situation. Additional questions from the Tokyo office although often pre-arranged draw upon abilities to prime i.e. mediate the most appropriate information for the occasion.

With the myriad of combinations of factors that merge from the contexts of the situation, the skilled news producer 'reads' a context and prepares accordingly. All other things being equal (such as the amount of information that they possess about a subject), news producers prime not just by reflecting upon their knowledge (mental models), but also and not least by communicating them. Negotiations have often already been underway through discussion with co-workers and personnel in Tokyo, which enhances awareness of the story content. An awareness of what they say when communicating mental models to others primes the unconscious in the same way that reflecting on them does. Whether it is reflections through retrieval and replay in interpersonal communication that bring mental models to the surface, conscious recall seemingly leaves an unconscious imprint. The more communication draws from the state of mental readiness that priming creates, the more comprehensive the information pool (mental schemes) becomes about a certain issue. The artfulness of communication lies in the ability to frame and make comments on-the-spot as good as the ones that could be later thought up (Goffman, 1986).

Frames in emotions and senses

Schema theory may also explain our emotional lives. It is important to explore the critical 'soft' aspect of enabling knowledge and communication. Because knowledge is so intimately tied to people, it is emotional and affected by our senses. The following shows how affective elements of cognition are important in knowledge processing, whether this involves the individual acquisition of information or social interaction.

> However we may feel about emotions, our emotional life is in fact modelled all the way down. (Shore, 1998:20).

People deal with sensory input through processes that in the terminology of the developmental psychologist, Piaget (1960), are referred to as *assimilation* and *accommodation*. These processes resemble schema theory in the way that inputs from the environment are assimilated and accommodated into pre-existing experiences of the individual through a combination of affective or sensory[51] stimuli.

Emotional schemes or models are described by Shore (1998:212) in the following way. The body is primed to model primary emotional states like fear, rage and surprise by a tattered marshalling of physiological responses to emotional experience. These responses include heart rate, blood flow, endocrine production and body temperature. People read some of the more visible of these body markers in others as models of their emotional state. And they monitor their own inner feelings by checking these signs in themselves. This way of checking inner feelings is a way of knowing how we are responding to the world.

Synaesthesia is an important kind of cross-modal sensory modelling by which people perceive sensory equivalencies between colour and sound, or sound and touch. While some individuals are far more likely to perceive synaesthetically than others, unconscious synaesthesia is a very important aspect of how we make meaning out of our experiences (one sensory experience reminds us of another and takes on a news meaning) (Shore 1998).

Less obvious than these more universal aspects of emotion modelling are *the specifically cultural models that we learn about how to feel and how to express our feelings*. Emotional states have their specific names, associations, body postures and related stories so that in large part we have to learn how to model our feelings (ibid). The cross-modal sensory model is interesting in the study of audiovisual material such as news. How do 'objective' news presentations affect the sensory system and how do the senses work consciously and unconsciously across to make meaning of audio-visual stimuli. While the empirical evidence to throw light on the sensory processes of synaesthesia is not within the reach of this project. The notions that emotional schemes may be culturally dependent is taken into account. And as there are culturally learned models for emotions, so are there learned ways to handle emotions professionally.

---

[51] Symbolic communication in face-to-face interaction is characterised by using the senses. The five human senses enable us to communicate embodied information with eyes, features and gestures. It is also characterised by immediate intentional perspective-taking, shared socio-cultural experience, and mutual knowledge between participants (Markova and Foppa, 1990).

A critical note on schema theory

As a final note, it deserves mention that schema theory may be criticised for its mechanical behavioural assumptions. The schema approach works from the top down, initially by formulating hypotheses concerning general cognitive procedures or rules, and then applying these to individual thinking through experimental or survey data. This theoretical framework may be compared to 'the algorithmic model of a computer, which fails to either integrate or account for the affective, context-dependent and interest-driven nature of human understanding - particularly in an area such as politics' (Crigler & Jensen, 1991:179). The 'laboratory' approach of cognitive studies has been criticised for being insensitive to contextual influences on information processing and for failing to deal with the affective and interest-driven nature of cognition, which is important in sense-making and the storage of information. It deserves mention that Graber several times throughout her book acknowledges emotions as an important motivation for watching news (See Graber, 1984: 107, 172). Graber also emphasises that interest (including cognitive and affective elements) supersedes formal learning in knowledge acquisition. However, the cognitive theories that she draws upon do not include the emotional element.

Varela, Thompson and Rosche (1991) likewise point to the limitations of the cognitivist view of human experience and suggest that cognitive experience is 'embodied action' rather than a mere representation of a world that is independent of individual cognitive systems. Their notion of 'embodied action' takes the five senses and their influence and specific ways of storage and recall of information into account. The aspect of senses[52] is paramount in perception and knowledge acquisition. It suffices for the present argument to say that there is a difference between learning by experience or learning in an intellectual fashion. The process of learning, however, is the same: it builds on existing knowledge. Why do journalists with very sophisticated knowledge not become superior journalists in the field? The implementation of knowledge depends not only on which knowledge (s)he possesses but also what he or she does with it – a difference between knowing and doing. How is knowledge applied? Practical knowledge and intellectual knowledge are thus two different forms of knowledge.

The present study takes its point of departure in the specific understanding of news voiced by interviewees in an informal, conversational context. It thereby moves in a *bottom-up* direction from the data. The present study does not intend to verify or falsify theoretical hypotheses about cognition. It merely employs cognitive theory as a theoretical framework. It applies a bottom-up approach, moving from empirical data, using cognition as an analytical tool to explain the circular process of meaning creation and interaction in news texts resulting from the production of these texts and knowledge in society.

---

[52] Senses and emotions as important cognitive elements are neglected aspects of management and organisation research, although sensual and emotional schemata are important parts of the cognitive apparatus and important for business and management competencies. Access to information about people's inner worlds concerning these issues is difficult and ultimately a methodological problem. (Chapter Four in this dissertation includes an analysis of the framing of visual images in news presentations).

Contextual framing

Inspired by the models of Shoemaker and Reese (1996) and Fairclough (1995), the present study provides a model including four contextual influences on news production strategies, namely the *global*, the *national*, the *organisational* and the *professional*. In the following these models of inspiration are discussed; secondly, categories of analysis that differ between Western studies and the Japanese case are presented; and finally, the 'domestication' model of the present project is introduced.

In an effort to analyse the forces that influence news content, Shoemaker and Reese (1996) depict a series of concentric rings representing five hierarchical levels with the point of analytical departure at the centre of their model. The rings represent the individual, the media routines, the organisational, the extra-media and the ideological level. Their model is based on an extensive listing of mainly American theoretical and empirical studies of news content. Shoemaker and Reese (1996) approach the analysis of content from a social science perspective. The British linguist, Norman Fairclough (1995), has developed a model for the analysis of media texts. Fairclough takes his point of departure in the text and considers the *discursive practices* (consumption and production[53]) and the socio-cultural environment in his analysis of news texts. Where Shoemaker and Reese (as social scientists) take content as a starting point and work forward in order to examine the effects external to and created by the message, Fairclough (as a humanist) takes content as a starting point and works backwards in order to understand the culture producing it. Thus, for the social scientist, content is part of a chain of cause and effect; while for the humanist content is important and the 'text' worthy of study in its own right. The cause and effect theories as discussed above assume a transmission model of communication. The assumed 'hyperdemic needle' effect, as argued above, is less sensitive to the dynamics and reciprocal influences between media and society. Against this backdrop, the present project is a study of media texts in a perspective of *interaction*. It is an exploration of contextual factors and actors influencing textual strategies. The study is 'grounded' in news production practices and content analysis. It takes its point of departure in texts *cum* production analysis and from an interpretative contructivist perspective uses humanistic tools to explain the influences on textual strategies and social processes in organisations where these texts are produced. The socio-political environment represents one of several influences on news production. The extra-media factors and actors of influence at the socio-cultural level are extended in the present project to include a 'global' perspective.

In relation to the research issues and categorisations at the different levels of analysis as represented by Shoemaker and Reese, some differed in the Japanese case study. The communicator's characteristics (religion, gender, ethnicity, and sexual orientation) and their personal background and experiences (attending journalism or film school) were not categories of analysis in the present study. Religion, gender, ethnicity and sexual orientation, which are overt issues in the US, are covert in Japan. The issues of religious rights and religious affiliation of employees is not an issue in the polo-theistic Japanese

---

[53] Although Fairclough does not attend to empirical studies of text reception and text production he emphasises the importance of studying 'discursive practices' (1995:59).

society. Ethnicity[54] and sexual orientation are seldom discussed in mainstream Japanese media and even less so in the work environment. The issue of gender was not covert, but it was not a mainstream issue. The issue of gender became a theme in the present analysis at the professional level (Chapter Four and Chapter Seven) because the focus of analysis is the production and framing of news from the UN Conference on Women in Beijing.

Educational background was not an analytical category because news producers in Japan have hitherto been hired (with or without a college degree in journalism) through general hiring procedures in the company. They have then been educated as journalists on-the-job (See Cooper-Chen, 1987 on communication and journalism studies in Japan).

Where *hiring and firing* were strong factors of journalistic socialisation in US media companies, the lifetime employment system in the Japanese companies caused a different form of professional socialisation. Following the collapse of the bubble economy the bankruptcy of big Japanese companies was seen as a welcome new source of employment. Headhunting initiatives were mentioned as innovative methods against the restricting system of lifetime employment.

In the United Sates as in Japan, government control through laws and regulations determine both who can own a broadcast media and what kinds of content will be permitted. The size of the market and its opportunities for profit affect content (Shoemaker and Reese, 1996:175, 219). (For a comparative analysis of the differences in the business side of media in Japan and the United States see Westney, 1996).

The notion of routines, which is not a cultural issue but a theoretical and empirical construct, was not employed in the present study. In the classic studies of news production introduced in the previous chapter news values, audience appeal, story structure and the use of sources are considered part of bureaucratic and functionalistic routines. These routines are found to *constrain* media workers (Shoemaker and Reese, 1996: 139). The concept of routines in the view of the present project (see discussion in Chapter Two) undermines the multifaceted and complex work of news production[55]. In the framework of the present study, news production is studied from a psychological perspective in order to describe the 'mental strategies' of news producers, which provide a more nuanced and heterogeneous view of work processes than that implied in the notion of routine. The embodiment of structures in this study may be seen as an opportunity for news producers to work according to own preferences rather than being a constraint.

Ideology as 'a symbolic mechanism that serves as a cohesive and integrating force in society' was a main issue in many US studies (Shoemaker and Reese, 1996:251). The present analysis is not adapting ideology in a paradigm of hegemony but rather treats ideology as political strands of discourse.

---

[54] The discussion in the Japanese media of one Japanese minority the *burakumin* (Japan's "Untouchables") remains almost taboo. People of *burakumin* heritage had ancestors who engaged in butchering and leather working. Unless they can keep their heritage secret, they have to marry only other *burakumin* and face housing and job discrimination (Cooper-Chen, 1997: 144).

[55] A large body of literature on news production as listed in the previous chapter uses the notion of routine to explain work procedures and dealing with an abundance of information. Furthermore, Giddens emphasises the role of routine in sustaining social structure and sketches the rudiment of a psychology of motivation in his notion of the "basic security system" as a fundamental component of the self. Drawing selectively on development psychology, Giddens contends that the control of diffuse anxiety is "the most generalised motivational origin of human conduct" (1984: 54). The means of such control is adherence to routine, and he points to the fact that the compulsion to avoid anxiety motivates actors to sustain the social encounters that constitute both daily life and social structure.

Where this section introduced the theoretical models of inspiration for the analytical levels of the 'domestication' model, it also demarcated issues that for cultural reasons and/or due to theoretical assumptions were not treated in the present project. The contextual levels of analysis in the present project are described in the following.

Text in context

Tveiten (1993) distinguishes between two different meanings of the term context: context in text which is concerned with how the various elements of the text are related to each other (intertextuality); and text in context concerning how the various elements of the text reflect the cultural framework of its production. Helland (1993) presents another meaning of context which is also relevant in this thesis – that of the context of the production of the text for example, organisational factors, or relations to the state and to the market.

In the present project the notions of 'text' and 'context' change according to level of analysis. At the global level 'texts' refers to the verbal and visual expressions in news output. The news texts are analysed in relation to their professional, national and global context. At the national level 'texts' are statements provided by media experts and executive news producers about news management and production strategies in media organisations. These 'strategy texts' are compared and related to a wider socio-political context. At the organisational level statements by news producers are analysed as texts; their context is organisational practices which are related to wider socio-cultural factors. At the professional level interviews serve as 'texts' about the actual production of the 'news texts' studied at the global level. In other words these text are studied in order to provide insights about social processes on location in the actual making of the specific news. These processes include negotiation of individual and professionally (organisationally) shared values.

The 'domestication' model

The 'domestication' model is based on the ontological assumption that in a world of infinite happenings only some become global events. There is a difference between the 'marked' and the 'unmarked'. Only when happenings are recognised by social actors and become *discursive* are they viable for distribution to local and global markets. This is where the initial process of selection and construction takes place. At first, international events come to the attention of news workers through international news distributors, or they may be 'marked' or and made discursive by Japanese journalists abroad. Or they may be a combination of both. Incidences happen locally but are made available to an international marketplace or sphere. The ability to gain access to local sources through own offices and correspondents around the world is determined by the financial situation and policy of the news media. In this case, the investigated media have financial means and connections worldwide to develop their own stories.

Following the concentric circles of the 'domestication' model, one may imagine the process of international news production as being influenced by actors and factors at each level. The hierarchical order of levels indicates the order of analysis and refers to the composition of chapters. Influences on *production strategies* are analysed at the global, the national, the organisational and the professional levels. The main issues addressed at each level are:

1. The *global* influences on international news output in national broadcast institutions: Themes, actors, communication form and formats, sources.

2. The *national* political, legal and technological environment.

3. The *organisational* differences at the public station and the private station

4. The *professional* values and journalistic standards

It is noteworthy that the model does not show how the overlapping factors and actors at each level. At the global level, for instance, the textual strategies are influenced by national, organisational and professional factors. At the national level, global actors and factors (the news agencies, technological and economic development) influence the national media environment and production practices at the national broadcast stations. At the organisational level, global trends in the new economy (leading to the

Figure 5: The 'domestication' model: Influences on news production strategies

marketisation of news), as well as trends in the national political and legal system, influence organisational practices; and finally at the professional level considerations are influenced by factors including all of the above. The model merely outlines on the analysis of factors and actors at each level.

Global context

At this level, 'global' discourses in news presentation in two national contexts (Danish and Japanese) are analysed in order to describe how concepts are incorporated or transformed in a European and Asian part of the world. The communication strategies, the choice of actors and the discourses are analysed in media texts in the two national contexts in order to describe the final product as an outcome of the national frame of

80

reference in production process. The analysis of communication strategies and 'aesthetic' elements is important in order to describe how 'discourse' (information) is transferred globally and mediated through the employment of conventional communication strategies in the news genre. It was found that aesthetic elements in news formats and narrative structures in news presentations were recognised in both contexts. The study of actors provided knowledge about prominent characters and their behaviour in political and national contexts. The construction of identities and choreography in news, the costumes and the coherence of verbalisations followed conventional patterns that were recognised across cultures. Finally, the framing of the global (UN) themes and the creation of global coherence were analysed as they were enacted through visual and verbal 'instalments' throughout the presentations. The social and professional actors represented different domains of historical, political and cultural knowledge, which became apparent through the analysis of verbal accounts.

The textual analysis of news in its final form brings insights to the understanding of production processes studied in the succinct chapters.

National context

International news production is aimed at political and social agents in a national context. The analysis at this level is concerned with extra-media factors in the national media environment. The news event may both include and concern politicians, sponsors, audiences, non-governmental organisations, competing media and ordinary citizens. The 'world views' of executive management in the international newsrooms at the public service and the commercial stations provide information for a description of the structural premises and the actors surrounding and influencing news content. The focus on geographic areas and the choice of news items and actors are influenced by the national positioning in the international economic and political community, as is the national self-understanding.

The international news agencies play an important role at this level for the proliferation of discourse. Firstly, the influence of Western discourse in Japan is evident as the agencies have already 'domesticated' news information to suit Western publics. Secondly, the main public and private stations are connected to Western national networks and international news wholesalers.

Finally, at this level, the audience is of importance in strategic news management. Audiences are the targets of news messages and the 'domestication' of discourse is done with an appeal to national audiences. In cognitive terms, global information is shaped in order to be assimilated and absorbed into pre-existing schemes of knowledge or models for world events within a given national framework of reference.

Organisational context

At the organisational level the micro processes and 'discursive practices' of news production are studied. The construction of news discourses and the assembly of visuals and texts include various editorial processes and organisational procedures at different levels of the organisation. The order of events is decided through a process of attributing priority to story ideas in newsroom meetings. The chosen events pass scriptwriters, news desks, correspondents, editors, producers, and anchors, newsreaders and satellite staff, who in turn contribute with their expertise in editorial work.[56] International events are framed while taking the interest of the domestic social actors into account. The organisational context provides a structure for the flow information and dynamics of interaction and negotiation. Communication strategies (the expression of discourse in form and content) are influenced by these structures. The human resources that give the structures life are in focus at this level. The capability and expertise of individuals are important in the production of international news in two ways. First, knowledgeable staff is necessary to recognise and interpret international discourse. Secondly, the activation of practical senses of shaping international discourse into news is necessary.

The concept of 'priming' is introduced at this level. It is connected to the concept of framing and relies on sensitivity to the audience. If context in communicative action is defined by framing elements of meaning to an implied audience, priming is a sensitive awareness of the mental models of the audience and the ability to prioritise information in an appropriate fashion to suit a given context. The awareness of the mental models and audience frames of knowledge make news producers able to shape and condense knowledge acquired in one context to suit another. There are two ways of framing: a 'proactive' and a 'retroactive' framing (Fairhurst and Sarr, 1996). News producers employ both when they account for happenings in the past and predict future developments and social change in the future.

Assumption in the analysis of organisational practices is that the organisational structures are understood as enabling expressions of knowledge. The hierarchical structures of decision-making are important in the assessment of value and authority of information. The role in the hierarchy of the newsrooms is important for the choice of issues and ability to set the agenda and consequently decide on the frames, time and resources allocated to certain issues. Access to decision-making fora and procedures are paramount in order to influence newsroom agendas. Professional and organisational structures are imprinted in the news producers' work in important ways to shape news, while news producers on the other hand continuously reconstitute and change structures.

Professional context

The analysis at this level concerns the mental strategies of the news producers as professional news producers. It is an analysis of their personal approach and strategies on location abroad, including the planning, research of events and the way preconceived ideas and impressions are dealt with in the situation of the event. It is an analysis of the news producers and their perception of organisational policies and structural factors described above. It is a study of the internalisation of the institutional and professional values that affect the strategies of production. The production of specific news events is followed from the planning to the final output and I describe the strategies of the individual news producer in negotiations with colleagues and superiors in the framing process which includes the choice of themes, actors and visuals for the final output.

The *professional* level in the present study includes an analysis of individual considerations of professionals in action. This includes a study of personal attitudes, values and beliefs about content, which are found to be indirect and operating only to

---

[56] Bell (1991) estimates, for instance, that in a moderate-sized press newsroom up to eight people may contribute to the production of a story, and the story may correspondingly go through up to eight versions. The journalist's first draft may be changed by the chief reporter, the news editor, the editor, the chief sub-editor, a page sub-editor, a copy sub-editor, or the check sub-editor (Bell, 1991:44-46).

82

the extent that the individuals hold power within their media organisation. The focus of this study on international news enhances individual influence on the production of news as each news producer is an *expert* in his field and thereby is allotted authority status in the interpretation of events.

The study of specific news (The UN Conference on Women) makes the issue of gender in national broadcast news, in media organisations as well as in Japanese society at large, a central theme at this level of analysis.

In summary, the complexity and inter-relatedness of the different levels and influence on news content are obvious and a challenge to media scholars. The question of where to focus is paramount. Most studies, like this one, deal with some combination of levels. The present research accounts for multiple factors and actors at each level, but with a narrow focus on the production *processes* of specific news events. The factors analysed at each level in the present project are not understood as hierarchical structural influences but as overlapping and interrelated.

Conclusion

In today's information society, the ability of news producers to negotiate a story successfully depends on their ability to 'frame' international information, in other words to make international events discursive through verbalisations and visuals. The 'priming' of knowledge, the choice of words and visuals depends on personal experience and the ability to prioritise and contextualise information.

The object of analysis of the present project is the framing of texts in context. Where explicit statement and mental representations are studied through interviews, cognition is used to map the inner worlds of the news producers. Experience and knowledge acquisition may be understood as schemes or schemata stored in memory over time. The stored schemata make models and inner scripts for our understanding of the outer world. The knowledge bases, understood as schemata, are imprinted cultural models for social behaviour. The newsrooms are understood as 'rooms of knowledge' where information is actively negotiated.

A synthesis of theoretical approaches provides a framework that encompasses and interconnects the contextual levels mentioned above: The framework is context sensitive, explains information processes, bridges between social processes at macro and micro levels and includes emotions in knowledge acquisition. A cognitive framework may be used across cultures, as theories of information processing as presented above may be applied universally. Cognitive theory includes schemes for cultural knowledge and the notion of 'domestication' relies on the theoretical construct that information is processed through already existing mental schemes in memory. Domestication is defined as a) the process of adapting and presenting 'global' news within frames of reference of *local* national audiences in the same socio-cultural setting (at the macro level). B) and as the process of transferring information in communicative action from one framework to another (at the micro level). 'Domestication' refers in both cases to the process of taking information home and processing it trough pre-existing knowledge.

The use of cognitive schema theory helps to break away from the categories often used to describe Japanese management. Japanese organisational and cultural studies have tended to focus on differences, which has made Japanese organisational cultural characteristics appear 'unique'. A cognitive approach such as the present opens up for descriptions of work strategies that do not take their point of departure in these conventional organisational cultural categories and therefore opens up for new ways of describing social processes in Japanese organisations in their heterogeneity and complexity.

The following chapters thus explore the mental strategies of news producers in processes of textual framing and professional interaction while it makes a systematic analysis of the influence of contextual factors of influence including the global, the national the organisational and the professional.

Part II

Chapter Four

Global news output in Denmark and Japan

News is a window on the world. Through its frame, [we] learn of ourselves and others, of our own institution, leaders, and life styles, and those of other nations and their people (Tuchman, 1978:1).

Introduction

Theories promoting the notion of 'global' news assume that broadcast news in any country because of technological development and the international distribution of news, causes the organisation and production of news to be universal. These 'global' news theories assume that the global infrastructure of media organisations and the inter-connectedness between suppliers of news influence content and result in a diffusion of homogenised news worldwide. However, systematic analyses of news visuals and texts, as presented in the present chapter, reveal that news content in important ways differs between nations and even between types of station (public versus commercial) within national media environments.

The present chapter is an analysis of *communication strategies, discourses and actors* in international news as they are presented in Denmark and Japan. The analysis is made with the assumption that content reflects the professional practices and textual strategies of international news production. News texts and visuals are analysed in order to bring insights into the practices and textual strategies of news production.

Where the following chapters concern news production in Japan, the present chapter provides a comparative perspective of international news presentations in order to highlight Japanese presentation forms.

It is assumed in the study that news presentations reflect a dialectic process operating between agenda-setting at the global level and agenda-setting at the local national level. International political discourses transcend national borders, while meeting the 'filter' in production processes in national broadcast organisations that reflect the particular conception of politics embodied in the political life of national society. The textual strategies of news producers not only differ according to the agenda of national broadcast media but also according to organisational and professional presentation practices.

It is concluded that strategies of communicating international news include elements that may be defined as both *global* and *local*. It is empirically difficult to distinguish between the two as news production includes elements that are nationally distinct as well as elements that are recognisable in news presentations worldwide. Nevertheless, it is attempted throughout the analysis to categorise these elements by highlighting similarities or *universal* findings with differences or *particular* findings in news content in the two countries.

The chapter is thus an analysis of discourses as presented in two media environments with different historical, political and cultural backgrounds. The chapter verifies the proposed hypothesis that international news is 'domesticated'. In spite of universal characteristics in communication strategies, content to a great extent includes elements that create meaning in a particular national environment. The notion of 'domestication' serves in this project as a counter-conceptualisation to the 'global' news theories mentioned above. It implies that news is 'made suitable for home audiences'. In cognitive theoretical terms, 'domestication' concerns the identification of elements of meaning construction in news texts that describe the *mental schemes* and *models* for news-making that render communication of political information possible. These mental strategies and professional models are based on a national cultural frame of interpretation, which is recognised by journalists and audiences alike. The 'domestication' of news in this context is defined as the means by which news is constructed within a framework of meaning which is recognised by news producers and viewers sharing the same socio-political background.

There is an increasing number of competing national and international channels offering news programs. This, however, has not altered the fact that television news broadcasting remains a prime source of information about the world (, 1992). Television news, therefore, is an important source of information about international affairs and an important public forum of study, which reflects international political affairs. The study of the flagship[57] news programs in the two countries offers insights about the socio-politically integrative character of national broadcasting, and makes the diverse interpretation of news information within different regional and national frameworks apparent.

The present chapter is thus an analysis of global events as they are presented within national boundaries. It investigates international news discourses and the communication strategies that involve the selection of themes, actors, visuals, angle of stories in the interest of national audiences.

'Global' news here refers to homogeneous information disseminated world-wide. 'Global' (as opposed to international) is understood as an international political discourse with an impact on nations worldwide. The United Nations Conference concerns policy-making which influences a majority of countries (184 members) in the international community. The focus of analysis is the textual strategies used in the mediation of global political discourse in the broadcast media in two UN member countries.

In summary, it is assumed in this chapter that ongoing processes at various contextual levels influence news production. The global standards of the news genre, the national political factors, relations with the outside world and connections to Western news agencies, the media environment, the public service and commercial organisational factors, and professional journalistic criteria are important influences on news production.

International news discourses (visuals and texts) are a combination both of standardisation i.e. 'universal' characteristics, as well as culturally 'specific' contextual traits. The questions asked in this chapter are: What characterises these traits and how are they implemented in the news texts? How do international media discourses enhance consciousness about global political affairs while making this relevant and appropriate for national audiences? How is the 'other' and own national identity constructed news texts and visuals?

A study of the public service and commercial news outputs in the two countries brings insights into organisational factors and provides answers to the questions: What characterises the communication strategies of public and commercial stations in different national contexts? One of the main findings was that the commercial stations allocated more resources to the coverage of the UN Conference, and that they broadcast

---

[57] The news programs studied were flagship programs of the national stations with the highest viewer ratings in both countries in September 1995. The public service station, NHK's *News Seven* and the commercial station, TV Asahi's program *News Station*, had viewer ratings of approximately 18 % (Video Research). The viewer ratings of the Danish Public Service Station DR1's *TV-Avisen* were 17% and the commercial station TV2's *Nyhederne* were 21% (Gallup). It deserves mention that the size of the audience differs, with populations of 120 million in Japan and 5 million in Denmark. Viewer ratings are measured in the population above 15 years old.

longer sequences about this event than the public service news programs in the two countries (See outline of news items in Appendix 1).

At the professional level the textual strategies were analysed in order to describe elements in formats that make them 'transnational' and journalistic values of news-worthiness that may be universal in order to answer the questions: Can strategies of 'factuality' and 'impartiality' of news information be traced in the news? How are these processes apparent in news texts?

The present chapter thus presents the analysis of international political news. It analyses the factors and actors that influence textual strategies at the *global*, *national*, *organisational* and *professional* levels. The observations are summarised and discussed in the conclusion of the chapter.

Framing international events

The strategy of analysis is threefold. First, it analyses the aesthetic elements in international audiovisual news communication. It analyses and points out how international news stories are presented in a communicative style (format), which has become recognised and 'natural' to viewers world-wide. Secondly, it investigates how international political discourses, while reflecting global occurrences and political dynamics are presented in the broadcast media in order to target audiences in a national context. It investigates how social identities and relationships are set up between national and international actors within the news presentations and choreographed in ways conventional in the news genre as part of the professional framing process. 'Discourse(s)' in the analysis are understood as visuals, verbal and written texts. Discourse at a more abstract level is understood as issues or domains of knowledge (Fairclough, 1995).

Thirdly, the representation of actors and their identities (roles) in the news are investigated in order to describe what relationships are set up between those involved? What are the relationships between reporters and interviewees, audience and experts, politicians and ordinary people. How is the symbolic social order maintained through this set-up?

The textual production strategies are presented through a systematic account of relating the public service and commercial Danish stations to the Japanese. The differences and similarities between the communication strategies, discourses and actors are then presented. By way of conclusion, the differences and similarities between approaches in the two countries, with regard to their different socio-cultural contexts are discussed.

The UN Conference on Women in Beijing

The opening day of the UN political meeting is selected for analysis as it represents the initial report of an ongoing world event. It exemplifies the framing process of a planned political event in its early stages when the background and premises of the event are being established.

The second day of the conference was used to exemplify a 'global' news story in chapter one. It was the last day of coverage for the Japanese public station (transmitting two short reports). This piece of news featured the speech of Hillary Rodham Clinton and attracted global media attention. The visual images of Clinton's performance were circulated world-wide and broadcast in Denmark and Japan with several sequences of almost identical visuals (Appendix 2). Why, then, was this not 'global' news exemplifying the homogenisation of global information, as theorised by some scholars? The visual images at first glance resembled each other but turned out to be assembled and edited differently. Furthermore, they were 'framed' and narrated with a 'spin' following production *formulae* for communication strategies of the national broadcast stations as presented in this chapter.

Figure 6: The UN agenda and Platform for Action

The Platform for Action (PLA) was divided into six chapters. These included the Mission Statement, the Global framework; the Critical Areas of Concern with twelve points; Strategic objectives and Actions; and the Institutional and Financial Arrangements. The PLA called for the integration of the gender perspective in all policies, and programmes and focussed on concrete measures to address critical areas of concern world-wide. These included: Women and Poverty and Training for women; Women and Health; Violence against Women; Women and armed conflict; Women and the economy. Others were: Women in Power and Decision-Making; Institutional Mechanisms for the Advancement of Women; Human Rights of Women; Women and the Media; Women and the Environment; and Girl-Child.

The PLA's objective was to remove all obstacles to women's active participation in all spheres of public and private life through a full and equal share in social, cultural and political decision-making.

Delegates from 180 countries gathered to contribute to the PLA. They had a variety of urgent concerns. While those from the Middle East were most interested in making child custody, divorce and inheritance laws more favourable to women, Latin Americans and Africans focused on poverty and human rights violations. North American and West European women wanted to talk about the absence of child-care facilities outside the home and the presence of corporate glass ceilings and other barriers to parity in the workplace. East Europeans worried about the economic upheaval that was eliminating their jobs and longstanding maternity and child-care subsidies, as well as provoking a suspected upsurge in physical assaults against women. Asians were caught up in the plight of women forced to feed themselves through prostitution, while Muslims objected to the Western representation of fundamentalism. Adolescent sexuality in Scandinavia was on the agenda as a concern in this region of the world. The official aim of the conference was to make a plan of action for gender equality to be implemented in the respective countries in year 2000. But as the outline suggested, the concern for policy on women's situation at the global level was varied, representing many interests.

(Compiled from "The Beijing Platform: UN Women's conference press releases": www:arcc.or.ke/gln./platform.html; Time, News Week, Economic Business Review, September, 1995).

The fourth World Conference on Women, henceforth referred to as the Beijing Conference, was held from September 4th to 15th 1995 in the People's Republic of China. The conference brought together two gatherings: the UN conference and the NGO Forum '95. With 17.000 participants, including 6.000 delegates from 189 countries, a host of international civil servants and about 4,000 media representatives, this was one of the largest global conferences ever held. Over 30.000 people participated in the NGO forum. The theme of the conference was *'Equality, Development and Peace'*.

The global Platform for Action (PLA) that emerged during the Conference was an outcome of earlier platforms drawn up by regions all over the world with specific perspectives on their areas. These platforms had been discussed prior to the major meeting in Beijing. The global Platform for Action reflecting the regional platforms emerged during the conference to become a political blueprint for women's advancement around the world. The PLA has since been globally recognised as a strong agenda for women's empowerment. The Beijing Declaration also emerged as a result of the conference. The declaration was an affirmation by world governments to declare their stand on women, their commitments to and concerns about women.

In view of the official UN policy and strategy for implementation by its members, and considering the differing concerns of its member countries, the coverage by the media becomes interesting. How did the media cover the event and discrepancy between official UN discourse and national interests? The following is an analysis of the presentation of the UN conference in Denmark and Japan, countries with very different global positions, and different socio-cultural trajectories and implementations of UN policies, but with similarities in their hybrid form of public service and commercial broadcast systems and their 'homogeneous' national cultural identity.

The findings of the analysis are listed in the display and will be resumed in the following. The quotations throughout the chapter refer to the visuals and transcriptions of the verbal accounts in the news presentations of the UN Conference on Women on the opening day (Appendix 7).

Frames in news communication

Communication strategies include the considerations of news producers when combining visuals and texts into coherent messages of signs and symbols. 'Aesthetic' considerations involve the textual strategies and the expressive tools and technical criteria and norms for communication in the news genre. The 'aesthetics', as discussed in Chapter Two, specifically refer to the studio-decoration, the format, the graphics (signs and symbols), the image of the program and of the news presenters, the props and cutting pace. These remedies and aesthetic effects are used to make information into the institutionalised form of audio-visual expression recognised as news.

Figure 7: Communication Strategies, Discourses and Actors

		Danish Stations		Japanese stations	
Communication strategy		Public service	Public service/ Commercial	Public	Commercial
		'Dramatic narrative'	'Dramatic narrative'	Information intensive *News*	Information intensive *News* and *views*
		Global standard	Global standard	Global standard	Global standard
Discourse		Negative spin Political rhetoric	Negative spin *Conversationalisation*	UN political rhetoric	UN and *domestic* political rhetoric
		Equal rights; Women's liberation	*Equality, development and peace*	*Equality, development and peace*	Equality, development and peace
		Anything *but* -	Anything *but* -	Poverty, violence and human rights	*Violence against women in war* 'comfort women' 'Stop nuclear testing'
		Event centred Negative account	Event centred Negative account	Pro government	Anti-establishment
Actors		*Danish* political elites	*Danish* political elites Ordinary participants	*Japanese* political elites	Japanese political elites Ordinary participants
		Danish professionals On location	*Danish professionals* On location	*Japanese Professionals* On location	*Japanese Professionals* On location
		Few voices	Many voices	Few voices	Many voices
		African political elite	African political elite	Mixed political protocol	Mixed political protocol

Formats

Casual viewers of Danish and Japanese international news from other industrialised countries will immediately recognise familiar elements of the news genre, and may experience a resemblance in news formats. The first glance thus confirms the notion of a universal format familiar to viewers world-wide. On closer analysis, however, distinctions appear. The 'global' packaging of informational products as well as its local distinctions are exemplified in the following.

As part of the branding and construction of programme identity, the news programs start with short music jingles and logos with the aim of distinguishing their news programs from the remaining program flows. Only the Japanese commercial station, TV Asahi, differs from the 'still' logos by showing an animation of a seagull flying over the open sea towards a city on the horizon. In the presentation of international news in both countries, the screens include symbols of the earth, globes or world maps and blue (the colour of trustworthiness and confidence) dominates the studio settings. A symbol of the Beijing conference is used in TV2 and NHK (and in the 18.30 o'clock DR1 news program). Denmark and Japan are naturally situated in the centre of the world maps signifying 'home', the place from which the global news is perceived. Happenings abroad are interpreted according to the political, economic and cultural context of 'home'. The verbal introduction and closing of international information demarcate the border-line between the outside world and the national 'now to news from abroad' and 'back to domestic news' ('og nu herhjemme igen'; 'kokunai no nyusu desu'). In the interim between global and local, the national cultural and political identity is defined in relation to the others in the news event. I will return to the national positioning and identification of 'us' and 'them' below.

Figure 8: News Formats in Denmark and Japan

DR1. *TV-avisen*. 19.00-19.30   TV2 *Nyhederne* 21.00-21-30

NHK. News 7. 19.00-19-30   TV Asahi. *News Station*. 22.00-23.18

As mentioned above, the national broadcasting systems in both countries are hybrid forms of public as well as commercial TV. The formats of the four programmes are designed and inspired by features in the news transmissions styles of the English public service station, BBC, and the US commercial broadcasters, ABC, CBS, NBC. The format of the Danish stations, *TV-avisen* and *News 7*, and the Japanese Public service station, NHK, resemble the BBC News Service broadcast style, which is characterised by a conventional opening sequence with a static view of the newsreader in the studio. The studio at the Danish commercial station, *Nyhederne*, is open with cameras in the background as is common in the US commercial broadcasts. *Nyhederne*, although *not* showing commercials during the news program like its Japanese counterpart, *News Station*, has incorporated other ideas from the US commercial stations. Flyers and stringers of advertisements between news items work as appetisers and invite audiences to stay with the evening program flow on the channel after the news. The presentation at *TV Asahi* is modelled on the co-anchorage style of the US commercial broadcaster's. This style was introduced in the 1980s in Japan, and commercial elements were introduced in the early 1990s in Denmark. The studio at TV Asahi is open and three presenters including a female anchor, a male anchor and a male commentator, comment on it through interaction.

In sum, the jingle, the opening logo, the marking of the international news section by a symbol of a globe and the introduction of the specific news, in this case with the logo of the Beijing Conference, guide viewers through the programs. These signs may be seen as instalments. They support the visual macrostructure of the program and provide coherence in the progression of the news. Just as the reader of a newspaper, glances at headlines and identifies different sections in the newspaper viewers use these instalments for guidance. Viewers may be partly concentrating on news presentations while engaged in domestic chores, eating or interacting, and quick glimpses at the screen guided by familiar sounds and visual signals enable coherence.

A Sense of Immediacy

An effort to make live on-site reporting, which creates a feeling of the immediacy[58] of events is another institutionalised communication strategy. As exemplified in the following, foreign correspondents report 'live' from the conference at all stations.

The DR1 correspondent describes the event from the middle of the opening festivities. She introduces the event partly whispering in order not to disturb the audience of the event. "With Chinese pomp and circumstance, colourful flowergirls,

Figure 9: Immediacy through 'live' reporting

DR	TV2	NHK	TV Asahi

brass bands, prominent speakers and big words the World's Fourth UN Conference on Women was declared open this morning *here* in the People's Hall in Beijing". The

---

[58] See Schlesinger (1987) Chapter One concerning the time factor in news production.

camera makes a panoramic view of the hall and zooms back to the journalist who is standing in front of 'colourful' Chinese dancers in front of a vast painting of the Great Wall of China. Where the DR 1 reporter is inside the hall, the reporter at TV2 is right in front of it. "Everything looks festive *here* in front of the People's Hall on Tiananmen Square. But behind the flowers and brass band music, an enormous surveillance arrangement of each participant is concealed". In relation to the Danish new journalism style that seeks to engage the audience, the NHK foreign correspondent makes a political commentary and forecasts the outcome of negotiations: "However, agreement is not likely to be easy on the issues of poverty and human rights. Many countries have different traditional values. And developing countries face a situation very different from that of in industrialised nations.". The TV Asahi reporter is in Huairou in front of the NGO office where she illustrates the freely distributed NGO newspaper's coverage of the Japanese domestic problem of comfort women. "Two thirds of the front page is covered with an article about the problem of the Comfort Women. The headline says 'We need reparations, not Comfort'. The construction of immediacy is high in all presentations. The sense of time and space is 'here and now' although the stories are edited in Beijing and are therefore *not* real time. (The time difference with Beijing is minus 2 hours in Japan and plus 8 hours in Denmark). The setting in this first report of a continuing news story is established through professionals on location.[59]

The dress code of the journalists on location is more casual than the formal attire of the presenters in the studio. The correspondent at DR1 is wearing a T-shirt and a flowery skirt. The correspondent at TV2 is wearing a flowery top. TV Asahi's correspondent is comfortably dressed in a white shirt. The dress code of the female reporters signals the atmosphere of the conference. The festivities and the heat invite a comfortable and more colourful dress code than the conservative appearance of the hosts back home in the studio. Only the NHK reporter in Huairou stands out in his formal suit and tie. The outfit is in line with his commentary and perspective on the UN conference, which is presented as an international political 'hard' news story. Where the Danish stories are built around reporting on location, including interviews focusing on the atmosphere of the event without analysis or background explanations, NHK's Beijing correspondent summarises the news and places it in an international political perspective. TV Asahi employs both strategies by presenting the longest presentation of more than five minutes including both political 'hard' news elements and interviews atmospheres and impressions from the conference. As a matter of fact, the female correspondents from all the other stations are flown in to cover the event, while the NHK foreign correspondent is stationed in China. This, in part, may explain the depth and insights of the political commentary at NHK. Another explanation may be the national political environment, the political stand of the station and the professional values and news criteria, which are elaborated further upon below.

Visual images

Visuals serve as an important source of documentation in broadcast news. Visuals are paramount, and they are carriers of any news story whether merely illustrating a

---

[59] Only TV Asahi stands out by referring to earlier presentations about the women's conference: 'Last week TV Asahi showed the NGO opening…today finally the time came for the opening of the official government conference'. Although the event was not considered 'big news' according to the production team, TV Asahi made lengthy reports every day for a week.

government meeting, official event, or interviews that support the narration of an event, as in the Japanese presentations or express action, as is the case of the more dynamic visuals of the Danish presentations.

The immediacy, involvement of the audience and the documentation effect of visual communication enhance the popularity of television news. As confirmed by professionals and researchers alike, events that provide interesting visuals are more newsworthy than events with unclear or ambiguous or with no visuals.

The co-ordination between visuals and text is in large part the challenge of news production. However, visuals are not merely representations of 'real' events. The choice and framing of a visual follows certain conventions and schemes used by professional to identify what represents an event (Chapter 7 presents the professional considerations behind visual framing). The following explores how visuals are framed and cut according to these conventions. Thereafter, the composition of visuals, graphics and language are analysed in order to explore how visual sequences are made coherent.

Visual cutting and coherence

As is conventional in the news genre (in comparison with sports or music videos), the cutting of photos is slow.

The average cutting pace of the pictures at all four stations was from 7 to 9 frames per minute except for the presentation on the 2nd day of the government meetings, where NHK's cutting pace was only 5 frames per minute. In comparison, the cutting pace at DR1 news programs in 1984 was also 5 times per minute, which was considered slow (Hjarvard 1999:100). The cutting in the Japanese news presentations was quicker than expected from the visual impressions. However, closer analysis showed that most shifts in the Japanese presentations were made between close-ups views of actors and panoramic views of audiences. These shifts made the presentations less dynamic and the message of the news more focused on the verbal account, which resembles the 'newspaper style' of production discussed below. This 'newspaper style' is newsroom terminology and refers to the traditional frame of mind at NHK of keeping the news presentation information intensive relying heavily on verbal accounts, while the visuals are assembled to fit these accounts.

Whereas the visual sequences in the Danish presentation tell a story connected by an overarching theme, the composition at NHK and the first part of TV Asahi's report is based on narration. Visuals merely support the narration not *vice versa*. This production technique, which is mainly employed at NHK resembles the production of newspapers.[60] The on-site NHK, correspondent makes a voice over report and the visual overview merely serves to illustrate his narration. The photo sequences of the Japanese news about the government meetings may be characterised as 'protocol accounts'. Protocol accounts are thorough presentations of dignitaries present at the event. The cameras move at a slow pace from one dignitary to another, combining close-up picture of actors with audience panoramas. The cutting pace and dynamics of the pictures pick up slightly in the report of the commercial presentation in a sequence about 'Comfort Women'. However, as most of this story is built upon interviews, the camera rests upon

---

[60] An interview with NHK Foreign Correspondent, September 11th, 1997, supported the notion that news production is conceptualised as making stories for the written press. In other words, there is more emphasis on the verbal account than the visual expression. Although visuals are of great importance, the verbal message guides the production and editing of visuals and texts and not *vice versa*.

the interviewees for long sequences. By contrast, the Danish presentations clip visuals of passing Indian women in colourful saris into an interview, which adds excitement and colours to the visual impression.

The visuals in the Danish presentation seem more dynamic although the cutting pace in total does not differ from the Japanese. Some passages of the Danish presentations are slow but passages of pictures in DR1 of an interview with Winnie Mandela show a quicker cutting pace, and the actions are lively, festive and dramatic with an entertainment appeal. The visuals of festivities, turmoil outside, and interviews create an emotional engagement on the part of the audience. The photography is a mix of panoramic views of the audience in the People's Hall and close up pictures of individuals.

In the TV2 report, the Great Wall forms the background for a long sequence of Chinese dancing and singing. Overall, the report conveys an exotic and stereotypic image of China. The visuals that illustrate the strict security at the conference show a Chinese sign (for no parking), Chinese Guards wearing hats, emblems, computer checks, more guards wearing hats and uniforms and a hand obstructing the camera. The visuals are supported by the voice-over: "In spite of Chinese promises the participants can not move around freely without being filmed and shadowed by Chinese with hats and blue glasses". The photography is a mix of close up pictures of Chinese guards and interviewees (facing away from the camera) and wide-angle views of crowds outside. The use of TV2's own visuals adds to the feeling of immediacy and being there.

The Danish reports are produced with mainly own visual footage.[61] DR1's correspondent outside and the 'live' filming of the festivities inside are filmed with own cameras. TV2 microphones are in the picture on two occasions. Where the Danish visuals are clearly from own cameras, it is more difficult to estimate the origin of the Japanese sources, especially in the extensive reports about government speeches by the Japanese stations, described below. These visuals may be from pool arrangements[62] or from international news agencies or own pictures (See Chapters 6-7 on the use of sources in news production). The use of own visuals adds to the experience of the event as immediate and 'real'.

The visual expressions and ways of capturing events through the camera lens follow genre conventions. The camera sets up relations between viewer and event. In other words, the physical distance between the camera eye and the object in focus is an indication of the relationship between audience and actors. The visual framing of actors may be divided into six main categories: intimate distance, close personal distance, *far personal distance, close social distance, far social distance* and public distance, of which the most commonly used in news are emphasised. Tuchman: 1978:118-119, cf Edward Hall 1966, my emphasis) The three distances most commonly used position actors at a comfortable business relations distance and not at a personal intimate distance (which is common in post-modern films). The effect of this distance between the camera lens (the viewer) and the actors in focus is a sense of impartiality and

---

[61] The origins of visuals are only noted on rare occasions. Therefore it is difficult to determine the original source. In the 18.00 o'clock DR1 report, an interview was made with Winnie Mandela showing DR1 and TV2 microphones, indicating that this is own footage.

[62] The Japanese pool arrangement includes the five main TV stations in Japan: TV Asahi, Fuji TV, NTV, Tokyo TV and NHK, which have an arrangement to take turns a month each to take pictures of big events and press conferences abroad. This agreement includes following the Emperor, dignitaries and state officials abroad. The visuals are distributed to all pool members. (Interview, NHK Satellite section manager, September 11th, 1997)

detachment. Intimate and close personal distances are 'un-newslike' and rarely found in news presentations. TV2 on one occasion makes a close up of a Chinese guard which almost seems intruding. The fact that the Chinese guard looks to the side and not directly into the camera makes the intensity and intrusion into personal space acceptable. The distance is important in news because the intimate distance captures emotions at the cost of objectivity (Tuchman, 1978:119). The public distance frame is so distant from actors that it depersonalises them and is used mainly to film large crowds. The public distance is used frequently in all presentations to capture the audiences at the conference. Government meetings often do not provide exciting action visuals, and the shifts between speaker and audience add a sense of dynamism.

In conclusion, technology makes it possible to cut and paste the visual material in order to create continuity in the visual flow of the story. Technology also makes it possible to edit heavily and manipulate the visual material. However, there are clear conventions for how far news may be 'manipulated'. The cutting of news film is done according to certain rules. Slow cutting with controlled camera movement is part of the choreography. Pictures in slow motion, as are often used in sports reports, are not credible in news presentations. Pictures that are cut too quickly, on the other hand, rely too much on the visual story and leave less time for the information load expected in proper news reports.

The following shows how the coherence in news text also involves the employment of graphics and subtitles.

Graphics and subtitles

International news production revolves around making complex information easy to comprehend. The public stations (including the commercial Danish station TV2, which is partly financed by the government) are obliged as public service institutions to inform and address viewers as political citizens.[63] Attempts to make social and political informational messages clear are described in the following.

At the public stations in both countries, efforts were made to make messages clear not only for mainstream viewers but also for specific groups. In the DR1 presentation, there were subtitles in Danish throughout the program as is customary for *TV-avisen* at 19.00 o'clock. NHK as a public station offers a bilingual service. The news program is synchronised in English, and audiences with bilingual TV are able to choose between English and Japanese.

In all presentations, foreign speeches were translated into Danish and Japanese and presented in subtitles, as were titles and names of correspondents and other actors in the news. Interestingly, the Japanese creation of coherence between visuals and text included the use of headlines in news announcements. The use of headlines is found in China and the literate cultures of Asia that, like Japan (which has employed a simplified version) makes use of Chinese characters. This introduction to news through written headlines was not found in the Danish presentations.

---

[63] It is found in reception studies that watching news regularly does induce an awareness of social and political issues. In the study by Kawabata (1999), it was found that Japanese viewers who regularly watched news had an awareness of and critical attitude towards, for instance, the environment. Whereas viewers who were not in the habit of watching news regularly imagined nature to be beautiful, as depicted in aestheticised commercials.

The graphics and subtitles of *News Station* stand out in the analysis. Since the programme's start in 1985, it has been part of its production strategy to make political and economic news easy to understand even for even 14 year olds. There is frequent use of props,[64] visual aids and detailed titles of correspondents, speakers and interviewees. A prop in use in the news under analysis was a detailed schedule of the conference on a large piece of carton. It was used to explain in detail the time tables and events of the NGO Forum and the Government meetings. The detailed itinerary was also used divide the news into two parts: a report about the opening of the government meetings, and a report about the 'comfort women'. Other visual signs and symbols included a close-up picture of an NGO newspaper. A close-up gave the audience an opportunity to read the headline for themselves: "Reparations, not Comfort". Another visual symbol was a poster in English and Japanese the 'Japanese government must compensate for the Wartime Military Sexual Slavery". Graphics, props and pictures were integrated in order to make the news easier to understand, and occasionally provided supporting evidence for the argument or 'spin' of the story.

In sum, the above shows how 'meaning' is created in news through a composition of aesthetic elements including logos, framing of visuals, graphics and props. The communication of political information, it is found, follows framing procedures that are recognised in both media contexts.

The following moves beyond the anchorage and relaying of meaning through aesthetic effects. It focuses on global coherence and strands of discourses through an analysis of the framing of global issues (themes) in the national contexts.

The framing of UN discourses in Denmark and Japan [65]

The official themes of the Beijing conference were *'Equality, Development and Peace'*.[66] These were implemented as overarching themes in the broadcast media in the two countries, with some variation. The follow shows which issues are brought up and how they are presented linguistically and rhetorically. More specifically, the sequences of the reports are analysed in order to see the local meaning construction in relation to the global coherence of the news story (Van Dijk, 1991). The overall themes are related to the official UN themes in order to determine the how they are implemented in the two countries.

The DR1 news is divided into three happenings: the exotic Chinese festivities inside the People's Hall in Beijing, turmoil outside due to Winnie Mandela's denied entrance into the People's Hall and an interview with the Danish Minister of Social Affairs about

---

[64] The anchor, Kume Hiroshi, uses dolls that resemble social actors to act out political and economic events or scandals. In this reconstruction of events, the good guys and the bad guys are easily distinguished and the disputes are acted out at a level where everyone can follow the arguments.

[65] The politician interviewed in DR1 uses simple easily understandable language starting out with political rhetoric "(..)[N]ice words are not enough".
The language used by the TV2 journalists is informal and conversational. All actors in the news are female. The minister who is interviewed speaks in very colloquial terms. The language at TV Asahi is formal. The rhetoric style is factual, highly informative with elaborate protocol accounts of participants at the event. The narrative structure is a mix of voice-over conference speeches and interviews.

[66] Promote and protect the human rights of women by fully implementing all human rights instruments, especially the convention on the Elimination of all forms of Discrimination against Women; Review national laws to ensure implementation of all international human rights agreements; Ensure equality and non-discrimination under the law and in practice; Achieve legal literacy.

98

her speech the following day. The three events are set up as *negative* accounts. The Chinese hosts are reported as being against the intentions of the conference and in favour of anything *but* equality, development and peace. "While the Conference declared women's liberation the last big issue of the millennium.. the Chinese hosts are violating human rights". Further, "Chinese security guards have problems with the press and freedom of speech". The Danish Minister's speech concerns issues from the Platform of Actions.

The Minister accounts for her upcoming speech in colloquial terms in what Fairclough (1995) refers to as *conversationalisation*. According to Fairclough this conversational form characterises the present style of rhetoric by experts and politicians who appear the media. The conversationalisation style is particularly prevalent in the Danish presentations where news presenters and politicians both use ordinary language. In the NHK and TV Asahi presentations news readers, caster and politicians use the polite forms of language although polite form are becoming less used in the Japanese media (and a move toward a more feminine use of the language in media speech is taking place).

In the Danish presentation the Minister will make recommendations to eliminate cultural attitudes and practices that are against girls. She will recommend that the discrimination against girls in education, health and nutrition is eliminated and that the status of the girl-child improves within the family: "My message is that nice words are not enough – that governments have to go home and act. They have to make sure that little girls[67] get the same upbringing as boys, that they get the same food and education as boys. They have to make sure that grown-up women are not treated like the property of men, but have rights on equal terms with men and that they have the opportunity in economic and other ways to live their own lives". The content of the Minister's speech thus concerns the 'girl-child' and problems mainly of the developing world. The Minister addressed problems of gender in the developing world seemingly inspired by the issues of the neo-feminist movements in Scandinavia and other Western countries, who are concerned about global issues rather than specific gender issues in Scandinavia. Interestingly, behind her statements there are assumptions that human rights can be implemented world-wide, even in countries that combat problems of poverty with different cultural, philosophical, religious and ethical values. Within the interpretative framework of the news her speech, which is a negative account of the opening event, there may also be an indirect criticism of the Chinese government and its violations of human rights through actions at the conference and through its one-child policy.

The TV2 story likewise focuses on criticism of Chinese authorities. The description contains predominantly negative nouns and adjectives: "(..) a conference at risk of drowning in protests and conflicts, because the Chinese security police constantly watch and shadow the participating women". 'Thousands' of security guards, 'irritation', 'panic', 'boycott', 'provoke', 'unacceptable', 'aftermath'. The words connote conflict and drama: "The surveillance is very provocative, especially at a conference where the headlines are *equality, development and peace'*. The story is divided into four sequences of drama: festivities outside, drama and demonstration to get Mandela into the People's Hall, interviews and a section on surveillance with pictures of guards, detective machinery, computers, security emblems, "Chinese in hats and blue glasses". A Mexican NGO participant expresses: "We come here to work together and to generate dialogue between the nations. It is not possible to work here". A member of the Danish

---

[67] The reference to children is also found in Izmad Kitani's opening speech in NHK's presentation.

delegation, Minister Helle Degn, protests: "It is totally unacceptable..". The recipient address is dramatic, appealing to audience emotions and involvement. As in DR1's presentation, the Chinese who are under scrutiny are not interviewed. The Danish reports are dramatic accounts of the experiences of actors at the event presented with a negative 'spin'.

Compared with the dramatic set-up of the Danish presentations, the Japanese are formal, using political terminology. The framework of NHK's presentation is international politics: "(..)..a ceremony was held in Beijing today to welcome government delegations". The news is divided into several sub-themes drawing on 'equal rights' discourse. It is presented as an account of the agenda of a political meeting, referring to every point in the UN Plan of Action: The 'aim' is "to improve women's social positions and achieve equality between men and women". Following the 'aim' is an account of the 'slogan', the 'platform of action', 'obstacles and opportunities for women's rights', 'implementation' of the plan of action in 2000. Finally, the '12 main issues' on the agenda are listed. Among those are *poverty*, *violence* and *human rights*. In the summary of the report, the Beijing office correspondent concludes that developing countries and industrialised countries have different values and problems concerning 'human rights' and 'poverty'. He does not mention 'violence' or violence against women in war, which is one of the main themes in the coverage by the private station. The question of violence is of concern for Japan in relation to its war crimes and problems with demands for compensation from the 'comfort women' (*jugun ianfu*) in the neighbouring countries. It is not possible to determine whether the 'ellipse' is intentional in order to avoid alluding to the contested issue, which includes much criticism of the Japanese government.[68]

The issues are presented at NHK in politically rhetorical terms. The UN platform of action is described thoroughly, and it includes statements of the Japanese government's intentions concerning its implementation (the Japanese government did in fact take political measures in order to implement the UN Platform of Action. See Chapter 8).

The TV Asahi presentation, which lasts more than twice the length of the other presentations (5.34 minutes) is divided into two parts. The first part, the official opening of the UN Conference, concerns 'equal rights'. General Secretary Mongella expresses in feminist rhetorical terms that " We are facing a historical moment, we have to change the injustice of equal rights". Benazir Bhutto: "We are not alone in our search for empowerment – women across continents are together". The second part of the TV Asahi news concerns 'violence against women in war' more specifically the NGO Forum's treatment of the 'comfort women' issue. The TV Asahi presentation is a collage of views critical of the Japanese government: "The Japanese government should apologise, take on responsibility and pay individual compensation for the wartime military's sexual slavery" (Poster). The voice-over account draws attention to the fact that "A country like Japan with its specific memories cannot allow itself to ignore this motion" (Appendix 7). Finally, concluding a longer sequence of critical voices against the Japanese government, the *News Station* anchor concludes, "Certainly, the Japanese Government's idea that the 'comfort women' issue is a problem of the past does not

---

[68] The problem of 'comfort women' is formally raised in the government speech by Nonaka Koken the following day. Nonaka states that in sincere remorse for its past history the Japanese government intends to extend the greatest possible co-operation to the "Asian Women' Fund" (a private foundation). Japan already contributes over $600 million to the development of women....(Government speech). The issue of comfort women is discussed in more detail in Chapter 7.

100

hold true." (Appendix 7). Besides bringing the 'comfort woman issue to the agenda, TV Asahi also mentions in visuals and text the issue of nuclear testing.

In summary, the stories in both countries are framed within the UN themes *'Equality, Development and Peace'*. The understanding of equality between men and women is strongly connected with the concept of human rights. The Danish stories are communicated in negative frameworks describing the situation in China in direct contrast to the UN themes: The Chinese organisers exemplify everything *but* 'equality' 'development' and 'peace'. The UN concepts are not related to the conditions of equality in Denmark but concern conditions in the developing world. These discourses are thus not appropriated and related to a Danish context. The 'domestic' elements of this international news include the Danish actors on location the impressions and experiences of news producers, the Danish politicians and NGO participants.

The Japanese presentations (NHK and the first part of TV Asahi's presentation) draw upon general political rhetoric (as directed and defined by the UN) concerning equal rights. The concept of human rights is used, and at NHK detailed political rhetoric defines the plans for implementation of policy. It deserves mention that the Japanese stations do not make any criticism of China.[69] TV Asahi brings nuclear testing on the agenda, but this reflects the political agenda of TV Asahi, which is critical of nuclear testing, and is not a deliberate strategy to criticise China.

The Japanese stations treat 'equal rights' discourse in politically rhetorical terms. NHK expresses government policy and endeavours concerning the implementation of the Platform of Action. TV Asahi elaborates on the theme of 'peace' in its criticism of the Japanese government's handling of war victims, the 'comfort women'.

'We' and 'other(s)'

Part of the process of framing international news events is relating our own national actors to foreign actors and explaining our involvement in the event. This positioning is twofold and includes the national positioning in relation to other nations at the global level, and national political and social relations to the event. The positioning of self is a basic element in personal communication and involves the construction of 'other' as well as of 'self' (Mead, 1934). The study of personal pronouns thus brings insights into the national self-understanding and the premises for 'domesticating' international information.

Apart from the positioning of 'we' concerning national placement in a global and regional context, the positioning of 'we' within the presentational context also refers to the views of the broadcasting organisation and to the relations set up between professionals (studio host and correspondents) and viewers. The identification of self and other differed according to the socio-cultural background and geographical position of the two countries. The following describes how a sense of closeness and *proximity* to some countries and actors as well as distance to others was created linguistically.

In the DR1 presentation, the Chinese 'others' are described as 'colourful flower girls' with a "sense for pomp and circumstance". The DR1 attitude towards China and the

---

[69] In the government speech, Nosaka Koken expresses appreciation to the government and the People's Republic of China for the efforts to ensure the success of this Conference. 'It is indeed significant and an opportunity that the Fourth World conference on Women should be held in China, a country that has achieved remarkable economic progress, and a country where 'women hold up half the sky'. Statement by H.E. Mr.Koken Nosaka. Head of Delegation of the Government of Japan. UN Press release, September 5th, 1995.

official organisation of the conference is critical and ironic "prominent speakers and big words... flower girls and brass band music" (Appendix 7). China is seen from Denmark - a country far from the event. 'Others' include Winnie Mandela and 'other governments'. The Danish Minister has expectations of other governments but contrary to NHK's presentation above she does not promise any efforts towards implementation on the part of Danish government. South African actors are significant others in the Danish presentations. They are not mentioned in the Japanese.[70]

NHK positions itself as the spokes-channel of Japan, or more specifically the Japanese government. In political rhetorical terms, NHK's voice-over assures that "At the conference, Japan (*nihon wa*) will make it clear that it will actively contribute to the improvement of women's status in society – and to promoting their greater participation in society" (Appendix 7). The source of information is not referred to in the news, but the wording resembles the seven-minute introductory speech by the Japanese government spokesman, Nonaka, on the second day of the conference (Japanese Press Release, 1995). NHK indirectly quotes government policy, which leaves the viewer with the impression that NHK speaks on behalf of the government. The study of production practices in chapter 8 confirms NHK's attention to government policy in production strategies.

The presentation is a protocol account. The protocol systematically introduces the speakers at the conference. In the NHK report, Japan is positioned in relation to the outside world in different ways. One 'we' refers to the Japanese people and the Japanese government. 'We' in a global perspective refers to Japan and the US as part of the industrialised countries versus 'others', the developing countries. Japan is identified as a developing country in the 'in-group' with the US. NHK is close to Japanese government policy in its positioning of statements. The NHK news is seen from the perspective of the political system. The voices are passive.

TV Asahi, on the contrary, identifies with the people. 'We' refers to the people while the 'other' is the Japanese government. 'We' (the Japanese people), says a female NGO participant, want other people in the world to know that the Japanese do not agree with the Japanese government's way of handling the 'comfort women' issue. In a global perspective, 'we' refers to Japan, the Philippines and Korea who are co-arranging a symposium. 'We' when Japan asks China to stop nuclear testing refers to Japan, while the 'other' is China. Finally, there is a construction of Japan as 'we' and the US as the 'other'. TV Asahi makes a distance to the US, as opposed to identifying with the US as in the NHK presentation.

In sum, the identification between system and people differs according to the communication strategy of the station. The organisational differences between public and commercial stations were found to influence the production of news in both countries. I will elaborate on this below. The relationship with China differs according to geographic proximity and historical ties. In the Danish news presentations, China is constructed as a distant other. For Japan, China is important for socio-economic reasons

---

[70] Strong Danish NGO and political activity against apartheid has kept the awareness of South Africa high in the Danish consciousness. Danish Diplomatic Relations with South Africa have been positive since the embargo lift in the 1990s. The political awareness of South Africa on of both the Danish stations is shown by microphones placed in front of South African rep., Winnie Mandela. The incident with Mandela and other participants denied access to the conference is mentioned in *News 7* the following day as 'some women'. It is not a theme in *News Station*'s presentation.

(see chapter 7). Thus, the global positioning of the countries is important for the choice of themes and actors and is reflected in the verbal set-up of the news presentations.

Myths and cultural stereotypes

Myths and cultural stereotypes with an exotic image of China are plentiful in the Danish news. TV Asahi shows a short clip of the Opening singing and dancing but there were no verbal references to Japanese or Chinese cultural stereotypes in the Japanese presentations. One reason may be the cultural proximity between Japan and China. China is geographically and historically close and the cultural heritage may be too familiar for exotic images. Another more viable explanation in the case of NHK may be the professional news values that prioritise political and economic themes and ensure the coverage of 'hard' news in its news presentations.

TV Asahi presents visuals of Chinese cultural activities but there are no verbal references to generalised conceptions of Chinese or Japanese culture. Instead, European myths of military strategy and psychological warfare are at play. The male commentator[71] at *News Station* presents a Greek anecdote as a suggestion to resolve the problem of 'violence against women in war'. He presents the ancient Greek play by Aristophanes, where women make an agreement to go on a sex strike, which ultimately leads to peace. As a solution to the problem of sexual services, the commentator advises modern women to revive this classical wartime strategy. He argues that armies need 'service', but if this 'evil device' is handled cleverly wars will cease. How is this analogy 'received' by the two anchors of *News Station*? The male anchor (Watanabe who is substituting for the famous Kume Hiroshi) watches without comment. The reaction of the female anchor is merely occasional comments of 'aha', 'huh', and '*hai*'. Seemingly taken by surprise, she does not make a sustained commentary on his anecdote (as is customary in her approach). On one hand, the proposed idea may be considered brilliant, that is, if women in war have the mental surplus and physical power to enact the strategy. On the other hand, the commentary may seem anachronistic for those contemporary urban men and women who are seriously concerned with fate of the 'comfort women' or for those who struggle with their own problems of 'gender empowerment' in their professional and private lives. The interaction and commentary in this news is not pre-rehearsed. The scene is set and acted out in line with the strategy to produce 'live', exciting and unexpected commentary about news.[72]

In sum: contrary to expectations there were no references in the two countries to domestic or Chinese cultural myths about women and women's liberation. However, these became plentiful as the week progressed and more issues and events from the conference were brought up. Anti-McDonald's and anti-cultural imperialism demonstrations, lesbian rights demonstrations with strong feminist slogans were brought by the Danish stations and presented as curiosities of the past. In the Danish

---

[71] The commentator has spent much time in France in his youth and as a foreign correspondent, which affects his outlook on the world. In an effort to internationalise his fellow Japanese and share his knowledge and experience with TV Asahi audiences he provides them with international perspectives on any occasion (TV Asahi, Commentator, August 21st, 1997).
In the opening of News Station on September 5th, he makes a personal speech about his disappointment over the French Nuclear testing in Mururoa.

[72] In interviews with News Station's anchor (November 25th), commentator (August 21st, 1997) and producer (June 11th, 1997) they state that commentary is not pre-rehearsed. It is left to the individual to prepare their commentary in advance or 'play it by ear' while News Station is on air.

presentation of women's liberation as a historical myth lies an implicit understanding that Denmark has a leading position in international standards for equal rights. The strategies behind Japanese production included a curiosity to explore how Japanese conditions for gender equality compare in relation to international standards. Issues of anti-cultural imperialism and homosexuality were not presented in the Japanese programs. Japanese feminists have been concerned with other issue than fighting Western imperialism. The legal right to use the pill, which was only recently admitted and only in cases of a physical disorder, exemplifies one area of concern. Homosexuality is not a public issue in Japan. Feminist issues and homosexuality are still marginalised issues. The focus of TV Asahi (NHK only made reports on the first and second day of the UN conference) was the Japanese NGOs (6.000 participants). A story was made about men's activities at the conference, another covered foreign reactions to the fact that the Japanese spokesman was male.[73] The strategy in the coverage was to present issues that were interesting for women *and* men. TV Asahi therefore did not investigate women's issues in full as part of a strategy to making the news entertaining (see analysis Chapter 8).

Language import through news

Although the event took place in China, English dominated the available information according to the Japanese production crews. As the vehicle of communication in most international events is English, documents including press releases and government speeches had to be translated into Danish and Japanese, respectively. UN concepts such as 'equal rights' 'peace' and 'development' were replaced with Japanese synonymous expressions.

As was expected, borrowed foreign words were used in the news presentations. As an example, politicians and professionals used the English expressions 'mass hysteria' (*masu hisuteriya*), 'sex strike' (*sekkusu suturaiku*), 'feminist' (*feminisuto*). These words were imported directly from English into the Japanese language. The examples were all found in the commercial presentation of *News Station*. The fact that an import of English expressions was only found in the commercial presentation may be interpreted as a sign of liberal language policy. The language policy of NHK *News 7* is conservative, with the result that there were no examples of loaned words in its news. Although, the expressions were used by elder politicians and professionals, the fact that they were not deleted in the editing process as they may have been at NHK bears witness to a liberal language policy driven by an aim to address younger audiences, who are fascinated with English expressions. Although imported and appropriated with the English pronunciation, loaned words in Japanese remain distinct as they are written in *katakana*, a phonetic alphabet for loaned words.

From a perspective of 'global consciousness', the import of foreign words through news may enhance processes of globalisation. That English is used as a global communication vehicle may, in the opinion of some, enhance English 'linguistic imperialism' (Phillipson, 1996). However, in Japan loaned words are not usually imported in their original form. The visitor to Japan may be surprised to learn that the

---

[73] The month before the Women's conference Nosaka Koken was appointed Minister for Women's Affairs. As a goal of Japan to create a society in which there is an equal partnership between women and men, the post of Minister for Women's Affairs, to be held concurrently by the Chief Cabinet Secretary, was created three years ago. In addition to 6.000 Japanese NGOs, twenty four Diet members participated in the conference (including four male members).

pronunciation of foreign loanwords (mostly English) are local and occasionally not recognisable in their new form. In some cases, loaned words are also attributed local meaning. The effect of this 'creolanisation'[74] (Hannerz, 1996) or blending of languages makes communication across borders possible in theory. However, in practice, communication may become even more difficult. When the meaning of *katakana* words cannot be traced to its original English meaning and the uses of English expressions are not 'grounded' in the Japanese system with a consensus about pronunciation and meaning, *katakana* words become 'floating expressions' without systematic ascribed pronunciations or consensus about meaning. English 'linguistic imperialism' and the progression of language import due to modern technology in information-based societies is challenging national language systems. The fact that English is the linguistic vehicle of globalisation may be considered a problem by some. Nevertheless, a more serious problem is the fact that these terms may be appropriated locally with slightly different meanings. This becomes a challenge not only to Japan but also to other national governments. Globalisation and new technology have kept attention on language import though new media. Language policies are an issue at the national broadcast stations with NHK adhering to a conservative and TV Asahi to a liberal language policy.

Where the Danish presentations were in a dramatic narrative form on-location, the Japanese presentations related the UN themes to domestic politics.

Frames for interaction

The final part of the analysis concerns the interaction between actors and the set-up of relations and social identities in news. The professional actors (newsreaders and correspondents) as co-ordinators and station authorities are analysed in the following.

The actors in DR1 represent international political and social elites: South African Winnie Mandela is shown, and Karen Jespersen, Minister of Social Affairs and leader of the Danish delegation is interviewed. The representation of actors in the commercial TV2's presentation is higher. Danish politician, Helle Degn, member of the Danish delegation and an NGO participant Luz Gonzales from Mexico are interviewed. Their statements are used as bricks in the presentation supporting the theme of criticism of the conference arrangement. As mentioned above, the Chinese security guards are passive in the Danish presentations. In TV2 Chinese security guards flout the UN conventions. This "will have political consequences in the UN" according to a statement made by Helle Degn. The story is told from the perspective of individual participants in the conference and the audience is able to identify with the unreasonable security measures. Individuals are NGO members, African and Danish politicians.

The actors in the Japanese news represent the Japanese and international political elite. NHK presents Chinese Prime Minister, Jiang Zemin, the Japanese Socialist party member, Doi Takako, the conference leader, Gertrude Mongella, and Pakistani Prime Minister, Benazir Bhutto. The voice-over informs that Chief Cabinet Secretary Nosaka Koken will lead the Japanese delegation, and US First Lady Hillary Clinton[75] is

---

[74] Creolanisation is a socio-linguistic metaphor used by Hannerz (1996) in order to describe the blend of cultures. In this text it adheres to its original meaning, namely to describe the blending of languages.

[75] Hillary Clinton's speech at the UN Women's conference, which is critical of China, exemplifies a single political actor, who 'highjacks' the global media scene on 5th September. In her speech, Hillary

introduced (without visuals) as amongst the speakers the following day. "Many people are looking forward to hear what she has to say about human rights issues at the conference", states the NHK voice-over. TVAsahi likewise announces the speech by Clinton, which illustrates the Japanese preoccupation with US activity. Although most of the 180 UN country delegates are female, the only 'active voice' in NHK's presentation (besides the newsreaders and foreign correspondent) is that of male UN Deputy Secretary, Izmad Kitani:"They [the children] will look for concrete signs that Beijing in 1995 was followed by real action. Let's not disappoint them. Let's not disappoint ourselves. Together we will follow our words with our w[d]eeds.".

The protocol account of dignitaries and audiences at *News Station* resembles the NHK presentation. The Chinese Prime Minister, Jiang Zemin, the conference leader, Gertrude Mongella of Tanzania, the Socialist party member, Doi Takako, Izmad Kitani, and Benazir Bhutto are presented. However the editing, focus and perspectives of the two reports differ.[76] TV Asahi is the only station showing visuals of Hillary Clinton on the opening day of the conference, although NHK refers to her. Hillary Clinton is shown to departing from Washington DC on September the third together with Madeline Albright. Another 'exclusive' with TV Asahi is the Cabinet Secretary, Nosaka Koken, shown in a meeting with a Chinese government representative. "Late this afternoon upon arrival he [Nosaka] met with the Chinese State of Affairs Representative suggesting an end to nuclear testing".

The *News Station* report about the 'comfort women' issue includes a female correspondent on location and interviews with experts including NGOs and ordinary participants: A male representative of the Japanese Lawyers Council, an ordinary Japanese participant, a female Japanese NGO participant, Hayashi, a Lawyer. Three ordinary participants in the NGO forum from Jamaica, Canada and the US are shown. Their statements are all bricks in a critical account of the Japanese government's handling of the 'comfort women' issue. Ranging from "It's unbelievable. To "I don't understand why it is so difficult for Japan [the Japanese government] to apologise for something that happened so long ago. It is very, very important to the 'comfort women' and their families". "I think the attitude of the Japanese government is extremely…uh unacceptable". The actors reinforce TV-Asahi's critical view of the Japanese governments handling of the 'comfort women' issue. The 'spin' of the presentation is critical and anti-government.

In sum, the TV Asahi report is people oriented. Well-known *and* ordinary people, global and locals talk to the camera. Although the statements of interviewees are strongly opinionated and appeal to the emotions of the audience, it deserves notice that the communicative relationship between the professional staff and the audience remains paternalistic and authoritative.

In the international news, the actors are mainly representatives of the political elite. The opinion of 'ordinary' people is included according to the production strategy of the

---

Clinton criticises the Chinese government directly and indirectly. Symbolically, her speech represents criticism from the perspective of women in general, but more so it is used politically in US Chinese government relations.

[76] The visuals may be from international news agencies or from the NHK affiliate, ABC (NHK, Reporter on location, August 20th, 1997). Visuals may also be from the Japanese pool arrangement. The difference in framing, however, shows that NHK and TV Asahi use different sources. The visual output is a combination of close-up pictures of politicians and panoramic views of the audience and podium. The News Station camera crew was at the NGO forum in Huairou 52 kilometres away from the official conference in Beijing (TV Asahi Reporter on location. July 16th, 1997).

106

stations. The public stations feature representatives of the system, where the private stations, especially the Japanese, are multi-vocal. Social elites *as well as* ordinary citizens are included. The choice and orchestration of actors reflects the political and ideological views of the broadcasting organisations. Where the public stations in the two countries represent the system and a pro-government ideology, the set-up of actors in the commercial station presents the people and an anti-government ideology. The political tendencies are most pronounced in the Japanese broadcast news.

At the global level the actors to a great degree reflect the regional affiliation of Denmark and Japan. The Danish journalists do not position the Danes and Denmark very strongly. The Chinese 'other' is far away and the language used for description is stereotypical and negative. [77] South Africa is a significant other in the Danish presentation[78]. The Japanese presentations do not criticise China. The reason for this is investigated in Chapter 7. The United States is clearly a significant other in the Japanese presentations. Where NHK is in favour of US, TV Asahi is critical.

It may be concluded from the analysis that interaction *within* news presentation is minimal. The monologue form of news reading keeps information controlled and it is generally presented unambiguously with clear one-sided opinions. Occasional dialogues through interviews [79] are presented; these are controlled and questions often pre-rehearsed (except for the TV Asahi commentary, which after all is performed by skilled professionals).

Although news may be regarded as a medium for interaction between politicians, this interaction is mainly symbolic. As it appeared in the presentations, political interaction *within* the news was minimal. Dialogue and interaction between participants (except news producers) did not occur. Rather, news is a medium for political interaction. The set-up of relations, and the representation of social identities in news thus maintains the symbolic social order. The set-up of heroes and villains (for and against issues) was choreographed and played out guided by professional news producers. But who then were accessible as actors or, importantly, who had access as participants in the news?

In Chapter One, I argue that access should not be seen merely as a bureaucratic routine which privileges elites. This does not mean, however, that social elites are not privileged. The public service stations mainly features elites, whereas the commercial stations, and in particular TV Asahi used, multiple voices of both elites and ordinary people. In the Japanese commercial stations, actors represented not only bureaucratic and political power according to pro- and anti-establishment interests but also the voices of ordinary participants and a variety of organisational representatives. The incorporation of voices, however, did not make 'impartial' 'fair' and 'unbiased' news.

---

[77] The diplomatic crises between Denmark and China since have led to trade boycotts and heavy criticism of the handling of human rights in China. US citizen Harry Wu, a human rights activist, is released a few months before the conference after 19 years in a Chinese prison. The imprisonment of human rights advocates is openly criticised by Danish politicians. This political attitude may affect the critical rapport although the Danish political view on human rights in China it is not made explicit.

[78] Since the 1960's, the Danish public has been following NGOs and political activity to keep the trade embargo on the apartheid regime. South Africa, therefore, has a clear spot in the consciousness of the Danes.

[79] Even in interviews, except for DR1, the questions are cut and not obvious to the viewers. In a TV Asahi report, the interviewer's head is nodding heavily to encourage the 'ordinary' person to elaborate upon aview. The nodding signals full acceptance and encouragement to the interviewee. Although unanticipated answers occur, editors select the comments that are most appropriate for the framing of the event.

Rather, the social actors uniformly represented an anti-establishment political stance (the political character of news is discussed in Chapter 6).

Conclusively, although different voices are represented, access[80] is not a privilege of any individual social actors. Actors are carefully briefed and/or screened before they perform and contribute with suitable opinions for the program. Editing takes care of unorchestrated creativity and comments, which are not in line with the organisational policies and framework of the news story. Access at the public service stations may still adhere to elitist representation; however, the private stations include a broad spectrum of different voices. In spite of the 'emplotment' (Cottle, 2000a) of ordinary voices, these do not enjoy free access but are only included if they fit the story frame.

Another 'icon' and evident part of news presentations is the professional staff.

Broadcast professionals[81]

As described in Chapter One, a habitual use of television over time gives media personnel a prominent position in the consciousness of the viewer. In cognitive terms personal characteristics, appearance, gestures and voice are perceived and stored as information and knowledge in memory. News presenters are important representatives in the identification of a news programme. They are protected and celebrated staff in their companies (see Chapters 6-7), and often keep a low profile in other media spotlights in order to maintain the proper impartial, factual and authoritative image.

A commonality in the staging of television personalities in the Danish and Japanese presentations is their proper dress. The studio hosts are conservatively dressed in suits, discrete ties or scarves. The newsreader in DR1 is wearing a conservative grey suit. His blond hair and well-groomed beard contrasts with a light blue map of the world in the background. The newsreader uses formal language to introduce the event. The newsreader in TV2 is wearing a suit. Her appearance is conservative. The reporting style is factual, although her language is informal. The newsreader at NHK is dressed in a conservative short-sleeved woman's suit. She is herself an icon or a symbol of *News 7* through more than a decade of reading the news in this program. The presenters at TV Asahi also wear conservative suits. They radiate authority but also friendliness. Most of them have been in the program for more than a decade. The facial expressions of the news presenters change suitably with the content of the news items expressing small nuances of emotion but never emotional outbursts.[82]

Common to the Danish and Japanese national broadcast styles is the set-up and image of the news presenters. They are well groomed, good-looking and uniformly dressed. They appear Danish and Japanese. In other words there is no representation of ethnic or minority groups.[83] The staging of a 'national' look, in my interpretation, has two aims. Firstly, national broadcasting accommodates the broad majority of national audiences and therefore a perceived general look appeals to most people. In other words, these are business-related considerations. Secondly, ethnicity or minority representation

---

[80] News Station used e-mail responses from viewers about the Nuclear tests. However, all the televised comments were critical of the tests and urged the Japanese government to be more critical as a 'peaceful country'.

[81] See Cooper Chen (1997) for an introduction of popular Japanese news personalities.

[82] The News Station anchor, Kume Hiroshi, differs in this respect. He laughs out loud and even leans over the table in expressive outbursts over political conditions.

[83] A black Danish person is the weather forecaster on DR1 and a foreigner presents the sports on TV Asahi)

may connote meanings that divert attention away from the news information and thus ruin pre-established (institutionalised) communication contracts with the audience.

In sum, in both commercial and public service programs the newscasters radiate objectivity and authority. Their appearance, personality and clothing include no strong colours or individual character, which might take away attention from the news information. The didactic paternalistic way in which information is presented, the use of modalities, the factual ways in which news is read is characteristic of the news genre in the national broadcasting of the two countries. The impression and atmosphere created in the news programmes signal factuality and trustworthiness.

Public figures like TV personalities may become 'intimate' friends through their presence in the everyday life of viewer's in private spaces. News watching is understood by audience researcher as an 'active' process[84] of reception, which makes it comparable to a form of social interaction or para-social interaction (Horton & Wohl, 1997). Combined with the fact that most people use television news as their main source of news and watch it on a regular basis, the discursive expressions and *conversational* form in news make this relationship even more intimate. From very formal language use in the 1980s, the marketisation and commercialisation of news information has made news presentation a combination of expressions from the public *and* private spheres. Complicated political news is explained through the use of everyday conversation and metaphors from the viewers' everyday lives, which resembles forms of interpersonal communication.[85]

In their mediation of political *and* social drama of the day, TV personalities not only provide cognitive stimuli but also affective experiences. However, although viewers on occasions feel as though they are actively involved in interpersonal communication, and although reception studies claim that news information *is* received through active processes, the communication must nevertheless be characterised as *monologue*, as there is no reciprocate interaction. At any rate, TV personalities in their role as mediators of news information and emotional experiences that people need and want are important figures in the newsrooms and have an important position in the awareness of viewers who turn to broadcast news in order to be informed and/or entertained[86].

---

[84] The 'virtual' sense of activity is exemplified in Japanese reception studies (Clausen, 1997). A Japanese viewer of News Station expresses the relationship: "In News Station the casters make comments, and you can sit and think with them, and decide whether this is wrong or right. You are active" (Clausen, 1996:56). Another finds that it is an opportunity to say "Oh that's just what I think" (ibid:56)[84]. The people who like clearly formulated *and* critical opinions of the government enjoy *News Station*. In News Station not only the anchors but also experts voice their opinion. Many viewers welcome this. Audiences who prefer what they refer to as 'sure and accurate news' watch NHK's 'intelligent, reliable people'. Viewers who prefer NHK are less interested in 'silly comments' and 'variety show' news (*Waido shou*). Another advantage of the NHK presentation form as expressed by NHK viewers is that they like to make their own interpretations of the news. The viewers attribute the difference in style between the two stations to the sponsorship situation. NHK is public and sponsored by the country '*okami*'. News Station is commercial and sponsored by private business. "News Station has to think about sponsors. NHK does not. What NHK staff have to think about is the comments of their superiors" according to the viewer (Clausen: 1996:59)

[85] This form of *conversationalisation* (Fairclough, 1995) as discussed in Chapter One, is described by others as intimisation, privatisation and personification (Hjarvard, 1994, 1997; Meyrowitz, 1985); Giddens (1991) attributes this room for of intimacy and para-social interaction to what he terms the dis/re-embedded social relations of modern society.

[86] Reception studies in Japan (Clausen 1996) showed that people arriving home late after a long day of either working, after-work drinking with colleagues or long commuting, would relax watching *News Station* at 22.00 o'clock. In all families (ten), men would watch the news as a natural privilege. The

It deserves mention that TV-Asahi includes personal commentary and the views of its anchors. It differs in this respect from the traditional form of 'objective' reporting of the other stations. The 'opinionated' form is distinct for TV-Asahi and in comparison with the traditional news reading style of the NHK international news, information is presented quite differently. The staging and roles of news presenters attributes different meanings to the presentation of news. In the framework of the present project, it may be concluded that the different presentation styles in significant ways make the 'domestication' process differ even within the national media environment.

Conclusion

The belief that the content of news programs is similar across nations due to universal technologies and access to international news through international news agencies, as assumed in the 'global' news theories, is shown in this chapter to be a misconception. Although formats and framing processes may be similar in some respects, the communication strategies, the discursive (compositions of visuals and verbal accounts) and the choice of actors include elements of 'domestication' that make news content differ according to national socio-political contexts. Even within national contexts, content may differ from station to station according to the organisational and professional production formula.

The systematic analysis of communication strategies, discourses and actors in this chapter exemplifies elements both of global and local influences. In other words it is found that the phenomenon of *'domestication' of international information is universal*. However, the strategies for 'domestication' differ according to national, organisational and professional factors.

More specifically, is found in the analysis that the communication strategies of national public service and commercial broadcasters in different parts of the world 'package' news presentations (form, studio-decoration, narrative style) and create the 'brand' image (the station profile, message) according to similar global formats. The Danish and Japanese broadcasters apply universal 'generic' formats as a result of similar professional and organisational practices.[87] The 'aesthetic' expressions and the 'choreography' of actors in the presentations are done carefully in line with the conventions of factuality in the news genre. These conventions include the employment of actors and the ritual performance of socio-political actors and professional news presenters, the cutting pace, the framing of visuals, the immediacy effect of 'live' reporting, interviews, use of graphics and props. These conventional practices are grounded in professional values that ensure 'real' and 'objective' interpretations of news through incorporated 'objectivity claims' in textual production Helland (1999) or institutionalised use of sources in a 'web of facticity' (Tuchman, 1978). The outcome of these institutionalised practised for communication (based on mental schemes and models for news production among news workers) in turn meet the expectations of viewers, who accordingly draw upon their internalised schemes of knowledge for interpretation.

---

women would view sporadically while doing domestic chores. The effect on cognitive storage of information was that women remembered little or no information about the events in question. Their answers were primarily emotional considerations about related issues. Men, in general, remembered events and/or were able to derive information from memory through inferences and prior knowledge.

[87] Imitation or 'isomorphism' in new institutional theory (Dimaggio and Powell, 1991).

However, although based on similar strategies to factual mediation through universal formats, the presentation styles of the programs differed. The Danish style approaches an 'infotainment' style of communication, where the Japanese is information intensive. The appeal of the Danish DR and TV2 (and to some extent the Japanese commercial station) were *affective*, whereas the appeal of NHK and TV Asahi was *cognitive* and based on political information. The commercial station, TV Asahi, included explicit views in an appeal to engage audience emotions.

The framing of information targeted audiences in two ways. The mediation of political information, on the one hand, addressed audiences as political citizens who were equipped with a certain amount of prior knowledge of international and domestic political issues 'global consciousness' and certain values.[88] However, the 'aesthetic lay-out' and emotional appeals set up the viewers as consumers in the strategic planning of news presentations (consumers, who count in viewer ratings, attract sponsors and secure the commercial stations financially and public service stations in budget negotiations with their government ministries).

The 'commercialisation' of news commenced in Denmark in the late 1980s during the break with the state media monopoly (following the European trend). The trend was initiated in Japan by the inauguration of 'news magazine' style infotainment programs in the mid-1980s. The commercialisation and *marketisation* (Featherstone, 1991) of news information has gradually had an effect on news production strategies in at public service and commercial stations in both countries. However, the affective appeal is more pronounced in the Danish public service station than the Japanese, which is still driven by traditional hard news production criteria.

The international political agenda proposed by the UN was appropriated in all news presentations and referred to as 'universal' concepts. The UN official themes were implemented as headlines and frameworks of narration. The themes were literally translated into Danish and Japanese equivalents. Although these concepts have various meanings according to the specific geopolitical areas, they were appropriated locally without explicit definitions and implications in the national countries. The Danish presentations were framed with a negative 'spin'. The UN issues were not directly related to the socio-political situation in Denmark. The concepts of *peace, equality* and *development* were associated with third world countries (China) and 'other' governments.

NHK was detailed in its implementation of the Plan of Action, representing the stand of the Japanese government. In political rhetorical terms, the notions were implemented with one modification. It was noted that there was a great difference between these issues in the industrialised (including Japan) and developing countries. TV Asahi elaborated on the *peace* issue in a critical assessment of the Japanese government's handling of Japanese domestic concerns namely the 'Comfort Women' issue. The UN platform of action was thus mediated differently in Denmark and Japan due to national, organisational and professional conceptions of the issues. The political engagement was markedly pronounced in the Japanese presentations. This point will be investigated in the following chapter.

Conclusively, although the news in question was considered 'global' in the International News Flow studies, it was presented quite differently in the two national

---

[88] It is found in Japanese reception studies that audiences of news programs are more critical in environmental issues than audiences of entertainment programs. Entertainment and commercials present and leave their audiences with imagines of nature as beautiful and unspoiled (Kawabata, 1999).

contexts. Cultural and political proximity were influential in the framing of the news. In spite of the emerging strength of the international agencies as international news distributors and the competition of satellite and Internet news, the national broadcast media relies on its ability to frame world events intelligibly for national viewers. In an information society suffused with news, national media are no longer authorities and the sole suppliers of information. However, as is seen in the study of content, the national broadcast stations implement 'domestic' elements in news and thus maintain a national integrative character.

The present chapter is concerned with news presentations at the *global* level, investigating *how* information is framed in two national contexts. The following chapter concerns the Japanese *national* level and analyses how factors and actors in the Japanese media environment influence the production of international news.

Chapter five

The National Media in a global perspective

Every one in the Japanese media will insist that they are not engaged in politics, and in reality that is what it is all about. (TV Asahi, Chief Director, November 25th, 1997)

Political and legal influences on strategic management

The present chapter is a description of the Japanese broadcast environment at the *national* level. The analysis is based on interviews with Directors of international news departments at the five national Tokyo-based national broadcast stations: NHK, TV Asahi, TBS, Fuji TV and NTV and media experts from the Japanese Reporters' Club. The interviews were conducted in 1997 in Japanese and translated into English by the author.

The questions asked were: What are the extra-media factors that influence the production strategies at the national stations? How do these extra-media factors influence the 'world views' and mental strategies of the news producers in their composition of texts and images of international affairs? How do these factors influence the process of 'domesticating' international information?

International and domestic politics, legal regulations, competition, economic change and technological development were verbalised as the main factors influencing the processes of news production, which are incorporated in the everyday working processes of international news making.

The chapter is divided into four parts. The first offers an introduction to the political and legal aspects of the Japanese media environment, which forms the background for political influence on production processes. The second part is an analysis of the presentation forms and content of the national broadcasters, which result in different ways of 'domesticating' international information. Thirdly the 'global' influence of the international news agencies is explored, and finally the increasing demands on international news producers due to general changes in market trends and technological development are highlighted. A discussion of the *global influence on domestic strategies* and the *marketisation of political information* in Japanese news production concludes the analysis.

This analysis of the Japanese media 'ecology' provides background for analysis at the organisational level at the public station, NHK, and the private station, TV Asahi, in the following chapters.

The political character of the broadcast media

A noticeable difference in the Danish and Japanese news presentations in the previous chapter was the political 'spin' on news which was most prominent in Japan. The reason for this is explored in the following.

In Japan as everywhere, much research has been done concerning the relationship between the media and politics (see Chapter One). These studies are to a great degree based on media content analysis. Few studies in Japan besides Krauss (2000, 1996, 1995) who like the present study focuses on NHK and TV Asahi, have examined newsroom practices and news production processes. Where Krauss in his earlier work is concerned with coverage between the US and Japan based on content analysis and a historical account between the political system and NHK, the present study is concerned with the coverage and production of specific pieces of 'global' news and the perceived difference in strategies between public service and commercial stations in the choice and production of international news.

The Japanese broadcast system has been dual since the US-led Allied Occupation Forces poured their energies into demilitarising and democratising Japanese society. Pre-war censorship laws were repealed after the end of the war. With the San Francisco peace treaty in April 1952, Japan regained its independence and the major newspapers and news agencies began to expand their overseas news-gathering networks. Most of the broadcast stations as described in the following were started by newspaper companies. The dual structure (NHK and commercial broadcasters including TV Asahi, TBS, Fuji, NTV and TV Tokyo[89]) and the broadcaster's linkages with the print newspapers characterised the Japanese broadcasting system.

The public service station, NHK, is financed by licence fee[90] and the five private networks are financed by commercials. Each private network is related in terms of capital and personnel to one of the five major national newspaper companies.[91]

Newspaper companies started most of the commercial stations at both national and regional levels. The local stations are affiliated with the local newspapers, and the national networks have their flagship station affiliated with the national newspapers.[92] Thus, Nippon TV (NTV) is with *Yomiuri*, TV Asahi with *Asahi*,[93] Tokyo Broadcasting

---

[89] Tokyo TV is a latecomer. It differs from the national networks in its business structure and size. It is briefly described in this section but not included in the interview survey.

[90] The Diet deliberates and approves the budget, operating plans, and capital plans submitted by NHK every year. The Minister of Post and Telecommmunications is able to comment on the settlement of accounts. NHK is referred to as a public interest corporation (Foreign Press Center, 1997) while the European organisations are referred to as public service. The commitments are described in similar ways.

[91] Dentsu is one of the indispensable actors in the audio-visual landscapes in Japan, whether public or private. Dentsu is one of the biggest advertising agencies in the world. It represents 35 per cent of advertising receipts in Japanese television. In 1986, Dentsu became one of the partners of SogoVision, created by the public television network, NHK, together with Mitsubishi and NTT. According to Mattelart (1991), NHK was anxious to get into the commercial arena in order to fully exploit its production facilities and large library of programming, but hesitant to appear to be going commercial (Mattelart, 1991:122-23). In 1989 Dentsu reorganised its management and personnel to create a new business division, the Visual Software Division. This division managed News Station (reportage and light entertainment) among other television programmes.
See Westney (1996) for a description of Japanese mass media as business organisations. The issue of business evokes anxieties about the potentially contradictory roles of mass media: as providers of the critically important public goods of information and values, and as businesses that buy and sell. Wolferen describes what he calls a cozy relationship between Dentsu and the LDP "The ninth bureau absorbs over one-third over of the PR budget of the Prime Minister's office and some 40% of that of the other ministries. Dentsu also has a near monopoly on disposal of the LDP's PR budget. ..A role of the major 'advertising agencies' as servants of the system illustrates admirably the impossibility of drawing a line between the private and public sectors in Japan." (Van Wolferen, 1993: 236-7). It serves notice that Wolferen's "The Enigma of Japanese power: people and politics in a stateless nation" is a thorough but often overly critical appraisal of the Japanese system.
5 The circulation of the five biggest newspapers in millions; Asahi (12.6); Mainichi (5.8); Yomiuri (14,4); Nihon Keizai (4,5); Sankei (2,8). With 5 national papers and 102 local, Japan by population has relatively fewer daily newspapers than most other industrialised countries. The shortage of newsprint and the desire to manage the news during the war led the government to encourage consolidation until there was only one newspaper per prefecture. A pattern that basically remains unchanged. (Foreign Press Center, 1997).

[93] In 1996 Rubert Murdoch and son Masayoshi together bought 21% of Television Asahi. Believing that this was the first move in a broader game plan for media dominance, the newspapers quickly rushed to enhance their own cross-media capabilities, including Asahi Shinbun's buying the pair's stake from them at cost. At the same time, concern has been expressed that the newspapers, by virtue of their very close ties to the broadcaster, may have forfeited their claim to special protection and may now be regarded as just another business (Foreign Press Center, 1997).

System (TBS) with *Mainichi*, TV Tokyo with *Nihon Keizai* and Fuji TV with *Sankei*. These five national newspaper companies and NHK dominate Japanese news. It is generally said and has been empirically supported in case studies (Ito, 1993:71) that the Yomiuri Shimbun and the Sankei Shimbun are conservative or pro-LDP (The Japanese Liberal Democratic Party), the Asahi Shimbun and the Mainichi Shimbun are anti-establishment or pro-JSP (Japanese Socialist Party, now the Social Democratic Party). The political stances of Nihon Keizai Shimbun and NHK are middle of the road (Ibid:71).

The political views of the TV stations resemble their newspaper affiliates. According to the renowned Asahi journalist, Matsuyama Yukio, TV Asahi is the most liberal, and the most critical of the Japanese government. The Asahi group, TBS, and the Japanese news agency Kyodo News belong to the liberal side. Fuji TV is the most conservative. NTV and TV Tokyo and the Japanese news Agency Jiji Press are conservative and close to the LDP, the ruling government's views. Compared with this, NHK, as a public broadcasting company, tries to ensure impartial and neutral reporting (Matsuyama, interview August 11th, 1997)

A placement of the broadcasters as political actors as shown in the model poses difficulties. Although Article 21 in the Japanese constitution guarantees freedom of speech, Japanese broadcasters are obliged to be 'politically neutral' because the broadcast law prohibits partial political stances. Article 3 of the Broadcast Law sets out four ethical principles that should govern editorial policy: (1) Programming should not be detrimental to the public order or to good customs, (2) programming should be politically neutral, (3) programming should be truthful, and (4) programming should make an effort to present all sides of controversial issues (Foreign Press Center, 1997). Compliance with these ethical principles may make obtaining a new licence possible. Licenses are valid for five years and broadcasters have to reapply in order to secure a new licence every five years. The Ministry of Posts and Telecommunications (MTP) is in charge of the broadcasting licences.

The Japanese broadcast law thus requires political neutrality. The violation of the law can cause the licence of a station to be withdrawn. In spite of the 'impartiality' clause stipulated by law, the following, based on research and scholarly findings as described above, is an attempt to make a model of the political spectrum of the Japanese news media based on empirical evidence.

Figure 10: The National TV Stations with Their Newspaper Affiliates

Political spectrum	Liberal (JSP)		Neutral	Conservative (LDP)	
Newspaper TV Station	Asahi Mainichi		Nihon Keizai	Yomiuri Sankei	
	TV Asahi TBS		TV Tokyo NHK	Nihon TV Fuji TV	
News agency	Kyodo News			Jiji Press	

In practice, several events have made the political engagement of the broadcast stations evident. A strong case exemplifying political engagement was the political turmoil and the fall of the LDP in the election in 1993. The fall in the view of media scholars and

116

experts was greatly influenced by unprecedented political activity in the media (Altman, 1996). The political involvement was in conflict with the existing legal prescripts of the broadcast law and the question of whether the government should be responsible for licensing and enforcing broadcasting laws was raised and debated widely on this occasion. Based on the US experience where the Fairness Doctrine was abolished in 1987,[94] Altman (1996) raises the question: Should political fairness be regulated at all? A problem in the view of liberal critics was the allocation of power to the Ministry of Post and Telecommunications to determine whether the ethics are maintained or violated. This ministry may render any criticism of the government unfair and irresponsible. As the government since the Second World War has been headed by the LDP, except for a coalition with the socialist party in the short period from 1993-95, the Liberal Democrats, in the view of some, inevitably influence interpretations concerning the renewal of licences. The imbalance in political influence on licence renewal has been debated widely.

Unlike the broadcast stations, the Japanese newspapers are not regulated by law. According to Matsuyama Yukio, the newspapers strive to be impartial by imposing self-regulation. Unlike the American press, who in times of elections support individual candidates, the Japanese Press refrains from this kind of direct involvement.

> Law does not regulate the newspapers but they try to be impartial. Unlike the New York Times for instance. The Americans seem to be dissatisfied with a non-partial, non-partisan press. In times of elections, the New York Times did not hesitate to support Kennedy instead of Nixon or Dukakis instead of Bush but Japanese newspapers refrain from supporting particular candidates. Even conservative Yomiuri or Sankei do not take a stance. Many subscribers will stop buying the papers. So our opinions seem to be a bit abstract. (Matsuyama Yukio, Interview, August 11th, 1997)

The non-partisan attitude of the press, according to Matsuyama, is connected to the business strategies of the newspapers. Business strategies were also given as the reason why broadcasters refrain from political activity (see statement by the Fuji TV Director, Chapter Three). Political involvement, according to business logic, turns away subscribers and viewers. Opinions of the press, accordingly, are somewhat 'abstract' (Matsuyama, interview, August 11th, 1997). Nevertheless, in the 1993 election according to the research of Kristin Kyoko Altman (1996), the activity of the television stations made the political process clearer and closer to people than ever. According to Altman, politicians who understood the importance of the broadcast media made use of it and political leaders were increasingly concerned with image and performance. As a result, the triangular relationship between television, politics, and elections that characterises American politics began to emerge in Japan (Altman, 1996).

The fact that three new parties were able to round up 103 seats, surpassing the JSP to become a new political force, was due in important ways to television. No election in Japan had ever felt the impact of television, as did the election of July 1993 (Altman, 1996: 175). The three new parties were the Japan Renewal Party (*Nihon Shinto*), Japan

---

[94] In the United States, the Federal Communication Commission, a neutral party, regulates broadcasting. Until 1987 the FCC had a Fairness Doctrine, similar to Japan's Broadcasting Law. With the spread of cable television, the Fairness doctrine was abolished on the grounds that it stifled freedom of expression and thought (Altman 1996).

New Party (*Shinseito*), and New Party Sakigake (*Shinto Sakigake*) (all from factions within the LDP). The leaders of these three dominant reform parties: Takemura, Hosokawa, and Hata, respectively, appeared daily on television. Their characters were strong and they were for the first time addressing an 'image-conscious generation' (ibid.) by using the exposure of television to promote their ideas for reform. The heavy TV coverage in part encouraged the loss of majority power of the LDP for the first time since the Second World War in the elections on July 8th 1993.

But how did the broadcasters manage to be political under the restrictions of the broadcast law? According to Matsuyama, the content of tele-visual media is difficult to regulate by the Ministry of Posts and Telecommunication. The fleeting nature of television makes documentation and control tedious and once images are on the air, they cannot be called back. Some newscasters took advantage of this and severely criticised the LDP. During the election, TV Asahi criticised LDP leaders openly and supported LDP politicians that were promoting political reform. [95] However, their activities did not go unnoticed, as described in the following.

The fundamental attitude of TV Asahi is anti-establishment. [96] Because of the style of the anchor of *News Station*, Kume Hiroshi, the *News Station* program has become one with strong opinions. A public poll conducted at the beginning of July 1993 in Tokyo shortly before the historic election showed that on this occasion 60.2 percent of Japanese watched *News Station* for political news, while 38.3 percent watched the NHK news. [97] Thus indicating that the opinions of the TV Asahi newscaster on this occasion were echoed in the majority of Japanese homes.

At the time of the election, the Asahi paper did not hesitate to criticise the LDP, and Kume Hiroshi was also active on this occasion.

> Mr. Tsubaki encouraged Mr. Kume to condemn the LDP's arrogance. At this time the paper did not hesitate to criticise the LDP and Mr Kume criticised Kanemaru (the don) and other members of the LDP. Mr Tsubaki was the director general. He expressed his opinion that the LDP should lose its seats in the congress election in a closed meeting. The content was leaked and the LDP were exasperated. TV Asahi was by no means impartial, which was against the law. Mr Tsubaki was only expressing everyones thought at the time. But a high-ranking person should not express political views. (Matsuyama Yukio, August 11th, 1997)

---

[95] As an example, TV Asahi made extensive coverage of and interviews with Sakigake leader, Minister of Finance, Hata, concerning his participation (on holiday) in anti nuclear demonstrations in Australia in 1995.

[96] The anti-establishment attitude of TV Asahi is exemplified in the presentation of the French Nuclear testing. After almost half a century of LDP leadership, a coalition government with the Socialist leader, Matsuyama, as Prime Minister was in power from 1993-95. It may be expected that TV Asahi would have supported a socialist leader of the Cabinet. On the contrary, Matsuyama is ridiculed and shown dancing with two companions (Japanese young women in uniforms with uniform, anonymous but pleasant appearance). TV Asahi was dismayed that the socialist party had changed its old policies and made a lot of compromises in the coalition government. In the view of TV Asahi, Matsuyama did not explain the change in socialist politics to its supporters - the people.
According to the chief editor, TV Asahi has changed its policies over the years. The Asahi newspaper has changed. The Asahi group does not protect any political side. It adheres to a liberal goal: to protect the grassroots and the people, thereby promoting a democratic system. The journalistic goal is to dismantle power and to stand on the people's side. Nevertheless, the people's side, the human rights side and the liberal side equal the socialist side. (TV Asahi, Chief Director, November 25th, 1997).

[97] Altman, 1996: 171. Cf. Shunji, 1994:49.

Thus, in a closed meeting at the Japan Commercial Broadcasting Association (Nihon Minkan Hoso Renmei), the head of TV Asahi's news department, Tsubaki Sadayoshi, expressed the opinion that the time was ripe for the LDP to lose some seats in the congressional election. The fact that TV Asahi had broken the impartiality rules of the broadcast law by encouraging political action against the LDP had serious consequences. Tsubaki was summoned to the Diet and in a subpoena he had to apologise. The initiation of political activity by high-ranking media executives had its consequences.

The Tsubaki statement became a problem and ignited a fierce discussion about politics, power and media. The Tsubaki statement split the media into supporters of the conservative Sankei, Yomiuri and the liberal Asahi. The regaining of power in 1995 by the LDP resulted in a backlash. Before the LDP lost its power experts were invited to talk freely on different subjects, even the sensitive political issues of US military occupation of Okinawa and security problems with North Korea. After the Tsubaki affair, according to several interviewees, critical views have been less in demand even in TV Asahi programs. Talk shows and political interviews screen opinions through rehearsals before the programs and leave out experts with controversial views.[98] The LDP's control, according to critics, is felt in the mass media at large. The LDP learned its lessons and it will not lose its power as in the 1993 election.

The above analysis of the political character of the Japanese media makes the political stances of the national media apparent. But why are the Japanese broadcasters so political and why are some of the commercial broadcasters so anti-establishment? Three plausible reasons are found in a paper by Matsuyama Yukio "Mass Media and Democracy[99] in Japan" (1993), which attempts to explain the anti-establishment attitude of the Japanese press. Firstly, Matsuyama argues, the constitutional system of checks and balances by comparison works better in other democracies than in Japan. Japan has adopted the separation of powers dogma, but the Executive Branch remains superior to the Legislative and the Judicial, which means that the Prime Minister, backed by the overwhelming majority of the LDP is almost in an autocratic position. These conditions, according to Matsuyama, put pressure upon the press, which he refers to as the 'fourth estate' to provide effective opposition 'based on the conviction that power corrupts' (Matsuyama, 1993: 6). The notion of the 'fourth estate' or the 'watch dog' role was expressed as a professional ideal by many of the interviewees but was seemingly only put into practice in rare cases. While the investigative character of the US press is consistently exemplified by the Watergate affair, the Japanese press has initiated coverage of the Lockheed payoff scandal, the Recruit bribery scandal in 1988 and the Kanemaru tax evasion scandal. However, although scandals are covered almost excessively by media organisations once they are revealed, it deserves mention that few

---

[98] Personal communication, August 1997.

[99] It deserves mention that the notion of democracy has been debated fiercely in Japan as some argue that the Allied Powers enforced a constitution upon Japan, which has not since been amended. Others refer to the freedom of speech the free election system and to the fact that the Japanese are free to change their constitution and enact their legal system as they please, and that Japan due to these circumstances is a democratic country. According to Ito (2000) although 'individualism' and 'democracy' are ideologies originated in the West, the development of communication technologies makes these notions empirical phenomena which are ubiquitous. In Japan, the proliferation of information, Ito argues, brings information within the reach of the common people and enhance democracy. The new forms of social interaction due to the development of communication technology seemingly break up Japanese traditional patterns. Family ties, for instance, are according to Ito, decreasing in importance and replaced by 'individual' networking across traditional groups of belonging such as family, place of employment and class.

are initiated by the media. The attitude expressed below, therefore, may be regarded as somewhat idealistic:

> Investigative journalism and scoops can make situations different. Sensation does not make the world change. A scoop may change situations because the airing means that attention is brought to a problem and the politicians have to make policies. (NHK, chief desk, interview July 17th, 1997)

In the NHK international newsrooms there was an eagerness to get scoops, i.e. to acquire information and visuals first; however, the scoop strategy differs from the notion of investigative journalism. A hindrance for investigative journalism in foreign news coverage may be the considerable reliance on international news agencies for news agendas. Once the news has broken, investigation is too late. TV Asahi made an investigative journalistic attempt to cover the French nuclear testing. The TV Asahi news director, who is a native French speaker, conducted a telephone interview with French military officials concerning the nuclear tests. However, this piece of news, although investigative in its approach, did not reveal much beyond the information that was already in circulation.

Secondly, an important reason for the anti-establishment attitude of the Japanese press, according to Matsuyama, was that the Japanese newspapers, even the Asahi Shimbun, which is the most liberal, co-operated with the military government during the war. As a reaction to this experience, it has become the instinct of newsmen, after the war, not to do favours for the government or any part of the power-establishment. The 'power-establishment' and strategies to work against it were prevalent at TV Asahi as exemplified in the following chapter. Thirdly, according to Matsuyama, the Japanese government has displayed erratic policies and conduct that invite for criticism. Matsuyama refers specifically to reluctance to liberalise agricultural products, bribery and a poor social security system.

In conclusion, the political character of the Japanese media system, according to the interview survey, is due to different circumstances. Although based on democratic elections, the Japanese political system of checks and balances provides the Japanese ruling party with great power. Since the Second World War the LDP has been the ruling party except for a few years from 1993-95 (it deserves mention that the LDP includes a wide spectrum of political fractions). The newspapers as categorised above cover a large spectrum of political views, which resembles the political press of the European countries. However, the anti-establishment strategies of the commercial broadcast stations stand out by comparison. The anti-establishment attitude of the commercial stations (mainly TV Asahi and to a lesser extent TBS) has developed over time as a counter measure to the strong position of the government.

The political power of television news personalities

The political nature of broadcast news and an 'opinionated' style of news presentations may be credited to initiatives by individuals.

As discussed in Chapter 4, TV personalities have a strong affective impact on audiences. In Japan because of political articulations they have according to Matsuyama, become even more influential as opinion leaders than their European and American colleagues.[100]

> All private broadcasters are supposed to be neutral because the broadcast law prohibits a partial political stance. But under these restrictions, Kume and Chikushi try to express their own opinions, which sometimes causes resentment or frustration on the part of the LDP and in business circles (Matsuyama Yukio, August 11th, 1997).

Under the restrictions of the broadcast law, the two most popular newscasters, Kume[101] Hiroshi from TV Asahi, and Chikushi Tetsuya[102] from TBS, express critical political opinions. Both are progressive and do not hesitate to criticise the government. Kume and Chikushi are influential newscasters and they have a considerable impact on public opinion. However in comparison with the popular US newscasters, James West and Walter Cronkite who are considered heroes, Kume and Chikushi are, according to Matsuyama Yukio, although very influential newscasters not perceived as heroes in Japanese society, possibly because of their one-sided political critique.

According to Murayama, the Japanese public welcomes critical opinions, however, the influence by a few individuals, especially through the 'at times superficial medium' of television gives reason for concern. According to Matsuyama, the two newscasters have personal influence on the production and presentation of domestic as well as international news.

> Kume and Chikushi easily influence people who are not familiar with political issues. They comment on the situations from Washington to Tokyo in black and white versions and for audiences who often do not follow politics in the newspapers but use television as their main source of information, the one-sided reporting is a dangerous tendency. Stories are often presented one-sidedly. (Matsuyama Yukio, interview August 11th, 1997).

---

[100] See Cooper-Chen 1997 for a description of the most popular news anchors in Japan.

[101] Based on Chen-Coopers (1997) description, Kume Hiroshi was hired by TBS from Waseda where he had studied politics and economics. In the "Doyo Waido" (Saturday wide) he unfolded skills as a program host. Later, as a free-lancer he hosted four programs in one of which he often discussed current news with co-host Tetsuko Kuroyanagi (author of Totochan). His presence alone guaranteed high ratings. At age 41 Kume became the host of News Station and added his personal opinion, questions and reactions to this well-researched top rated news program. It was not uncommon to see him making grimaces and laughing out loud. With respect for individual initiative, he felt a duty to represent citizens concerns, while stating that journalist should not think of the national interest but report facts. He brought 40 staff from his own company with him to News Station to research and fact check. In 1995, the French weekly Le Nouvel Observateur named Kume as one of the world's 50 most influential people. (Cooper-Chen,1997:123)

[102] Chikushi Tetsuya a former editor of the Asahi Shimbun is a graduate from Waseda in political science and economics. He was a special correspondent stationed in Washington in 1971 covering the Watergate affair. As an anchor of 'News 23' on TBS at 23.00 o'clock, he is noted for his liberal viewpoints and regarded as one of Japan's most trustworthy journalists. (Cooper-Chen, 1997: 125)

Where the newspapers allocate much space to unfold stories, Kume and Chikushi's versions, according to Matsuyama, are simple but reach tens of millions.[103]

In conclusion, where NHK's *News Seven* leaves facts for individual interpretation, TV Asahi's *News Station* is a program of clear opinions.[104] The 'opinionated' style in news programs was introduced by Kume Hiroshi in *News Station*. Other national broadcasters have adopted this style. In the following, the flagship programs of the national broadcasters are divided according to their style of presentation into 'news' and 'views' and according to their content into 'hard' news and 'soft' news.

The national broadcasters[105]

The 'news and views' display (Krauss, 2000, 1995) describes the content and style of presentation of Japanese broadcast of US news.[106] The display is based on *content* analysis, however, it is included here as it supports and illustrates the interview statements of the news directors at NHK and the commercial stations about their professional strategies. The incorporation of 'views' in news presentations differs from the traditional news presentation style in most countries where the 'objective' news presentation style is dominant (See discussion of 'news objectivity and new(s) epistemologies' in Chapter 2). The 'domestication' of news in the Japanese case, thus, is influenced not only by *political framing* as described above but also by the *style of reporting*. The news and views reporting styles differ considerably between the public service station and the commercial stations. The present chapter provides an overview of the spectrum of news presentations of the Japanese national broadcasters, which serves as the background for the analyses in the following chapter of organisational factors at TV Asahi, which includes 'subjective' commentary and NHK that strives for

---

[103] The impact of television on audiences is a world-wide concern, however, cognitive oriented studies of have produced generally more optimistic judgements of how much news information is acquired by audiences. Learning from broadcast news depends on the pre-established knowledge and motivation of the viewers. (Graber, 1984, Iyengar 1991)

[104] It was stated in several interviews that Kume Hiroshi is thriving on the 'indecisive character of the Japanese'. A reason why individual anchors have gained power is their courage to voice their opinions. Japanese people, it is believed, do not voice their opinions and this lack of self-assertion is likewise ingrained in management practices. Traditionally, the top leadership in Japanese politics, bureaucracy and the business world has been assigned on a rotation basis rather than encouraged by personal ambition. There is generally no focus on strong leaderships or front figures. This accounts for media organisation too. High business profiles such as Murdock or Turner are not found in Japan. The presidents of most media companies are not opinion leaders, neither are they front figures and symbols of the company. Rather they are part of the 'consensus' of the company. Kume thrives on the ability to make criticism in this environment. These statements resemble the reinforced stereotypes and self perceptions of the Japanese. While it may be true that some leaders seemingly are part of the 'consensus' of the company, others are strong symbols and leader figures in their companies or political parties. This notion of inability to express oneself is one of the misconceived notions of nihonjinron (see criticism in Chapter Three).

[105] Global change is an issue which is difficult to understand comprehensively. The influence on NHK is that leadership is much more important than before. A strong, active top leader is vital (NHK, Vice Director and Staff Correspondent, interview July 10th, 1997).

[106] Because of the complicated and time-consuming task of translating broadcast news from Japanese into English (Miller 1994), most content research focuses on only a few of the major stations.

'objective' news reading. The 'hard' news refers to economic and political issues while 'soft' news are social issues with a human-interest approach.

It deserves mention that although *News Station* includes opinions and is conceptualised as a 'news magazine' style with a mix of light entertainment and well-researched reportage, the international news and special reports follow strict journalistic guidelines (See analysis in the previous chapter).

In short, as the model shows, NHK and TV Asahi present mainly 'hard news' i.e. political, economic, business, military and international affairs. The two commercial stations, TBS, Fuji and NTV show a higher rate of 'soft news' including social, human-interest, disaster and crime stories.

Figure 11: International Broadcast News Presentation Styles at the National Networks.

	Content tendency of News	
	'Hard news'	*'Soft news'*
'factual'	NHK	FUJI [*NTV*]
Style of News		
'opinionated'	Asahi	TBS, NTV

Source: Krauss, Ellis K (2000) NHK, *Broadcasting Politics in Japan: NHK and Television News*. Itaka: Cornell University Press p. 234. Printed with Permission

NHK and Fuji present their news in a factual, neutral way, whereas TV Asahi, TBS and NTV include, opinions and commentary by their anchors. Where the political implications of the 'news and views' presentation styles are discussed above, the discussion in the following concerns the 'news and views' 'hard' news and 'soft' news communication strategies, including *news criteria, presentation style* and *audience considerations*.

NHK

NHK has public obligations and strict standards for programming, which includes news. It is an integrated procedure in the production of news to present news impartially (see production procedures in Chapters 7and 8). Besides being impartial in its news reports, NHK is obliged to spend an equal amount of airtime on each political party. This has some advantages. All parties from the LDP to the small parties are heard. However, this neutral political stand, according to the NHK Vice Director, can be frustrating and a barrier to getting things moving. NHK is a big bureaucratic[107] organisation in this

---

[107] In a self-critical assessment of news production, NHK finds that the quality of reporting is low. Many of the senior reporters are qualified, but there is a shortage of these. It is recognised that there is a need to educate new talents and measures are taken to 'internationalise' the education of journalists (NHK, Vice Director, Staff Correspondent). NHK had 13.060 employees in 1996 (Japans Mass Media, 1977).

respect (NHK, Vice Director, July 10th, 1997). Although the NHK information level in news and the journalistic standards are considered high, news broadcast according to the Vice Director is to a great extent guided by emotions. It has to be in order to being effective. What kinds of emotions are at stake in political, economic and social news reporting? According to the Vice-Director, for instance, the coverage of the French Nuclear Tests was based on the emotional sentiment of the Japanese people and professionals alike. The fact that Japan became a victim of the only atom bomb attack on civilians is a historical tragedy, which is present in the mind of even the younger generation. The sympathy with the people in Nagasaki and Hiroshima was the emotional background for this news and the coverage of the event was a priority and turned into hour-long reports (appendix 1). In relation to the present study, the news about the French nuclear tests was 'domesticated' to a great extent in Japan both quantitatively and qualitatively. The stories were told within a Japanese historical framework appealing to the sentiments of the Japanese audiences[108] and the reports were lengthy.

In general, the news presentation style at NHK is described as 'factual' and 'neutral'. (See nuances of these terms in the content analysis in Chapter Four and production practices in Chapters Seven and Eight). According to the NHK executive, NHK is seeking to achieve a high quality control and efficiency check of its programming, which includes news.

> It is difficult to get rid of a bias. Misconceptions are carried on and ideology forms company policy. Human rights, democracy and freedom of speech cause different problems of interpretation. And implementations of these concepts cause the main problem of quality control. (NHK, Vice Director, July 10th, 1997)

According to the Vice-Director it is difficult to get rid of biases and preconceived ideas. It is difficult to change integrated company policy. Quality reinforcement advised from above, he asserts, takes time to incorporate into the strategies of individual employees. At any rate, according to the Vice-Director, news producers cannot be controlled. The outcome of news reports depends on the reporter's point of view. The NHK executive's assessment of the reporter's freedom to express his point of view only partly explains production practices. In some cases, journalists feel they are able to present events as they intend; however, most refer to self censorship learned through practice and negotiation with superiors over time.

NHK's news programs are based on objective news reading and do not offer opinions. Instead NHK makes programmes like 'Shitenronten' (Views and Opinions) in which experts give their personal opinion about political issues. This is a way for NHK to provide a forum for discussion. Experts, also with controversial opinions (anti-establishment and therefore against NHK's neutral stand), are invited. NHK gets around the public's offence at critical views by letting participants talk for themselves, not

---

[108] An Australian study, also based on the News flow in the 1990 material, of the French Nuclear Testing in Mururoa supports the domestication hypothesis. "Less than 20 % of the stories in the Australian sample were event-focussed. They were primarily concerned with describing an occurrence. Over 80% of the sample material was primarily concerned with interpretation and commentary. In these latter stories, the sites of interpretation (both geographic and ideological) and the subsequent circulation of these interpretations had greater significance than the original dispersion of information about the event itself " (Putnis, 1999).

NHK. The Dutch journalist, Karel van Wolferen (1991), calls these programs "pseudo discussions". However, scholars and political commentators who have appeared in the show have felt that they could voice their opinions freely. As one example, the scholar in international politics, Gregory Clark has participated with opinions about the Northern Territories, which are against NHK's official view on the territorial conflict with Russia.

> I have been allowed to appear on 'Shitenronten' to give my view on the problem. My view on the Northern Island territorial conflict with Russia is very different from the government's. It is very critical. NHK does not mind that. But they themselves will not go too far from the government position. (Gregory Clark, August 14th, 1997)

According to Gregory Clark, NHK at times is careful and at other times is quite critical of government policies in its reporting. He exemplifies an instance of where NHK has been critical of the government.

> On questions of war guilt (*sensosekinin*), NHK is one of the best. It has some very good analysis of the war and Japanese behaviour in the war, which sometimes embarrasses the government. In particular, NHK exposed the government lies about forced labour (*kyoseirinkosha*) three or four years ago and managed to change government policy. (Gregory Clark, August 14th, 1997)

Gregory Clark concludes that NHK is critical in reporting on government foreign policy and neutral in domestic political matters. Matsuyama Yukio has appeared several times with opinions that contradict NHK's politically neutral stand.

> Even NHK wants to present opinions. NHK has the program of Views and Opinions (*shitenronten*), where I have frequently voiced my opinion. When NHK receives telephone protests from the general public they refer to the personal opinions of Mr. Matsuyama. NHK has nothing to do with the content. NHK has 10 minutes every night with view and opinions. (Matsuyama Yukio, August 11th, 1997)

'Shitenronten' has been broadcast every night for more than a decade. It has generated numerous telephone protests from the general public. NHK has counterfeited the criticism by presenting the controversial statements as the opinion of the participants and not the official NHK. NHK, although hosting merely social elites (as opposed to giving access to ordinary citizens), has in this way provided a public forum for discussion.

The NHK's news content is categorised as hard news without views. The NHK news reading was the conventional reporting style at the commercial stations, until the introduction of a new format by TV Asahi in October 1985.

TV Asahi

In 1985, *News Station* went on the air for the first time. The 'news magazine' style was a new concept introducing new ways of presenting news. The concept was a break away from the traditional news presentation style of NHK, and the new approach influenced the presentation and news production strategies at the other commercial stations.

TV Asahi created *News Station* in cooperation with Japan's largest advertising agency, Dentsu, and according to the Chief Director the new format went from a traditional production-oriented focus on professional journalistic standards to a focus on what audiences were perceived to demand. The previous NHK style of presentation resembled what the Chief Director referred to as 'newspaper production style'. According to the Chief Director at TV Asahi, no one had previously paid attention to the fact that TV was based on audio-visual perception. The traditional news reading was informative, standardised and complex. The anchor, Kume Hiroshi's, style did much to change this. He was a former pop-show host and was not inhibited by journalistic rules. Kume was an exceptionally skilled TV performer.[109] According to the Chief Director Komiya Tetsuko, the long time female anchor (see Chapter 4) picked up the techniques from Kume and soon mastered the art of introducing and speaking about complex news themes in an easily understandable manner. In the beginning, according to the Chief Director, it was difficult to carry out the more investigative, explorative kind of journalism because the *News Station* staff had previously been trained to write news stories like newspaper articles with much emphasis on information and less on the visual message.

Feature stories (*kikaku*) were the next development. They were connected to the so-called 'window' format of *News Station*. The program was divided into several windows or sections, which were separated by 5-7 minute slots of commercials. The first two sections of about 18 to 20 minutes were dedicated to 'straight news' i.e. political happenings of the day such as the Yamaichi Security and other scandals. The third section presented a feature story, and finally there were sections with sports and weather forecasts. The feature stories, which normally lasted 10-12 minutes, required a large budget. They were time-consuming and costly. Because of the budget and because of the traditional reporting style, the staff did not make feature stories about straight news (current and breaking news). The number and length of the different sections has changed several times over the years.

The most difficult hurdle which had to be overcome, according to the Chief Director, was to convince the TV Asahi management to make a prime time news program. Earlier, the prime time broadcasting hours were reserved for entertainment programs and the audience was accustomed to this. But the *News Station* innovators decided that the time was ripe. There was an audience demand for longer news entertainment programs in the prime time slot. The budget for *News Station* was the biggest ever. Late night, early morning, late evening do not make good commercial turnover. However, the prime time programs from seven to eleven o'clock in the evening bring in considerable sums of money from commercials (See Moeran 1999, Cooper-Chen, 1997). No one believed that a news program could succeed, but the TV Asahi management made a decision and the 'news magazine' went on the air.

Although TV Asahi is commercial, with opinions and subjective commentary, the international news content primarily concerns politics and economic issues. As argued previously, the economic ability of NHK and TV Asahi enhances the ability to

---

[109] Kume Hiroshi was on holiday during the tape recordings of the International News Flow Material in 1995. However his special talent as an anchor was mentioned several times by his colleagues, as indicated in Chapter Seven.

'domesticate' news. It enables Japanese-held cameras world-wide and allocation of competent staff and resources to make thorough reports.

TBS

TBS is categorised in the model as presenting 'soft' news including opinions. According to the statements of the Director of Foreign News, TBS is adhering to the hard news line in its production strategy. A discrepancy between the professional strategies as expressed by top executives and the analysis of content is found at the commercial stations. The professional ideals are eventually compromised for business strategies, as discussed below.

The TBS Director of Political News lines up two audiences of consideration: the economic and political social actors and the Japanese general public. Like many of his colleagues, he identifies with the economic and political establishment; however, the content analysis of the early evening program shows a 'soft' approach to news. While the TBS news management staff imagines its viewers to be interested in international news, it is produced with the awareness that the average Japanese does not think about exchange rates and the rise and fall of the yen in his everyday life. Rather, according to the Director of Political News, the political and economic establishment relies on international information, to make economic and political decisions. In this respect, international news mediation is important. As part of the identification with the political and economic elite in news selection, the Director states that Japan's position in the international community affects the considerations behind news production:

> If Japan were a world power like the US it could concentrate on internal matters. It would not have to be so interested in the world around it. Japan by comparison is a small, weak country with no national power. Japan is perceived to be a powerful economic nation but it possesses no vital resources [oil, gas, steel] for its production and is therefore dependent on the outside world. Because of its dependency, Japan has to be on top of moves around the world. This is a major premise for the very existence and destiny of Japan. (TBS, Director of Political News, July 11th, 1997)

In the view of the Director of Political News, the importance of international news updates is a reason why 62 per cent of the TBS budget is dedicated to international coverage and import of international news. Most TBS managers would prefer to allocate 70 per cent of the budget to domestic news, as it is more appealing to audiences (TBS, Director of Political News). TBS considers its role as an informant of international affairs seriously and this according to the Director is reflected in the international news budget. Concerning Japan's international status, it may play a minor role in "world culture" (Mattelart, 1994) but it occupies a leadership position in the world economy. The self-perception of Japan's position in the world expressed above therefore does not match the image of Japan in the international community. The Director of TBS Political News expresses an ambition to mediate international information at a high level. However, as mentioned above, TBS news is categorised as 'soft' including opinions. The ambitions expressed by the Director may refer to the late evening program, which caters to a more mature audience, as described further below.

FUJI TV

Whereas NHK, TV Asahi and TBS executives expressed an ideal of keeping the public informed as political citizens, NTV, like Fuji news, base their strategies entirely on perceived audience demands.

According to the Director of Foreign News, Fuji TV works with three basic criteria for the selection of international news. Generally, domestic and international news is chosen very consciously with the audience in mind. In many instances international news does not influence daily life directly and has no meaning for the audience. Considering this, international news is presented so people know how it affects their life and daily activities. Secondly it is a news criterion or a presentation strategy to estimate which international developments may have an influence on the future life of the Japanese. This estimation is made in order to present news that *makes the public feel informed.* [110] The final criterion for international news selection includes rare phenomena that people have neither heard nor seen before. These criteria are based on perceived audience demands. It was stated that an important element in the production of international news was the creation of a sense of closeness.

> We try to get our news from a variety of sources. Among these the actual stories that are chosen are dependent on the criterion above. In order to explain this in brief, if for instance there is a story about the EU currency and at the same time a story about the US (*kambatsu*) drought, which may cause damage to the rice crop, we will choose the latter. As a matter of fact, if something happens to the US harvest of rice and vegetables, the Japanese kitchen is in jeopardy. In this way we have a clear direction for the choice of news. (Fuji, Director of Foreign News, July 2nd, 1997)

According to the Director every household in Japan is affected by the US rice harvest. If a correspondent wants to make a report about how the same drought affects Brazil, the desk staff in Tokyo may hesitate. If there is great distance to an event the correspondent has to have a convincing idea. If an event is directly connected to Japan there is no doubt. 'Proximity' is not understood as a geographic measure. It is a measurement of the effect on the everyday life of the Japanese and the estimated interest in this news by the audience.

Fuji TV is placed in the 'soft news' column. The presentations are without opinions.

NTV

The production of international news at NTV, like Fuji TV, is totally audience based. According to the Editor of Foreign News, NTV only chooses international news items that are directly related to the audience in mind. The main international news since the Cold War according to the Editor of Foreign news, has been '*jiken jiko*' social events, accidents and natural disasters. This type of news reporting, in the view of the Editor of Foreign News, has been very popular. Social news in his opinion has been almost too dominant, but because visuals in this genre are plentiful they are easy to incorporate.

---

[110] 'To make the public feel informed' is a notion which takes its point of departure in the presumed audience demands, not in journalistic or public service criteria for how the public should be informed.

Until 1989 most foreign international news included economic and political analysis, which was connected to the cold war between the US and Russia and the situation in the Middle East. Until the fall of the Berlin wall political commentary was easily set up with clear distinctions between heroes and enemies. International political analysis is not popular any more and less of it is done for competitive reasons. When news stories get too complicated viewers switch to another channel. (NTV, Editor of Foreign News, July 4th, 1997)

This minute-by-minute attention to ratings, in the experience of the Editor of Foreign News, pertains to all stations except NHK. There is a tendency, in his opinion, among the private stations to focus less on hard news (*kouha*) and more on entertainment. News as wide-shows or variety shows is becoming popular. The social aspects such as accidents are getting higher priority. The line between entertainment and news is becoming less noticeable. The presentation of material, which gives the audience a form of broader knowledge or education (*keimou,* enlightenment) has changed to a strategy of serving entertaining, easy to understand news, which the audience can consume without putting thought and energy into interpretation. This type of news scores higher ratings. In the 17.30-19.00 o'clock NTV news program, salary men have not arrived home yet. It is mainly produced for children and housewives as entertainment while they eat supper.

> We have surrendered to this conspicuous (*gimonteki*) strategy because the effect is better ratings. The problem at large is the scale of the station and the amount of capable staff which NTV is capable of acquiring' (NTV, Editor of Foreign News, July 4th, 1997)

In other words, two important factors namely economic capability and human resources, influence the production strategy.

NTV is placed in the 'soft news' and 'views' category in the display above. The display of Krauss is based on content analysis. According to the veteran newscaster, Mayama Yuichi, the presentation form is formal and the commentary is without personal opinions.

> In each program a piece of news is picked for special explanation in a so-called 'News point corner' in order to make issues easier to understand. The interpretation is often connected to visuals that are already speaking for themselves, but the 'point' in the 'News Point Corner' makes it even easier to remember and enjoy news. The audience can space out while eating and still get the point. (NTV, Anchor, September 7th, 1997).

Although the news is made easy to understand the explanations are *not* based on the personal views of the newscaster as illustrated in the display. This places NTV in the 'Soft news' without views category.

In sum, interviews with the top executives at NHK and the commercial stations showed a variety of news programs and styles of presentation. It also showed a gap between the journalistic ideal (production perspective) and the perceived viewer's interest in news (audience perspective). The discrepancy between the professional ideal and business strategies affected the editorial decision- making processes. While some of the executive managers expressed high ideals and stressed the importance of international hard news coverage, the perceived audience interests were often prioritised in order to make the right appeal (to maintain or gain market shares). The following elaborates on these audience considerations.

From public service to market strategies

The awareness of audiences as receivers of news information varies among news producers as discussed in Chapter Two and Chapter Seven. The investigation of audience awareness is an indicator of production strategies because it provides insights about the processes of framing and the awareness of local audiences, which are assumed in this project to be the communicative basis for the 'domestication' of information. In other words, news producers perceive news through the eyes of their audiences when they select issues, choose visuals and words. Further, the analysis of audience awareness brings insight into the *commodification* of news.

The notion of 'public interest' (Foreign Press Center, 1997) has been questioned in Japan and criticism has been raised concerning whose interest the media does and should serve. In the case of the newspapers, they have less of the special privileges they have had previously as public interest media, including advantageous tax treatment and other allowances. There is an emerging tendency to treat newspapers as a *commodity* both politically and within the companies. The trend is similar in the analysis of broadcast news strategies below. There is a discrepancy in the strategies of the news producers between the *public interest* and the *market orientation*. The audience considerations of NHK and TV Asahi are not included here as they are analysed in the following chapter.

As described above, the professional interest of the TBS production staff concerns international politics. However, audiences for the early evening program are interested in news, which they can understand immediately (without prior knowledge). Erosion in the mountains of Kagoshima with a number of casualties or homicides in Hyogo prefecture are visually comprehensible. Cambodian civil wars and Asean meetings require prior knowledge. Although the TBS news producers find the political dynamics in this story interesting because the civil war in Cambodia affects Vietnam and Thailand and becomes a broader Asian issue,[111] there is a gap between the professional interest and the demand for information by the ordinary viewer. The average salary man, in the view of the Director of Political News, is not interested in this news. International news of interest to the audience at the time of the interviews in 1997, was information about the lack of rice in North Korea. TBS had acquired pictures through their foreign correspondent in China from the border between China and Korea. They expected this to be a scoop[112] because the Japanese audience had an *emotional* interest in North Korea because a number of Japanese women were married to North Koreans during the

---

[111] In 1997 Cambodia applied to enter the Asean Corporation, but was not admitted. News management staff saw the Asean decision as important in Asian regional politics. TBS foreign correspondents in Cambodia and Manila were alert and investigating developments in the relationship between Cambodia and the Asean countries.

[112] In the increasing battle for scoops, the discussion of ethics is important. From the Asahi journalist who made a cross in a coral reef in the southern islands of Okinawa, to the journalist who endangered the hostage case in Peru, to the TBS deal with the AUM religious sect described below, which cost human lives, the Japanese media has had its share of ethical problems (See Foreign Press Center, 1997). Ethics was a big concern in 1997 and a new manual based on Western national broadcast manuals for news production ethics was in progress at the National Broadcasters' Association (NAB).

Japanese occupations leading to the Second World War. The Japanese wives were never able to visit their home country again. Within the right emotional framework a sense of proximity and relation to Japan was created.

The international news update is costly. TBS spends a considerable amount of money on international news but eventually mainly broadcasts domestic stories. The younger generation is interested in computer games and not in news unless it is instantly stimulating and shocking, according to the Director of Political News. They require *visual experiences*. Background information and analysis is not of interest. Chikushi Tetsuya, popular anchor mentioned above, hosts a late night *News 23* program at TBS, which caters to a more mature audience. The average viewers of this program are highly educated and most are above 45. The maturity of the audience means more insight into domestic and international political matters. This audience is not satisfied with what the Director of Political News refers to as 'sensational' news.

According to the Fuji Director, the audience is perceived as being as knowledgeable as the production staff because of 'sophisticated' access to information through newspapers, the Internet, documentaries, movies and foreign friends. It is therefore important to 'pick the right part of a story' and make it worthwhile though elaboration and explanation. Although the Fuji TV news producers work with the notion that the audience is well informed, the staff pays close attention to the wording and pictures.

> The wording is slow and the explanations are easy. It is important to put an interesting spin on the story. (Fuji, Director of Foreign News, July 2nd, 1997)

According to the Director Of Foreign News the spin in stories may lie in the dramatic conflictual forms that are well known to the audience. As an example he mentions the 1997 appointment of the US ambassador to Japan. Rather than repeating the well-known information that the decision making was prolonged, a story about the tactics of the two Houses of Representatives in the decision-making process was set up. The story was presented, as a conflict between the two US Houses of Representatives which in this case had consequences for Japan.

NTV news production management likewise perceives its audience as highly informed. The editorial process of the late evening news is geared to highly informed viewers. However, the viewers at the time of NTV broadcasts at 17.30 are mainly housewives. Around dinnertime they have to do work in the kitchen. According to the Editor of Foreign News, intellectuals, public employees and politicians watch NHK. In his words, this is general knowledge among professionals. Other executives supported his notion:

> An intellectual person would never watch the commercial networks for news information. High government officials get their information from NHK. (TV Asahi, Chief Director, November 25th, 1997).[113]

This is the kind of hopeless (*nasakenai*) situation NTV is in. The housewives may be knowledgeable but not very interested in international news. Domestic news such as the Aum religious sect's crimes was broadcast thoroughly and prioritised over international news for several years. Straight international news is mainly broadcast in the morning

---

[113] Nevertheless, the government follows the news at TV Asahi closely. Not least in order to measure the criticism and the possible effect on audiences.

and noon programmes. This is partly due to the time difference, which affects all Japanese stations (as seen in production processes Chapter 7). Due to the time difference, most European and US news is broadcast in Japan the following day in the early programs. When evening comes, it is not news anymore but a summary or interpretation.

The main observation concerning news production strategies in this section is the gap between what news producers estimate to be news for an informed public according to normative news standards (chapter 2) and what is essentially aired. As a whole, the executive news producers claimed that the evening programs at all stations were geared towards a younger, less educated rural mainly female audience. This had the effect that if broadcast at all international news was made clear and easy to understand, preferably with a human-interest approach and a focus on social themes. An appeal to emotions, expressive visuals and recognisable narrative forms were used as framing devices mainly at the commercial stations. The programs later in the evening were made for the working, urban, higher educated males who return home from work late. *News Station* also catered to this audience segment but attracted a younger audience including many female viewers. The late evening news programs, according to the executive staff at TBS, Fuji and NTV, presented more 'hard news' and international stories. The concentration on audience demands in the early evening programs would often compromise journalistic ideals of 'harder' news. Although the budget for International news was higher than the budget for domestic news in the above programs it was not prioritised very highly because of perceived low interest by the audiences.

The display by Krauss showed that while NHK and TV Asahi presented 'hard' news TBS, Fuji and NTV presented 'soft' news. In relation to these findings the executive news managers in most cases at first identified with professional 'hard news' standards, while admittedly had to compromise their professional *ideals* for business *reals*. In other words, they had lower their professional standards by succumbing to perceived audience demands in order to fulfil business strategies.

In conclusion, the trend of *commodification* of news described above is summarised well by Omori Yukio a Japanese press club member and expert on Japan's mass media.

> The main aim of the commercial stations is to get high viewer ratings so they can attract sponsorships and gain profits. News is a product. Entertainment (*goraku*) is the overall strategy of the private stations. The private stations merely think in profit. Compared with this approach the NHK news style is stiff and boring. A production trick is to drive on feelings of closeness of the viewers (*shitashimi*). NHK is not concerned with the *omshirookashii* production strategy. NHK has lower ratings than the private station but it has integrity and trustworthiness (*shinraikan*). In other words, where the private stations have (*shinkinkan*) closeness, NHK is (*shinraikan*) trustworthy and reliable. (Omori Yukio, August 11th, 1997)

Omori asserts that the market orientation and fierce competition between the national broadcasters to get high viewer ratings and sponsorship agreements encourages the treatment of news as a product. The entertainment strategy of the private stations is profit driven and their most important 'trick' is to create a sense of proximity. Against this, NHK may be rather stiff in its presentation form but it maintains its integrity and trustworthiness.

'News' and 'views' in perspective

Based on the interview survey, the strategies and news values at the national stations vary greatly. From the emphasis on economic and political news of NHK to an emphasis on social themes at NTV, the national broadcast stations offer a wide spectrum of news. The different styles of presentation of 'news' and 'views' further distinguish news programs and contribute with variations.

The Japanese media environment, like most European countries, provides a broad variety of news programs in terms of styles and content. By comparison, US network news reports (ABC, CBS, NBC) are often indistinguishable from one another in terms of content, signalling a conformity in news values (Surlin, Romanow, and Soderlund, 1988). The national news reports at NHK and NTV, according to the content analysis of Miller, offer a distinct difference in coverage (Miller, 1994:83). The US, in Miller's analysis, showed a consistency of news values and gate-keeping functions through similar hard news story selection on any given day. In the comparative survey, NHK and NTV newscast were only similar on one day in the composite week of investigation. Compared to the strict NHK hard news criteria on politics and economics, NTV newscast stories were described as 'sensational' and occasionally bordering on 'tabloid television'. (Miller, 1994: 87). These findings support the interview statements above in which NHK was found to prioritise political and economic themes in its international news while NTV at the other end of the spectrum concentrated on social themes with an emphasis on disasters and accidents.

In the study of US and Japanese coverage of the 'other', Krauss (1996) found that "…The Japanese style of television journalism in recent years differs both from American television and from Japanese newspapers. Instead of the neutral and factual style of Japanese newspapers or the neutral tone of the American anchor and correspondent, the anchors and correspondents of Japanese commercial stations provide much of the personal commentary and opinion about the other country…" (Krauss, 1996: 264). The American anchors and reporters according to Krauss do not refrain from expressing their opinion but do so by more subtle means of communication, such as facial expressions, body language, or tone of voice. US television news items are more likely (53 percent) than Japanese (33 percent) to contain opinions expressed by other people than an anchor or journalist. The US, thus, does not refrain from expressing opinions about Japan but they tend to be expressed by persons appearing in the segment rather than by the station's news staff (Krauss, 1996: 264). This indirect way of including opinions in segment rather than by news professionals was found in the present study to be incorporated in NHK's news production (See analysis Chapters Seven and Eight).

Against this backdrop, it may be concluded that 'opinionated' journalism is a significant characteristic of Japanese national commercial broadcasting. More universally it may be concluded that the so-called 'objective' journalistic style employs more sophisticated ways of integrating views as is seen in American commercial and Japanese public service coverage.

Global influence – extra-media factors

The political character of the national media and the competitive strategies were shown to influence the presentation and content of news. In the following, the global influence on news production will be analysed. The reliance on international news agencies was found to have a major impact on the choice of international news. Language was an issue in the 'domestication' of international news. Other consequences of global influence on news production, such as enhanced competition of informational sources, technological development and changing work conditions of news producers were highlighted as important factors in international news production.

The Japanese language[114] as a 'domestication' tool

Many of the directors brought up the issue of language, which was seen as important in the translation of scripts in the newsrooms and as an important communication tool for correspondents stationed abroad. The translation of events from English to Japanese is a considerable task in international news production. The issue of language was considered a challenge by most.

Some of the executive directors were critical of the Japanese ability to communicate in English. These statements resemble Japanese self-perceptions.

> Japan's insularity and the character of its people means that many Japanese are not accustomed to communicating with other peoples. Because of an education system with an emphasis on memorising facts, the Japanese are not brought up to express their opinion through presentations, speeches and debates. Compared with the majority of the world's population, which is multilingual, the Japanese do not speak foreign languages sufficiently.[115] The new generation may change but from the age of 30 years and above, despite great efforts, people still do not communicate well in English (NTV, Editor of Foreign News, July 4th, 1997).

This inability to voice one's opinion was a self-perception of most executives. It is one of the reinforced conceptions of Japanese self-understanding, *nihonjinron*,[116] which is

---

[114] Language was observed to be important in the production of international news. The scriptwriting staff in the Japanese newsrooms speak English fluently. Most of the scriptwriting consists of translating agency material from English to Japanese (see also chapters 6-7). Actors, themes and phrases that are familiar to the Japanese are foregrounded. The translation of news requires resources, but it is also an asset which distinguishes terrestrial broadcast channels from their international competition and appeals to national audiences. A certain world-view or mental processes was the basis for the choice and editing of the global news (See chapters 6-7) Nevertheless, the public service station was found to be conservative in the use of Japanese vocabulary, whereas the commercial station was more liberal. This was both found in the analysis of production procedures and in the news texts.

[115] The 1980s internationalisation efforts mainly focused on learning English. English conversation schools throughout Japan made great profit from their effort to converge the high level of memorised vocabulary and grammar into conversation ability. Acknowledging a need for innovation and creativity, the end of the 1990s have brought new internationalisation reforms in the school system encouraging English learning and other education, which should foster more creativity in the new generation.

[116] These conceptions surface in interaction with foreigners. Yoshino Kosaku exemplifies how these cultural stereotypes are reinforced in English language education, in tourist brochures and academic writings. Such cross-cultural comparisons, according to Yoshino (1992), have emphasised Japanese

based on the US as the comparative other. Matsuyama Yukio, who was stationed in the US for many years as an international correspondent, Bureau Chief in New York and Chief of the General Bureau in Washington D.C., likewise compares Japanese to US communicators.

> Japanese English speaking ability lags behind. Japanese students use their mental energy on technicalities behind speaking instead of conversing. Assertiveness is not a virtue in Japanese culture, so verbalisation and discussion have not been encouraged in the school system (Matsuyama, interview August 11th, 1997).

Similar conceptions are expressed in the studies of Krauss who argues that language is a problem facing journalists abroad. According to Krauss (1996), Japanese reporters in Washington still see language as a major problem. The problem of spoken language often induces Japanese journalists to use more Japanese sources, especially embassy personnel, than they otherwise might (Krauss, 1996: 261). From interviews with former correspondents in Washington, Krauss formed the impression that while American reporters tended to use their embassy to establish their government's "official line" before moving on to alternative sources, the Japanese reporters were more likely to use the embassy as a final source. The norms of Japanese journalism that constrain reporters at home also constrain those abroad according to Krauss. (For studies of data gathering through the Japanese press clubs see Feldman, 1993)

Among the correspondents at NHK and TV Asahi, several had been to Washington D.C. or other US destinations. They were seemingly competent English speakers with outgoing personalities, but according to their experience, it was difficult at times to establish social relations and information networks. This was problematic as much information is obtained through personal connections and unofficial networks. Language was not perceived as the main obstacle (See Hattori et al. 1995 for an account of the US 'other' from a Japanese point of view).

The official set-ups abroad vary greatly from China to Europe to Washington D.C. The capability and experience of the staff and the economic size of the broadcast station vary too. NHK is aware that it needs to educate its correspondents to tackle the language and cultural barriers better. (NHK, Vice Director and Staff Corespondent). New measurements are in the 'think tank' in order to produce innovative and creative staff.

Views on language and cultural barriers seemingly depend on the cultural knowledge and experience of the staff. The Chief Desk of the NHK International newsroom who spent many years in New York and following that was stationed in Berlin never felt that language was an obstacle (NHK Chief Desk, July 17th, 1997). Whether language was felt like a barrier or a challenge, translation of scripts (from English to Japanese) is the main task in international news production and the translation process is in itself a vehicle of 'domestication'.

As observed in the newsrooms, the main task of news production included information co-ordination and discussion between the desks, scriptwriters and editors about words and phrases in order to '*shape* the news properly'. In the process of

---

uniqueness to the extent that commonality between the Japanese and non-Japanese is forgotten (Yoshino, 1992). From a Danish perspective non-native speakers naturally vary in their English language proficiency. The Japanese self-perception does not provide a nuanced picture of the difference in proficiency among the Japanese (of whom many are excellent English speakers) because Japanese are compared to native English (US) speakers. See critique of theories of Japaneseness (nihonjinron) in Chapter Three.

translation, scriptwriters and desks would often communicate and discuss the translation of concepts into Japanese. Dictionaries were often less helpful than person to person exchanges of experience and reference to prior examples.

Reminders of the implementation of new vocabulary were occasionally posted on signs in the newsrooms. These signs carried translations of foreign concepts and international organisations (EU for example) that had been agreed upon at meetings at management level, and were posted in the newsrooms for some time until the concept was incorporated in news reporting.

According to the European correspondent, informal procedures keep the Japanese language subject to preservation. National broadcasts cherish Japanese, even though many Japanese since the 1980s economic boom and internationalisation strategy in education have made much effort and spent considerable amounts of money on learning English. This preservation strategy is an attempt by NHK to restrict in their programs the import of foreign loan words (mainly English) that proliferate in Japanese discourses in general.

> We always broadcast in Japanese. Japan is a united (*touitsu*) homogeneous country and we treat the Japanese language with care. Ideally, one channel should be 24-hour news like CNN but geared toward the Japanese audience. It would be an information channel. The problem is that it has to be transmitted in Japanese. English news is too difficult for most viewers. There is a news program in English at 10 o'clock. It has full subtitles in Japanese (NHK, European Correspondent, August 21st, 1997).

Translation is very costly and according to the European Correspondent 'gearing news towards a Japanese audience' requires manpower for editing and commentary. Nevertheless, it is one of the main forces and *raison d'etre* of the national broadcasters.

A main challenge in the translation process is that many terms do not translate well or directly. As it is seen in the following, the materials (in Japanese) from the Japanese agencies JIJI Press and Kyodo News are used frequently to verify information from the international agencies. Also, agency material is used to double check language translation to match Japanese terms and vocabulary in the translation of news scripts.

International news agencies

The most significant extra-media factors that influence the 'global' news in the distribution of international news in Japan is the agreements between Western national and international networks and Japanese national broadcasters.[117] The agreements result in close relationships and mutual use of footage between the Western networks and their

---

[117] The use of sources differs between domestic and international news production. The most important press clubs in Japan are the *Hirakawa Club*, which covers the LDP; the *Shakaito Club*, which covers the opposition; and the *Nagata Club*, which covers the Prime Minister's office. The *Kasumi Club* is attached to the Ministry of Foreign Affairs, and there is a group of journalists attached to the Ministry of International Trade and Industry (Feldman, 1993). These clubs are important in order to get information about Japanese political reactions and actions in foreign affairs. This coverage is the responsibility of the political department (*seijibu*). The international newsroom, which is investigated in this study, is mainly responsible for covering international affairs outside Japan. The final news output is influenced by the negotiation of interests of the different divisions in the news production department. As an example, a Cambodian women's group was followed before the UN conference on Women. A report on the Japanese women's groups would have been the responsibility of the social department (Chapters 7-8).

Japanese affiliates. The agreements cause close cooperation and exclusive deals on materials. The following describes the general use of international agency material. The use of sources at NHK and TV Asahi is described in detail in the following chapters and is therefore only briefly mentioned here.

A set working principle at NHK in its choice of material is that the station's own production is prioritised before the agencies'. Visuals from AP and Reuters are considered the most reliable and used most frequently.

> We have many sources but the most important are Reuters and APTV and ABC. NHK is affiliated with ABC (News One). And we are affiliated with or have free passes to Danish TV. They can get free pictures from us. (NHK, Chief desk, July 17th, 1997)

NHK Foreign news material is acquired from AFP, WTN, Interfax, ITAR-Tass, and the English Service from North Korea and the BBC. Besides being connected to the main public stations throughout the world with agreements for free exchange, NHK is affiliated with and has close co-operation with the American network, ABC. It is generally agreed among the production staff that each of the above agencies has its strong areas. According to the satellite manager, who receives and keeps track of visual material, Reuters and AP are the main international suppliers. NHK has 24-hour circuits, which enables checking of the schedules of the two bureaux. NHK is connected to a database where the arrival of pictures can be verified. If the schedule is not updated the staff calls London directly. The transmission with Reuters and AP is described as easy and smooth.

The affiliation with ABC is used considerably. ABC provides programming for the satellite news program, News One, and supplies NHK with a large amount of pictures. The ABC pictures are transmitted through the NHK New York bureau. There are three lines connected to the New York office and two lines connected again to Tokyo (via satellite). NHK receives news packages regularly. The Tokyo satellite staff orders special pictures from ABC by telephone to the New York bureau. The European Broadcast Union (EBU) satellite connection is only used occasionally. Eurovision news has set schedules for its release of pictures. Often the information does not come directly from Paris. NHK has two outputs, one in Europe and one in New York. A power signal is sent from Europe to New York in order to get packages from there as traffic directly form Europe is usually very busy. WTN supplies are few and there is no subscription agreement. On an occasional basis the New York office will call WTN for footage. Besides being connected to the main public stations throughout the world NHK is in close cooperation with ABC.

The TV Asahi international news section (*gaihobu*), which provides news for all TV Asahi news programs, mainly uses Reuters, AP, CNN and Jiji Press. The CNN Japan office is situated on top of TV Asahi in its headquarters in Roppongi, which enhances cooperation between journalists and exchange of information.

Fuji TV staff most frequently use AP and Reuters. For visuals they use WTN, Kronos and BBC. Fuji TV has a variety of contracts in order to get spots from different part of the world. AP and WTN are the most used agencies. Jiji Press and Kyodo News are also checked but they are seen as being slow and sometimes having mistakes in their translations. Fuji TV has foreign correspondents in 19 countries: Moscow, Seoul, and Singapore, Peking, Shanghai, Indonesia, Sydney, Bangkok, Manila, Hawaii, Los Angeles, New York, Washington DC, Paris, London, Cairo and Rome. The foreign correspondents are teamed with a cameraman in order to make their own visuals when possible. In case these do not suffice, the reports are supplemented with agency visuals. Most often the Tokyo office staff is involved in the editing process. Feature stories are made on location. Some events such as UN meetings and national elections are pre-planned and decided through negotiation between Tokyo and the local correspondent.

NTV has 16 offices abroad. The foreign news section (*gaihobu*) is in charge of international news. The foreign correspondents are the main suppliers of information. Reuters, AP, AFP. Jiji Press and Kyodo news are used as references. Recently, these bureaux have started to supply visuals too. NTV is connected to the American NBC 24-hour service. Most visuals are acquired from NBC, thereafter Reuters TV and AP TV. These three are the main NTV news sources (NTV, Editor of Foreign News, July 4th, 1997).

The display below lists the US network affiliations with NHK and the commercial stations. According to the interviews the affiliation with Western national and international broadcasters influences the choice of material. According to Bruce Dunning, CBS correspondent in Japan since 1979, the agreement and mutual exchange between TBS and CBS is exclusive. Therefore, both stations use the material of their affiliate when possible (CBS Bruce Dunning, July 14th, 1997). Close cooperation with their American affiliates was likewise expressed at NHK with ABC, TV Asahi with CNN and NTV with NBC.

Figure 12: The national TV Stations and their Western Affiliates.

Station	NHK	TV Asahi	TBS	Fuji	NTV	Tokyo TV
Affiliate	ABC	CNN	CBS	-	NBC	-

NHK further has agreements with BBC News Service and public broadcast stations world-wide.

Statistics of the amount of affiliate and agency footage may have provided an interesting overview of the actual use. However, as mentioned earlier such statistics are not available, as sources are most often not recorded. It is possible to estimate the cost of special deals and acquisitions through the accounting department; however, this was not investigated further in the present project.

According to the news managers, the mutual exchange of materials between the Japanese national broadcasters and their American affiliates is considerable. Material is preferred and used in news production when possible because of exclusive contracts. It can be concluded that the exchange and close cooperation with Western (mainly US) affiliates to a great extent influences the agenda and discourses in Japanese international news broadcast.

An additional factor of global influence in information networking is that the Japanese international agencies, Kyodo News and Jiji press,[118] besides their own thorough web of correspondents world-wide (see Cooper-Chen, 1997:72), are connected to the same international news agencies as the broadcasters. NHK and the commercial stations all subscribe to the two Japanese news agencies. The bureaux supply English and Japanese information about Japanese and international politics, economics, industry, finance, science, sports, social and cultural events. Little research has been done on the

---

[118] See Foreign Press Center (1997) for an overview of Jiji Press and Kyodo News affiliations.

exchange of information between the national broadcaster and these influential mediators of words and pictures. Less research is done concerning production processes in the newsroom of the two bureaux. Henningham (1979) has researched the gate-keeping processes in the Kyodo newsrooms with emphasis on the production of English news for overseas 'export'. But no research has been concerned with the use of sources and their connection to national broadcasters from inside the Japanese international agencies.

Jiji Press and Kyodo News have contracts with the same international news agencies as the national broadcasters (See Foreign Press Center, 1997). The Jiji Press and Kyodo News association with the US agencies dates back to pre-war times. Domei Tsushin-sha, which had been active during the war, voluntarily disbanded, to be replaced in November 1945 by Kyodo News (Kyodo Tsushin-sha) and Jiji Press (Jiji Tsushin-sha). After the San Francisco peace treaty in April 1952, Japan regained its independence and the major newspapers and news agencies began to expand their overseas news gathering networks. Pre-war legacies and linkages remain even today (Cooper-Chen: 1997:83).

Research investigating the interconnection between agencies and the use of sources in the production processes at both the national broadcasters and the agencies may throw light on the multiple connections and compositions that form the final broadcast outputs.

The interview statements show that the reliance on agencies in the Japanese newsroom at NHK and the commercial stations is considerable. Coping with the abundance of incoming information has resulted in the reliance on a few sources in the daily processes, which make the influence of the trusted agencies strong. With this significant knowledge about sources of information, the following is a description of the strategies and foci of international reporting.

International focus – return to Asia

As a reflection of the 'global consciousness' and world views of the Japanese national news managers, a regional level of influence on news production may be inserted in the 'domestication' model as a buffer zone between the global and the national. In an increasingly interconnected world of media infrastructures and circulation of information, the executive managers claimed that a regional sense of closeness is increasing in Japan. And a focus on Asian issues is prevalent in future news production strategies at the management level. Japan's modern history as discussed in the introduction may, since the Meiji restoration and the reopening of Japan in 1868 after 250 years of isolation may be described though the notion of Western Techniques Japanese Spirit *wakon yosai*. Japanese history has moved through periods of 'Asianisation', 'Japanisation' and 'Westernisation' and may now be making a full circle. The description of Japanese international news production below provides evidence of a 'return to the Asian' through management decisions to move the focus of foreign coverage from the West to the East.

Hitherto, even the smallest US political reflections had been seen to inflict great impact on trade negotiations between the US and Japan. The US-Japan trade frictions have been big international news for decades. Minor US internal affairs have sometimes become major news in Japan although it is hardly broadcast in the US. The more US involvement affects the everyday life of the Japanese, the higher the news value of the event. This international focus counts for all broadcasters, from NHK to NTV.

The production strategy at NTV has focused on the mediation of two kinds of US reports, namely news from the White House and 'topics'.

> Topics are interesting, different and strange happenings with good impressive visuals. In the intense US news reporting the news producers take advantage of the general awareness of US happenings through years of accumulated knowledge about the US. (NTV, Editor of Foreign News, July 4th, 1997).

However, although NTV has broadcast regularly from the US, this news according to the director is loosing its attraction. The main area of interest (at the time of the interviews in 1997) was moving towards Russia, China and the Korean peninsula. The remaining Asian countries were considered less important. NTV has correspondents in Beijing, Shanghai, Seoul, Manila, Hong Kong and Bangkok who may produce two and a half-minute feature stories about the everyday life and cultural aspects of these geographical areas. Straight news is mainly from Seoul. Interest in Russia was news connected to Yeltsin's health and the general domestic situation. The most pressing international news at the time of the interview was the situation in North Korea.

> Although it is difficult to make a picture of the North Korean situation it is a major matter of concern. Chinese and Korean news is important even if it is only 30 minutes. Special assignments of two and a half minutes or more are not granted in the evening news. The 'Today's happenings' (*kyunodekigoto*) late night program is more apt for a heavy schedule of hard news. I am pushing to do much more of this kind of reporting from the actual location. But because the ratings are affected immediately if the point is difficult to get across, these kinds of news items (*neta*) are only occasionally used. ((NTV, Editor of Foreign News, July 4th, 1997).

In the Fuji international Strategy, the European countries and the US have hitherto been the most important areas for news but there has been a change in focus. The Fuji international production staff places more and more interest on Southeast Asia.

> Europe and the US have hitherto been the important areas of news coverage but from 1996 we have changed our focus. Southeast Asia has become a place that we would like to know better. This has meant a change in bureaux and manpower from Europe to Asia. At the same time we are trying to make contact and contracts with local stations and stringers in South East Asia. The communication strategy is moving from reporting and data gathering in Europe to Asia. At the time the strength of the US coverage stays the same. This is not meant to change. Rather, the focus of Europe changes. The Berlin correspondent is going to be moved to Asia and so forth. The EU currency problems are interesting and important economic news but for us Cambodia is even more important. (Fuji, Director of Foreign News, July 2nd, 1997)

In other words, the EU currency problems are interesting and important economic decisions in the view of what audiences from a management point of view 'ought to know' but the Cambodian news by this comparison is even more important[119] in relation to what they 'would like to know'.

Thus far, TBS has invested a lot of resources in US and European coverage. The TBS international strategy has mainly been based on coverage from these two areas.

> The US-Japan trade frictions have been mayor international news. Even the smallest US political reflections are seen to have a great impact on trade negotiations. Therefore, minor US internal affairs have sometimes become mayor news in Japan although it is hardly broadcast in the US. The more US involvement affects the everyday life of the Japanese, the higher the news value of the event. This news value counts for every station from NHK to TV Asahi (TBS, Director of Political News, July 11th, 1997).

Recently, TBS like NTV and Fuji has also turned its focus on Asia. In the future, the efforts of TBS will go to Beijing and to North Korea's Phon Yang. TBS correspondents will still remain in the US and Europe in order to take advantage of the extended knowledge about these parts of the world. However, the instability and unsettled economic and political situation of many Asian countries make this region more interesting as news.

> The Cold War reminiscences of course play a role in the coverage of for instance Nato affairs. But the way Japan is affected (*kakawaru*) by the New World order and the new Nato model is rather ambiguous. Therefore this news has little value. Korean affairs, by comparison, are more interesting. (TBS, Director of Political News, July 11th, 1997).

China is of special interest because of its coming challenges of adjusting to the international community. Japan has just been through this stage of growth and adjustment and it is interesting for news staff and audiences alike to see how China develops in many respects. According to the Director of Political News, important questions are. How will China deal with union and labour problems? What kind of consumer market will China become?

> The last 50 years we have been dedicated to the West, the next 50 will focus on Asia (TBS, Director of Political News, July 11th, 1997).

In its efforts, TBS will strengthen its coverage of Thailand, go to Delhi and cover India more. From there, it will strengthen China, North Korea and also South Korea. As a bonus of this strategy, the concentration on Asia will mean fewer expenses in flights and satellite cost. Compared with the budget allocated to international news, this coverage is relatively small. TBS has offices in 15 countries with 30-40 foreign correspondents stationed abroad.

---

[119] Although international economic moves are considered the most important news for Japan, NHK is the only station with a bureau in India although Japan has made significant financial investment in India recently. Fuji does not plan to have a correspondent there. In this one case, economic interest does not determine news (Fuji executive).

62 per cent of the budget is used in order to make international coverage. 32 per cent is spent on domestic news production. As a matter of fact foreign news per cent is even smaller than this, less than 20 per cent. Foreign news is a 'money losing' enterprise (TBS, Director of Political News, July 11th, 1997).

Although operation in Asia is less costly, information is often difficult and even dangerous to acquire. Coverage in Asia is more complicated than in the EU and Europe. In China, Hong Kong, Russia, Thailand, the Korean Peninsula, Indonesia and places where American freedom of speech does not prevail and in countries with internal friction, it is often difficult to get information. There are many events that the press is not welcome to see, hear and report on. In the case of dangerous and politically sensitive news, management makes the decision of whether to cover it or not. In some cases, according to the Fuji Executive Director of News Department, the private companies end up breaking the law. If the story is newsworthy, they deliberately go ahead. It is problematic to make decisions that endanger the life of journalists. At the time of the interviews in 1997, there were no dangerous places. Nevertheless, although it was peaceful to walk in the streets of Phnom Penh, a shoot-out may suddenly be life threatening. It is uncomfortable for the management staff to have to make the decision to send people to some of the unstable areas in Asia. Fuji TV recently lost a correspondent this way (Fuji, Director of Foreign News, July 2nd, 1997)

Only NHK stands out in its future planning. NHK plans to improve its news coverage of Europe. In the management view, there are lots of stories to present concerning the integration of Europe. Europe is not close to Japan mentally and spiritually but the European Union offers a wide variety of economic and political issues which are of interest to Japan, particularly in the light of its Asean membership. Living standards are similar to the Japanese and technological, industrial and democratic developments and EU integration are followed. NHK plans to cover Asia more thoroughly in the future. 40% of NHK's international news production budget is invested in Asia (NHK, Vice Director, July 10th, 1997). As a merit of this plan, many journalists volunteer to go to Asian countries.

The United States is always important for us. The United States is the most important area for us. The United States' economic crises, politics and involvement abroad are areas of priority. These are important foci, which have been unavoidable since the war. (NHK, Chief desk, July 17th, 1997).

The Japanese concern for rice has been in the back of the minds of foreign correspondents for a decade according to the European correspondent. European and US trade conflicts have been seen in the light of a supposed effect on the Japanese rice situation. The Japanese ongoing battle with the United States has centred on trade restrictions and US demands for a liberalisation of the import of rice. Japanese correspondents in Europe and the US have concluded many reports of conflict by analysing the effect of a crisis on the Japanese rice situation. In the European correspondent's account, the extensive coverage did not take into account whether NHK or the Japanese media were emphasising a real threat. It was a matter of making a 'spin', which could relate the news to Japan and capture audience attention. The issue of rice was a concern of every Japanese person as it is their main dietary ingredient. Due to images that were kept alive by the media, US imported rice was deemed of lower quality than the traditional Japanese sorts and this led to many media initiated consumer boycotts, according to the European correspondent. US rice has since been sold as a generic brand without US declarations. While the issue is now outside the media agenda, the anti US rice sentiments have cooled down.

In conclusion, the US has and will continue to have high priority in the production strategy at all stations although there is a shift in priority to Asian affairs. Thus far news from the United States has been more important than the remote areas of Japan. The heavy emphasis on US news means that Japanese citizens, who also receive a fact-oriented education, are kept remarkably well informed about American behaviour and trends that affect Japan. According to Krauss, "Ironically, they may be too well informed about the United States, especially American political life in Washington. If we drew a cognitive map of a Japanese citizen's view of the world based solely on the information provided by the mass media, the United States would probably occupy a large proportion of the globe" (Krauss, 1996: 264). The high coverage of the US, according to Krauss, overestimates the US's impact on Japan and feeds the intensity of Japanese reaction to even the most trivial or ephemeral event. This is especially a problem in relation to the perception of the United States because political events and "friction-related" (ibid) incidents receive more coverage than background analysis or stories about US society outside Washington. The perceptual reality in the totality of information about foreign affairs which the average Japanese citizen receives is, according to Krauss, based sometimes on insignificant Congress bills, without further context (ibid). The exaggerated emphasis on US news as described by Krauss very well reflects the importance attained by US affairs as described in the above interviews.

China is second in the international coverage and Europe is third. The Japanese are not familiar with Islam, so very few people are interested in the cultural and social happenings in the Middle East. Only crises concerning oil put this area on the agenda. Oceania is becoming a place of interest. Australia only has a one-hour time difference so it is convenient to go to Australia. After Australia split with the Commonwealth it has turned to Asia. The relationship has developed from both sides. Peru is continuously on the map because its President, Fujimori, is of Japanese decent. Regionalisation or the turn to Asia may be concluded in short as stated above, *the past 50 years of international journalism have been dedicated to the West, the next 50 will focus on Asia.*

In spite of the fact that international news flow studies show that political, economic and military conflicts dominate the content of international news (Ito, 1998), *trade* is the greatest concern of the daily managers at the national broadcast stations. There are several reasons for this. The trade frictions between Japan and the US have been top international news issues since the 1980s. US demands to lift trade barriers and to liberalise the Japanese market have featured as foreign news. The economic consequences for the Japanese farmers, and the consumer dissatisfaction with imported *rice* have been recurring issues in the media. According to Matsuyama Yukio, the Japanese are not proud of their politics and engagement in world affairs. Accordingly, the aim is to try to have good relations with Japan's world trading partners. This concern influences the coverage of international news and places the focus on trade (Matsuyama, interview August 11th, 1997). Another explanation may be possible. The question of defence is too sensitive. Too much is at stake for Japan in discussions about military threat. This is evident in the analysis of the coverage of the French Nuclear Testing, which brings the question of military threat and the Japanese 'peace' constitution onto the agenda.[120] The coverage of trade issues, by comparison, is less politically sensitive.

International news frames since the end of the Cold War

It is the impression of the NTV Editor of Foreign News that the rate of international news in the 1970s and 1980s was generally higher than in the 1990s. Before the Cold War the international arena in his view was polarised and easier to explain. Accordingly, international news was easier to convey. The concern with international news framing and the lack of frames since the end of the Cold War is a general concern expressed by the international news managers.

> Foreign news coverage has changed dramatically since the Cold War. We do not have the shadow of the big powers in the regional conflicts, so we are less interested in regional conflicts. For instance, in the conflict in Yugoslavia there is no shadow of the United States or Russia in the background. When these players disappeared from the back stage this regional problem lost interest for Japan. This news is taking place in a very remote area of the world for us. But during the Cold War if such a regional conflict took place, the US and Russia would be in the background and this influenced our situation. So after the Cold War our attitude to such regional conflict has dramatically changed. Recently, if something happens in Yugoslavia it has nothing to do with us. Before it was a serious place (TBS Director of Political News, July 11th, 1997).

The political interpretation and commentary is gradually disappearing. This is not because people have greater knowledge of the world. Rather the average person is not interested. This tendency is spreading to the inside of news production too. The international production staff is only mildly interested, the domestic staff is even less so and the viewers are not interested at all (NTV, Editor of Foreign News, July, 4th, 1997).

TV Asahi staff were looking forward to a more international orientation after the fall of the Berlin Wall. But contrary to predictions nothing happened. The Japanese have become more self-centred. Two high-ranking staff expressed concern for what they call a 'new nationalism' (for elaboration on this point see Chapters 7-8).

An NHK desk staff also expressed that there was little interest in international affairs. The reason was that Japan is a centre world economy. "The greater and more secure the role of a country is in the international community, the less interest in international news". There is no empirical evidence supporting this assumption. According to Cooper-Chen the US percentage of "pure" international news is higher than Japan's. Cooper-Chen and Kanayama (1998: 39) shows TBS coverage of 13,9 percent in 1993 and 15.3 per cent in 1996. US network news reporting foreign news abroad has remained quite stable at about 20 % for almost a quarter century.[121]

It is a general perception among the Directors across stations that the percentage of international news coverage is low. This is seen especially in light of invested resources.

---

[120] As the 1993 election divided the press and broadcast media, the bill for a change to Article 9 to enable Japanese Peace-Keeping Organisations (PKO) to be dispatched, caused a division of the media between LDP conservative and JSP leftist supporters.

[121] Research on news content analysis in the United States and Japan is plentiful. However, the comparison of findings is problematic because of the difference in context and because this research is often made on the basis of a few selected stations, cases or time periods.

144

The statistics of three independent studies show that the percentage of foreign news, albeit perceived as low, has been rising steadily from the 1970s to the 1990s. The percentage of foreign news at NHK was 5.2 percent in 1974 (Shiramizu, 1987 cf. Cooper Chen and Kanayama, 1998: 35), 9.2 percent in 1984 (Miller 1994), and 14.5 percent in 1993 (Cooper-Chen and Kanayama, 1998).

The fact that international news is not automatically prioritised means fierce competition in the newsrooms between the social, political, economic and international sections to have their stories included in the news programs (Chapters 6-7). The strong world powers and division of the world between the East and West during the Cold War provided a commonly recognised view of the world against which international political news was easy to frame. Overarching news frames similar to this have not since been incorporated in international news production

Technological advance and journalistic challenges

Technological developments and access to sources of information in 'knowledge based society' bring challenges and new demands for national broadcasters. The new satellite possibilities are changing journalism in several ways. From being mass communication production the development is going in the direction of person to person communication. The Internet possibilities and the many news satellite channels bring about a change in communication forms. This includes news information.

Although news is presently geared to mass audiences, according to the TBS Director of Political News, the content of the news channels in the future will have to suit individual needs. This will be a challenge to national broadcasters according to the TBS Director of Political News. In the development of new channels, TBS is considering a 24-hour international news channel. In preparing for year 2005 when the revolutionary person-to-person communication will take shape, TBS is planning to provide services for smaller audiences more closely directed at certain segments.

According to the TBS Director, the technological development opens for the possibility to make 'news on demand'. Audiences will be able to watch the most recent news at the times they want. This means expanding and educating competent independent news correspondents who can mediate complex news information.

> The *Japanese perspective on events remains important in the new business opportunities.* TBS therefore seeks to strengthen its system of cooperation with native news workers abroad. Presently, TBS has stringers in Mexico, Lima, Argentina, Baghdad, Teheran and Sydney and other places where it does not have its own offices. Some of these news workers only speak English. Some speak Japanese well. Since most are non-Japanese, the challenge is to convey the Japanese sense of news to these journalists. TBS calls its stringers 'home' for study programs in Tokyo in order get them acquainted with the Japanese state of affairs which enables them to return with the ability to see events from a Japanese point of view. (TBS, Director of Political News, July 11th, 1997).

According to the Director of Political News, the ability to produce stories from a Japanese perspective from a newspaper, in for instance, Lima requires a great deal of insight into the Japanese context. Study tours to Tokyo further the familiarity with what makes a good story in Japan. It is an advantage to have natives provide information. They have great knowledge of local affairs. Besides they know the language and have local networks.

According to the Fuji TV Executive Director of News, the conditions of the foreign correspondents have changed with new technology. A correspondent can be reached almost everywhere instantly through mobile phone. Expectations are higher and control is much stronger. The days of 'my pace' work are past because of the new technology. News is expected immediately and aired quickly.

The news agencies constantly feed information, which is taken into consideration. In breaking news incidents and in the case of pre-schedule political events, the foreign correspondents are involved in the stories. There are pro and cons in using material from both. According to the Fuji TV Executive Director, agency material is often checked with the foreign correspondent. Sometimes the stories are similar and sometimes they differ. It is up to the desk to decide which side of the story is closest to the 'real' event. And to double check information in order to avoid mistakes. It is not possible for the desk to look through all incoming information. The main news is listed and the rest is only glanced through.

> The correspondent constantly feeds ideas for stories. In the editorial meetings the foreign desk tries to sell the idea to the rest of the production staff. Tokyo makes the overall decision and overviews the projects. A working premise for effective production is that the Tokyo office is on top of things. Usually Tokyo gets the information first, when something happens. The foreign correspondents can give advice about the local situation but because of the online news, the Tokyo office is continuously informed by the international news agencies. There are single incidents where the foreign correspondent picks up news first but these are rare (Fuji TV, Director of Foreign News, July 2nd, 1997).

The advantage of using foreign correspondents is the ability to judge the local interpretations of the event, which are not available to the Tokyo desk. According to the Director, the coverage by the foreign correspondent will most likely be less biased to the local country than news edited in Tokyo. The findings of Krauss (1996) support this hypothesis. Reports from correspondents in Japan and the US were less likely to blame the 'other' than stories filed at home: "Japanese stories with a US dateline were much less likely to ascribe blame to the United States than those with a Japanese dateline. Similarly, American stories with a Japanese dateline were less likely to ascribe blame to Japan than those with a US dateline. In other words, *journalists based in a foreign country seem to be less critical of that country than their colleagues at home writing on the same issue.*" (Budner, 1993:19, cf. Krauss 1996, my emphasis). In-depth knowledge of another country makes a correspondent able to see events in a broader perspective and enables him to explain the event from within its own premises. In cognitive terms, knowledge from experience on location enables journalists to overcome original stereotypes about the other country and paint a more detailed picture.

On a whole, technological development does not make international correspondents superfluous. On the contrary, the status and value of foreign correspondents with intercultural experience is enhanced.

Reporter career patterns

The Japanese salary system with its life time employment restriction is inhibiting the developing of elite (*yuushuuna*) correspondents and news workers.[122] Attempts have been made at TBS to develop human resources by hiring people from the outside and developing inside staff with special talents.

According to the TBS director, elite journalists and commentators are presently employed by NHK. TBS and most of the commercial stations do not have similar economic means to use their expertise on the screen. Most experts advance into management positions. The TBS international news producers work as reporters and correspondents until they are 45. Hence, they may be placed in a totally different part of the company. The journalists who work on domestic news reach their peak when they are 35-36 years old. In other words, the production staff are engaged from their mid-twenties to mid-thirties. Staff above this age are moved to totally different sections of the company. There is no room for them as editors or commentators. The newspaper companies and NHK, according to the TBS Director, are able to employ people and provide them with a good career path because they have more departments. Age is therefore not as important in a company the size of NHK.

In the view of the TBS Director of Political News, in principle, 'any event is potential news'. Coverage according to this statement thus depends on the ability of the foreign correspondent to *frame* the event. Audio-visual reporting according to the TBS Director requires several abilities of reporters. If a correspondent is skilful he is given great responsibility and the perspectives on events are often left to **him**[123] because he has a deeper knowledge of local affairs than the Tokyo desk. The sense of news and the journalistic skills differs greatly among the foreign correspondents. Some are good at editing and some are good at performing. It is very difficult to gather people who are good at both. Expert knowledge does not necessarily guarantee good performance. As a general rule, according to the TBS Director, the most important skill is the ability to make a news report. The 'acting' comes second. Standing reports are common work procedures and almost everyone is able to do this.

As mentioned above, experts in international affairs may not have the skill to sense and mediate information as news. The talent of the foreign correspondents is important in developing their designated part of the world. However one of the weak points of the Japanese lifetime employment system according to the TBS Director is connected to the collective hiring system (after university graduations in February, almost all companies take on new hires in April). Because their employment does not depend on experience

---

[122] One of the strong points of the Japanese system, seen from the TBS management position, is the fact that unions are weak. If the news producers want to move a camera or cross their field of expertise, this is not a problem for the union. This is one advantage. When the Japanese teams make coverage abroad, the American stations such as ABC will meet with tons of equipment and production people, whereas the Japanese get by with a few. This is only possible because of weak unions. The Japanese TV stations can also employ cheap labour and stringers abroad without problems with the unions.

[123] The reference to male employees was not explicit in the interviews as personal pronouns are omitted in Japanese. The reference is a deliberately presentation strategy by the author based on the observations that female journalists were scarce in the international newsrooms at the five national stations. The issue of gender is discussed in chapter seven and eight. It serves mentioning here that Japanese newspapers employ approximately 25,000 reporters (about 40 % of their total work force). Of this, 8% are women. (Foreign Press Center, 1997). Supporting these statistics, the Yomiuri Shimbun's planned hiring for April 1995 included 85 men and 10 women; the Asahi's, 98 man and 13 women; and the Mainichi's, 32 men and 8 women (Chen-Cooper, 1997: 202, cf. "News Companies", 1994)

and ability but on which university is attended, it is difficult to estimate the abilities of new staff. The Japanese employment system was not very productive in a competitive environment such as news production, where human resource development is vital. This account of the disadvantages of the Japanese life-time employment system was generally shared by news managers and media experts.

Headhunting

After the downfall of the bubble economy job-hunting has become more usual. The economic problems and bankruptcies of big Japanese companies have opened up for new constellations in the job market. According to the TBS Director of Political News, TBS has recently started to recruit people from NHK and other stations who are dissatisfied with their positions.

> Recently we have also started to recruit people from NHK and other stations who are dissatisfied with their positions. Rather than employing students with no experience from the universities we can strengthen our organisation by headhunting staff from other broadcast companies. It is not only in the media world that this trend has started. After the downfall of the bubble economy job-hunting has become more usual. (TBS Director of Political News, July 11th, 1997).

The unions and the journalist organisations are not yet familiar with employment in alternative ways, 'entering from the side' (*yokokaraheitekuru*). They are still only using the traditional annual hiring procedures. According to the TBS Director of Political News, the Japanese organisations traditionally operate under the ideal of 'poor-blooded-ism' (*junketsushugi*), which refers to an inbred system where one's career path is predetermined. From the beginning off their career, young graduate students enter TBS. They have lifetime employment arrangements and stay with TBS, make friends within TBS and its network relations (*keiretsu*). These news employees (*shinshain*) only get acquainted with people outside of TBS whom their superiors recommend and introduce them to. They do not make friends with staff from Fuji TV, NHK or NTV. This is the traditional way of operating.

> When you have been in a place for years inspiration dries out. Only some of the people hired in TBS develop into top quality staff. Without inspiration from the outside no one develops. Out of 250 employees, TBS has 45 people who are employed from other companies. Only a small per cent of the people who are employed directly from university manage to develop and climb the career latter successfully. Some are moved around to different sections but you cannot count on the fact that they will flourish. (TBS, Director of Political News, July 11th, 1997)

It is difficult to assign people with certainty to a set career and it usually takes a long time until their ability develops. Even then, they only have access to the TBS view of the world. Against this backdrop, employing people from the outside is stimulating and refreshing. The new employees often have prior experience and have gone through hardships and survival strategies which make them an asset to TBS.

In conclusion, according to the statements of the news production executive, there is a change in the market and conditions for news producers. These changes follow general employment conditions and confirm employment trends found in other research. More and more young reporters see their work not as a calling but as "just another job" (Foreign Press Center, 1997) and are increasingly dissatisfied with the irregular hours that the reporter's life imposes. It is not uncommon for young reporters unable to tolerate the rigors of the work to quit their papers after only a few months on the job. In a way, this is because economic growth has expanded employment opportunities and there is increasing acceptance of mid-career job-hopping. There is also some mobility among middle-aged reporters moving to other papers in search of better working conditions. Thus, there is a re-examining of the traditional life-long employment pattern (in which employees are expected to stay with the same company until retirement at the age of 60) for reporters as well as for other professionals.

It was claimed that in addition to life-long employment, reporters' identification with the company has also been buttressed by the fact that the newspapers and broadcast stations have traditionally been closed and that the young reporters traditionally joined the enterprise union after being hired. At the same time, as mentioned above, Japanese employment practices are not conducive to the development of veteran or specialist reporters. In the past, there was considerable room for the development of specialist staff reporters who were not on the career track for promotion to management, and it is imperative that personnel policies revive this system to produce experienced specialists rather than treating everyone as management candidates. Even more important than the development of specialists, however, is the development of good reporters knowledgeable in a wide range of fields. It is increasingly important and increasingly difficult for the media to develop the kinds of reporters they need in today's diverse media environment. Conditions are changing for reporters, not just in what is expected of them but also in the powerful technology they have at their disposal. Laptops, hand-held computers and cameras enable reporters to file stories online. While this is a great convenience, it also demands greater efficiency and precision of the reporters, especially in the mediation of international affairs.

Conclusion

The above describes the socio-political environment that influences the gate-keeping process and production strategies in the Japanese national broadcast organisations based. Based on interviews with executive managers at the five national broadcast stations and media expert it reveals how how extra-media factors (legal, political, sources, market trends and technological development) influence the strategy for selection and processing of news at the management level in the national broadcast institutions. Various 'stakeholders' including public and commercial broadcasters, politicians, sources, professionals, audiences are parts in an interdependent social ecology that forms the national media environment. While the extra media aspects do not solely determine the coverage of international news, the interview provides predictable explanations for the patterns of production of media products. The analysis of the patterns of the national media environment forms a basis for further analysis of production strategies at the organisational level in NHK and TV Asahi. The most important observations in an international perspective are outlined in the following.

According to the 'domestication' thesis, the Japanese regional belonging with its specific historical and cultural background, and its present political and economic position in the international community influences the choice and framing of news.

Further, the domestic political environment and the political character of the broadcast media provides news coverage with a 'political spin', while the competitiveness of the media influences news production from a focus on mediation of political and economic information to a more emotional appeal with a focus on human interest stories. This commodification of news or what you may refer to as the *marketisation of political information* in Japanese news production is reflected in the management concern with audience ratings and their strategies to make news appealing to as many viewers as possible. The market orientation causes different strategies of 'domestication' in which the main effort concerns making international news seem 'proximate' to Japanese audiences. Opinionated journalism is another strategy of emotional appeal. The categorisation of 'news and views', as described above refers to a specific profile and presentation style of the Japanese national stations. The presentation styles of Japanese national broadcasters cover a spectrum of communication strategies, from hard core economic and political 'news' to entertainment oriented production including 'views'. These presentation styles have an impact on news content and affect the 'domestication' process differently in Japan than in other countries.

The dual Japanese public-commercial system is found to provide the Japanese viewers with a variety of news programs. Despite, the legal aspirations to keep broadcast news politically neutral, domestic politics shape the production formulae of text and images in the production of international news. As a provider of political information in the perspective of the governing elite, NHK represents one end of the spectrum, while NTV as a provider of social information in entertainment form based on audience demand represents the other. It was found in the analysis that the news values and standard of reporting at NHK was highly esteemed for its professional standards. However, the aim to keep market shares and obtain high ratings, which is the goal of all stations regardless of style, brings about a constant battle between journalistic ideals of what the imagined audience 'ought to know' and what they are imagined to 'want to know'. Because of the continuous effort to maintain and gain viewer loyalty, journalistic ideals are often compromised.

The most significant observation of this chapter was the close connection between the Western networks and the Japanese national broadcasters. Through cooperation and exclusive agreements, the Japanese broadcasters are closely connected and rely on their affiliated sources for what they perceive as 'reliable information'. The availability of material and professional connections with these suppliers means that when possible the Japanese networks will use material from their affiliates. Thus, from a globalisation perspective this is potentially a strong factor of Western influence on international news production. The extent of use of these affiliates in production practices is analysed in the following chapter.

In sum, the challenge of international news presentation and production is threefold. One is to mediate global information in more or less 'distorted' versions *as public information or as a cultural commodity.* News production strategies have gradually moved from a professional focus to an audience-based focus. Another is to maintain and promote national identity. The processes of globalisation through the presentation of international events were met with 'domestication' efforts. The strong audience awareness and catering to the pre-existing knowledge of the viewers was part of an effort to make events feel 'proximate'. Narration techniques and the use of event models that were well established with the viewers was part of this effort. Thirdly, future strategies followed trends of regionalisation. A (re)turn to Asia was part of a strategy to fulfil audience demands and awareness trends of the Japanese public. In short, as stated by one executive: *The past 50 years of international journalism have been dedicated to the West, the next 50 will focus on Asia.*

As the interviews were conducted in 1997 after the 'global' news event they do not concern the specific strategies behind the 'global' news events, nor do they provide concrete examples of *global influence on domestic strategies* in the production of the specific news events. The Chapter rather contributes with general insights about the influence of extra-media factors from the point of view of news management and outside experts.

Whereas this chapter has provided an account of the extra-media factors that influence news production at the *national* level, the following chapter explores the news making processes and editorial decisions at the *organisational* level. The chapter is a comparative analysis of NHK and TV Asahi's general production of international news.

Chapter six

Public service and commercial organisational factors

All institutions are frameworks of programs or rules establishing identities and activity scripts for such identities." (Ronald L. Jepperson, 2001: 146)

One must try to form an image of a group's framework or frameworks, its belief system, its cosmology"… (Goffman: 1986: 27)

Introduction

The present chapter is an analysis of the organisational factors in news production at the public service station NHK and the commercial station TV Asahi. It explores the editorial decision-making processes, the interaction among staff and the business considerations behind production strategies.

In Chapter Four the analysis of news presentations in Denmark and Japan showed both similarities and differences in public service and commercial news output. Similarities included the 'system' perspective and the top- down approach of the public service stations and the 'people' perspective in a bottom-up approach at the commercial stations. In both countries the commercial stations gave priority and allocated many resources to the coverage of the UN Conference on Women. It was concluded that popular issues such as the UN Conference were prioritised by the commercial stations for business reasons. Differences between the countries included the choice of themes, actors and communication strategies according to the socio-political background of the two countries.

In a comparison across cultures the Danish news organisations were almost indistinguishable in their political approach and presentation style. The Japanese stations, by contrast, offered oppositional political views and very different presentation styles. The present chapter explores the organisational factors and 'house' values behind the differences in public service and commercial organisation approaches to news production.

Frame 'ba'

'Frame' has hitherto been defined as cognitive schemata and mental scripts shared by organisational members about professional processes. Frame in the study of organisational context is referred to by Japanese management researcher as 'ba'[124].

---

[124] The Japanese sociologist Nakane Chie (1970) defines frame (*ba*) as 'a locality, an institution or a particular relationship, which binds a set of individuals into one group' (1970:1). Nakane (1970) makes a distinction between 'attribute' and 'frame'. The classification of Japanese relationships according to the distinction of Nakane depends on cultural pre-dispositions (ibid: 1) and not their social practices as are in focus in the present study. The 'group' notion is analysed by Nakane within a structural functionalist theoretical framework, in which frame is a constant and stable institution. The object of Nakane's analysis is traditional hierarchical systems in households (*ie*) and Japanese corporate organisations (see criticism of the uniqueness of Japanese management and communication models in chapter three). The analysis of micro processes in the present study brings insights into interaction and personal strategies in news production. The analysis pays attention to personal attributes by focussing on the multi-faceted establishment of professional networks within hierarchical positions of 'groups'. The traditional vertical ranking system where the strict order of superior and subordinates (*sempai-kohai*) relations are central in the traditional Japanese corporate structure (*ie*). The vertical relations and the notion of 'consensus', which is highlighted as one of the most unique traits in Japanese management literature, do not sufficiently describe the dynamics of decision-making in international news production. Editorial decisions are negotiated across positions in the hierarchy, editorial positions are rotated among qualified staff, while *ad hoc* groups are assigned to do different tasks. *Frames of interpretation therefore are multi-*

154

The present chapter introduces the notion of 'ba' inspired by researchers in comparative knowledge management.[125] Von Krogh, Ichijiro and Nonaka define 'ba' as an 'enabling context' or 'a place in which knowledge is shared, created and used' (Von Krogh, Ichijo, Nonaka, 2000:49). Their notion of 'ba' (which they translate as 'place') is suitable in the present chapter, as it is extended to combine *not only physical space (an office) but also virtual space (e-mail, intranet, teleconferences), and mental space (shared experiences, ideas, emotions)*. 'Ba' in this interpretation is also a network of interactions determined by the care and trust of participants. The broad definition of Von Krogh, Ichijiro and Nonaka is applicable in the present analysis of production processes of informational products.

International newsrooms are physical spaces in which interaction and information sharing takes place while much information is transferred through TV monitors, e-mail and telephone. The attention to 'mental space' relates well to the present project's aim to describe the mental processes, schemata, scripts and models for news production as acquired and shared by news producers. The organisational frame 'ba' thus refers to a combination of the physical, the mental and the virtual 'space' of interaction. 'Ba' is the organisational context explored in this chapter and it refers specifically to frames of reference of professionals in action within the international newsrooms (in the following chapter this frame is on site reporting).

It is argued in the present chapter that in a study of micro processes in Japanese newsrooms, 'routine'[126] does not suffice as an analytical category to explain the decision-making processes and the complexity of negotiations of information and composition of news. A conceptual shift from routine to 'practice' and 'strategies' behind practice is necessary.

The present chapter thus explores communication 'practices' in order to provide insights into the 'considerations' and 'strategies' behind action. Considerations and strategies as discussed in chapter three include the intentions and emotions of news producers. The considerations of individual news producers are based on the acquisition (internationalisation) and knowledge of organisational factors. The study of organisational practices in this chapter uncovers the *shared* strategies of news producers and reveals their models and scripts for news production.

---

stranded and continuously changing in the ad hoc constellations of international news work. The organisational hierarchy, thus, is a formal structure, which comes alive in various combinations and dynamic constellations of social practices.

[125] The notion of 'ba' is, in Von Krogh, Ichijiro, Nonaka's account, inspired by the Japanese philosopher, Nishida Kitaro (1921/1990, 1970).

[126] It deserves mention that theories of 'routines' are well established in news production studies (see Chapter Two). Routines are used not only to describe working processes in mass communication organisations but in any organisation. Routines help explain the flow of work (of informational and material products). The notion of routines provides ways to categorise and create regularity and manageability in a job that is inherently unmanageable. Although news producers, as found in previous studies, are trained to be able to handle unexpected moments by being able to 'tame the information tide' and to 'routinise the unexpected' (Tuchman, 1978), the observation of production processes is not explainable through the notion of 'routines'. Production processes in a cognitive perspective entail multiple readings of situations into pre-existing schemes of knowledge, and notions of 'routine' do not suffice to explain the complexity of meaning making and framing processes. In other words "The explanatory reliance upon organisational routines as the prime mover in news production tends towards a form of organisational *functionalism* and, in consequence, emphasises the determinacy of bureaucratic 'needs' over journalist *agency*" (Cottle, 2000a: 22. Original Italics). The structuralist approach positions journalists as mere bearers of the organisational system, rather than as active and thinking agents who purposefully produce news through professional practices.

Method

The aim of the analysis is thus, to explore the production practices at two national broadcasters in order to ascertain how differing practices make different news output.

The analysis is based on interviews with 19 news production staff at NHK[127] and 12 at TV Asahi including all positions in model one and two from scriptwriters, editors (desks) and foreign correspondents to chief editors. The interview transcripts and observation in the newsrooms form the basis for the analysis. The factors explored are the international news production strategies, including newsroom practices and editorial decision-making procedures, expertise and authority and finally audience considerations and segmentation.

The focal point in this chapter is thus, the study of general production procedures and decision-making processes in order to describe the 'production formula' at the two stations. The interaction between staff as well as the possibility of individual influence on production is analysed in order to describe the possibility of using organisational factors. The analysis further explores the reliance on international news agencies, in order to estimate the influence of the international agencies as 'agents of globalisation'. Following the descriptions of production processes at the two stations, similarities and differences are discussed. The production strategies of the two stations are summarised in a model.

It is concluded that the framing of international news information differs according to the different organisational practices and production strategies observed at the organisational level. This supports the hypothesis that *international news is diversified and 'domesticated' not only in an international perspective according to national socio-political agendas but also organisationally within national media environments.*

I. NHK

The following introduces the general procedures in the international news department in order to provide an overview of the production practices and decision-making processes of *News Seven,* which is the NHK flagship program broadcast from 19.00-19.40 on week days.

The model below shows the interaction and hierarchical structure between actors in the international newsroom. The executive management is placed highest in the hierarchical order but located outside the international newsroom (on the first floor), as indicated by the stipulated line. Members of the executive staff occasionally frequent the newsroom. The circles below the stipulated line show the hierarchical order in the newsroom as described in detail below. The lines between the staff symbolise the flow of information and interaction in the formal decision-making hierarchy. The senior commentator (who is a main actor in the analysis below) is outside the international news room decision-making process indicated by the stipulated line.

---

[127] The news producers are quoted by their position in 1995, which is an individual agreement with each interviewee.

The observations and interviews about production practices were made from August 1996 to November 97. The 'global news' stories were broadcast in September 1995. Thus, the description is a retrospective account of happenings.

Figure 13: The Hierarchical Structure of Decision-Making at NHK

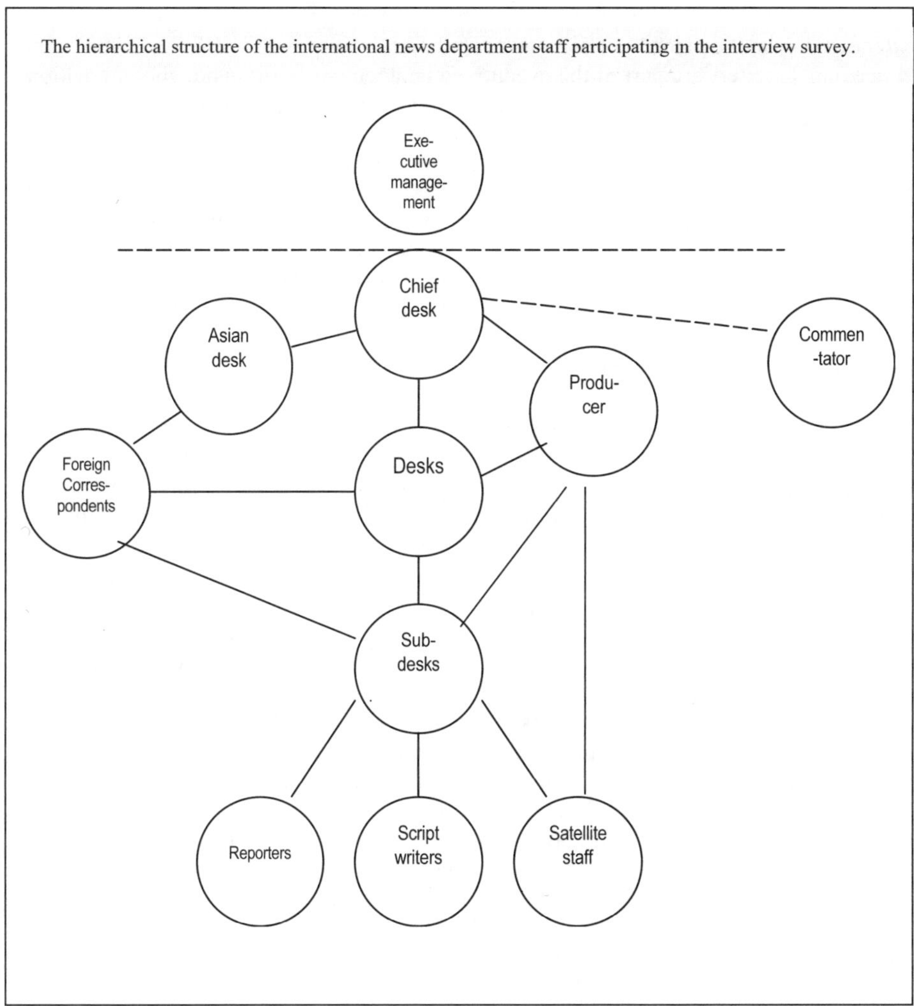

The 'desks' are positioned in hierarchical order of chief desk, desk and subdesk. The Asian desk is one of several area experts. The foreign correspondents are placed in a line of communication to the desk or the sub-desk. Foreign correspondents would in an extended display be placed in positions according to seniority at NHK. Their superiors in personnel matters are part of the executive management staff outside the international newsroom. The desk and sub-desk positions are assigned on a rotation basis between staff qualified for the position. The desk positions and assignments abroad are dependent on personal attributes rather than seniority. The scriptwriters are placed in the hierarchy with the satellite staff and the reporters. The circle marking reporters refers to trainees who are assigned two years of mandatory training at local NHK stations in the countryside. Reporters include correspondents who are acclimatising in the home office between assignments abroad. Satellite staff may be divided in an extended organisational chart into several positions within the satellite department

International news room practices

The NHK chief editors of the news department are the top decision-makers and are responsible for the final editing. There are four editors in charge who take turns in having the final say. One from each of the sections in the *news centre*: the political (*seijibu*), the economic (*keisaibu*), the social (*shakaibu*) and the international (*kokusaibu*) section decide the order of the news in a morning meeting. They work out a tentative list of news ranging from top news stories to less significant inputs. In their own view, they do not exercise independent power but discuss with the staff in charge of each specific news item. They describe the production process as a matter of negotiation and consultation. The model shows the structure of decision-making in the international news department, which is an independent unit in the *news centre*.

The international section supplies news stories to all of NHK's news programs. International stories are constantly developed and presented in different programs throughout the day. The production staff which plan the *News Seven* program choose from incoming events from early in the morning until the program is broadcast at seven o'clock at night. The following day, the morning news program examines *News Seven* and uses the main news as a guide for its presentation. If there is news that could have been shown more extensively, it is re-edited and shown later.

Where the producer at *News Station* has the ultimate responsibility for the news program as described further below, the role of the producer at NHK is to co-ordinate the news input from the different sections. The producer checks the international visuals in order to reconfirm the news list from the international department. The visuals from AP and Reuters are displayed on a monitor and recorded. As soon as the producer receives the plans from the international department, he double-checks the scheduled times of incoming visuals. The satellite department, which is part of the international news department, is in charge of visuals for news, sport and music. The editing of news stories involves combining the scripts, which are made in the international department with the visuals tape-recorded on the VCR monitor from AP and Reuters. The final editing is done in the editing department. The main duty of the producer is to co-ordinate the news pieces and to communicate the development of news in the four sections.

In the daily work of the producer, there are several combinations of co-ordination. The main responsibility is to combine scripts and visuals. When the news scripts are ready for broadcast the various outlets are checked again for visuals. If there are no visuals available the archives are checked. In rare cases if there are no visuals the production staff put something visual together. (NHK, producer, august 23rd, 1997)

The editing department decides on the subtitles, which means that they ultimately insert the cues in the framework they find suitable. The international department makes its own props for international news (the props for domestic news are made in the political department).

News about foreign affairs arrives with the person who is in charge of the desk. The 'desk' and 'subdesk' refer to both a position and a location. The other 'desks' refer to positions in the work hierarchy. The 'chief desk' manages the department. The 'chief desk' is the manager of daily operations of the International Department (*kokusaibu*). The chief desk at the time of observation was constantly present in the newsroom and participated in all meetings during the day. He only interfered and 'overruled decisions' or made additional suggestions in rare cases. He was a visible leader, aware of news developments and available for discussions and advice. Only the department manager is above the chief desk in the hierarchy. The American, the European, and the Asian desks (the area specialists) are next in the hierarchy. The desk and the sub-desk are in charge of the daily operations. The desk and sub-desk are located next to each other with the scriptwriters in front. They often stand up to confer across their computers. The person in charge of the desk delegates top news items to staff with special knowledge in the field. The less significant non-headline news is divided between two or three scriptwriters who translate information from the foreign agencies and rewrite it. Upon completion, the scripts are mailed to either the desk or the sub desk, where they are edited again or returned to the scriptwriters for additional research. The final scripts are registered and listed electronically with the signature of the scriptwriter. The scripts form the basis of the international news output. They are rewritten, extended or shortened throughout the day[128]. The daily duties of the desk and the sub-desk are to follow international news developments and edit the incoming scripts. Meanwhile the desks are in constant contact with the foreign correspondents and the visuals department.

One of the duties of the sub-desk is to establish connections with the foreign correspondents and stay in touch with them. In case of important decisions and negotiation the desk takes over and the chief desk may be consulted. The visual department continuously reports on expected and incoming visuals. After the morning meeting, people split hurriedly in order to research and prepare as much as possible before the 11.00 o'clock meeting when the international desk meets with desks from the other sections to make a tentative list of priorities for the seven o'clock news. As domestic news generally has a higher priority than international news, the arguments have to be well prepared.

The desk staff relies on the Japanese agencies to compare information with other agencies and also to be on top of foreign and national coverage. The scripts from the agencies are circulated across computers and important points highlighted for

---

[128] At NHK, records of news scripts are kept systematically. It is easy for professional and researchers alike to check the wording of each piece of news. The scripts are maintained and the final news program is recorded and filed. In some cases the news program differs slightly from the scripts. The order of news items may have been changed or the scripts shortened or not aired altogether. Like everything else at NHK, the documentation of news programs is very thorough and the easily accessible original scripts may encourage future research on content analysis.

incorporation in the scripts. If there are no foreign correspondents in the area of an event a reporter may be dispatched or a correspondent from a nearby news bureau flown in. Decisions concerning staffing are made by the chief desk and executed in this cast by the desk. The desk is also in charge of the content of news. If the main point of a story is not expressed well, the desk may change anything from the headline downwards. The reporters are instructed beforehand about what should be the focus and the length of a story. When the desk submits a piece of news it is considered final.

News is broadcast at 12.00, at 19.00 and at 21.00 o'clock. Each program has a senior editor. Until the program is over, he may decide whether news to be broadcast or not. Much effort is put into making a piece of news. Only in rare cases if the news is not developed enough and because of lack of time is it not broadcast. Usually this is due to a sudden accident and there is a reasonable explanation, why it was not aired. The chief editor does not have to ask the desks when he 'sacks' a piece of news. However, the scriptwriters have the opportunity to protest if they believe their story was more important than the ones broadcast. This perceived influence is important for the self-worth of the journalists as their criterion for success naturally depends on whether their piece of news has been aired or not.

At the nine o'clock meeting before the shift between night and daytime staff, the priority and choice of news is discussed. Staff from the whole 'house', the satellite, radio and educational departments, gathers in order to be informed about the agenda. The sub-desk runs through the list of important news. For each piece of news she or he announces the sources. The sub-desk supplements the announced run down of the desk with news that is preliminarily researched. Hence, the responsibility for news items is negotiated. In some cases, ideas or perspectives are brainstormed, but usually it is left to the desk and sub-desk to negotiate with the journalist or scriptwriters about the angle and content of news.

> Basically, a piece is not re-edited after it leaves the international department. But because time is limited in a news programme, it may be necessary to adjust the length. If an important change is required in our report, the editorial staff asks the opinion of the international section. The duration of a piece of news is normally somewhere between 30 seconds to 2 minutes. If it is big news, it will be extended. It depends on the day how much time is allowed for international news. (NHK, news desk, September 8th, 1997)

Limited time is the main reason for 'sacking' (*botsu ni suru*) a piece of news. The producer of each news program, in this case *News Seven*, has the authority to change the news list or reject a piece of news. When a piece of news has made it all the way to the final list, a rejection is usually due to lack of time. If the producer estimates that this will not make the seven o'clock news it may be used in the nine o'clock program. The airing of a news item is a measurement of success, and it was a concern expressed by several news producers.

The correspondents abroad are responsible for feature stories. The correspondents in New York, Washington, and London have their own editing machines and send home news packages. The one-person bureaux just send the scripts, the voices and the pictures separately and the editing is done in Japan.

The sub-desk follows the wire services closely and is responsible for incoming news. When he (one woman was trained for this position at the time of observation) finds important news, which has to be made ready for broadcast, he gathers the scripts from AP, Reuters AFP, Jiji and Kyodo and passes them to the scriptwriters.

> The scriptwriters write the scripts and the sub-desk checks to see if they are *shaped* in the right way. The sub-desk may confirm information by telephone, or ask for additional information. Sometimes the desk has a different view on certain subjects. It happens sometimes that our scripts can be changed to totally different scripts. But we always talk about it. The desk always has to consult with the correspondent when he changes the script. (NHK, scriptwriter A, August 19th, 1997).

After a series of writings back and forth from subdesk to scriptwriters to desk, the scripts are made available on the net to the different programs. These programs include general television (GTV) satellite and radio. The editors of the different programs may cut the scripts, but they never change words or expressions without consulting the responsible scriptwriters or reporters. The visuals are co-ordinated and edited according to the scripts. The announcer finally reads the script on air. She (the female anchor for over a decade) sometimes shortens the script, but she does not change its contents.

Two or three scripts are aired on the *News Seven* program every day. Program directors are in charge of feature stories, which are longer than the ordinary straight news. The correspondents provide information and scripts and the program director is in charge of the visuals and the structure of the news story. In feature stories, the visuals are important. High quality visuals and good interviews will be shown if possible. The combination eventually depends on what scripts, visual material and interviews are available.

As described above and expressed by several news producers, international news has to be 'negotiated with convincing arguments in order to make the daily news list' (NHK Chief Desk, July 17th, 1997). International news is not a priority, and is minimal compared to the amount of domestic news. The notion of news values is elaborated upon further below. Within the seemingly strict hierarchical work structure of the work process at NHK, the employees claimed that they had the opportunity for individual action. From the perspective of the individual, their decisions greatly influence news production, as elaborated upon below. The individual inputs, however, undergo negotiations in the framing process and eventually the news agenda in general is not affected greatly by individual inputs. The following elaborates on the sense of individual influence.

Individual influence

Sociological studies in newsroom practices analyse and describe news production (see discussion in chapter two and above) as routines. From the perspective of the news producers, including trainees and higher level management staff, the production procedures are described as 'flexible' as discussed below.

The general selection process as described by the producer below includes five elements in the decision-making: area of interest (news worthiness), negotiation between correspondents and desk personnel, hierarchy of decision-making, individual judgement and deadlines.

There is no one standard or rules for deskwork. It is flexible. It is very difficult to describe how we make a judgement about news. It is centred on the basis of individuals. We decide between the reporter in the field and the desk. Very occasionally, the chief desk might propose a topic of news. On a regular basis, the news desk will make the final decision. The chief editor of the whole program decides the order of the news. The final decision ultimately depends on time. (NHK producer, August 23rd, 1997)

A resource and possibility to get assignments approved was in many cases based on financial strategies. In August 1997, for instance, during my observation period at NHK a story on Greenland's fight for independence from Denmark was aired. The news featured an ongoing problem between Greenland and Denmark which was not a media event in Denmark or anywhere else in the world at the time. Sharing this point with the chief editor made him laugh and comment that it was possibly a nice holiday opportunity for the London correspondent. This incident, of course, does not characterise news production in general. Nevertheless, it addresses an issue of personal career opportunity in a professional environment. The incident further shows how a random decision made information from a corner of the world available to 10 millions of Japanese viewers by a professional tool of framing which made the information fit to become news.

The personal inputs and subjective interest are here exemplified. The sub-desk accounts for his choice of news:

> I am interested in Chinese events and not at all in the US, for example. If the desk is a US expert it evens out and we discuss back and forth. *Naturally, the choice of news is very personal.* You cannot help thinking your own area is the most interesting and include news from this part of the world out of the many incoming issues. (NHK, Subdesk, August 26th, 1997. My emphasis)

The Asian desk expresses a similar example of the perceived ability to influence production.

> As an Asian desk, I have been involved with and lived in Asian countries for 16 years. I automatically pick news from these countries. *The news program looks different when I am in the office.* NHK has multiple wire services and a very solid international staff. NHK news aims to be objective. It is difficult to make objective news. In the selection process we tend to prioritise our special field. (NHK, Asian Desk, August 19th. My emphasis)

The trainee asserts that all journalists in the NHK Tokyo office have the opportunity to pursue their fields of interest.

> We propose a story and if it is accepted we go abroad. I am trying to work on a 30-minute program on landmines and the things going on in Oslo. There will be a final treaty in December in Ottowa, Canada. I want to take the opportunity to do something. The timing is right. In order to do that I have to do research on landmines in Cambodia, Bosnia, Angola and the Korean peninsula before I go abroad. (NHK, trainee, September 17th, 1997)

In order to get permission to go abroad, the journalists have to make a proposal, which includes a financial estimate for the production both of news and feature stories. The trainee presents a proposal which includes items for the NHK General TV programs as well as the 21.30 o'clock program, *Close Up Gendai*, a high level current information program (hosted by the brilliant female host, Kunihiro), which also features foreign current affairs. Several pieces of news for the daily news programs are proposed in his package. Financial awareness and the ability to make a budget (i.e. translating their news work into economic discourse) gives them strong arguments to get assignments though the first round of negotiations with the chief editor. In the second round, after the programme managers have approved the budget, the framing of content is worked out. Professional ability and budget awareness enhance career opportunities. Strategic planning and awareness of structural factors in other words is a resource.

Only one individual mentioned restraints in information processing as caused by a tendency to keep knowledge to oneself. Transparency and the willingness to share knowledge in the opinion of this news producer would enhance cooperation and make information flow more easily.

In sum, news producers at all levels, from scriptwriters to the chief editor express an ability to influence the gate-keeping process. Nevertheless, from an analytical perspective, individuals do not influence the final output in obvious ways.

The above concerns personal preference over institutional expectations and shows how institutional expectations are used by individuals as resources for personal preferences. Awareness of such technicalities within the organisation (decision-making processes, hierarchical structures, financial planning) as knowledge acquired professionally plays a role in the negotiation of individual interests. The point will be elaborated in the conclusion as part of a final discussion on personal empowerment and models for (inter) action, as they differ at the two stations.

In relation to the domestication argument, it may be concluded that the low priority given to international news in the *News Centre* keep international news producers alert and enhances their awareness of the relevance of information to Japanese audiences. The explanations alone provide evidence that audience awareness is heightened through interaction in the newsrooms, which is a core point in the domestication hypothesis.

NHK style visuals

The NHK style visuals were perceived by several news producers to have a characteristic 'house' style. This was similarly found in the analysis of Japanese news presentations in Chapter Four, which showed a strip of slowly cut 'political protocol' visuals. The NHK visuals served as documentation of the political event and strictly adhered to the agenda of the political meeting with *emphasis on the verbal account*. The following exemplifies the framing of visuals from a production point of view and explores the NHK style of visuals that are characterised as *traditional, slow views with priority given to the documentation effect and the information intensive verbal accounts*.

A European correspondent describes the specific visual image of NHK. The correspondent made weekly reports about the development of the European Union and Nato. The transmissions were mainly a combination of interviews and on-location narration from the European parliament. For visual arrangements the correspondent used the NHK's special deal with a Belgian studio to use ad hoc camera crews. The cameramen in this particular studio had worked for NHK for 10 years so they are accustomed to making the pictures NHK style, which means making *beautiful static pictures*.

> The nature of the picture is different. NHK's pictures are in general aesthetically organised to be beautiful, quiet and the cutting is slow. The focus is meant to be on the content of the news and not an exciting visual experience. (NHK, European Correspondent, August 21st)

As is customary (see above) in the large NHK bureaux abroad, the European correspondent edited the reports himself and included visuals from the local television station in the news package sent to Tokyo. In case of special reports the European journalists went back to Japan to put a Japanese crew together.

In sum, NHK visuals are described as aesthetically organised, beautiful, quiet and slowly cut. Visuals serve in the NHK production strategy as documentation of political events and the focus is on the content of the news rather than on an exciting visual experience. This observation is confirmed in the study of Ellis S. Krauss (1996), which compares the visual images at NHK to US visual production. In American network news, professional storywriters are responsible for writing scripts. In some cases, the stories are filmed first by the camera crew and then rewritten by the scriptwriters. A determining factor in visual production in the US is the visuals themselves, and the story line, which is moulded by non-reporter producers and scriptwriters. At NHK, the writing of a script is always the responsibility of the reporter covering the story, who then transmits it to the newsroom to be edited by another reporter at the main desk. The camera crew films the visuals while accompanying the reporter, and the visuals are edited in the newsroom according to the reporter's draft. The norm that guides the process of filming and the visual editing is the story written by that journalist. Visuals, in the NHK mode of production, it is concluded by Krauss and in agreement with observations in the present study 'rarely have priority on their own merits; rather, they are designed to illustrate the reporter's story and to be an adjunct to it' (Krauss, 1996: 115).

Traditional, conventional and reliable

In the previous chapter NHK news is described by executive management and media experts as being reliable, adhering to traditional news criteria. NHK is admired broadly for it high professional standards. Supporting this outside image, the NHK news producers describe NHK news as traditional, conventional and reliable. Many of the NHK news producers expressed great pride in working for NHK because of these ideals.

> I can compare with other correspondents in other companies. I think we are doing a good job. We have many journalists and we have good craftsmanship. (NHK, Trainee, September, 17th, 1997)

A few interviewees mentioned that the salaries could not compare with the private stations but seen in the light of the sensationalism and recent scandals at the private stations, many news workers were happy with the high degree of journalistic professionalism and high ethics at NHK. The neutral and factual image (traditional, conventional and factual) was a presentation profile which was described with pride by most news producers. Although the 'neutrality' and 'factuality' of news seems somewhat naive in the light of the almost unavoidable bias through professional procedures in the construction of visuals and language as described above, it was strongly believed to be a characteristic of NHK's organisational identity. Many news producers had the impression that NHK viewers appreciated and trusted the NHK line. It deserves mention that while there have been no ethical cases raised concerning NHK news coverage, NHK documentaries have been found to distort facts by including fictive scenes (*yarase*) (see Cooper-Chen, 1997:207). The issue of ethics, although a big issue in the Japanese public, is outside the scope of the present project.

The incorporated audience 'mechanism'

It is assumed in the present project that the effort to 'domesticate' information is included in the framing process as a consideration of news audiences. There were differing ideas of the imagined audience among the news producers. The news producers identified mainly three audience segments. One segment was the urban population *as well as* people in the countryside. This catering to the farming population maintains the traditional and conventional form of news reporting. The rural audience was described as people interested in economics and politics. The second audience segment was the political and economic system i.e. government employees and business people. The third segment included the Asian neighbouring countries, which were perceived as a target group closely following NHK news for Japanese political moves. The nine o'clock news was described as more 'sophisticated' aiming mainly at professionals and politically interested (urban population) audience members. It deserves mention that *News Seven*, because of its target group, does not have a high percentage of international news. Its main priority is domestic news. *News Nine* presents more international news items (Clausen, 1996). The morning programs as described above present the largest percentage of international issues due to the time difference between Japan and the West. When the sun rises in Japan, yesterday's events in Europe and in the US are televised for the first time in the morning news. The low priority of international news was regretted by news producers, who were advocates of international political and economic news.

In relation to the 'domestication' hypothesis, the European correspondent describes the audience awareness of foreign correspondents abroad.

> The most important fact when considering the news value of a story when abroad is the estimated effect on Japanese people and on Japanese politics. We have incorporated a mechanism which automatically takes the audience into consideration when making news. (NHK, European Correspondent, August 21st, 1997).

Part of the audience 'mechanism' includes an awareness of the distinction between the communication strategy of NHK as a public interest station against the strategy of the commercial stations. The correspondent believes that the fact that NHK news is not biased and is presented in a neutral manner is the main attraction for NHK viewers and an important guideline for the correspondent. The European correspondent imagines the viewers to be loyal to NHK because of what he refers to as the 'neutral' presentation form, and works accordingly.

NHK does not prioritise entertainment in its news as the commercial stations do. The viewers will have to choose whichever style they prefer. The audience we have in the back of our mind is a faithful one. Our viewers are steady. They have followed our news for many years and they are used to our presentation. They know that our news is not biased. It is presented in a neutral manner. (NHK, European Correspondent, August 21st, 1997)

The statement of the European correspondent resembles statements by several news producers who seek to legitimise news as public interest information about international political processes. Viewers are in these public interest strategies positioned as citizens (rather than consumers). It deserves mention that the correspondent refers to frames of 'economic consequence' in news reporting (De Vreese, 1999). News presented in the economic consequence framework concerns the economic effect of government policies on ordinary families. The approach resembles the human-interest frames of the commercial stations. The consideration of viewers in the framing process is, according to the correspondent, a result of the importance paid to ratings. It is a challenge and at times professionally less satisfying for experts in economics and politics to be obliged to mediate news in general, easily comprehensible terms.

The trainees were very explicit in their expression about audience considerations and communication strategies. Lessons from two years of practical training at the local stations left communication strategies fresh in mind, while the shift to international news production provided a new perspective on news mediation. One of the trainees expressed a sense of obligation to make news understandable to the general public as follows.

In *News Seven* and *News Nine* programs news producers aim at the general public. As a public station NHK is obliged to broadcast to the general public. Other programs may be more specific about politics and business news. NHK news has to be understandable for teenagers as well as 70-80 year olds. Every word has to be carefully considered to target both the young people as well as the older generation. (NHK, Trainee B, August 19th, 1997).

The translation from English to Japanese, which differs from the process of making news at local Japanese stations, was described as a 'cumbersome endeavour'. Much news vocabulary which was understandable for members of the younger generation with a knowledge of English had to be replaced. Borrowed words (mainly from English) had to be replaced with Japanese vocabulary for the sake of the older generation.

Conclusively, imaginings of the audience were varied. Most news producers had a very abstract and a general view of their audience. Many referred to 'a sense of news' which was expressed in terms of professional news values and production practices rather than imagined audiences. The fact that NHK news is ideally supposed to target the Japanese public from the young to the older generation makes its language policy conservative, preserving existing Japanese expressions. Foreign expressions were not only 'domesticated' and taken into the Japanese language, as is policy at the commercial station, foreign loan words were replaced by Japanese equivalents.

166

A summary of NHK's organisational characteristics

The above describes the general production procedures in a day in the NHK international newsroom. There are three important differences in international news that make the institutional processes at the public station different from that of the commercial station analysed below. These differences include the hierarchical structure of the decision-making processes, the news values and the production *formula*. The latter refers to a combination of strategic efforts to make traditional, conventional and factual news.

There is a strong hierarchical order of decision-making both within the news sections (the social, the political the economic and the international) and in the international newsroom. The hierarchical structure is based both on years of experience *and* the 'sense for news'. The two complement each other in some cases and are often but not always linked. In Japanese companies employees are traditionally promoted according to years with the company and not according to personal attribute. This is also the case at NHK. However, the international news production career, which requires expert up-to-date knowledge and strenuous assignments abroad has an age limit, and seniors are moved to other departments of NHK when they reach the age limit (approximately 35 on the screen and 45 behind it) as described in Chapter Four. NHK, as a large news corporation, has much talent to choose from. However, the development of talent and skills especially of the new employees (*shinshain*) was a concern among NHK management, and initiatives were in the pipeline at the time of the interviews.

The NHK production processes are characterised by negotiation. International news producers, in particular, have to be able to present their news ideas in order to convince the *News Centre* of the importance of their stories. In a cognitive light, this keeps framing and priming mechanisms alert and enables great awareness of why events are suitable for the programs. A less pleasant effect is that this pressure adds to the many other pressures in their daily practices.

News production, and international news making in particular, is accomplished through personal attributes, competence and (tacit) knowledge through experience. It is expressed high and low in the hierarchy that everyone has the opportunity to pursue personal interests and argue for the importance of their ideas. The personal freedom, however, as I observed it was strongly connected to the ability to socialise and understand the rules of NHK. A good sense of what was news within the NHK traditional news framework was a way to advance from the less independent work of script writing to desk positions and assignments abroad.

The trainees (three) were eager to think up projects and establish an area of expertise. With English fluency they were looking forward to going abroad. The correspondents in the newsroom were back from years of assignments abroad getting readjusted or preparing for new destinations. The scriptwriters were more settled in their positions. Seemingly, the scriptwriting positions were assigned to journalists less motivated to challenge the field. The sub-desk, desk, chief desk, editors and above were included in the decision-making meetings. The 'desk' position and positions above participated in the daily evaluation meeting after the program.

While emphasising that there is a strong hierarchical system in the newsroom, the interviewees expressed that there was room for personal decision-making and development in their work. The NHK journalists were proud of the high standard of journalistic handcraft, although the money was less than offered at the private stations. Most news producers were experts in economic and politically related issues and/or expert in a geographic area. The production practices were based on strategies to make factual news. NHK *News Seven* stories were characterised as reliable, conventional and objective.

The following is an analysis of international news production at TV Asahi. Conclusively the two approaches will be compared.

II. TV Asahi

The *News Station* production strategy differs greatly from that of *News Seven* at NHK. A basic difference is the financial background of the stations. The market orientation and sponsor considerations influence the overall strategies of the production. First, the *News Station* program was conceptualised in cooperation with Japan's largest advertising company, Dentsu, to become a money-spinning venture (see previous chapter). Second, given the high priority at TV Asahi, the production of *News Station* is an autonomous unit in the company structure with its own employees and strategies. Where NHK *News Seven* is produced by the NHK News Centre, which supplies international news to all NHK news programs, *News Station* is an independent production unit. Third, where *News Seven* production staff members are regular NHK employees, *News Station* staff includes personalities from the TV Asahi Broadcasting Company as well as independent production companies. Fourth, the role authority in the production hierarchy differs. Fifth, the focus on a few individuals in news presentations is reflected in the preparation and arrangement of the program. Finally, the emphasis on feature stories makes work processes and final news presentation differ at the two stations. These factors will be elaborated upon the following.

The model below illustrates the organisational structure of *News Station*. The model shows the hierarchy of decision-making and the flow of information news production staff. The producer at *News Station* is in charge of the daily operations. The President marked at the top of the hierarchy indicates that the communication line is direct from the producer to the president. This signifies the importance of *News Station* within TV Asahi. The management is placed below the president in the hierarchy. Management is logistically separated from the daily operations of the newsroom, which is shown by stipulated lines. *News Station*, as stated above, is an independent unit with its own national and international news production. Where the observation point of analysis at NHK was from inside the international newsrooms, the point of observation and interpretation at TV Asahi is the production of *News Station*. The foreign news department in stipulated lines marks an outside function as a supplier of news. The producer, the commentator and the anchors are at the top of the hierarchy of the decision-making line including the general desks in the decision-making meetings. The desk positions are placed in hierarchical order. The desks are operated on a rotation basis. The foreign correspondents are in frequent contact with the general desk. Their hierarchical position depends on seniority and personal attributes. The program directors are next in the hierarchy and report to the 'desks' in charge of their story. The A.D. staff has a hierarchy of its own independent of the *News Station* newsroom, and finally the scriptwriting position includes reporters. The following presents in detail the work procedures and the interaction in the newsroom.

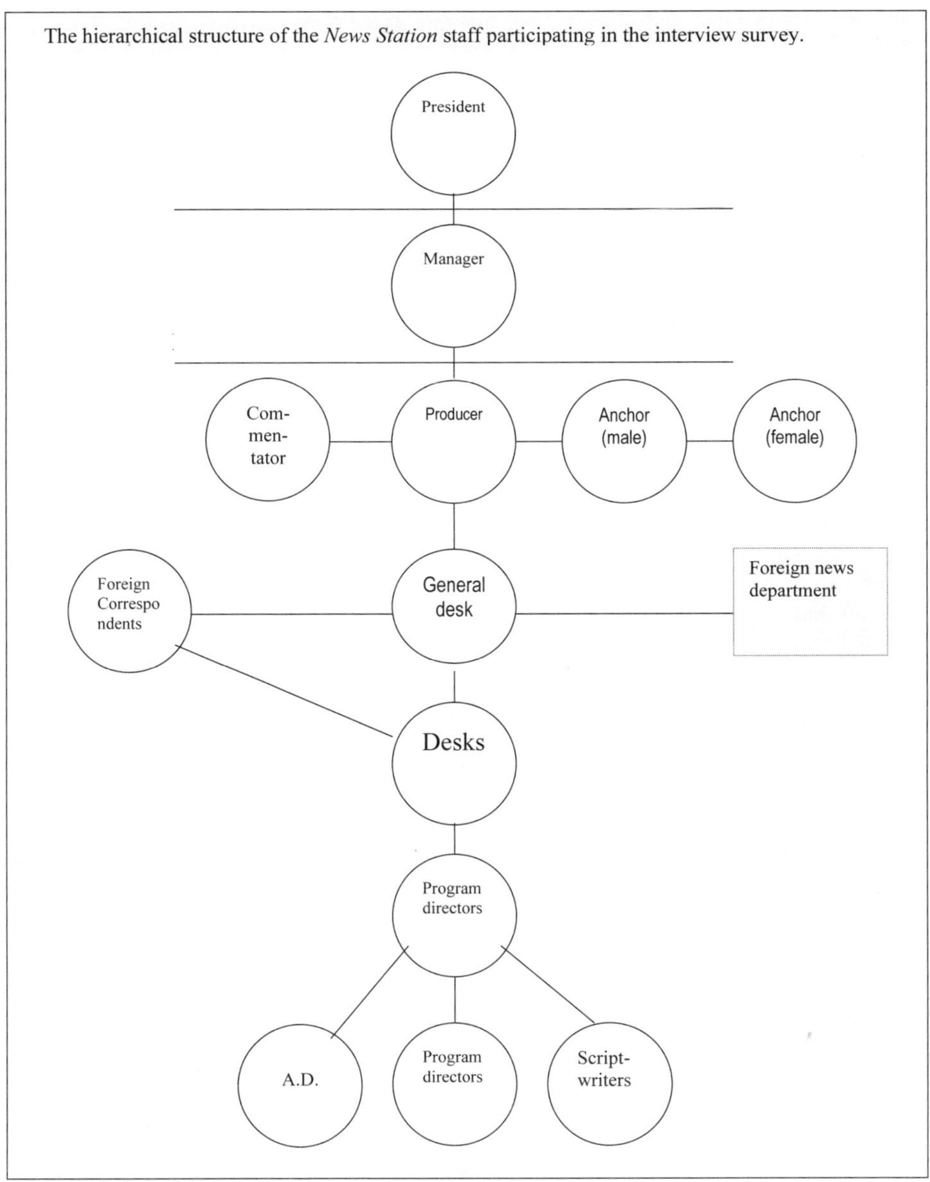

Regularly 105 people are employed [129] in the production of *News Station*. Approximately fifty employees are engaged in each news program. The other fifty are divided into two groups who work in shifts. Ad hoc teams are assigned to do domestic

---

[129] TV Asahi employs roughly 1300 people. Female employees number a few hundred. In the whole news section with 200 employees 50 or 60 are female.

or international news according to the shifting agenda.[130] In each shift of 50 people, about seven or eight are female. Several women hold middle management positions, but in the upper and executive management they are few.[131] Approximately 20-30 people work as program directors on special assignments.

Straight news is made at the foreign news section (*gaihobu*)[132] and made available to *News Station*. In the information department (*hodokyoku*) there are three departments: the social (*shakaibu*), foreign information (*gaihobu*), and planning (*seikeibu*). These departments supplied scripts and footage to the various news programs throughout the day such as the twelve and six o'clock news and *News Station*. The *News Station* production staff either decides to use this footage or to make its own.

News Station staff produce most of its feature stories (*tokushu, kikaku mono*). The foreign department (*gaiho*) generally supplies the straight news. The first three segments of the *News Station* program are usually news segments. The news is mainly rewritings of scripts from the foreign news department. The greater part of the *News Station* program is straight news. The program includes a few feature stories. There is a sports section, which is very popular, and a weather report finishes the program. Commercials divide the segments. International news is scarce but still considered an important part of the *News Station* program.

Decision-making

There are different types of employee at *News Station*. Some are engaged for the program and others are Asahi Employees. The Asahi employees the so-called *salary men* and *office ladies* (O.L.) are employed full time by the Asahi Company and can be transferred anywhere from production to accounting. The impact of this is flexibility.

Five people are in charge of the production of *News Station*. Three of these are 'desks' in the news section. A 'desk' can be a set location but not necessarily. Most often it refers to a chief or person in charge of a section of the news program. The anchorperson, Kume Hiroshi, is referred to as 'the master of ceremony'. The news program is built around his personality. The producer is the last person in the decision-making group. The group of five meets one or twice a day and occasionally three times in order to discuss what themes should be included in the evening program. The female anchor has an important position in the program profile but she is not mentioned in the

---

[130] As an example, the Israeli assault was major news during the field work activities. Almost 25 people were engaged in this news.

[131] Very few women held editorial positions, which in the light of the statement of the news producers affected the decision-making process specifically in the choice of issues and allocation of resources. The seriousness of the UN Conference on Women was not appreciated fully and many of the plans at both stations did not make it through the decision-making process. Even so it was mentioned that the reporting this time was far superior (*mashii*) to the amount and quality of reporting of previous Conferences on Women's issues. The percentage of female managers in the 1995 statistics show that the ratio of regular female employees at *News Station* was 15-16 percent, compared to an average of 8,7 percent of the total work force at NHK (Cooper Chen, 1997:221). Women held managerial positions on an average of 2.2 percent, with commercial stations having more female managers than NHK. (ibid: 211). Managerial positions were held by 1,7 per cent at NHK according to the senior commentator. Very few women were stationed abroad for a longer period of time. This was a serious hindrance to career advancement to management positions in the international news section and ultimately further in the organisational hierarchy.

[132] In spite of its name, the international department (*kokusaibu*) is not concerned with news and international affairs. It deals with international co-productions and import of international TV items.

170

gang of five. At the meetings future, events ranging from events next week to events scheduled next year are also discussed.

Particular to the *News Station* production line is that important decisions and problem solving do not pass through middle and upper management but are communicated directly to the top of the hierarchy to the President of TV Asahi. Such cases are rare.[133] Full competence is given to the daily production team.

> As for the news program, special assignments, international news, sports events, weather or anything concerning the content is up to me exactly. But there are other issues such as budget or personnel. I have to talk to my superior (*hodokyokucho*). I have to consider the opinion of the president. There are other executives but I go all the way to the president. Directly yes, because *News Station* is a very, very big project. (TV Asahi, Producer, June 11th, 1997)

News from the international agencies and proposals from the international correspondents first arrive at the general (*soogoo*) desk. Here, the planning of the overall structure of *News Station* takes place. The news desks are responsible for the parts of the programme, allocated by the general desk. Under the supervision of the news desks there are 3-4 program directors. Each director is responsible for one piece of news for a certain part of the programme. The production team and staff of *News Station* work closely with the directors. The directors work in shifts. They are allocated different responsibilities on a weekly basis. The program directors are engaged in all forms of duties from writing texts to producing, researching, receiving satellite, one-minute video props, etc.

The desks and the program directors meet at 7.00 p.m. the night before a news program. They make plans for the following day and necessary preparations start then. There is another meeting at 12 p.m. on the day of the presentation, where a more detailed plan is made. At the 7 o'clock evening meeting the final decisions are likewise made concerning the content of *News Station*, which is broadcast at 22.00 o'clock.

The news desk is responsible for the news on the day of assignment. The news producers in charge of the general (*soogoo*) desk co-ordinate the program and decide the itinerary of the news list. There is a rotation of people who handle the strenuous work of the desk. As was observed at NHK, only regular full time employees are assigned to the news desks. Whereas the entire staff at the NHK *News Centre* include specialists and experts in their field, the *News Station* desks are generalists. Their duties are to maintain an overall perspective of the program flow and, importantly to have an understanding of the concept of the program. As mentioned above, all news desk staff are Asahi employees. The anchors are employed by independent production companies. The commentator at the time of the interviews was from the Asahi newspaper. The news desk decides what is newsworthy, gives future assignments, negotiates and fits breaking news into the program. The news desk staff also writes the schedule and decides what is top news.

---

[133] The importance of *News Station* is illustrated in the following: "The producer and the news desk staff make the daily decisions. At CNN and CBS, the producer makes the final decisions. At *News Station* the producer reports directly to the President of TV Asahi *hodokyokucho* or even to the president of the entire Asahi Network (*shacho*), if there are problems." (Program Director, June 12th, 1997).

News room practices

According to the producer, news presentations have become more spontaneous since the inauguration of *News Station* (see description in the previous chapter). The coverage of news focuses on 'live' reporting, which is enabled through satellite transmission. The viewers have become used to seeing things 'live for themselves' and great efforts are made to cater to this wish. *News Station* is affiliated to CNN, which means that CNN's feed can be used freely. CNN is situated on top of the TV Asahi building in Roppongi, which enhances cooperation through the exchange of material and communication between news workers.

As it was observed at NHK, news producers at *News Station* claimed that the main and only clear production policy was to convey facts. Much research and double-checking is involved in the preparation of reports. Verification strategies depend on individuals. Although most news producers try to verify information in order to present stories as close to the original event as possible, the constant battle with time often makes news decisions and story angles arbitrary:

> Much time is spent on research and preparations. But news making is a constant battle with time. Time considerations influence the many small calculations and decisions. Often random decisions are made. It is impossible to paint an exhaustive picture of the many layers of decision that go into a piece of news work. A lot of time spent does not mean that the outcome is perfect. And there are many circumstances to take into account. The single fact that news production is not a one-man show means that every event comes out differently than originally thought. (TV Asahi, Program Director C, June 26th, 1997).

Even editing is not the program director's job alone. It is always done together with an editor and sometimes with technical staff. In this process, small intentional and unintentional changes and additions are made. Often, a director is in charge of one specific news item, but he may also have more responsibilities such as making video inputs and props.

Much concern was expressed at both stations about the approval and airing of news, which is the means of measuring accomplishment. According to the News Director the hard work usually pays off. Most prepared pieces of news are broadcast. Lots of preparation goes into making a piece of news and it is most often broadcast. Of course there is always a risk. Daily news cannot be broadcast again, but most documentaries or specials make the news list because they can be rescheduled.

Easy to understand, people oriented, anti-establishment

The main characteristic of *News Station* production strategies is the focus on individual personalities and their contributions to the program. The production practices and content revolve around the personalities of anchors and commentators, as described below.

The host, Kume Hiroshi, has been a major cause of the popularity of the program. In the words of the program director, most participants find it an honour and pleasant to appear in the program because of Kume's personality. He is a frank, witty interviewer, who makes people relax.[134] Foreign guests have included Margaret Thatcher, Gorbachev, Fujimori, Mandela, movie and sport stars. In interview situations, Kume has the role of audience representative. He asks questions (often very direct) that the viewers might ask.[135] (TV Asahi, program director). The people-oriented strategy was reflected in the analysis of news presentations (Chapter Four), in which *News Station* presents many 'voices'.

> One of the cornerstones in the strategy of *News Station* is to include guests from all walks of life. People who make news are part of it. Prominent guests are interesting for the audience, so their appearances are considered important in the planning. (TV-Asahi, Program Director A, June 12th, 1997)

According to the program director, *News Station* makes an effort to presents the visits of foreign and domestic dignitaries as news and not as promotion for their personal projects or visits to Japan. This supports the notion that news is choreographed according to set norms. In this case, social actors appear in the *News Station* program as official public figures.

Another aim of *News Station* and an important part of the production policy is to enable the viewers to relate complex themes such as economic and international news. The goal is to make news understandable for middle and high school students without being condescending. This is done through frequent use of aids and props, such as models and maps. As an example, dolls of politicians and economic players may be used by the anchors to play out events. Props are thought up by the program directors and created in the art section. Another important means to make news easy to understand is the choice of commonly used terms in financial and political news. The *New Station* studio has the cosy atmosphere of a home and the anchors and commentator converse following news outputs.

The fundamental attitude of TV Asahi is anti-establishment. Because of Kume Hiroshi's style *News Station* has become one with strong opinions. According to the Chief Director of TV Asahi the casters are not active in real politics. Their attitude, which reflects a general consensus at the Station, is to be on the side of people and anti-power holders. To 'be on the people's side' means to present news as consequences for ordinary people, people with weaknesses and minorities. The Japanese broadcast law (as presented in chapter six) stipulates impartial reporting, and political activity is therefore not overt.

> If I accept an interview with a Japanese magazine and I admit a political engagement, I lose my position. That is the way it works in Japan. If the magazine makes a point of the fact that TV Asahi staff are not neutral we really have a problem. (TV Asahi, Chief Director, November 25th, 1997).

This, the Chief Director continues, is why the Tsubaki's statement (see chapter six) became such a problem. The incident became a discussion about politics, power and

---

[134] His sense of timing is an important asset in his skilful news casting.

[135] In my reception study a viewer, while watching NHK News Seven, said "Kume Hiroshi would have said something like…". Another stated that "Kume's comments are not always the greatest but it is always fun to match your own opinion against his" (Family interviews, November 11th, 1995). The study concludes that Kume Hiroshi is considered an important 'member of the family' in many homes. Even people who are critical of his style are curious to hear his opinion.

media. Everyone according to the Chief Director believes that the Japanese media has to be independent. That is the ideal. But for historical reasons the Japanese media is influenced by political power.

> You could say that *News Station* is leftist to a certain extent. But, I would not look at *News Station* in terms of left and right. *News Station* is typically anti-power. In politics you have the power of opposition. No matter whether the government is right or left this party is in opposition. The power of opposition in politics is not a party that actually wants to achieve something. It just wants to be against the power holders and always criticise something. This is the idea of *News Station*. (TV Asahi, Program Director B. October 27th, 1997)

According to the program director, the anti-power attitude can be frustrating at times in the sense that it is easy to find people's faults and to criticise. A similar concern was expressed by the anchor, who felt that criticism was an incorporated remedy at *News Station*, and it was now expected by its audiences. However, in the long run, she did not always find this critical spin productive.

> The one goal of *News Station* and the main way in which *News Station* distinguishes itself from other news media is by being against (*hagai suru*) the government. (TV Asahi, Female Anchor, November 25th, 1997)

The message of the program according to the female anchor is that the government is a ruling and suppressing authority. However, *News Station* shows that *Nagata-cho* (the area where the government buildings are situated) is not superior. The people are the sovereigns and the ones who hold power. In order to convey this message politicians from left to right are made fools of. This has been the production line concept from the beginning and it has become a habit to present the world this way. However, this attitude is not productive after a while. The female anchor believes that the *News Station* team needs to commit itself in certain issues and get ideas for improvement instead of just criticising.

> *News Station*s is a specialist (*tokui*) in destruction. We can split everything into pieces but we are not good at building up anything. It is not good to broadcast in this one-sided destructive and critical style. I personally do not like the destructive way and I would like to continue in a different path. Until today the program has had this destructive approach. It has got to change in the future. Times have changed and it is time to create instead of breaking down. It is difficult to change. The audience, too, is used to our style. They like the idea; destroy, destroy! (*kowasee, kowasee!*), which is very entertaining (laughs). We have a trustful relationship with our audience. So it is up to us to change our ways and do our work properly. (TV Asahi, Female Anchor, November 25th, 1997)

The long-term effect on audiences she finds problematic. If ordinary people only criticise political decisions and get in the habit of making a fool of politicians they lose faith and interest in politics. In a way *News Station* is responsible for this trend by exaggerating too much. The times in her view are changing. 'Earlier it was right be against the government and politicians under the assumption that in a democracy people need to be strong as voters. They need to be strong to keep the politicians down and get power in order to get ideas through'. However, she considers that these ideas of emancipation, which have Marxist overtones, have to emerge through ideas of construction rather than destruction.

Live, spontaneous broadcast by individuals

The reporting and production at *News Station* relies on the personality of individuals. This not only pertains to the front figures of the news casting but also to production staff behind the scenes.

> We do not generally have fixed criterion or a basic style of reporting at *News Station*. Each individual director makes his/her own programme. We do not even plan in how we are going to approach a report before we start. The reports carry each director's point of view and originality in them. (TV Asahi, Program Director A, June 12th, 1997)

The originality of news reports and the room for individual influence was also referred to by NHK staff. However, whereas the newsreading at NHK is prepared minutely, the presentation and commentary at *News Station* is up to the individual. According to the *News Station* staff the news presentation is not rehearsed.

> We do not rehearse beforehand. We all prepare our own contributions. Sometimes I also get the facts wrong. I apologise for this (laughing). But this is also one of the good sides of live transmission…(TV Asahi, Female Anchor, November 25th, 1997)

The female anchor at *News Station* prepares herself by consulting newspapers and watching TV news. She watches the news at noon and reads through all the national newspapers. The daytime is often busy with interviews and report making. When she arrives at the station late in the afternoon, she reads the papers again and watches several news programs.

> You have to keep in mind that we are not professional journalists (*puro*). I only have general knowledge about news. I have to be able to convey the point. The point is the key word. We have to have the ability to grasp the main content of the news. But we do not have to know the information in detail. That is what our journalists and program directors research. I just have to be generally informed and convey the points of news. (TV Asahi, Female Anchor, November 25th, 1997)

The ideas and opinions of *News Station* are formulated by its own staff. Kume Hiroshi and Komiya Etsuko are the opinion leaders. It is perceived as one of the basis concepts of *News Station* that it represents individual ideas and opinions. The general perception among the staff is that TV Asahi does not influence the ideology of *News Station*.

> I am not briefed to have certain opinions. I am not a spokesman for *News Station*. I am employed as myself. The opinions I state are mine personally. I do not state my opinions as a newscaster. Through my job as a caster I get to voice my personal opinion. Actually, I do not have chances often enough to give my opinion (laughs). (TV Asahi, Female Anchor, November 25th, 1997)

Although ideology is not perceived as imposed on the staff, it is as described above difficult to break from its influence not least due to the perceived expectations of the audiences.

The preparation of the commentator who has been with the Asahi newspaper for many years as a writer of editorials and leaders includes attending numerous meetings at the newspaper in order to stay informed. He starts writing editorials based on different arguments. He makes his own decision about commentary by a 'sense of news' as defined above.

> *News Station* does not have a systematic way of preparing or briefing the staff. Not the people on the air anyway. For people outside it may look like this but we don't. Kume is usually the one who sets the atmosphere. He is the front figure. The members of the news team basically make their own preparations. Possibly these dynamics are what makes the program interesting (TV Asahi, Commentator, August 21st, 1997)

News Station is not staged or pre-rehearsed which is an ideal way of making a program according to the participants. Though it has its pluses and minuses. An obvious advantage according to the commentator is the fact that the staff is free to voice its opinions. In the newspaper work at Asahi, the commentator is obliged to listens to the opinion of 30-40 people at the editorial meetings. By considers the different angles and the opinions of everyone 'everything ends up rather neutral' (TV Asahi, Commentator, August 21st, 1997). It is an important and positive point according to the commentator that *News Station* leaves the presentation up to its employees. And that it is 'live'. Once comments are on the air they are irrevocable. There are no chances of editing or cutting sequences, which editors do not find appropriate. The live presentation of *News Station* is risky at times but the excitement makes it interesting. (TV Asahi, Commentator, august 21st, 1997)

In some situations, the live approach is problematic. Especially when it leads to strong audience reactions:

> Under the cabinet of Prime Minister Hosokawa, I really had the intention of rocking the boat in Japan. In Japan the voting age is 20, compared to 18 in most countries. In France the voting age is even down to 17. I had pondered for a long time how to bring this up. Kume agreed to bring up the issue and during a discussion about young people and politics I suggested to bring down the voting age. Kume supported the argument by suggesting that we could lower the voting age at the other end, by limiting the number of the older generation in return for votes from younger people. This caused a telephone storm. Thousands and thousands of older viewers called in to complain. (Laughs). (TV Asahi, Commentator, August 21st, 1997)

The commentator only intended his idea to be a joke but the effect was quite serious judged by audience responses. At NHK the audience reaction to 'out of line' reporting was likewise expressed as a major concern. Whether this is to be interpreted as an expression of an empowered and active Japanese audience is difficult to estimate.

The commentator brings ideas from the editorial meetings at the Asahi newspaper to the evening news program. He verifies information about current events through political journalists directly involved with the issue. In order to make proper commentary, the use of different sources contributes to an overview of events. The commentator consults with Asahi newspaper colleagues and follows other media reports in order to make the right judgements. The fact that the newspapers are divided in their opinions (as described in chapter six) provides a differentiated political view. Insights into opposing arguments help the commentator interpret events. In the case of international news the commentator is an expert and authority because of his long-term stay and many connections in Europe (see elaborate exemplification of personal strategies in the following chapter).

Sponsor considerations

Although NHK is concerned with ratings, its income depends on licence fees and not commercials. The commercial stations have more direct pressure to please their client sponsors.

Some of the senior journalists at TV Asahi expressed a wish to replace the current emphasis on entertainment aspects with the high professional journalistic standards they encountered at NHK.

> Sometimes I would like to work for NHK or the Asahi Newspaper. The newspaper reports straight news, but our conditions as a commercial network are totally based on high audience ratings in order to sell commercials and secure the budget. When we have our budget set we can start concentrating on news presentations. These are the conditions of commercial stations. (TV Asahi, Chief Director)

From the time when the TV Asahi management was convinced that news programs could get high ratings, *News Station* was allocated a large budget, the biggest ever for a news program.

News programs late at night, in the early mornings and evenings do not make good commercial turnover. However, the prime time programs from seven to eleven o'clock in the evening bring in enormous amounts of money from commercials.[136] The employees, although having to negotiate budgets in their proposals, found that money was not an obstacle in their assignments. *News Station* in this respect has been a major 'cash cow' and the feature stories and documentaries of *News Station* are accordingly allocated resources, which enable thorough reporting.

Only a few news producers saw the responsibility to sponsors and the commodification of news as a constraint in news production. They belong to the elder generation of journalists who were trained before the introduction of *News Station* and adhere to the traditional journalistic ideals employed at NHK. They watch the marketisation of news with scepticism. The female anchor does not feel restricted by sponsor considerations in her daily work. She pays attention to what she imagines her audience wants to know before she considers how sponsors would react.[137] Most news

---

[136] 'The importance and influence of sponsors in the market driven commercial stations is not to be underestimates'. (Press Club Member, August 11th, 1997)

[137] The only taboo at *News Station* (and in the media in general) is criticism of the Royal family. The only means to criticise the Imperial House is by not broadcasting anything (*mushi suru*). Social control in this respect is considerable. The right wing (*uyoku*) has its own measures concerning issues that are taboo.

producers did not reflect on the sponsor influence on programs; these strategies were made at management level.

The quantitative analysis of news presentations (appendix 1) bears witness to extensive coverage of popular themes related to the UN Women's conference in the *News Station* program. The lengthy coverage of women's issues is concluded with commercials by the cosmetics company, *Shiseido* (See appendix 7). The perceived audience interest in certain issues and enhanced sponsor interests in placing advertising following popular news segments may influence the selection of news items. This may hinder the investigative role of the news media in business and economic sector issues. Secondly, 'interesting' themes and presentation forms may highlight entertainment and neglect information about political processes. In a more positive light (as concluded in Chapter Four) the commodification of news in some cases encourages the coverage of are as outside the hard news criteria of political and economic news. In the present study, women's issues are covered extensively by the commercial stations, while it is covered as straight news at NHK. It deserves mention that NHK did make extensive programs about the UN Women's Conference. However, these were broadcast by the education TV channel, which is seen by a small segment of the population and not by the general public as is NHK *News Seven* program, which has national impact.

International news values

From the perspective of news producers who strive to produce news with and international perspective the efforts to 'domesticate' and produce 'proximate' international news is problematic. As observed in the present study (and this is not exceptional to Japan) domestic news is prioritised above international news in the newsrooms (Gans, 1980; Helland, 1993, Hjarvard, 1995a). The following sections discuss international news values and trends in the selection of international news themes.

> *News Station* is becoming more and more domestic. It is unbelievable. For instance, when huge things recently happened in Zaire, Congo, only in the very last minute, did they decided to cover it. From an international perspective, the ranking in their top news place very minor domestic subjects way before big international news. So my frustration often is that it is extremely domestic. But of course when something really big in the world happens they cover it. (TV Asahi, Program Director C, June 26th, 1997)

The program director, who is experienced at working at the incoming desk, describes three important guidelines in her selection of international news.

> When we choose a news topic, the distance may be of higher priority than the seriousness of the incident. If a news item is from abroad, we decide whether it is in the interest of Japanese viewers or not: Suppose there was a riot in Africa which

---

When the president of TV Asahi announced that the Emperor had cancer before his death in 1989, he was threatened. Warnings are allegedly given to foreign journalists who bring up critical issues. The audio-visual presence of the right wing activist in the public domain is overwhelming. As an example, political demonstrations demand attention when hundreds of black trucks with full extension loudspeakers drive through the streets of Tokyo. Affiliated motorbike groups race the roads in Tokyo neighbourhoods late at night with roaring engines.

killed 100 people and there was a riot in Korea, but it was not as serious as the one in Africa. We may spare 10 seconds on the one in Africa, but we may report the incidence from the actual scene in Korea. Secondly, it is difficult to make TV news without visual images. Thirdly, important news does not necessarily mean interesting. Political and economic news is very important and has to be reported even though it is both complicated to report and to understand. I strive to achieve some kind of balance between hard and soft news. (TV Asahi, Program Director C, June 26th, 1997)

Her criteria for selecting stories resemble the classic criteria for international news: Proximity, Japanese involvement and good visuals. Further, in her selection of news she tries to keep a balance between soft and hard themes. In her opinion, political and economic news is not very interesting but a necessary ingredient in the formula. She represents the younger generation's consumer driven or more 'female'[138] entertainment approach, which emphasises human-interest stories. A strong group of her colleagues still adheres to the old school of journalism, which prioritises hard core economic and political news themes.

The newsworthiness of accidents, natural disasters and war is judged according to a measurement of the number of deaths of one race against the number of deaths of another. This estimate or what may be referred to as 'calculated value of life against viewer rating' is connected to the thesis of proximity i.e. perceived feelings of closeness towards the victims by national audiences. The interview transcripts present numerous examples of this estimate, which resemble the above calculation. Although this sense of newsworthiness is universal and exemplified in many studies (Paterson, 1998), it represents a rather morbid side of decision-making in news production.

Timely, proximate and interesting

The special assignments (*kikaku mono*) are planned at a weekly documentary meeting. At these meetings it is evaluated whether a news story is 'timely', that is, in tune with current happenings and whether it is 'proximate', i.e. has something to do with Japan. 'Interesting' is an important criterion but it does not suffice in the assignment proposals unless the other criteria are included. Besides, the definition of interesting has many nuances, according to a program director. The program director is Swiss and the only foreign full time member of staff (*senshain*) in Japanese broadcast media. As a foreigner, his understanding of the word often differs from the general consensus.

My proposal for the Swiss program was just on the border (*girigiri*). But it passed because Switzerland is Japan's dream country. Denmark would not be a place where you could dig up news. It is simply too far away from Japan and not even in the category *interesting.* At the planning meeting you can present your own idea and usually it is accepted. Sometimes you are assigned a shoot. (TV Asahi, Program Director C, June 26th, 1997).

---

[138] The 'female' view is based on the 1995 reception analysis, noted above where it was found that most women in the 10 families did not recollect much actual information from the international news stories. However, in their account they recollected emotions perceived during the news presentations. More 'human approach' not so much 'business' and 'politicians dressed in suits' stories were requested. (Clausen, 1996)

Contrary to the belief of the Swiss program director, and as shown on several occasions throughout the book, news may be 'dug up' from any part of the world. A story from Greenland (Under the Royal protection of Denmark) among others (see above) was covered by an NHK journalist. The story was not 'timely' according to the agenda of the international agencies at this time but it was made 'interesting' through processes of 'domestication': a connection was drawn from the problems of self-government of Greenland to the sensitive problem of the Japanese Northern Territories.

The definition of an 'interesting' story was not immediately expressible in words according to the program director.

> When you ask me, what I look for you put me in great trouble because I am not a journalist. When I pick a subject I sit down by the database and pick a place where I would like to do a push 'search'. I sometimes *find* a scoop. It does not always work like that but many stories initially happen that way. (TV Asahi, Program Director B, October 27th, 1997).

In the experience of the director, many news topics are initiated through personal networks around the world. The program director has 'found good ideas' for documentaries by knowing people and getting hints from them. The Internet is another resource. Ideas may come from anywhere and he is allowed to do anything he wants. The only and most important guiding principle in news work at *News Station* is that 'the facts have to be correct'.

> Sometimes, I do assignments that are very *timely* like the Nuclear Testing and I did a story on what the people expected from their government. I try to do everything. I decide the perspective of the news. I do the editing by myself. I have an editor who does the technical part but I make the decisions. I write the voice over. I speak it myself. I do it all by myself. I do the subtitles by myself. It is very exciting and fulfilling but it is unbelievably time-consuming. (TV Asahi, Program director C, June 26th, 1997)

Two points stand out in the account. Firstly, news is 'found' and 'picked' which provides evidence that world events are not inherently news but can become so through processing. The notion of 'getting the facts right' bears witness to the positivist view of the world which characterises the view of most journalists. Most news producers, like the program director, envision news as a window on the world rather than a social construction of professionally processed information. Secondly, the fact that he perceives the production of news as an individual accomplishment is interesting. The fact is that he relies on advice through the entire process from the producer that accepts his proposals to the production team that accompanies him on location, to the interaction with interviewees to the co-commentary with colleagues in the final presentation. Most news producers describe the production of news as involving many different actors and factors. However, everyone describes his or her contribution to the process with a point of departure in their own experience, which gives meaning to their 'strips' of experience and places their perceptions of events as prior to others (Goffman, 1986).

The Swiss Director is a former novelist and one of his skills, he asserts, is that he 'knows how to pick a good story'.

180

Feature stories

The production and length of feature stories (often more than 10 minutes) is one of the main characteristics of *News Station*. The following exemplifies the production of international feature stories. It shows, in particular, how it is 'domesticated' and framed according to preconceived ideas. Further, it exemplifies how the 'domestication' of stories is made possible through the elaborate budget of *News Station*.

According to the program director, the assignments to make feature stories may last for several months. The following illustrates that although the staff enters news production with a 'grounded' approach and intention to make news as it presents itself, preconceived ideas and models for adequate mediation of material as news influences the framing process.

An assignment about the Swiss bank secret system became a 13-minute feature story. Forty tapes of 20 minutes were shot for the story. The story production was based on the statements of interviewees. All tapes were transcribed and the visuals studied again and again. However, although the story was documented and developed through interviews, only the material that fit into ideas about what 'makes a good story' was chosen. Material that did not fit the prescribed formula was left out.

> I try not to think about what I am going for, when I interview. If you want a certain comment from a person, you try to bring the discussion back every time, he says something. Often they have something unexpected and those are often the best lines. But it takes a lot of tape rolling. And tape rolling means that you are going to spend a lot of time by yourself writing it out. (TV Asahi, Program Director C, June 26th, 1997)

The program director made a four-hour interview with a Swiss man, whom he refers to as a 'cliché of the May 1968 leftist'. However, although the interview was continued for several days and although the interviewee was 'good', he was too emotional and did 'not appeal to our journalistic goals'. In other words, although the program director went into the reporting with what he refers to as an 'open mind' the final materials were selected from a 'secure sense of what was fit'. The interviewee did not perform according to preconceived ideas and eventually his statements were not broadcast. The generous budget allowed for extensive research and interviews across borders. Much of the material was not put to use and the work process illustrates (in cognitive terms) the vast amount of knowledge necessary in order to make simple news claims.

> The only limitations, I feel at *News Station*, is that it is always very superficial. If I had shown the Swiss documentary in Switzerland people would have laughed because it was just the surface. There are so many aspects behind what I did. And I filmed so much. I could do a two-hour program about how the international Jewish community is working behind that, the problem of Jewish assets in Swiss banks, how the Swiss banks try to protect the Swiss banking secrecy system and why it is like that. There are so many aspects. (TV Asahi, Program Director C, June 26th, 1997)

Besides the fact that the subject is covered superficially in his view, he also finds that a lot of material is wasted. With the same material Swiss television would have allotted him several hours of broadcast time. CNN by comparison would allow for just a few lines.

> I have unlimited, incredible budgets to go and shoot. For instance, if I worked for Swiss TV, I could never go to Poland or Israel to do a few stand-ups. Never. I would get an hour or even an hour and a half of airing time. But for *News Station*, I have unlimited resources but very little time. So my only limitations are not a limitation of content but a limit of time. I have 15 minutes at the most. I worked with CNN. CNN is even worse. The announcer will just announce that 'this is a very difficult problem'. That is it. So it is really the essential. Everything I said in the news program was true but for a Swiss person, it is also true that the Swiss government is doing a lot to make amends for the past. They created humanitarian funds. They created a historical research committee. In a Swiss news program you would talk about this too but it does not fit in a Japanese program. So preparing a feature story is always a mixture of frustration and excitement. (TV Asahi, Program Director B, October 27th, 1997).

Many of his colleagues, who have been stationed abroad, share the dilemma of wanting to share more than just the tip of the iceberg of their knowledge of local cultures. The Swiss program director is even allocated a generous amount of time when doing special assignments compared with the short straight news stories. While the presentation of feature stories as exemplified above is not agenda-set by the international news agencies, it enhances the difference in news mix at the national stations.

The following elaborates on the interpersonal communication of information between staff with different experiences and levels of knowledge about foreign affairs.

Communication between Tokyo and overseas staff

While NHK merely have area specialists and news experts in their desk positions, the New Stations desk personnel as described above are generalists. The news producers assigned to the 'gates' for incoming news at the two national stations thus differ in professional expertise. Some news producers see the knowledge gap between foreign correspondents (who are mainly expert at both stations) and the Tokyo office as a challenge; others describe it as a hurdle.

The depth of local knowledge of well-integrated correspondents abroad is, by some news producers, considered problematic, especially if the desk is not equally acquainted with foreign matters in general or their area of expertise. In reverse cases as described by a program director, 'the correspondent loses touch with the visions of the Tokyo office'.

> It is sometimes difficult to see the seriousness of an incident if we do not know the background of it. There are occasions where a correspondent sends me a news topic, which he thinks is newsworthy, but I do not think so. But more often the case is that the correspondent cannot see things we find interesting, as s/he is so used to living in that particular country. (TV Asahi, Program Director A, June 12th, 1997)

The situation is described by a foreign correspondent as a double dilemma between on one hand becoming integrated in the new surroundings and on the other of keeping in touch with the home office. While trying to become integrated locally, the correspondent, who was stationed in European countries for 16 years, returned to Japan every year in order to stay in touch with Japanese issues. He also made an effort to listen to the radio, watch Japanese TV, read newspapers and weekly magazines. Staying in touch was important professionally, however, the effort to stay close to Japanese happenings he felt may have taken energy from becoming integrated locally.[139]

The initiation to cover events differs. The desk in the foreign news department (*gaihoobu*) may initiate assignment for coverage. Alternatively, foreign correspondents may suggest a piece of news to the foreign news department desk. Correspondents have to get permission from the Tokyo desk, as coverage is ultimately a financial decision. If expenses to produce a story are high, the international news desk gets the director of a particular programme to approve proceedings. A proposal has to be accepted in the schedule before it is pursued[140]. The costs of special assignments are considerable because they require a production team of 3-4 people.

In the production of straight news of 1-2 minutes, visuals from news agencies are often used. But if news is of great concern to Japan, the foreign correspondents produce their own visuals. The final editing of straight news takes place in Tokyo. The foreign correspondent instructs the director in Tokyo about editing. According to the European Correspondent, it quite often happens that the editor in Tokyo re-arranges the material. The length of a story is almost always negotiated before the reporting starts but the editing is negotiated until the story is on air. The communication between the Tokyo desk and the overseas staff is a challenge. The notion of trust was mentioned as a bridge between information gaps. In cases where information did not transfer successfully across continents, the desk would base decisions on earlier experience and rapport with the correspondent. Stories by experienced foreign correspondents easily pass the Tokyo 'gate-keeper'. In such cases, trust in expertise and experience bridges over gaps of knowledge between communicators.

Familiarising information through the use of cultural clichés

The communication of complex information is a challenge in interaction with colleagues as it is a challenge in interaction with audiences as imagined in the composition of news. The barrier of 'not knowing what other people know, and wondering how to present what you know so that they will understand it' is a major challenge in news production, according to the Swiss program director. The assumptions and guesses about the imagined audience are even more difficult for a foreigner, he asserts.

According to the program director, the broadcast medium is limiting proper presentation and the use of cultural stereotypes in the visual and verbal expression a necessity. The broad focus on a general mass audience in his view makes news superficial. However, the dominating strategy in news making is business considerations and news producers make an effort to give audiences what they want.

---

[139] TV Asahi now has a rule that correspondents have to return to Tokyo after two years of overseas activity.

[140] It is costly to send news via wire. The use of Aircard is the least expensive. For ten minutes it costs 1,000, 000 yen, but because of technological developments it now cost 100,000 yen for the same transmission. (TV Asahi, European Correspondent)

> Actually I do not picture the audience. My stories, except for the outdoor stories or
> the sport stories, are a bit intellectual. It is difficult because on the one hand this is
> more than enough information for these people [the audience]. On the other hand
> there are people who are very, very sharp and you should not talk down to them
> (*namechaikinai*). (TV Asahi, Program Director C, June 26th, 1997).

The 'intellectual' image of the productions of the program director was also held by co-workers. Nevertheless, the strategies behind his presentations included considerations of the general audience as exemplificd in the production feature story concerning the Swiss secret bank system. The program director perceived a gap between the investigated story and the knowledge level of the general audience. He tried to make a balanced report between what he perceived as ideal and the fact that some people did not know anything about the issue. He started the report on top of the Jungfrau Mountain. This was only one of many visuals and verbal 'clichés' or national stereotypes employed to make the story comprehensible and interesting. The use of well- known stereotypes or metaphors is an important tool in framing (Fairhurst and Sarr, 1996).

One of the biggest communicative dilemmas and greatest personal insights in the 'business of making television' according to the program director was that 'you should never take for granted that people know what you know' (TV Asahi, Program Director C, June 26th, 1997). While this statement is very banal it exemplifies the very challenge of communicative action. The program director found it difficult to present facts that were very obvious (redundant) to insiders but new(s) to the audience.

Skilful 'domesticators'

One of the roles of news professionals as argued throughout this book is to mediate and familiarise complicated information to audiences. The skills of priming are mastered exceptionally well by Kume Hiroshi, the anchor of *News Station*. International information at *News Station* is mediated through his particular way of familiarising and 'domesticating' news information. As a provider of idiosyncratic interpretations of complex international information, Kume and the other anchors and the commentator provide their audiences with interpretations of international affairs.

The charismatic anchor, Kume Hiroshi is exceptionally good at 'priming' information. In the terms of Goffman, Kume Hiroshi is able to say something at a given moment better than could later be thought up (Goffman, 1986). The ability to prime is particularly valuable in news production, where conditions are to communicate contextualised information under time pressure.

Kume was on holiday during the recorded news in 1995, and consequently did not feature as the *News Station* anchor in the 'global' news material. Nevertheless, he is a central figure in many of the interviewees' accounts and reportedly an important consideration in the preparation of news. Many of his co-workers imagine what his response and commentary would be while preparing a story. Some of Kume's biggest assets, besides his wit, are explained by the program director as his 'sense of timing' and the 'ability to express the essence of a story', which are two important elements in the notion of priming. The following exemplifies this.

According to the program director, he gets so involved with a story and its details that he forgets the original perspective. The bottom line of the Swiss story, as an example, was the abstract notion that 'neutrality is a legal concept'. The program director has the ambition to explain 'neutrality' in detail to the Japanese although it is a complex issue even for European viewers.

> We are in the middle of the news commentary and have to provide a minimum of information. 10 seconds are left to communicate the most important point and what do you do? 'Sensote nan demo ari'. "In a war rules don't count"!, Kume said. And that is the bottom line. In two seconds, he can think of something to say. His brain works speedily. We could have unfolded the discussion about Copernicus and the concept of neutrality in the 1700 hundred. But the reality is that when war happens, people try to survive and do terrible things. Kume is a genius in some ways. He is so fast it is scary. Every time I do a story, I get very involved emotionally. I get attached and totally absorbed in it. And when I am on the set it never fails. Kume always comes up with one sentence like that. (TV Asahi, Program Director B, October 27th, 1997)

Another example is Kume Hiroshi's sense of time.

> If Kume is asked to say something in 23 seconds he talks for 23 seconds. He has a clock in his head. On air I was so nervous that I just kept talking. When the commercial came on Kume said 'You were five seconds over'. I went home and I timed it. It was five seconds over time. It is unbelievable. (TV Asahi, Program Director C, June 26th, 1997)

While Kume Hiroshi was described as an important opinion leader by media experts in chapter six, his intelligence in sensing time is mentioned by colleagues as a great advantage in this chapter. Many news producers referred to the charismatic personality and special skills of Kume Hiroshi.

Conclusively, the fact that international news is produced around and through the subjective commentary of Kume Hiroshi makes global news content and its audience effects of *News Station* programs differ from other national news programs. His ways of priming and framing news for domestic audiences is unique.

A summary of TV Asahi's organisational characteristics

The chapter describes the working processes of news making. *News Station* is a privileged program within TV Asahi. It has it own production staff and is able to draw on the capacities of the foreign news department and its own correspondent abroad. Besides the fact that *News Station* is a commercial success and a major 'cash cow', it is also the flagship program of TV Asahi. It is important for the image and reputation of the Asahi Corporation. *News Station* was a pioneer program and many of its ideas are news: interaction between newsreaders and anchors, commercials, longer news sequences; and the other commercial stations have adapted the use of props. International feature stories are costly and in that respect *News Station* is ahead of other commercial stations with large sums of money to invest in producing the program. Other private stations rely more on agency material, as they do not have the means to make elaborate coverage and feature stories.

The awareness of the entertainment value of news is integrated in the strategies of news production at *News Station*. While the *News Station* program provides much straight news in the traditional journalistic style, the dominating strategy of the program is to gain viewer shares and thereby attract sponsors.

The core decision-making is centred around a few people and based on the personality traits of individuals. Under the 'group of five' in the top of the hierarchy there are many positions and *ad hoc* groups who support the production. The chapter describes the negotiation between staff to prepare the 'spontaneous interaction' between the news events. Without pre-rehearsing scripted lines, the inputs are previewed and information is exchanged. The anchors and commentaries are central figures in deciding or influencing the way news is put forth and presented to its viewers. The master of ceremony, Kume Hiroshi, has a special skill in time and communication management, which is considered by other staff in their preparation of stories.

In an effort to make news understandable, a big responsibility of anchors and commentators is to communicate economic and political issues in an easily understandable manner. It is an explicit strategy to bridge the gap between the complexity of political processes and the everyday life of the viewers. Being non-experts and free from the professional limitations of journalists, the role of the anchors is to interpret information from the point of view of their viewers. Props are often used to illustrate economic and political news events.

The analysis of production procedures describes the challenges of communication between journalists with different country expertise, and the challenge of communicating in-depth knowledge to large audiences in general terms. The employment of a foreigner in the production of news adds an international perspective in the newsroom. The internationalisation efforts of TV Asahi have consequently provided *News Station* with a view on international affairs that differs from the gate-keeping criteria of native employees. The analysis of statements by the foreign news producer provided insights about framing and domestication processes that were implicit in the statements of his Japanese colleagues.

Many of the news producers at TV Asahi are not educated or trained as journalists in the traditional sense. Rather, authority is given to generalists who understand the concept of *News Station*. While some senior news producers in the foreign news department adhered to traditional 'hard' news criteria, the younger generalist who take turns in co-ordinating the desk positions at *News Station* represents a 'soft' line of news with an emphasis on human interest stories, entertainment and instant gratification appeals. *Timely, proximate* and *interesting* are criteria for news selection, while national metaphors (stereotypes) recognisable by many guide the mediation of international information.

It is described in the chapter that the main challenge for international correspondents is to simplify vast resources of knowledge while staying in tune with Japanese trends. The working process is a continuous negotiation between *selecting what is interesting, or alternatively, making what is selected interesting.*

The basic attitude of *News Station* is anti-establishment. Whenever there is a chance, the news turns into criticism of the Japanese government. This angle is strengthened by the courage of the anchors to speak up and voice their opinions. The critical attitude and the comments of Kume, Komiya and the commentators have become a natural part of the production formula and an ingredient expected by the audiences. The critical and anti-establishment attitude is ingrained in the production strategies and news output is greatly influenced by this formula. The anti-establishment attitude has become the *raison d'être* of *News Station*. But according to some news producers a less 'destructive' attitude would be a welcome challenge. Critical commentary with 'constructive' suggestions symbolises this challenge. However, it is believed that it is difficult to change the critical style, as a new approach would confuse audiences.

News Station produces news for everyone but the staff envisions younger viewers for its sports section and *salarymen and women* (company employees) who have incorporated viewing into their schedule when they return home from work or from drinking late in the evening.

The above social processes together create a certain *formula* (practices and strategies) for the production of *News Station*.

Conclusion

In conclusion the display sums up the differences in organisational styles at the two stations: It shows the basic elements in international news production strategies and decision-making processes based on observation in the newsrooms and the perceptions of news production by staff at the two stations. It was concluded in Chapter four that NHK news may be characterised as factual (information intensive), while the news of TV-Asahi is more emotional (info-tainment) style. The analysis of the Japanese media environment at the national level showed that NHK supplies economic and political 'news' while TV-Asahi supplies economic and political 'views'. The analysis in this chapter highlights some of the differences in organisational factors that influence the content and style in the international news presentations.

The business foundation of the two stations was found to impact production strategies in important ways. The fact that NHK is financed by public fees turns the focus of NHK news mediation onto political processes and public interest concerns. The fact that *News Station* in the original set-up was conceptualised as a money-spinning program based on commercial income influences the overall strategies of the program (See previous chapter). Where NHK *News Seven* is produced by the NHK News Centre, which supplies international news to all NHK programs, *News Station* is an independent production unit.

Where *News Seven* production staff members are regular NHK employees, *News Station* staff includes personalities from the TV Asahi Broadcasting Company as well as independent production companies. The NHK News Seven news producers are specialists, while the *News Station* news producers are generalists. The news producers at NHK are responsible for several news programs, while *News Station* has its own production crew. The role of authority in the production hierarchy differs according to the organisational structure at the two stations. The focus on a few individuals and their personalities is reflected in the preparation and arrangement of *News Station*. The integrity and objectivity of the newsreader at NHK symbolises credibility.

The members of the international newsroom at NHK are educated as journalists within the company as opposed to the variety of backgrounds of the production team at the commercial station. This has important consequences for the framing of issues, as the transmission process at NHK is influenced by the priority of traditional journalistic news values. News values at NHK may, in short, be characterised as traditional, conventional and reliable. The production practices involve preparations to present 'objective' news from a system perspective. The *News Station* criteria are proximate, interesting and instantly gratifying. The production practices prepare subjective, people oriented and anti-establishment news.

Figure 15: News Production Strategies

	NHK *News Seven*	**TV Asahi** *News Station*
Business foundation	License fees Public	Commercials Private
Newsroom practices	Part of company production flow Specialised journalists Expertise focus Consensus NHK employees Rehearsed	Independent unit Generalists Personality focus Individual TV Asahi employees *and* Production company staff 'Spontaneous'
News values	Traditional, conventional and reliable Knowledge accumulation Objective, factual System oriented Information intensive, complex	Timely, proximate and interesting Instant gratification Subjective, interpretative People oriented Easily understandable (14 year olds)
Audience Considerations	General public Educated older viewers Farming population Public interest concern	General public Younger viewers *Salarymen* and women Sponsor concern
Political views	Maintain status quo Pro-government Neutral	Change Anti-establishment Liberal
International news agency influence	Agenda setting Own visuals preferred	Agenda setting Own visuals preferred

The world-views of the journalists at NHK are connected to their area of expertise. Many news producers acquire a general overview and flair for news production over time, but the level of the international news coverage at NHK requires in-depth knowledge of an area. The NHK news producers have a high level of expertise. Although an audience perspective is supposedly incorporated into the journalistic 'sense' of what makes information fit as news, the final news presentation is a product of high professional standards with descriptions of political processes. The diversity and generalist background of production staff at *News Station*, the mix of straight news and longer feature stories although based on the same journalistic standards results in more popular presentations and choice of issues. The models for news production as reflected in the production practices, reveal the different mental strategies of the staff at the two stations. The mental models and scripts for news production differed concerning newsroom practices, editorial decision-making, news values and audience aims.

Concerning the ability to adapt abroad, the journalists were operating between a spectrum of total integration in the local society to short term use of already established formal channels through the Japanese business and local diplomatic enclaves. The production of international news depends on the human resources i.e. the information mediation ability and knowledge of the news workers. Their personal experience and judgement in news is the very core of news production. In principle, news can be made from anywhere in the world. The ability of the stations to make their own reports when possible makes the stations less dependent on the agenda setting and materials of the international agencies than their competitors. The financial capacity of both stations enhances the means to frame news for a national audience. Accordingly, the degree of 'domestication' at the two stations is high.

Conclusively, the difference in production practices and models for news framing differed greatly at the two stations. Against the notion of homogenisation of information through 'global' news transmission, the processes of information at the two stations show that news events even within the same country are 'domesticated' differently with different political content, appeals and audience aims.

The above focuses on general production procedures, decision-making hierarchies as they influence strategies for news production within organisational structures at a public service and a private station. It is concerned with production processes from an *organisational* perspective. In contrast to these organisational factors of influence, the following chapter focuses on the implementation of strategies of individual news producers in action at the *professional* level. While the present chapter focuses on general organisational practices, the following chapter analyses the professional considerations in the production of a specific piece of 'global' news, namely the UN Conference on Women in Beijing.

Chapter Seven

Professional Strategies

Reporters have special "glasses" through which they see certain things and not others, and through which they see the things they see in the special way they see them. (Bourdieu, 1998a: 19)

There is no set way to make news. News is chosen experience and a sense for news (*kan*). With regard to international news it is chosen with the Japanese in mind. (TBS, Director of Political News, July 11th, 1997)

Introduction

The present chapter is an analysis of the *professional* aspects of news production. It is assumed that the media environment and organisational characteristics described in previous chapter are incorporated and in play in the production of specific news. The present chapter is thus an analysis of how news producers 'see things' and how their special way of seeing things as part of their national and organisational background influences their framing of news. Their outlook is influenced by previous experience and models for professional action. It is also influenced by personal motivation and values.

The event in focus is the government meetings of the UN Conference on Women in Bejing from September 4-8, 1995. While Chapter Four provided specific examples of strategies of domestication in the framing of this 'global' news through content analysis, the ensuing chapters provided insights about the influence of extra-media and organisational factors on news production. The present chapter is analyses the actual production of the particular news.

The chapter explores professional considerations and negotiation on location in the production of the above news. The journalistic professional aims against personal interests and efforts to 'domesticate' are of particular interest.

Professional strategies are defined in this chapter as norms, values and criteria for newsworthiness in the profession[141] of journalism. Hitherto the legitimisation and credibility of journalism has been sought through claims of a shared professional ideology of 'objectivity'. The notion of 'objectivity', I argue in Chapter Two, is however, a theoretical and empirical orthodoxy as it refers to a wide range of news interpretations. Consequently, 'subjective' new terms of journalist are needed to describe professional criteria particularly in commercial media organisations, where the commodification of news tends to include more subjective and emotional elements than the classical professional values allow for.

Personal values in this chapter refer to individual strategies of the actors influenced by the interests, opinions and motivations of the news producers. The professional norms and values of the news organisations tend at times to conflict with personal intentions, as exemplified in the chapter.

The analysis is based on interviews, made in 1997, with news producers at NHK and TV Asahi including foreign correspondents, reporters, producers, executive management staff, editors, commentators and anchors. (See organisational charts in previous chapter).

---

[141] In "The Sociology of the Professions" Keith M. MacDonald (1995) describes the professional norms and ethics for doctors and lawyers. Although journalism is not one of these established professions it has it own values and claims of professionalism.

192

The chapter provides an analysis of the social processes in international news production as experienced by individual news producers in their professional environment. It is an analysis of the process of framing at the individual level with an emphasis for the efforts to 'domesticate' information to local audiences. The analysis involves four elements of investigation, as described in the cognitive framework in Chapter Two. Firstly, the chapter explorers the negotiation of professional values of the organisation against personal intentions and knowledge domains in the planning process. Knowledge domains and schemes of knowledge of individuals are analysed against the professional values and production formulae of the organisations, as described in the previous chapter. Secondly, it investigates the processes of decision making and information negotiation in order to cast light on hierarchical structures and responsibility attributed to roles and positions in the organisation. Thirdly, personal information processing, involving the measurement of preconceived ideas against perceptions of events on location, are investigated. Fourthly, the personal evaluations of strategies, from the planning of the event to the final coverage, are included as a measurement of strategies against the intended results.

As concluded in previous chapters, the framing process and the news output at the two stations differ. The allocation of resources to the coverage of the event due to the political and legal factors of the Japanese media environment and the business foundation of the media organisations differ. The public service station, as an example, covers the event for two days with two-minute reports while the commercial station makes daily reports for a week of up to 5 minutes a day. *The issue at the public station is treated as another 'straight' international piece of political news while the coverage at the commercial station is popularised with a much broader focus on popular themes concerning women's issues.* The implementation of the differing strategies at the public service and a commercial station are analysed below.

It is not within the realm of this project to review and make a sustained discussion of women's issues in Japan. The analysis in this chapter is concerned with *how* international news is produced rather than *why* it is produced like it is. Nevertheless, besides providing insights into the social processes and individual considerations in the production of the particular news, the interviews naturally provide insight about schemes of knowledge and attitudes towards the issue in focus. The chapter maps articulations of gender in media discourse and within media organisations. Issues specific to the Japanese socio-cultural context in a 'domestication' perspective were the Japanese government's intended implementation of 'gender politics' at the public service station and the issues of 'comfort women'[142] and the Japanese gender situation

---

[142] According to meeting protocol of the UN Commission on Human Rights in 1991, Japan had not provided compensation for its war-rape victims. As many as 200.000 girls and women were part of the Japanese programme of "comfort women" (*jugun ianfu*). More than half of these girls and women died as a direct result of the treatment they received. Many survivors were detained in the programme for 3-5 years. About 500 women have come forth for apology and compensation. The draft of women and their conditions became more violent as the war prolonged, leading to physical and mental illnesses. The first Japanese Prime Minister to make an apology, after the refusal of his predecessors, was Socialist leader Miyazawa. A 'private' fund was made for compensations but the contributions from corporate Japan were less than expected. Many Japanese right-wing organisations have been against Japanese apology and compensation. They claim that Japan was not responsible for the war and that human rights were denied to all under wartime conditions. They further claim that many women have been motivated for economic reasons (because of Japan's economic success) to come forth with demands for compensation (Hicks, 1995). The issue of comfort women has been debated fiercely in the Japanese public and the awareness of

in a global context at the commercial station. Issues that were not familiar to the Japanese public, as concluded in this chapter, were not made discursive in the Japanese media.

Mechanisms of 'domestication' are understood at the professional level of analysis as being implicit in the decision-making processes. They are implicit in the negotiation of meaning at the individual level in an attempt to familiarise information to imagined audiences. The process of domestication is implied in individual strategies from the initial planning phase to the actual organisation of 'strips' experience (Goffman, 1986:11) at the conference. The analysis of 'domestication' strategies in this book involves the global national, organisational and professional levels of influence. The 'domestication' process at the professional level includes an analysis of audience considerations in the framing process on location. The 'domestication' of information is an ongoing process initiated through stimulation of previously stored schemes of knowledge about events and activated in the moments of sense-making on location. In other words, events are perceived through pre-existing mental schemes acquired through cultural and professional experience. They are stored, negotiated, recalled and primed and mediated in a new context.

The verbalisations of production strategies at the two stations are analysed in turn. The observation and statements at NHK are analysed first. The following TV Asahi observations are accounted for in relation to the findings of work procedures at NHK. In conclusion, the professional values of the news producers against personal interest and knowledge are discussed.

I. NHK

In the NHK newsroom there were differing and contradictory opinions about the news value of the Women's conference. In light of its importance as the biggest UN world conference ever and considering the number of Japanese participants at the conference, which amounted to more than 5.000, the senior commentator found that the news was under-represented. The Beijing commentator, who was the reporter on location, found that the conference could have been covered better on its own terms by focussing more on women's issues than on the international political aspects of the conference. The producer of *News Seven* concluded that the report was sufficient based on NHK news criterion. And finally, the young female reporter[143] (the only female reporter in the

---

its importance in the consciousness of the Japanese audience was reflected in the expressions of the news producers at both NHK and TV Asahi.

[143] She was the only female reporter in the international news department during my three months of observation. Experience abroad and in the trusted sub-desk work signalled high status in the international department. At the beginning of the interview, the female reporter asserted that there was no difference in the working conditions and selection processes of men and women. She went to the convention in order to cover not only social issues but also to report on the political and economic implications of the conference. She was following the values of her male colleagues completely. Her strategy was to distance herself from the term 'feminism' in fear of the reactions if she had reported on the convention 'as if hysterical women gathered together and complained about how terrible men were'. Upon return from China, she was asked by many NGOs to report on her experience. She was made aware of a letter of critique (also send to NHK) of the Japanese media's scarce coverage by disappointed NGOs. In the light of the fact that the platform of action was to be implemented in Japan in 2000, she found in retrospect that it had been an obvious chance for the Japanese media to report on aspects and the estimated consequences of this gender equality plan.

194

international department during the observation period) thought the amount of coverage had improved compared with earlier coverage of women's issues. These different views on the newsworthiness of the event are accounted for in the following in order to estimate how they influence production processes and the final presentation.

Planning the UN Conference on Women

For NHK as a whole, the UN conference on women was a big event. The directors from the satellite department and the directors from the educational channels sent crews to Beijing. Every department had its separate strategy. Some female correspondents were stationed at the conference in order to cover the main events and themes such as Women's Rights and violence against women. However, the NHK flagship program, *News Seven*, which has been a focus of study in this project, merely included two pieces of news about the issue (see Chapter Four). According to the producer, the conference was not at first considered important among the editors in the news department. It was eventually decided to cover some aspects of it. The bureau in Beijing, which was under the supervision of the international news section, was engaged with camera staff, reporters and a director in charge. The reporter from the news bureau in China filed interviews on the scene and a female reporter was sent to China from the international news section in order to make reports.

> The two events that were covered for the *News Seven* program were accounts of the Japanese government's intentions concerning implementation of the Platform of Action for Equal Rights and the US criticism of the clash between human rights and the Chinese government. The issues were framed in a political and not particularly gender specific way. (NHK producer, August 23rd, 1997).

The recollection of the framing of the specific NHK news perfectly matches the frames found in the content analysis of this news in Chapter Four. As part of the preparation for the coverage in the international department, the female reporter went to the United States twice in order to cover campaigns related to the convention. Investigative reporting as in this case according to the female reporter required a lot of preparation and research before leaving Tokyo. Before the Women's convention, she went to Cambodia where she reported on a women's group that later participated in Beijing. The Cambodian women's group was favoured before the Japanese NGOs due to basic news criteria in the international department to convey information from abroad. A structural factor thus determined the coverage in this case. A report on the preparations of the Japanese NGOs would have been the responsibility of the domestic economic, political or social sections. Subsequently, no reports were filed about the 5.000 Japanese Women's preparation for the conference.

The female reporter filed ten reports while on location. None of these were part of the *News Seven* program. A story was filed about Japanese activities at the NGO Forum, which was broadcast in the morning news program. Time was given as a reason for the difficulty in making the seven o'clock news deadline. 'A part of the report had to be edited, before it was sent to Japan and it could not be done in time. Commuting from the NGO site to Beijing was time consuming and took almost two hours. That alone delayed many reports' (NHK, female reporter).

In the view of the senior commentator, the scope of the event alone should have been grounds for a proper presentation of the Beijing conference. The event gathered 50.000

people from around the globe, which in scale is one of the largest United Nations conferences ever. She made proposals for special presentations and special programmes about the matter. However, as she saw it, within NHK women, numbering less than ten per cent had very little opportunity to influence the plans. Further, she belonged to the commentators' room, which put her in a peripheral position to the decision-making process of the news department. The proposals that she made to the international news department were not accepted. She planned to take a vacation and pay out of her own pocket in order to follow the meeting in favour of the people in developing countries. At the last minute the satellite department stepped in and engaged her to cover the event. The situation was similar in 1994 for the UN Conference on Population and Development in Cairo. The procrastination, in her view indicated, the low priority of problems concerning the developing world and women's issues.

The NHK News Centre that produces *News Seven* made limited coverage of the women's conference according to the female reporter. However, considering the newsworthiness of the event, which was traditionally low for women's issues, she found that NHK did more than expected. In the past they would not have paid very much attention to this type of convention, but this time they treated it as important international news. The reason for the change in attitude she credited to an increase in the number of women in higher-level management positions. Contrary to the view of her female colleague and to the statistical evidence counting merely 2,2 per cent women in management positions at NHK, women in her view have become more noticeable.

The strategic planning in the international department thus involved different views. In retrospect, the producer found that the event was covered sufficiently according to NHK economic and political news values. The younger correspondent in Beijing expressed regrets that the event had not been covered more on its own premises, but it could not be helped because of his 'political spectacles'. The senior commentator, who was far from the decision-making process, found the UN event underrepresented in the main news programs. The young female correspondent, basing her evaluation on NHK professional news criteria, found that the event was covered sufficiently, even better than it would have been hitherto. As demonstrated above, the perceptions of women's issues differ not only according to gender but also according to age.

The following investigates the thoughts and intentions behind these views, or in cognitive terms the models and scripts drawn upon by the news producers in the production of the particular news.

A political perspective in mind

Economic and political news values are found in the interviews to be the guiding principles in the NHK coverage. A political framework was the basis for the professional strategies and the way in which the conference was perceived. Compared to the TV Asahi account below that focused on women's issues at the event, the NHK news producers expressed much knowledge about the conditions at the conference in relation to Chinese international affairs and China's international position. The NHK coverage of the event was presented in an international political framework, whereas the Asahi coverage more specifically concerned actors and events at the conference. The following elaborates upon the considerations at the conference.

The fact that the event was held in China influenced coverage in two important ways. The close but sensitive diplomatic relationship between Japan and China, to which I will return below, influenced the coverage of the event. The 'circumstances concerning the Chinese organisers' in the view of NHK staff took much attention away from the actual event but was nevertheless strongly felt by participants and professionals at the conference. Secondly, the diplomatic problems between the US and China over human rights guided the NHK's coverage and perspective of the conference, because of Japans close relationship to the United States.

'Equality, peace and development' were the main themes of the UN conference.

> On the second day the world witnessed how the concept of 'equal rights' was made interchangeable with 'human rights' through the influence of US first Lady Hilary Rodham Clinton's strong statement that women's right's are human rights. In a Western context from where these concepts and the political objectives derive there is a natural causal link between human rights and women's rights due to the considerable advancement of women's situation in equal rights questions. In third world countries and some developed countries where some human rights measures are not yet implemented according to Western standards and equal rights even less so, there is a vast gap between the meanings of these two concepts. (NHK, Correspondent in Beijing, August 23rd, 1997)

'Equal rights' was made a theme at NHK. It was adapted and covered in political rhetorical terms (see Chapter Four) with no specific reference to the UN definition of the concept, nor were the implications of this concept explained in a Japanese context. NHK instead took the opportunity to relate the issue of equal rights to women's position in Asia.

> Asian women's positions in the light of human rights are still not at the same level as other developed countries. Japan in this respect positions itself as a developed country. The conditions for human rights differ in each country. Equal rights of women are only partly incorporated in most Asian countries, in some respects this includes Japan. (NHK Correspondent in Beijing, August 23rd, 1997)

According to the Beijing correspondent, there were many reminders of the 'human rights' theme at the conference, especially because the action of the Chinese authorities in many ways went against it. The NHK correspondent in Beijing interpreted the situation in the following way. China is a growing economic power and its main concern is to be included as a big partner in international relations. The Chinese government is very conscious of its position in the international community. China has previously tried to host the Olympic Games, but did not manage to be chosen to hold the event, which is why it was even more important to make the United Nations Conference successful. The Chinese government thus had a strong desire to succeed, which was the underlying motivation for holding the conference. It was obvious that it was the first time for China to gather NGOs from all over the world, and the authorities wanted the conference to happen without any problems or negative happenings. In their great effort, however, they were less successful than anticipated. As one example, the government made a great effort to control human rights demonstrations in Beijing against the Chinese invasion in Tibet. The demonstrations were guarded and kept down as much as possible in order to prevent unforeseen chaos. The overall strategy of the Chinese was to keep the demonstrations against women's rights within the NGO camp and the NGO facilities were therefore moved to a small village outside of Beijing. This strategic measure, however, was 'very cautious planning' even seen from a Japanese standpoint. The Japanese standpoint here refers to the underlying NHK strategy not to criticise the Chinese arrangements. Even with this in mind, however, the move was seen as an unnecessarily cautious step.

According to the Beijing correspondent, the Japanese production team had great difficulties deciding how to report on the Chinese government's actions and on the event as a whole. The team had different alternatives. They could focus on the security strategy of the Chinese government, which would focus on plans of action if a problem should occur. Another angle was the reaction to the Chinese precautions by other countries. Finally, a plan was to make a report about the overall results of the conference in order to estimate whether it succeeded or not. These alternatives were concerned with issues related to Chinese organisational measures and not to the themes of the conference.

As the production team anticipated, the Chinese government was prepared for all kinds of happenings.

> The Chinese government was prepared for all kinds of groups to demonstrate against the Tibetan problem, human rights and the like. However, it was unprepared for the forcefulness and aggressiveness by which these human rights groups appealed for democracy in Tibet. Further, all participating countries made protest marches against the location of meeting places far outside of Beijing. The Chinese authorities were so eager to control the event that they considered it risky and unfortunate to let NGOs into the official conference. In the middle of Beijing the active NGOs would have a possibility to get in contact with ordinary Chinese citizens and the Chinese authorities were afraid that this impact would cause trouble. The chance that the Chinese citizens would start acting freely as a response to the NGOs could not be taken. (NHK Correspondent in Beijing, August 23rd, 1997)

The original plan was to include the NGO activities as part of the official conference in the middle of Beijing, but as noted above, the NGO forum was moved to a small village close to the Chinese Wall more than 55 kilometres away from the official Women's conference. This precaution, according to the senior commentator, contrasted with other international conferences she had attended where the official political meetings and the NGO forum are close to each other to enhance mutual lobbying and interaction.

According to the Beijing correspondent, the Chinese government was thus prepared for protests but was seemingly overwhelmed. It was a dilemma of on the one hand trying to make a successful event which would provide acceptance in the international community *vis-à-vis* improved diplomatic relations, and on the other hand trying not to reveal internal political problems. The government was confused about how to handle the situation. The reporter and mass communication staff could not help but focus on this clash between the NGO's fight for human rights on one side and the Chinese government's precautions on the other. Accordingly, the news presentations about the conference were not well balanced in the Japanese national broadcasts. This was not only a criticism of the Japanese media. Other foreign media also tended towards this one-sided coverage, according to the foreign correspondent.

In the senior commentator's view, the coverage of conditions in China was a true reflection of the turmoil at the conference.[144] However, this discussion took time away from the goal of the Women's Conference. The important points of the conference were 'equal rights', and issues directly concerned with women's every day lives in different settings around the world. She saw it as problematic that these matters were not treated sincerely. Blowing up an outside problem instead of exploring the core of the conference did not give the right picture of an event of this importance. The real message and seriousness of the event was undermined and therefore, she concluded, the nature of the convention was not mediated properly. The coverage was biased because Chinese matters became more significant than the women's conference. Even a general presentation of different issues would have been fair. Considering the amount of Japanese female reporters who filed reports and gathered information on the spot, remarkably little was reported in Japan. In her opinion even the newspapers did not make thorough reports.

> The Japanese media took bits and pieces, which fit into the existing Japanese discourses on women such as demonstrations by the Korean 'comfort women' and similar stories, but they did not get into the core problems of poverty, violence against women and equal rights. (NHK, Senior Commentator, July 23rd, 1997)

A focus of many Japanese presentations was the difficulty for Japanese media to move freely on location showing the audience in detail how difficult it was to make interviews with Chinese people. Often there would be a translator in between or there would be some kind of police present. But, according to the senior commentator, this and other security measures were to be expected in a country like China. A certain amount of restrictions were to be expected, and the coverage merely confirmed stereotypical views of China. There were demonstrations that were forbidden and interviews that were not possible, but there was too much emphasis on this kind of reporting. The media in general made a big issue out of human rights in this respect. In fairness to the on location experience, this may be one angle but it was a small part of the event. In the view of the senior commentator, NHK could have focussed more on women related issues at stake at the conference. Rather than concentrating on women's rights and freedom of participation in society and other issues central to the Women's conference, NHK tended to focus on the political aspect. In retrospect, the correspondent found that NHK over-emphasised its political focus. The NHK Chinese bureau chief had the same kind of reflections and stated that NHK could have covered more of the themes central to the women's conference.

Conclusively, the considerations of the NHK staff in China reflected a professional interest in political issues, the political situation in China, and Chinese internal affairs in a global situation seen from a Japanese perspective. The insights illustrate the NHK production staff's in depth knowledge about and preoccupation with political and economic issues.

---

[144] As a foreign reporter, it was not possible to get close to any civilians in restaurants or coffee shops. Even in the elevator there would always be someone watching to make sure foreigners and Chinese did not mix. Outside the hotel doors there were very young Chinese military people watching to prevent Chinese to enter rooms with foreigners. The commentator found it frightening to see that so many people were brought up to support the totalitarian system. Considering this, it was not a mistake to convey observations about these security measures.

'Global' media discourse

The following exemplifies the professional news values of NHK that assign priority to information about parliamentary processes from a non-partisan political point of view. Interest in international politics and international political friction was also behind the NHK coverage of the speech by Hillary Rodham Clinton. Although the speech of the First Lady addressed various problems of the women of the world, the US criticism of Chinese human rights enactment was in focus in the NHK coverage.

The speech by Hillary Clinton was televised globally. Her speech was the main topic in many broadcasts. The event was attractive in Japan according to the senior commentator as it concerned the political relations between China and the US, and the appearance by an American representative naturally attracted a lot of attention globally. (The news as presented in Denmark and Japan is analysed in Chapter Four).

As a contrast to the chain reaction of the foreign media, the only place where this news was not broadcast was in China. It was not even mentioned by the Chinese TV that Clinton had appeared. Only events and speeches in favour of China were broadcast and used extensively. Interviews with other country dignitaries (African communist leaders educated in China) who spoke in favour of the Chinese one-child policy were televised. The Chinese media used the event to their own advantage as a means of internal propaganda - as the foreign media used theirs.

From a women rights perspective, the attention paid to the speech by Clinton was important according to the senior commentator. She had the privilege to attend the entire speech although the facilities were extremely crowded, leaving hundreds of reporters outside. In her opinion, despite being critical of the Japanese coverage of the conference altogether, Clinton's speech was televised properly in Japan and in the USA and many other countries.

In summary, the evaluation of the conference, and the media coverage of it, were influenced by NHK political news criteria as well as personal impressions of the event. International politics, human rights and the political discourses of the international political elite were dedicated more broadcast time in Japan (and globally) than they deserved in relation to the themes and aims of the conference. The elite actors were given access to the international news arena and set the agenda for distributions of impressions out of Beijing. Consequently, the event was made discursive by Western voices (The Chinese were passive in all reports). Friction between international political elite nations was captured as the main theme by most media according to the NHK news producers. However, although excerpts of this news (visuals and texts) were televised word wide, it should be noted that reports may have been framed differently in different countries. In Japan at any rate the news was 'domesticated' according to production *formulae* that differed greatly even between national news media (see Chapter Four).

Where and what is news?

The process of making information fit as news, described in the following, is based on the accounts of the female reporter on location. She describes her preparation and negotiations with other staff during coverage. The reporter, as it turned out, had *two* audiences to consult: the general public and her male colleagues.

The reporter was sent to Beijing directly from the Tokyo office. Together with a cameraman from Tokyo and a Chinese interpreter they formed a group of three. In reports about the Chinese Government's reaction to the convention, the correspondents in Beijing assisted her. Other issues she covered by herself. The overall impression of the convention was overwhelming and the challenge of making it into news enormous. It was her original intention to avoid portraying the convention as a scene of hysterical women screaming; portraying an image of 'feminism' where women figuratively hit men she found outdated and simplistic.

> I did not want to report on the convention as if hysterical women gathered together and complained about how terrible men were. If I had done that, I could see what the reaction would have been. I wanted to avoid doing that. I wanted to report from the convention. Not only about social issues but also about the political and economical implications. (NHK, reporter, August 20th, 1997)

At the same time, she felt obliged to convey some of the central feminist issues such as equal rights. Her reports went through the Tokyo desk without any repercussions. Her male colleagues joked that they were typical, but they did not delete or rewrite her scripts. She interpreted this as sign that her male co-workers are getting more experienced in handling information about women's issues.

At the political meetings of the Women's Conference, the Japanese Cabinet Secretary (*kanbochōkan*) was the male government representative. The reporter found this to be a natural choice and a reflection of the 'Japanese ways'. The production team at TV Asahi, as described below, found it rather disturbing that Japan was the only country that did not have a female representative.

Before the reporter went to China, she submitted a plan with specifications for the reports she intended to make. Among her ideas was the 'comfort woman' problem. Her proposal was basically accepted. She went to one of the symposia about comfort women and interviewed some of the participants from North and South Korea. A piece of news was made about this. Other themes were added once in China. She was not prepared to make news about the Chinese reactions but made this in connection with the Beijing bureau. The chief desk had originally approved of her plans and she consulted him about additional ideas. She also talked with the news desk of the Asian section. She found the international divisions to be flexible and receptive to her ideas.

There were many activities at the conference. It was too overwhelming to cover for one person. Originally the reporter planned to cover the contents of the convention, but encouraged by her superior she ended up focusing on Chinese organisational problems, as described above. She found the change of her own agenda and original ideas to be problematic. The fact that her superior in Tokyo had access to the field through other media put her version of the event in competition with the newsroom impression of the story through other media. CNN reported on Chinese problems rather than the convention itself and her superiors suggested that she file stories with similar themes. She personally intended to focus on the convention but actual time spent on this was less than expected. According to her interpretation, her superior's decision was influenced by competitive strategies. He could not risk missing stories that may have become 'scoops' for the competition.

The coverage by other media penetrated work in the field in several ways. Being present in the middle of an event made it difficult to get the right picture (and get the picture right). She therefore checked other reports to make sure she was on the right track. If there were conflicting views in the material or if her personal opinion differed from interpretations of the situation in general, she would 'consult' other media reports. The news transmissions of ABC (with which NHK is affiliated and has an exclusive contract, see Chapter Four) were useful and perceived as reliable informants with interpretations useful in a Japanese context. The composition of information she described as a constant activity of trying to judge 'where and what was news'?

The reporter noticed that US media filed several reports about the Chinese attitude and reactions to the convention, portraying China as limiting freedom of speech and the right to access. This was one extreme. Another extreme may have been to describe China's first world convention as a learning experience.

> I couldn't simply say that the Chinese were doing their best and it was really good, but I couldn't say that it was totally wrong for China to take the measurements it did either. The whole convention I saw as a positive step taken by China. So I couldn't take either position. The trick when you have strong personal opinions and work for NHK is to learn the professional skill of being objective rather than opinionated. I tend to look at both sides in any case. A way to even out your own bias is by talking to your co-workers. I was constantly making contact with my boss in Tokyo. (NHK, reporter, August, 20th, 1997)

The instructions and monitoring from Tokyo were the ultimate decision-makers and of great influence. The authoritarian voice in Tokyo, as learned in the previous chapter, based his decision on the ability to market the idea to co-workers and top editors, not only in the international newsroom but also with the other sections of the 'news centre'. His personal judgement of the news of course made a difference in his willingness to invest energy in the negotiation of an idea. Time pressure was a decisive factor, working for or against an idea. In other words, the time factor could be used in negotiation 'at both sides of the desk'. The stories, according to statements by several news producers may be vetoed and renegotiated at any place in the hierarchy. Nevertheless, the female reporter felt that she ultimately made her own moment-by-moment decisions on location concerning the shaping of the material, although it was based on negotiations and inputs from superiors. The editors in the Tokyo office made adjustments in editing according to inputs from the reporter in the field. It deserves mention that the greater part of this piece of news was edited on location.

In summary, the on-location experience was described as a search for 'where and what is news'. The account of the reporter includes several elements of negotiation in the framing process: The negotiation between preconceived ideas (mental frames) and actual experiences of the event. The negotiation of her perception of the event against her colleagues' and superiors' preconceived ideas. And finally the negotiation between the perceived understanding of the experience in relation to the transmissions of CNN, ABC and other sources. This description lends evidence to the theoretical perspective that news is socially constructed and not merely a mirror of reality as understood in the positivist tradition. Much preparation is needed to understanding what is happening at the event. Following the cognitive rationale in Chapter Two, the knowledge taken into an event influences the way it is perceived and ultimately put together. As described above, the preconceived ideas (mental schemes and scripts) and criteria for suitable stories importantly influence emerging strategies in the coverage of news. The negotiation with co-workers and superiors influences this process. The reliance on competitors' stories and their interpretations of events as it is presented illuminates the chain reaction and creation of stories among media. News coverage in this perspective is not merely the mediation of novel happenings. As described in Chapter Four, the novelty criterion is constructed textually by use of communicative strategies such as 'live' reporting, commentary, accounts of progressions of events, 'here and now' narration, legitimisation of 'facts' through implicit or explicit interviews.

In the light of the 'global' news theories, the reliance on the international agencies described above for angles and story ideas in the framing process is considerable. Specifically, CNN and ABC stories are referred to as important agenda setters and sources used in order to measure ideas and judgement of the situation.

Considerations about audience impact

While the co-workers and superiors were perceived as one audience and bearer of organisational values in the production of news as described above, the general audience and the estimated impact was another audience concern, as elaborated in the following. The professional values of the organisation were at times in conflict with personal interests and convictions.

According to the senior commentator, the broadcast of the women's conference was not geared towards the audience for two reasons. As a starting point, the decisions were not made with the audience in mind in the NHK news centre. NHK, due to its professional hard news criteria, did not take its point of departure in popular interest in the Women's Conference. The satellite department and the educational channel, by contrast, presented different angles of the conference. These programs, however, were only seen by specific segments of the audience. The ordinary news programs seen by large numbers of viewers of the general public such as *News Seven,* broadcast two or three minutes. Secondly, it was a vast mistake not to make a media opportunity out of the fact that 5.000 NGOs from Japan went to the conference by neglecting to report on their efforts.

Supporting this view, the Beijing correspondent found that he had spent a lot of time covering problems connected to Chinese internal affairs such as Tibet and the NGO appeals for democracy and human rights rather than reporting about speeches and happenings at the conference. He concluded that 'the Japanese audience must have wondered what the conference was all about'. People who were not already knowledgeable about the Women's Conference were left with no impression at all in his opinion. The neglect of meaningful coverage in his view was the fact that TV crews were distracted from investigative reporting by Chinese organisational problems.

> In Cairo or in the US where previous conferences were held information flows more freely. If information were not so difficult to come by the presentation would have focussed more on women's issues. In a country like China with that many problems it could not have been otherwise. To have an international meeting in a country like China was very problematic in my opinion. (NHK, Correspondent in Beijing, August 20th, 1997.)

According to the senior commentator, it was only expected that NHK would concentrate on political aspects of the Women's Conference due to its professional values, but for some audience groups including the NGOs, it was a great disappointment.

The female correspondent was concerned whether the stories were comprehensible to the audience. As described above, there were different communiqués and appeals with direct Japanese involvement at the Beijing conference. She found it difficult to convey the results of these political meetings to the Japanese audience. The original intention was to transmit such conference moments to the Japanese people, but it was difficult to grasp the atmosphere and to convey the results. For the audience it must have been even more difficult to make sense of what was eventually transmitted, according to the female correspondent. (See alsoTanaka, 1995). The correspondent in Beijing shared her concern.

> I do not think we managed to inform them properly about the conference as such. The people who watched back in Japan got the impression that China has many problems. China still does not comply with human rights and tries to suppress groups fighting for democracy. It is a country without freedom. I believe it is a country without freedom and therefore I got so involved with problems of this kind. In reflection, I really do wonder if we managed to convey any of the central problems of the women's conference to our audience at home. (NHK, Correspondent in Beijing, August 20th, 1997)

The correspondent was concerned with audience reception. Ordinary people, in her view, probably did not understand the contents of the conference. If they only watched NHK news they would not have been left with knowledge about the central themes of the conference. The transmission of events was too scarce to provide a proper background.

The statements above characterise the audience considerations by NHK news producers. They may be summarised as follows. First, there was a general doubt as to whether the output was extensive enough to be comprehensible to the general audience. The doubt about audience comprehension is a general professional concern as exemplified in the previous chapters. Second, the news producers imagined audiences to be loyal to the NHK programs. Audience loyalty was likewise a characteristic perceived by TV-Asahi news producers as described below. Third, NHK news producers imagined their audiences to have the ability and desire to interpret news without subjective views. Consequently this justified the adherence to conventional professional news criteria and encouraged the coverage of specific issues as advised by the Tokyo office. It was expressed that the NHK professional news criteria did not encourage the coverage of the UN Conference to focus on women issue. Finally, it was emphasised that grasping the atmosphere of political meetings with intentions of mediation was a difficult chore.

The complexity of political events

The following exemplifies how complex events are negotiated in the mind and among news producers and formed through the professional criterion to file 'objective' political and economic news. NHK coverage, presented in Chapter Four, includes a traditional protocol list of elite politicians. A noticeable domestication strategy is to feature Japanese elite actors at any given opportunity. Another domestication strategy may be observed in the thorough account of the Japanese government's aims to implement the Plan of Action. The concluding commentary is a general statement about the difference in negotiation strategies between developing and industrialised countries. It is emphasised in the NHK news presentation that Japan belongs to the group of developed countries, along with the US. The news is thus framed within a broad international political framework focussing on parliamentary processes rather than the consequences for equal rights policies in Japan, which may have been another approach to this coverage, as suggested below.

Many happenings occurred simultaneously at the Beijing conference. Many events had complex historical and cultural backgrounds, which required in-depth knowledge in order to understand their significance. Prior knowledge was not only important in order to make sense for the reporter on location; it was also necessary in order to present the event within a suitable framework.

An understanding of the relationship between Japan and China was in the commentator's opinion a basic premise for reporting. The understanding of the political implications of government and NGO meetings was another. In order to mediate the politics and legal aspects of women's issues, the ability to interpret the wording of international law was necessary in order to make on the spot interpretations of the core points and to frame results of political negotiations in a comprehensible manner to a home audience. According to the senior commentator, it was only possible to make stories of events of this nature for reporters familiar with these cases.

NHK according to the senior commentator did not make sufficient coverage from the political platform. NHK only showed glimpses from the political Forum of government meetings. More coverage was made from the NGO Forum (in the NHK *News Seven* analysed in Chapter Four there is a story from each forum). One reason, in the view of the senior commentator, was that, the NGO activities provided better visuals. Another and even more important reason was the fact that political events require elaborate knowledge of parliamentary processes. Preparation for writing proper reports of political events includes the study of the drafts of the scheduled meeting in order to estimate its implications.

> The NHK news department made little coverage of the political meetings. They sent talented young reporters but no one had specific knowledge about women's issues. The reporter's insight and knowledge enables him or her to maintain the overview it takes to make independent decisions about the contents of a story. Knowledge of the material makes reporting of events from within its own universe possible. It makes the reporter better at informing the home office about events and following it makes him or her stronger in negotiating stories, and less dependent on the interpretations of competitors. For the same reasons, it makes the reporter more resistant to pressure from superiors at home to file a certain story or make a certain headline. (NHK, Senior Commentator, July 23rd, 1997)

According to the senior commentator, the Beijing office did not have any staff with this kind of in-depth knowledge. Although NHK has 3.000 employees around the country there were still only a few who mastered women's issues[145].

In a cognitive perspective, prior knowledge of events enables sense making and interpretation of an event from within its own premises. The next step in the communicative activity is to contexutalise perceived information into a new framework. The challenge is, in other words, to prime and frame information through the professional news values of the media organisation for a home audience. Expert knowledge, which is inevitably connected to personal interest and curiosity, may conflict with professional values of the media organisation as described below.

---

[145] The senior commentator gives an example of competent staff. For instance at the international meeting in Sweden about the sexual abuse of children, there was a reporter from the NHK London office who went to Stockholm and made an excellent coverage of the event. She was personally very interested in the subject and presented the story well. She claimed that the most important attribute of a reporter is to know the material well.

Expert knowledge and personal strategies

It was found in this study that news producers in the international newsroom were specialised in certain areas and therefore had high preference for certain topics. It was obvious from observation in the newsroom that the staff from 'desk's to higher editorial positions had successfully adopted the general norms and news values of NHK. In order to manage their positions, the ability to take in information and present it in verbal or written form was important. The ability to interact and exchange information between fields of expertise, it was observed, was an ingredient in successful communication. NHK, like any other bureaucratic organisation, has room for 'entrepreneurship'. Within the corporate hierarchical system of NHK, which is in part gender based (as pointed out in this chapter) in part seniority based, individual strategies and networks are at play in order to pursue personal ideas and ideals. The specific knowledge of the senior commentator is presented in the following.

The senior commentator's field of specialisation was labour problems and consumer politics. She was also engaged in the field of women's issues, family and children. Dealing with women's issues naturally involved political and economic matters. The senior commentator was called upon to make a political commentary about the Prime Minister Hashimoto's policy on women's issues in his administrative reform. She has knowledge acquired directly through engagement in government policy making.

> As a member of the government board of the Equal Rights Committee - collaboration for equality between men and women - we met with Mr. Hashimoto several times last week concerning the political decision last year [1996] in December to make a plan for equal rights in the year 2000. In this regard the board had an inquiry from the Prime Minister to consider the contents of this plan. There are plans within the administrative reform to make some efforts for the equal rights of men and women. The plan includes activities that could be the key to a great reformation within Japan. (NHK, Senior Commentator, July 23rd, 1997).

Other sources of information were the political reporters within NHK, whom she consulted on various issues. She generally acquired information from following the news, mostly NHK's. If she needed to reconfirm some information, she called the Prime Ministers press office for verification. There were different ways to get information but she never got it through the press club.

> I was an announcer eight years ago for five, six years about political matters, so I am very familiar with the political reporter and I know the different departments in the government and political system very well - I know where to ask and how. I know the system by heart and I do my best to use it to its fullest (laughs). If you are a political reporter you have to get the information from a younger reporter (*kohai*), who is connected to the press club.[146] When you are a commentator you

---

The reporters in the international department were recruited from the mayor universities Keio, Waseda, with majors in various fields. Most were recruited as general NHK employees and just happened to become reporters through on the job training, which is initiated by 2 years of fieldwork at a local branch. Recruitment of candidates with communications or journalism majors, which was hitherto more an exception than a rule, is becoming more common practice. After several years in a country district following a local politician or police station the new employees (*shinshain*) are trained as scriptwriters in the international department and slowly move to different positions according to their abilities. New

are free to create your own networks and routes of information. (NHK, Senior Commentator, July 23rd, 1997)

The knowledge of the commentator was used both internally and externally. She was involved in creating government policy because of her credibility as a well-known TV commentator. Meanwhile, she had access to political information through connections through informal channels to government offices. The exchange of information and knowledge through personal and professional connections was part of a unique personal network built over years.

> I am not an aggressive feminist. The times have changed. The objectives of Equal Rights are not only aimed at liberating women. They are also a means for men to get a better life. More equality and shared responsibilities in the work place and at home are an advantage for men. Japanese men work too much. Their life is based on work and this is not fulfilling. I do not believe that fist-fighting feminism can solve this problem. Men have to become aware of the problem and together men and women have to make an effort towards improvement. Therefore it is important to get more women into media and politics so that with the support of men they can influence politics in various ways and eventually make a more humane (*ningenrashii*) society. (Laughs). (NHK, Senior Commentator, July 23rd, 1997).

Her strategy was to mediate information and foster innovation through information and new ideas. Criticism in her universe was redundant and not productive. Her statement resembles the discourse of Japanese feminists who approach equal rights in a 'feminine' way as opposed to the 'masculine' rhetoric of their Western counterparts[147]. Her colleagues at TV-Asahi as described below similarly follow the strategy of refraining from making reference to feminism.

It may be observed from the above account that the capacity and expert knowledge of the senior commentator in relation to women' issues and government policies on equal rights were not taken advantage of in the *News Seven* program. The hard news criteria of the news department as well as being outside the ordinary decision making lines of the 'news centre', may explain why her expert knowledge was not incorporated.

---

approaches to this conformist training were underway in the NHK 'think tank'. A new effort was made in order to motivate innovation and creativity in these future employees. NHK reporters, however, were very proud of their extensive education in journalistic practice and when they insinuated that their salary was not at the level of the private stations, they soon expressed pride in their handicraft, which was 'objective', therefore proper, journalism. The new trend of headhunting from one company to another and the tendency to employ entertainers to present news which is characteristic of the private stations was seen as a negative development of news by NHK news producers. Older reporters and foreign correspondents in TV Asahi (TV Asahi European correspondent) also expressed this concern.

[147] Men *versus* women has not been the issue in Japanese fight for equality. Freudian concepts such as penis envy and castration complex, for example, have stirred little interest in Japan (Iwao, 1993). The proactive attitude of the feminist movement and the employment of the militant rhetoric of the women's liberation groups in the US and Europe in the 1970s therefore cause the word 'feminism' to have negative connotations in Japan as stated repeatedly in the interviews. In Japan pragmatism, non-confrontation, and a long-term perspective are the rules that govern change also within equal rights politics. Iwao (1993) has referred to the pervasive and dynamic transformation of Japanese society with women back stage referred to as 'the quiet revolution'. Women in Japanese society until today have had sovereign power in their homes.

Strategies of objectivity and facticity

Guiding principles and work ethics as concluded in the organisational analysis adhere to professional criteria that news must be factual and objective. These criteria are maintained through organisational processes of making news factual, as exemplified in Chapter Four. It is found in the present chapter that NHK news producers implement the 'objectivity' criterion as a working rule while they keep the 'myth' of investigative journalism alive. 'Myth' refers here to the fact that NHK reporters seldom do disclose controversial political information. This is also the case in international news coverage. NHK considers government diplomacy in its criticism of foreign countries and only indirectly makes criticism, as elaborated below.

Two important audiences are considered in the reporting of international affairs besides the general public and the Japanese government. The governments and people in the surrounding Asian countries are known to pay careful attention to tendencies in Japanese politics through NHK news because of the Japanese colonial past. The content analysis in Chapter Four shows that NHK *News Seven* coverage of the UN Conference on Women in China contrary to other foreign and national media did not criticise China. The seven-minute government speech at the conference in China "Where women hold up half the sky"[148] did not include criticism of Chinese human rights conditions either. The different 'spin' in news reporting poses questions as to news production. Is it a deliberate strategy in NHK news production to refrain from making negative stories about China[149]?

The Beijing correspondent asserts that he was not restricted personally in any way when making reports on China. There were no restrictions as to how far the reporters could go criticising Chinese activities. But unwritten rules seemingly existed, as unfolded below.

> Taiwan is a restricted area of reporting at NHK. NHK does not have a bureau in Taipei because of political diplomacy with China. Attention is paid to the political wishes of Beijing. This attitude is not only a reflection of the problems in Japanese and Chinese relations. It is a general diplomatic attitude that reflects the nature of Japan and the Japanese government. The attitude of Japan reflects Japan's original diplomatic ways. The Japanese politicians and diplomats are soft spoken. Japan as a country does not have much experience in foreign diplomacy and accordingly its policy is weak. (NHK, Correspondent in Beijing, August 20th, 1997)

The statement represents a tenet of the theories of Japaneseness (*nihonjinron*). The soft spokeness, according to these theories, is a characteristic of the unique interpersonal communication style of the Japanese. The hesitation and weakness supposedly is

---

[148] Government speech. UN Conference on Women. September 5th, 1995. Press release.

[149] Kim (1981: 145), investigating constraint in foreign coverage, demonstrated how Asahi newspaper's self-censorship involved deliberate omission of material, disallowing the publication of news or commentaries critical of *Beijing*'s interest. Kim concluded that intense competition among Japanese newspapers and what he referred to as 'traditional Japanese emphasis on formality' accounted for the acceptance of China's terms. It meant a great deal for a newspaper to be able to carry a story, filed by its own corespondent, datelined Beijing. The struggle to station a resident correspondent in Beijing apparently outweighed the concern for substance in reports coming from Beijing, the ethical aspect of the problem, the sense of public service, and freedom of the press. The above concerns may still be at work two decades later and explain the non-critical reporting of Japanese broadcast media in a competitive news environment.

reflected also in diplomatic communication. The 'not much experience in foreign diplomacy' of Japan refers to the fact that Japan was closed for 250 years until its reopening in 1868. In the light of Japan's position as an economic world power, the excuse is feeble. The Japanese have tried not to face their imperial past in Asia by camouflaging themselves as victims of the war. This has become part of a self-understanding, as expressed above.

The self-imposed restrictions, according to the correspondent, are ultimately a combination of NHK's professional production strategies (news values) and the fact that it is a public station. NHK differs in this respect from the private stations. NHK is aware of being a public station and although it does not obey government objectives blindly, they are taken very seriously. This way of expressing it is quite ambiguous but according to the correspondent, NHK staff at all levels of the hierarchy is strongly aware of being a public station. The fact that NHK does not touch upon problems with Taiwan, is an example. The public aspect also affects NHK's reporting on China as an economic power. There are many Japanese investments in China. Economically, the ties to China are very deep. In this case political and economic considerations are tied together.

> NHK is able to criticise to a certain degree but in serious matters it does not. When countries like the US criticise China, it is possible to report on this criticism. In the example of the Women's Conference the NHK reports did not make direct criticism and it was at no point as critical as that of the US. In effect, NHK reports would never surpass the criticism of the US. At the most, NHK would criticise as much but never more. (NHK, Correspondent in Beijing, August 20th, 1997.)

In cases of criticism, the technique of indirect criticism is applied. Whether the US was right in its criticism was another question and sometimes at doubt in the mind of the correspondent. The correspondent emphasised that he had his own opinion about this, which did not influence his work. While watching the US media, NHK reporters made their reports.

> In a naïve way - NHK did not make any criticism at all did they? (Laughs). In reality they do not want to. But the fact that we broadcast Hillary Clinton, Clinton's wife's statement is an indirect way of making criticism. And that suffices. If we had not broadcast it at all, we would have had a problem of credibility. (NHK, Correspondent in Beijing, August 20th, 1997)

Being credible in this account means fulfilling self-imposed 'obligations' to cover US events. For historical, economic, political, military reasons (see Chapters Five and Six), US news has dominated Japanese foreign coverage and NHK depends on the US government for action. The Japanese self-identification mechanism places the US first and Japan in a secondary position in international politics.

There are certain criteria for the selection and framing of stories, which are negotiated through practice in order to 'keep reporting under control' (NHK, Correspondent in Beijing, August 20th, 1997).

> When stationed abroad for one or two years both good and bad sides of this kind of self-control become evident. The overseas experience teaches what kinds of

stories are reportable and how to present them to an audience. Part of the lesson is to learn what superior staff in Tokyo consider a good story. In that respect there are restrictions that are learned by training. Even when you are not aware of it, I guess you always have some kind of self-censure. Self-censure is at operation when you think to yourself: I wonder if it is ok to report this? Censure works like this. Ideally, I think you should report on anything until you are told that this does not work. But in reality you conform and make these adjustments yourself. (NHK, Correspondent in Beijing, August 20th, 1997)

According to the Beijing correspondent, the economic power of China is becoming more significant in global relations. Japan has great investments in China and the economic and political relationship between Japan and China is interconnected in various ways. NHK is not a commercial station and is not dependent on China as a market. Economic news is covered in order to satisfy interested actors in the NHK audience.

> Maybe it is a form of restriction but when we broadcast we think about our own audience and try to imagine what kind of relationship our audience has with China. Many Japanese are getting stronger and stronger relations with China, we try to make news in their interest. We are aware of certain interest groups and try to cater to them. (NHK, Correspondent in Beijing, August 20th, 1997)

Conclusively, the considerations of the news producers were manifold. The on-location news producers in China considered first their superiors in the Tokyo newsroom and secondly Chinese Japanese governments (foreign diplomacy) and economic actors as they composed their stories. 'Self-regulation' and 'self-control' were expressed as an acquired knowledge about guidelines for professional behaviour and accomplishment. This knowledge was acquired through experience and learned through interaction with superiors. Concerning investigative journalism and critical reporting, NHK exercises a kind of self-control[150] or self-regulation (*jikokisei*). The regulation is strong in domestic affairs (Kim, 1981), but is likewise at work in the production of international news, as found in the present analysis. It may be concluded based on the above that the credibility and objectivity criteria in the NHK professional strategies are internalised complex considerations placing value on non-subjective and non-partisan reporting.

A summary of NHK professional strategies

The following reiterates the main points of observations in the analysis of NHK production strategies in relation to the four categories set up in the introduction. These categories included the following. Firstly, the negotiation of professional values of the organisation against personal intentions and knowledge domains. Secondly, the processes of decision making and information negotiation with colleagues. Thirdly, personal information processes involving the measurement of preconceived ideas

---

[150] In development psychology one strong position is learning through mimicking others. The more the self and its position within a frame is stabilised the more this person becomes a mirror for others in their learning of socialisation process. Trying to adjust is a 'manipulation' of mental structures or deep feelings. Failing to adjust causes 'cognitive dissonance' a feeling of imbalance between one's inner and one's outer world.

against perceptions of events on location. Fourthly, the evaluation of strategies against intended results.

The Japanese production team had great difficulties as a whole deciding how to report on the Chinese government's actions and on the event as such. The team had different alternatives. These alternatives were concerned with issues related to Chinese organisational measures rather than the themes of the conference. The knowledge about Chinese internal and external politics that emerged in the interviews illustrates the NHK production staff's expert knowledge, their detailed preparation and their preoccupation with political and economic issues. It was obvious from the interviews and observation in the newsroom that the staff from 'desks' to higher editorial positions successfully tried to adapt to the general norms and news values of NHK. The News producers referred to self-control and self-restraint as socialising factors learned over time though experience and communication with superiors. In other words motivation was strong to follow professional norms rather than personal interests. (Although personal agreements or disagreement were made explicit in the interviews).

The planning and negotiation of coverage of the Women's Conference were characterised by the hierarchical status of the staff, and the final output was influenced by the NHK professional criteria to report on political and economic issues. The knowledge about China was limited to a few specialists who were engaged because coverage of China is considered a delicate matter. In this respect the conference was considered important, however, it may be concluded that the themes of the women's conference were not prioritised in the planning of the event. The staff member most eager to report on the issue, and the expert among 2.000 employers on gender politics and women's issues was in the periphery of the decision-making processes and her proposals were not accepted.

The NHK staff was well prepared concerning Chinese international and external issues. As noted above there were several alternatives. The on-location experience was overwhelming and even though the news producers had own ideas in mind, the Tokyo 'desk' was strong in its pressure to cover certain issues. Its access to events through the international news agencies and CNN initiated suggestions to file stories with similar themes. Competitive strategies were thus dominant in the decision making process.

The statements of the news producers concerning professional and personal strategies reveal an intentional effort to report political and economic news following conventional professional news criteria. The news was framed in an objective and factual way. In all respects, the presentations stringently followed the NHK production *formula*, described in the previous chapter. The news producers had great knowledge of Japanese international foreign policy and this was reflected in the production and presentation of the news. The political and economic knowledge of the production staff was the driving force and determining factor in the choice and framing of the news. It deserves mention that US criticism was used as an indirect way for NHK to be critical of China without expressing views openly. Through this indirect criticism, NHK maintained its 'objective' non-opinionated 'news' style.

In sum, the news values and preferred framing of the news department were political and economic 'hard' news not allowing for 'soft' news such as consequences of the political meetings in relation to women's situation. It deserves mention that the number of women in the international newsroom was small. Besides O.L. (office ladies) and part time workers, only the newsreader and the journalist interviewed above were female. The predominant male editorial staff, according to the statements above, affected the decision-making processes by merely acknowledging traditional choices of themes. In cognitive terms, schemes of knowledge and professional mental models encouraged the passage of traditional issues through the (mental) gate-keeping mechanisms of editorial staff. As is exemplified in the TV Asahi strategies described below, deliberate strategies were taken by female reporter to mediate information about equal rights. A 'feminine' soft approach was adopted and 'masculine' feminist discourse avoided.

The communication, it should be noted, is aimed at an 'older more educated rural' and 'loyal' congregation of people expecting conventional, traditional and objective news. Possibly this may also have been a reason why the NHK reports did not present any explosive material, which would rock the patriarch as he was arriving home demanding his daily 'slippers, rice, bath'[151]!

It may be concluded based on the above that the production strategies at the largest Japanese public media organisation, were dominated by conservative professional news values attributing priority to news about parliamentary political processes from a non-partisan perspective.

II. TV Asahi

A few female news producers at *News Station* initiated the coverage of the Beijing conference. Their proposal for coverage for the first time directed attention at the event. Few members of the *News Station* production staff were interested in the meeting in Beijing before the proposal was made. The producer was just as unaware of the event as everyone else, but was easily convinced of its news value. He acknowledged that the Beijing event was 'interesting, valuable and of worldwide concern,' and immediately allocated resources for coverage. *News Station* ended up reporting on the event every day for a week. The following describes the production process experienced by the staff involved, including reporters, foreign correspondents program directors, producer, anchor, commentator, and upper level management.

Planning

One of the female reporters proposed going to China for two weeks. This was opposed in the beginning, as it would be too costly. The female staff member had many ideas and there was much negotiation back and forth. Among different possible foci, the producer chose the theme of the Korean 'comfort women'. After many meetings with discussions about possible stories and estimations of cost against coverage, one of the female initiators was allowed to go. However, in order to ensure what the producer

---

[151] The 'slipper rice bath' is one of many stereotypical examples of Japanese the father's role at home. The command illustrates the communication between spouses, which is reduced to a minimum of most important orders. Other stereotypes include: Men as a big piece of garbage (*sodaigumi*) The metaphor symbolises that the husband is only occasionally at home so when he finally returns he is alienated out of place and in the way. When the husband is healthy and off to work life is at its best. "Shujin wa genki de rusu ga ii". The Ministry of Education is working to achieve gender equality in the family, particularly with respect to the rearing of children. The Ministry actively campaigns for a new approach to home education based on gender equality, and provides subsidies to municipal boards of education that run parent education classes for fathers at the work place to afford to men opportunities to become more active in home education (Prime Minister's Office Japan, 1995).

referred to as 'well-balanced' coverage the reporter was asked to report the news 'with women's eyes *and* men's eyes' (TV Asahi, Producer, June 11th, 1997).

With this in mind, a production crew made preparations to go China. A cameraman, an assistant and the female reporter went. All three were female including the videographer. Contrary to expectations, being an all-female production staff was experienced as a problem. Even the videographer claimed that a purely female crew did not provide optimal work conditions. The fact that the crew was all women did not give the usual dynamics of working in a mixed group. The seemingly good idea to send only women turned out to be a barrier also when mediating information to Tokyo. According to the program director, the limitations in working with women only made her wish that some of her male colleagues had been present. Fuji TV had made a big deal about sending a women-only report team. They even had a press conference before they went. In the view of the *News Station* crew, this way of making sensation was a bit outdated. (TV Asahi, reporter on location, July 16th, 1997).

Another unforeseen challenge was the fact that she had prepared to go to the convention mainly to report on the issue of the Korean 'comfort women', as originally planned, but just before departure the producer suggested that a report should be broadcast from the conference every day. This called for much more in-depth preparation than she had anticipated. She did some homework, but upon arrival, she found her preparations insufficient to shoulder the difficulties of reporting on an international convention. At the convention there were many parallel sessions. She knew the program in advance, but it was difficult to estimate what the content would be until she attended. The convention site was enormous, and on top of this, the Asahi office was more than one hour away from the site. It was a battle against time to prepare a report everyday day. She had tried to plan the coverage before she went but had to decide on specific sessions when she arrived. Half of the time she chose from the 'atmosphere' of the sessions. Choosing from the 'atmosphere' was her means to intuitively assess whether a story was interesting and fit. However, the scope of the conference and the different 'atmospheres' were not easy to grasp. This is exemplified further below.

The material was edited roughly in Beijing and sent to Tokyo for final editing. A rather large amount of footage was sent every day and with an hour's time lag the Tokyo office stayed busy.

> Generally, *News Station* crewmembers in the field do not get specific instructions from the editors in Tokyo. It is up to the reporter to judge the appropriateness of the material. In the case of the women's conference, the Tokyo desk mainly asked for more background information in the news 'packages' from China and requested more issues to be covered. (TV Asahi, reporter on location, July 16th, 1997)

The original intention was to divide the responsibilities between two reporters. One was to cover the Korean pleasure girls issue, and one would report on the overall image and detailed reports on the convention. In the end, the reporters were divided into the first and the second part of the convention. The first concerned the NGO forum (August 30th –September 15th), the second the government meetings (September 4-15th).

The problem of 'comfort woman' was very much discussed in Japan at the time, as it is still an unsettled issue. But apart from this, the reporter acknowledged other world problems which were even more serious, concerning poverty, health and reproduction.

Problems, which the Japanese people could not even imagine. For her it was an eye-opener but it was difficult to mediate these problems to a Japanese audience or even to fellow staff in Tokyo.[152]

> I discussed with the staff in Tokyo about how to present issues to the general viewers that they did not know anything about, for example, the circumcision of women. The Japanese would not have understood what exactly that meant. If you do not know the background of the issue or the culture and customs of a particular country where the problem exists, you can't understand how serious the issue is. (TV Asahi, reporter on location, July 16th, 1997)

Thus, certain issues were not even considered and as a result, it was mainly issues related to Japan that were broadcast. The *wider world problems of women and poverty, health and reproduction faded into the background*. The following explains why.

Strategy on location

The following presents a clear example of a 'domestication' strategy. The program director that was sent to China during the NGO Forum planned to highlight Japanese women's problems in relation to women's problems in other parts of the world. Her idea was to 'make a map of where the Japanese *lag behind* in women's issues' (TV Asahi, Program Director C, June 26th, 1997).

Three people went as a program team. The team was supported by staff from the Beijing and Shanghai offices and by reporters from other TV Asahi programs. The team did not deal with the conference as big news, but reported small pieces of news every day. 'Only footage, produced by *News Station*'s own staff, was used in the final transmissions. Hardly any, if any news agency visuals at all were used'[153] (TV Asahi, Program Director C, June 26th, 1997). Against this statement, Clinton's speech was possibly filmed by one of the news agency cameras according to the TV Asahi reporter on location. Further, she recollected that the office in Tokyo occasionally used footage from AP and Reuters when the team could not get around to shooting it. As stated in previous chapters, it is not possible to reconfirm the sources of visual material. However, the fact that Japanese production teams are present at events enables interpretations from a Japanese perspective, which enhances the 'domestication' of information.

According to the program director, another strategy was to get *men* interested in the conference 'because women already know what problems they face as woman'. This approach was partly chosen to fulfil the producer's request advising the team to cater to men and women equally, and to avoid showing events from a 'feminist' point of view (feminism was likewise expressed in the NHK analysis as having 'grim' connotations). The program director had a feeling that Japanese men would not take a feminist approach to reporting seriously. In her experience, especially older men were limited by what she referred to as a 'male chauvinistic view', which surfaced particularly when women's issues were on the agenda.

---

[152] The difficulties of framing news are described in Tuchman (1978). One of her examples likewise concerns the coverage of women's issues.

[153] The news agencies are paid a lump sum rate for usage. Therefore the acquired visuals are not minutely registered. The origin of visuals is rarely recorded on the screen. It is further difficult to ascertain whether a picture is taken by a news agency or a station's own camera. Investigating the origin of visuals is difficult.

214

Several strategic measures stand out in the account of the program director. She intended to describe how Japan 'lags behind' in gender issues. Behind this statement lies an assumption that women's issues in Japan should be compared with the situation in Western countries. Like many of the news, producers, she referred several times to the situation of gender equality in the Scandinavian countries (this was seemingly general knowledge among female media professionals[154]). She specifically referred to problems in these countries concerning equal salaries and 'glass ceiling' barriers in work advancement for women (and ethnic groups). She did not compare the status of women in Japan with the surrounding Asian countries such as Korea, Taiwan and China[155] but with Western standards. I will elaborate on this point below. Secondly, her communication goal was to make men interested in the news because as she said 'women already know what difficulties they face'. Behind this statement was another assumption, namely that women's problems are universal, which judging by the differing issues covered by the media at the conference (see Chapter Four) and the discussion at the end of this chapter, they are not. And finally she wanted to stay away from covering feminist issues altogether. The following explains why.

'Anti-feminist' strategies

The following shows how professional shared news values at TV Asahi dominate the discourse on women's issues. Although some of the female news producers were aware of and engaged in the improvement of women's issues, 'feminism', they sensed, had negative connotations in Japanese society and within their media organisations. Accordingly, it was ingrained in their strategy to refrain from making reference to feminist 'rhetoric' and action. They did not frame presentations and commentary in feminist perspectives. They rather distanced themselves from feminist views.

The impression of 'feminism' in the mind of the program director was negative. This led her to avoid issues altogether which might highlight feminist action. While covering the event, however, she found herself in the dilemma of having to make distance

---

[154] The research of the American social psychologist, Linda Schaberg, confirms the supposition that Scandinavia is a role model in women's issues. It was found in Schaberg's interview survey (forthcoming) that interviewees referred to Scandinavian programs as models in gender equality issues. Scandinavian countries were mentioned in relation to favourable arrangements for working mothers such as flextime, health care facilities financed through taxes, participating fathers, maternity leave for both genders (personal communication April 2001).

[155] With the post-war introduction of women's suffrage and revisions to civil and criminal laws under the new Japanese constitution advocating equality in the eyes of the law, women were guaranteed the same standards of education as men, the same working opportunities and the right to determine their own lives. Social and economic transformation in Japan during the ensuing period of rapid economic growth changed life for women considerably. In 1994, the number of female employees reached 20, 34 million or 38.8% of the total number of employees. Women in managerial positions, were on average, 1% according to these statistics (Prime Minister's office Japan, 1995). The Confucian ethics, which have spread throughout Asia (from China to Korea to Japan) include three objects of obedience": Obedience to fathers when young, to husbands when married and to their children (sons) in old age (Iwao, 1993:5). The Chinese gender structure has deviated from these values due to communist ideas that women and men equally share work positions equally as said in the Japanese government speech at the conference "China, the country where women hold half the sky". Another Confucian ethic which has been adopted in Japan, "good wives and wise mother's" attributed power to the women in the household. Hitherto, Japanese women were in charge of the household. The result today of these historical influences is described as 'men superior, women dominant' (*dansei joi, josir yui*) (Iwao, 1993:4). Confucian ethics were upheld during the Meiji restoration but the post-war constitution clearly stipulates that all people are equal before the law.

between her own aspirations as a woman *vis-à-vis* her professional task. She tried, as she termed it, to 'see the wood for the trees' in order to present a larger perspective than her own ideas of equal rights. One of her ways of doing this was to report on how other nationals saw Japan. On the second day of the conference, she arranged interviews with several people in the audience of the Japanese government representative, Nosaka Koken's speech. Foreign and Japanese NGOs and politicians were asked to comment on the fact that the Japanese government representative was *male*. The program director did not incorporate her personal opinion in the reports but tried to be what she referred to as 'objective'. In her own words she tried to report the 'facts' and to present things 'as they were'. The reports, thus, did not emphasise feminist views of equal rights but intended to reflect a 'fair view' and not just women's points of view. Somewhat contradicting this claim of 'objectivity' she later stated that among the interviewees, 'two cabinet members' comments fit well into the intended message'. The former Socialist leader, Takako Doi, expressed that women *and* men must work together for the improvement of women's conditions. Another, LDP politician Tanaka (the daughter one of Japan's most powerful politicians the late Kakuei Tanaka) declared that nothing is gained through the 'mass hysteria' approach, thus making negative reference to feminist action.

In spite of her efforts to make the news appealing to men, she was disappointed to hear from a male colleague that because she was a woman, viewers interpreted whatever she did as if she were part of the women's group. She felt that if a male reporter had reported it, people might have taken the reports more seriously. Nevertheless, as she had intended, one of the reports covered men's activities at the conference. She focused on their involvement and reactions. Due to lack of time, however, only a shallow report was transmitted on this subject.

Other comments about the issue of feminism were made: The female anchor pointed out that she was well aware that the reporter on location had to use what she called an 'anti-feminist strategy'. According to her experience, this was the only way to be able to broadcast women's issues at all. Although women were among the audience and on the production team, the main decision-makers were men and this first of all affected the choice of issues and secondly the perspective of the story. In her role as an anchor she tried to make inputs from a feminist (equal worth therefore equal rights) point of view. The anchor was aware that in her work, she was able to represent the voice of women and she tried to say as much as she could through her position. Nevertheless, she constantly dealt with the fact that decisions were made by men and from their point of view.

> The reporter in Beijing thought reactions would be negative if the presentations showed female aggressiveness. She chose a soft line where she could involve men. She deliberately used this special tool in order to get men to watch the news. This is the trick. (TV Asahi, Anchor, November 25th, 1997)

The above accounts reveal the journalistic strategies and concerns involved in presenting women's issues. The main concerns were to avoid connotations of 'feminism'. In the mind of the female reporter 'feminism' invoked a stereotypical image of 'women hitting men' to get equal rights, which she did not sympathise with. For the program director and the anchor, the understanding of feminism was that 'men and women have equal worth and therefore equal rights'. In their personal opinion, feminist work requires a continuous effort to achieve equal treatment and equal rights not only for women, they emphasised, but for both genders. Where the anchor did her best to express work for feminist views when possible, the program director on location tried not to let it influence her reporting. The program director noticed many Japanese women's groups at the conference. One of the reasons for their large number may have been that China is a neighbouring country. There were also groups from very poor African countries but they were fewer. Hoping 'privately' that the Japanese women's groups would continue to work with the issues they presented at the conference after returning to Japan, the program director tried not to let her sympathy affect the perspective of the programme she reported.

The program director intended to produce reports which would focus on various aspects of women's problems, for example, comparing countries or pursuing specific themes. She successfully reported about women in Norway, emphasising how they work as politicians or in the industry. The criterion of success in her view was the fact that she made a point of showing how the Norwegian women were competent in their positions 'without making a big deal about being women'.[156] The issue of feminism in Japanese society at large is elaborated upon in the conclusion. The following concerns a Japanese domestic public issue about the treatment of women during the Second World War. The so-called 'comfort women' have recently stepped forward from former Asian colonies, in greatest numbers from Korea, demanding compensation.

'Comfort women'

The issue of 'comfort' women was a domestic issue pursued at both NHK and TV-Asahi in relation to the UN conference. While NHK did not cover the issue in *News Seven* it was covered by *News Station* in accordance with its critical *formula* (described in detail in the pervious chapter). The overall production strategy was to report on foreign governments who were *critical* of the Japanese government's handling of women's problems. This included the problem of the Korean 'comfort women', who were most numerous and most visible in their demands for compensation. The female reporter investigated the theme throughout her stay and made a report on the issue from the NGO forum.

In the view of the female reporter, the Japanese government was not sincere in making policies for improvement of the status of women in society. Her opinion was reconfirmed on this international occasion.

> The Japanese politicians and representatives of the government stayed for a very short time. They hardly had time to get the feel of the convention. The leader of the Socialist party, Doi Takako, who made a short statement about the convention in the *News Station* coverage seemingly considered her appearance more of a political occasion and photo opportunity than a forum for women's rights issues. (TV Asahi, reporter on location, July 16th, 1997)

The reporter was curious to collect international views about Japan. Through her interviews she found that some foreigners were very critical of the 'comfort women'

---

[156] It deserves mention that Scandinavian women do not climb career ladders effortlessly. There are 'glass ceilings' even in the exemplary gender egalitarian Scandinavian countries. However, foreigners inquiring into women's issues in the Scandinavian countries will naturally be met with discourse and national pride supporting the 'myth' of gender equality.

issue and some were even very emotional about it. Others were not particularly
interested in the issue and yet others had strong reactions to the speech by the Japanese
Government spokesman Mr. Nonaka. While contemplating which view to emphasise,
the report ended up as a collage of different perspectives. (See Chapter Four). During
her stay she encountered many favourable responses from foreigners. She interpreted
the positive reaction to Japanese media as an effect of the remarkable number of
Japanese women participating.

She found that it was easier for Japanese participants to talk about topics like the
'comfort women' and nuclear weapons that were related to the Japanese domestic
situation than topics like discrimination and poverty. Hardly any of the Japanese NGOs
mentioned the latter issues. Most groups at the convention, and especially the Japanese,
she found, did not have time for other groups, because they were busy organising their
own activities.

> Not many participants grasped the overall view of the convention. Reporters like
> us certainly did not get it. But I grimaced at the size of the world, when I went to
> see some of the African exhibitions. They had problems, which I could not even
> believe. I did a little reporting on poverty. (TV Asahi, reporter on location, July
> 16th, 1997)

News production is described above as a continuous process of adjustment between
preconceived ideas (general perceptual schemata) and impressions at the conference
(more specific schemes of knowledge). The issue of 'comfort women' was an important
and current Japanese domestic issue, which was treated elaborately by *News Station*.
Issues of poverty and development (like the issue of circumcision mentioned
previously) faded into the background. The Japanese NGOs did not discuss these issues
and the *News Station* staff, in an effort to 'domesticate' and choose issues that were
'proximate' within a Japanese interpretative framework, selected issues and actors with
a relationship to Japan. The mix of interviews although found by the reporter to be
representative of different viewpoints, ' a collage of different perspectives', was critical
of the Japanese government following the production formula described in the previous
chapter (see also Chapter Four).

Most comments about women's issues, as exemplified above, were volunteered by
female news producers. Men were eager to comment, but their engagement and
knowledge about the issue was not as elaborate as their female counterparts. The
following is an account of women' issues from a male point of view.

'Womanism'

A former foreign editor at the Asahi newspaper was the commentator in the *News
Station* programme at the time of the interviews. As an expert in international affairs,
the role of the commentator has been to familiarise international information for
Japanese audiences for a decade. Consequently he was responsible for the comments
and 'domestication' of news during the UN Women's Conference.

It is a personal and professional aim of the commentator to provide the Japanese
people with a diverse outlook on the world. Many years in France and England are the
basis for his perspective on Japanese issues from an outside perspective. Events are
channelled through his European experiences.

218

The insularity of Japanese society means that people are not used to seeing things in a larger perspective. I try to provide a larger perspective through another side of the argument. If there is criticism of a certain foreign or domestic event, I try to represent the other point of view. This makes a good contrast to the anchors who do not have experience in the other side of the argument. (TV Asahi, Commentator, August 21st, 1997).

In the perspective of the globalisation discussion in Chapter One, most people are not exposed to the 'other side of the argument'. In spite of times of 'globalisation' and 'cosmopolitans' travelling the world, a majority of citizens live local lives. Their knowledge about other cultures may be based on intrinsic interests, news information and international connections, and trip abroad. The *News Station* commentator thus contributes with knowledge about international affairs and is able to provide the Japanese audience with an international perspective on world events. Importantly, his view of the world is familiar to Japanese viewers as the 'other side of the argument' is observed through the eyes of a fellow Japanese. The ancient Greek military advice put forth in the commentary on equal rights, however, does not reflect the present European accomplishments in this matter.

The *News Station* commentator made an active contribution to stories about the Beijing conference at the end of each presentation. On air, after the videotaped news input about the Korean 'comfort women' (see analysis Chapter Four), the commentator makes reference to the Greek play by Aristophanes, in which the wives plan a sex strike, which allegedly stops the war. 'There is no strategy behind this commentary' he asserts laughingly during the interview, '*News Station* lacks a strategy altogether'. His personal strategy is to assist the Women's movement to get as far as possible with their message. He only refers to the strategy of the old Greeks in order to demonstrate that women's power is so strong that it can even stop even war.

> It [sex strike] is a strong weapon at the family level and at the educational level all the way to the top level of the state. In a historical perspective from Napoleon to the Second World War the most important issues for mankind was to stop war. If his story had been applied it may have stopped many wars. (TV Asahi, Commentator, August 21st, 1997)

The intention of the commentator was to convey the Greek military wisdom by making this point. He strongly supports what he refers to as a 'feminisation of society'. He wishes women to 'step up' into higher political and bureaucratic government positions.[157] *Womanism*[158] as he calls 'female influence in society' will have to change

---

[157] The number of women at work has been increasing since 1975, marking a record high in 1995, when the ratio of women in the entire working population reached 39.7%. The ratio of women in managerial positions was also increasing: in 1995, the ratio of women general managers, section mangers and senior staff, respectively, accounted for 1.3%, 2.8% and 7.3%. In a survey in Tokyo among female members of the Tokyo Metropolitan or municipal Assemblies, females in administrative positions of the Tokyo Metropolitan or Municipal Government Offices, and female leaders or board members of a national women's groups were asked about obstacles against women seeking for political and social gender equality. The results were: Structures and operations designed in favour of men (71.6). Consciousness on women's side to accept the traditional stereotyped gender roles (25.4). Consciousness on men's side to take the stereotyped gender roles for granted (33.3). Lack of support and assistance by family members (5.3). Heavy family responsibilities imposed on women (22.2). Lack of personal networks (17.7). Lack of economic networks (15.8) (Tokyo Women's Foundation, 1995).

the Japanese masculine ways. Change is underway, he states, referring to the only female Ministers in the government cabinet[159] at the time.

In spite of this positive attitude it is not possible to estimate whether the audience appreciated the intellectual depth and intentions of his comment. In the specific case concerning the Korean 'comfort women', the younger generation may find his advice slightly anachronistic and difficult to relate to. First of all because the war problems are not part of their upbringing. The history books for one do not provide knowledge of the past from an Asian point of view (Rohlen, 1983). In spite of his intention to help the women's cause, the anecdote rather obscures the fact that 'comfort women' in most cases were not in a position to strike. From the point of view of modern Japanese women the historical perspective did not give concrete advice in their situation as working women. What were they going to do to overcome and improve their situations in conflicts/war at home or in the workplace? Sex strike?[160]

The political messages most effectively communicated through the media from the UN conference was the speech of the US First Lady, described below.

Elite actors and professional news criteria

As described in the NHK strategies above, the speech by Hillary Rodham Clinton was mandatory coverage and became agenda setting for media coverage at the conference. The speech was part of the international political parliamentary process. The participation of an elite actor was a determining element in the professional criteria of newsworthiness.

Clinton's seven-minute speech or parts of it were televised globally (except in China). Clinton convincingly hammered home the message that 'women's rights are human rights'. Her criticisms of China, especially the one child policy, were a welcome point of friction, and this part of her speech caused a chain reaction among foreign correspondents. Consequently, this message echoed worldwide.

According to the TV Asahi reporter on location the news was considered an important contribution to women's issues. The US first lady, Hillary R. Clinton, was the prominent guest speaker on the second day of the official government meetings. Clinton's speech included many specific and personal experiences with women worldwide. A full section was devoted to criticism of China's one child policy, including its abortion and sterilisation practices, and this part caught attention for two

---

[158] 'Womanism' was the original expression of the commentator. The interview was conducted in English.

[159] In international comparison Japan scored a 37th place in the UN development Programs index to compare the level of women's participation in policy decision-making processes, especially in the public sectors. "The ratio of female members in the Diet" and "the ratio of women in administrative and managerial positions" were factors that determined the low ranking. (The Present Status of Gender Equality and Measure. Report on the Plan for Gender Equality 2000. The Prime Minister's Office, 1997)

[160] The values of the new generation of women are changing. The mother complex '*mota kon*' is often used to describe the psyche of Japanese men. The attention, love and adoration a mother gives to her impeccable 'little prince' creates a constant need for some comfort for Japanese men brought up under Confucian values valuing little boys higher than girls, who find it difficult to find a 'mother' among the independent Japanese working girls. For young women the cute (*kawaii*) fashion, on the other hand, is also a reaction that contradicts values central to the organisation of Japanese society. By acting childish, Japanese youth try to avoid the conservatives' moral demand that they exercise self-discipline and responsibility and tolerate server conditions whilst working hard in order to repay their obligation to society. (Kinsella, 1995).

220

reasons. Firstly, she was inspired by many of her colleagues to make a report on this theme and secondly the statements of Clinton were assertive in the improvement of women's rights. The fact that many reporters were voicing similar thoughts,[161] she felt was a supportive element in her choice of theme. She had picked a different topic every day but found it difficult to make government meetings into news stories. Often the crew had to make side steps from the actual topics and report on related issues. 'The speech by Hillary Clinton was welcomed as a clear-cut message'. (TV Asahi reporter on location, July, 16th, 1997). A related report was made on the 'one child policy' in China with emphasis on women's fundamental right to give birth, a right also emphasised in the Clinton speech.

The Clinton news exemplified how classic international news values (Galtung and Ruge, 1965), including *elite nations, elite actors, individual action and negative events*, made the event newsworthy and easy to frame.

Framing the atmosphere on location (*ba*)

From the perspective of considering the conference an opportunity to bring women's issues into the public debate through NGO activity, it did not have much impact in Japan according to both NHK and TV Asahi news producers. Attitudes towards Japanese NGO accomplishments differed greatly among the producing team members, as described in the following.

According to the TV Asahi female reporter, it was clear that equal rights issues have not yet reached beyond grass roots level. This stage of awareness was reflected in the Japanese involvement in the conference.

> The Japanese workshops and exhibitions were eye-catching but the content was shallow. By comparison, the foreign workshops did not have any decorations but they debated their issues very seriously. The purpose of the Japanese groups with its fine decorations seemed different from other groups. The production team tried to catch this difference by shooting a scene with Japanese women doing a tea ceremony and then turning the camera to the scene of a foreign workshop where people were having a heated discussion. It was difficult to convey the atmosphere through the eye of the camera. You had to be there to experience the contrast. (TV Asahi, reporter on location, July 16th, 1997)

Similar observations were made by the TV Asahi program director:

> The Japanese women had a good reputation at the conference for their sheer number of participants but their exhibitions were more sophisticated in their wrapping (*uwabe*) than in content (TV Asahi, Program Director C June 26th, 1997).

---

[161] The speech by Hillary Clinton was also an inspiration to the reporters in the commercial station in Denmark. TV2 broadcast an English documentary program 'Death rooms' about the miserable fate of female orphans in China as a result of the Chinese one child policy. The following day, TV2 reported on political reactions in the Danish parliament, 'Folketinget', criticising China's one child policy as a reaction to the documentary. The US criticism was followed by critical reporting in other parts of the world.

While in China, the reporter wanted to make a critical report on the activities of the Japanese women's groups, but she refrained. It was obvious that they had spent a lot of time on the organisation of workshops. At the same time she was afraid that she had misjudged their intentions, as she had not studied them long enough. Some of the Japanese participants were conscious that they did not do as well as other foreign participants. But they emphasised that they had learned something from participating in an international conference for the first time and that reflection on their activities would make them progress from there. After all, the main theme of the convention was 'to put it into practice' so the reporter left it at that. Whether the perceptions of the Japanese NGOs were guided by the critical formula of *News Station* or actually reflected the exhibitions cannot be determined. At any rate the NHK coverage was made in an optimistic tone.

The theme of the morning news at NHK concerned Japanese women and their ability to speak up. It was in part a follow up on previous women's conventions, where Japanese women were criticised for their soft-spoken ways. This time there was a remarkable change in the attitude of the Japanese, according to the NHK reporter. The change in her view may in part have been due to the effort and preparation of 5.000 NGOs. It may also have been a feeling of confidence in being women of a world power or it may merely be attributed to the fact that Japanese women have learned to speak up. Working for non-governmental organisations and doing volunteer work has become more popular and heightened the awareness of women's situation in Japan. Japanese women have become confident and affluent world travellers. They are 'good learners'[162] in the sense that they are curious to know about women's situation abroad and just as curious to measure their own situation against that of women in other nations.

Besides the impact through the direct involvement of the NGOs, there were comments from viewers in Japan who had followed the coverage throughout the week. Where only a small percentage of the Japanese population reads the newspaper editorials (in spite of the largest circulation of newspapers in the world per capita), *News Station* targets a much larger population and reaches the average Japanese person (TV Asahi, commentator). The female reporter was surprised to be approached by many who had watched her reports. Especially middle-aged women followed the coverage throughout the convention. Some just happened to watch and continued to follow it. Her colleagues, on the contrary, the Asahi staff, were not interested in the convention, which made her conclude that men in general must have been even less interested.

Some, according to the female reporter, perceived the event in an overall category of 'women's things' and they were not interested in specific information about the state of affairs of women around the world. In retrospect, she found that the footage sent from China did not carry the weight of the issues. It was not possible to make in-depth coverage for various reasons. Firstly, time was limited. The typical three to four hours a day of active information gathering at the conference were too little to seriously grasp the content of the event. Secondly, there was a language barrier which made the cutting of sound and interviewing difficult.[163] Finally, it was difficult to grasp the atmosphere

---

[162] The Japanese success as 'latecomers' to international society is partly due to being 'good learners'. (Robertson (1992). This ability also characterises Japanese women.

[163] The language was a barrier in the reporting of the event in China. The female reporter was inhibited by the fact that her English was not good enough. Throughout the stay the production team had to work through two sets of interpretation: one between English and Japanese and another between Chinese and Japanese. This meant that the team was limited to report on only those sessions, which used the two languages. Sometimes questions and answers went through several layers of translation, which was very

of events. Consequently, the conference was only covered superficially according to the reporter. In her view, the Beijing conference was just another event and it did not have much impact.[164] Originally, she intended to follow women's activities up until the convention and to report on the Japanese women's preparations rather than just reporting from the convention.[165] Unfortunately, she said, time and resources were spent on two domestic disasters: the Kobe earthquake and the 'Aum' incident, which overshadowed the event in Beijing.

A summary of TV Asahi professional strategies

TV Asahi reported daily on the Women's Conference. The news was not treated as 'big' news, as much effort went into the coverage of domestic events at the time. However, compared with the coverage at NHK *News Seven*, the production strategy and planning allowed for lengthy and varied representations of themes and voices.

The following summarises the main observations in relation to the four areas of analysis. Namely, the negotiation of the professional values of the organisation against knowledge domains and personal intentions. The processes of decision making and information negotiation in the hierarchical order. The process of information involving the handling of preconceived ideas (general schemes) against perceptions of events on location (specific schemes of knowledge) and finally the personal evaluations of strategies from the planning of the event to the final coverage.

The areas of knowledge that were made discursive in the TV-Asahi interviews were related to the UN Conference on Women. The headlines above list the main themes including 'comfort women', 'anti-feminist' and 'womanism'. These themes do not exhaust the lists of gender- related issues that were verbalised in the interviews. Compared to the NHK international political knowledge domains, the TV-Asahi news producers focussed on the UN themes at the conference. In spite of the fact, however, that the production team went with the intention to report on women's issues, it was stated that professionally shared news values at TV Asahi dominated personal interest and motivations to cover these issues. Most of the female news producers were knowledgeable about women's issues, and some actively engaged in the improvement of women's conditions. They were aware, however, that 'feminism' has negative

---

time consuming. It was also frustrating to sense that somewhere in this process the speaker's intentions were lost. It was generally agreed at the conference that the fact that the Conference was held in China posed a problem. Simple information like times and places of meeting was difficult to acquire. This was unusual at international conferences of this size. Another problem was the interpreters sent by the Chinese organiser. The interpreters supposedly did not translate everything, which was discussed. They even suggested which questions to ask. Further, participants in the Chinese Human Right's Group were selected by Chinese authorities, and not volunteers like participants from other countries. The answers they gave were said to be prepared. If she had spoken Chinese she would have been able to double check for herself whether their answers had been fixed or were genuine. She found it impossible to get in direct contact because of the language barrier. The result of this barrier is that news producers consult the international news agencies and affiliate Western national broadcasters for their interpretation of events. One consequence namely, 'linguistic imperialism', is discussed in chapter nine.

[164] According to the research of US scholar Jean Renshaw (1999), the conference did have a positive impact. In a, estimate of the future conditions for Japanese female managers, Renshaw lists multiple examples of women who have been stimulated by the Beijing International Women's Conference to get together, exchange information, to start their own consulting companies and make leadership courses for young women.

[165] *News Station* staff cover both domestic and international events. These areas of responsibility are not divided, as was the case at NHK.

connotations in Japanese society *and* within their media organisations. Accordingly, they incorporated 'anti-feminist' strategies into their professional practices and refrained from making reference to feminism and feminist activities in news concerning women's issues.

The organisation of experience and the communication of the 'atmospheres' of events were described as a challenge. As a contrast to the political focus at NHK, TV Asahi news producers stated that some political themes were given up, because they were too complicated even though the reporters were well prepared. Other themes were excluded as they were interpreted as calling for higher levels of knowledge among Japanese viewers and fellow staff. Eventually, they stated, supporting the 'domestication hypothesis, that stories directly related to Japan or Japanese involvement in the conference were chosen.

The 'critical formula' of *News Station* (as described in the previous chapter) was followed stringently. The statements of reporters referred to critical attitudes and witnessed a critical frame of mind in the choice of themes and perspectives. In one instance, however, the critical approach was set aside. This was in order to spare "well meaning" Japanese women's participation in the conference (Their 'pretty decorations and lovely tea ceremonies' were in great contrast to the heated discussion of poverty and war in other seminars).

At TV Asahi, an all-female crew was sent to China. As this turned out, it was not the ideal working situation. First of all, the staff missed the feedback and usual work dynamics of working with men. Secondly, it proved difficult to negotiate ideas with superiors. This, of course, was partly due to the complexity of the issue and the challenge of framing generally, but it was also due to the overall strategy influenced by the producer's advice to view the event from *women' eyes and men's eyes*. The fact that the perspective of the story was determined in advance without reference to the event itself, made it difficult at first to decide which news would fit within the given framework (Covering an ASEAN meeting with a similar working itinerary "see this from a men's *and* women's perspective" may equally cause some confusion and readjustment in the cognitive apparatus of the correspondent). Thirdly, female reporting, according to the news producers, reinforced a stereotypical image of women's issues by co-workers and audiences. Perhaps a male reporter may have contributed with a different impression.

In conclusion, views on feminism as expressed by TV Asahi staff resembled Western liberalist feminist views of 'equal worth therefore equal rights'. The statements about women's issues were plenty. The points of view among the female staff varied from being against the 1970s slogans and stereotypical images of 'women hitting men', to interest in clarifying the Japanese status of women compared with other countries (Scandinavia), to active feminist positions and work professionally and privately to enhance equal rights. Male as well as staff news producers expressed that the Japanese society as a whole needed improvement of gender politics in order to enhance the quality of the professional and private lives of women *and* men. However, it became apparent through the interviews that anti-feminist strategies were applied in news production. 'Anti-feminist' strategies were likewise apparent in the content analysis (see Chapter Four). Where the Danish programs made friendly, almost humorous reports about 'anti cultural imperialism' and 'lesbian rights', the Japanese refrained from filing reports about feminist issues in fear of negative connotations.

The focus on women's issues and the extensive coverage at the private station was not merely a sign of change in gender politics and a reflection of improvement of women's situation. It was also a *commercial consideration*. It was no coincidence that the news presentation geared to women *and* men faded into a commercial for perfume by the biggest Japanese cosmetics company *Shiseido*. Conclusively, the commercial interests in this case strongly influenced the production of news discourse and public debates.

Conclusion

In the following, the production strategies are concluded upon in relation to the four points of analysis. Firstly, the exploration of the negotiation of professional values of the organisation against personal intentions was a meaningful distinction that reflected the dual considerations of information processes within professional news producers. It was observed that the professional values and production *formulae* of the organisation were continuously negotiated against personal preconceptions and intentions. Secondly, the analysis of processes of decision making and information negotiation threw light on the agenda setting for strategic coverage and provided insights about responsibility attributed to roles and positions in the organisations. Thirdly, the investigation of personal information processing involving the estimation of preconceived ideas against perceptions of events on location allowed for descriptions of information processing as perceived by individuals. Fourthly, the personal evaluations of strategies from the planning of the event to the final coverage made intended results against outcome explicit.

Herbert J. Gans (1980) in his study of US reporters found that reporters with conscious values were in the minority and the media he studied seemed to attract people who kept their values to themselves. They had no prior values about the topics which became news, nor did they always develop them about topics on which they were working (Gans, 1980: 184). In the present study, news producers were found to have personal interest in and opinions about issues in focus. The news producers at the public service stations in particular were experts in their domains and made discrepancies between personal and shared professional strategies at their organisations explicit. The news producers at the commercial station had incorporated an opinionated critical style into their professionalism. Their personal and professional views were not always identical, and the organisational critical *formula* was questioned by some. Nevertheless, influential bearers of this attitude as well as perceived audience expectations made this professional value persist.

The strategies at the two stations differed greatly. At the public service station, the reporting of the UN conference was treated just like any other economic political news. The reporters went with a political perspective in mind and the news was covered accordingly. Views on the coverage of the news were varied, but eventually conservative journalistic criteria for news production were employed. By contrast the commercial station allocated much airing time for coverage and according to the themes in this chapter the coverage including 'feminism', 'womanism', 'comfort women' issues about women were varied and reflected in the news presentations. Themes that were important at the conference but not part of Japanese general knowledge were not covered.

The knowledge made explicit at NHK concerned international political issues and Chinese internal and external political affairs. The interviews revealed insights about international political diplomatic relations and parliamentary processes and consequences of the UN conference in a global perspective. They brought insights about the implementation of UN political discourse a the national level, and about work strategies and knowledge domains enhanced by professional criteria in media organisations at the organisational level. Finally the interviews brought insights about the negotiations of professional strategies and individual knowledge against personal views and motivations from the perspective of the individual actor. The knowledge made explicit at TV Asahi concerned gender issues and equal rights. The interview revealed insights about the notions of women's issues of the UN at the global level, gender in media discourse and in society as a whole at the national level, gender in relation to work conditions in media organisations at the organisational level and finally as individual knowledge and working strategies of the news producers at the professional level. From a 'global' perspective on news mediation, the fact alone that international news enters the gates of Japanese society through Japanese national media organisations that prioritise knowledge domains this differently in their professional strategies make processes of 'domestication' differ. The difference in knowledge domains with the strategies of 'objective' news presentation at NHK and the subjective idiosyncratic strategies of TV Asahi enhance differences in domestication processes.

The study at the professional level showed how the production formula described at the organisational level (in the previous chapter) was incorporated into micro processes in the framing of international news. A significant observation in relation to the 'global' news theories was the importance assigned to international news agencies in the framing process and the on-location implementations as well as the Tokyo office awareness of stories and story angles of the international agencies. The bureaux enjoy high status as objective and credible news suppliers (Paterson 1996). The strategic use of agencies was very prominent. The trusted affiliates, colleagues from the affiliate agencies and networks were reliable sources of angles and story perspectives on location, while agency supplies were constantly checked at the home offices, where the latest developments in the conference events were used to direct reporters on location.

Specifically, the NHK news producers adhered to 'objective' news production and factual commentary, which was carefully considered in the production process. The political economic news values and the consequences of the UN agenda on domestic policy-making were important considerations in their strategic work. NHK news producers strategically framed news as a government spokes channel and therefore sought to make little criticism of government action and less of international political partners of interest to Japan. In the case of criticism (as in the US criticism of China), they would be less critical than the international news agencies and only make indirect criticism through use of agency material. The NHK reporters were merely voicing knowledge about Chinese and Japanese political and economic relations and their spectacles were focussed on system political processes. The Asahi news producers, by contrast, were not guided by professional values and expert knowledge directed at economic and political news. Their frame of mind was to cover the events of the conference via a popular approach though observation and interviews. Entertaining critical informative reporting on the unfolding events describes their effort to frame the atmosphere of events. The TV Asahi reporters were eager in their 'domestication' effort to measure gender issues in Japan against foreign advances. They made much effort to cover the 'comfort women' issue with critical remarks against the Japanese government's irresponsibility in war crimes, criticism of human rights implementation and nuclear testing in China. They expressed critical views of what they referred to as 'superficial non-confrontational appearance of the Japanese NGOs' and were critical of the gender of the *male* Japanese government representative and criticised the many female politicians for using the event mainly as a 'photo opportunity' without political engagement in women's issues. The above exemplify the critical professional strategies of TV Asahi.

The analysis at the professional level directed attention at the connection between media, gender and politics. Elaboration upon this connection lies outside the scope of the present project, but may be investigated in further research.

In relation to the 'domestication' hypothesis, the analysis shows that the concepts and visuals of 'global' events may be the basis for news reporting; however, the final output highlights national contextual factors and actors. International events were presented differently within national contexts because of differing political and legal systems, it was produced differently because of differing strategies within national media organisations. The analysis of mental processes and negotiation of information between news workers illuminate the multiple factors and actors at play in decision-making processes. Although intentional explicit strategies were at work, some decisions ended up being arbitrary while others emerged as news was filed.

In conclusion, it is noteworthy that the analysis of production strategies of the public service station exemplified the traditional news values of 'objective non-partisan news' while the commercial station exemplified the new(s) epistemologies of 'subjective partisan views'.

The present chapter was the last of four empirical chapters. The following chapter summarises analytical observations at each level of analysis in relation to the 'domestication' hypothesis and concludes upon the implementation of the theoretical framework and the operationalisation of the analytical concepts.

Chapter Eight

The culturally integrative character of national news production

The process of making foreign news from its origin until it is aired is completely the same in every country. (Ikuo Wada, chief desk, NHK)

Introduction

The final chapter highlights the main observations in the analysis of international news production. It describes the conditions and challenges of news producers in 'information society'; a society characterised by fierce competition for market shares in which international news producers play an important role as mediators of information about international political processes in relation to national institutions. The observations are presented systematically related to the main argument of the book. Namely that international news is 'domesticated' and made intelligible to home audiences. In other words, it is argued that the 'global' distribution of news does not have a homogenising effect as theorised by some media scholars.

'Domestication' is explained in this book through a cognitive framework. The process of information acquisition involves the adaptation and elaboration of pre-existing knowledge schemes in the memory and thus includes models for appropriate communication in one's socio-political and professional environment. It is assumed in cognitive theory that information is processed through schemes of knowledge acquired through previous experiences. The fact alone that news events are perceived through pre-existing schemes of knowledge and made discursive for mediation according to the models and scripts (Van Dijk, 1991) of individuals is the first step in the 'domestication' process. In other words, *it is essential in the 'domestication' argument, that information acquisition happens through processes of adapting international news information into pre-existing schemes of knowledge.*

The process of 'domestication' is exemplified from the macro level of international news flows to micro levels of news production to news processing at the individual level. 'Domestication' in this project is defined as communication strategies in international news production. Within a cognitive framework, 'domestication' refers to the processing and effort of making information intelligible to a certain audience in a certain context.

Thus, the production of international news and the communication strategies of international news producers are the foci of analysis in the present project. The analysis is based on statements made by executive management at the five national stations and media experts, as well as observation and interviews with staff from foreign correspondents, scriptwriters, producers to chief editors at the public service station, NHK, and commercial station, TV Asahi. The findings at the *global*, the *national*, the *organisational* and the *professional* are highlighted in the following.

The global level

The analysis at the *global* level includes a comparative analysis of the framing processes, as they appear in news presentations in two national contexts. The content analysis of 'global' news presentations includes quantitative and qualitative methods and exemplifies how news is 'domesticated' according to national frameworks of interpretation. Although formats and framing processes were similar in the Danish and Japanese presentations in some respects, the communication strategies, the discursive compositions (of visuals and verbal accounts) and the choice of actors included elements of 'domestication' that made news content differ according to national

230

sociopolitical contexts. It is worth mentioning that even within national contexts content differed from station to station according to organisational and professional production *formulae*.

Figure 16: 'Domestication' Strategies in International News Production – a Japanese Perspective

Contextual levels	Factors enhancing the processes of 'domestication' in the selection and production of international news
Global	• National economic and political position in the global community • National interest in socio-political actors • National historical and socio-political background
National	• Broadcast system (public and private) • The political character of the media (pro-government, anti-establishment) • Affiliation between national broadcasters and international news agencies • Regionalisation strategies
Organisational	• Public interest versus commercial business strategies • Organisational factors • News' and 'views' production *formulae*
Professional	• Traditional 'objective' versus new subjective values • Generalist versus specialist knowledge domains • Political/economic versus popular framing approach

Specifically, the analysis provided examples of how national public service and commercial broadcasters in the two countries 'package' news presentations (form, studio-decoration, narrative style) and create the 'brand' image (the station profile, message) according to similar global formats. The Danish and Japanese broadcasters apply universal 'generic' formats as a result of similar professional and organisational practices.[166] The 'aesthetic' expressions and the 'choreography' of actors in the presentations are done carefully in line with the conventions of factuality in the news genre. These conventions include the employment of actors and the ritual performances of socio-political actors and professional news presenters, the cutting pace, the framing of visuals, the immediacy effect of 'live' reporting, interviews, use of graphics and props. These conventional practices are grounded in professional values that ensure

---

[166] Imitation or 'isomorphism' in new institutional theory (Dimaggio and Powell, 1991).

'real' and 'objective' presentations of news through incorporated 'objectivity claims' in textual production (Helland, 1999) or the institutionalised use of sources in a 'web of facticity' (Tuchman, 1978). The outcome of the institutionalised practises of communication (based on mental schemes and models for news production among news workers) in turn meet the expectations of viewers, who accordingly draw upon their internalised schemes of knowledge for interpretation.

In conclusion, the systematic analysis of communication strategies, discourses and actors in news content in Denmark and Japan exemplifies elements both of global and local influences, and suggests that *the strategy of 'domestication' of international information may be universally applied.*

Besides depending on global positioning and part on world affairs, the strategies for 'domestication' differ according to national, organisational and professional factors, as discussed below.

The national level

At this level four observations serve to illustrate the 'domestication' idea. Firstly, the variety of news presentation styles provided by the Japanese broadcast stations from public service to commercial news cause difference in content. Secondly, the political character of the Japanese media offers differing views of the parliamentary processes in news programs. Thirdly, the exclusive agreements with international news agencies and national Western broadcasters cause differentiated influence by Western sources. Finally, regionalisation strategies falsify the 'global' news thesis. The observations are described below.

The dual Japanese public-commercial system is found to provide Japanese viewers with a variety of news programs. Firstly, despite the legal aspirations to keep broadcast news politically neutral, domestic politics influence the production of text and images. Secondly, the public service and private broadcasters provided very different styles of news. As a provider of political information in the perspective of the governing elite, NHK represents one end of the spectrum while NTV as a provider of social information in entertainment form based on audience demand represents the other. It was found in the analysis that the news values and standard of reporting at NHK were highly estimated for their professional standards. However, the aim to keep market shares and obtain high ratings, which is the goal of all stations regardless of style, brings about a constant battle between journalistic ideals of what the imagined audience 'ought to know' and what they are imagined to 'want to know'. The political character of the Japanese media and the differing agendas between public and private stations thus provide different strategies for 'global' news processing.

A significant observation of this chapter was the close connection between the Western networks and the Japanese national broadcasters. Through corporation and exclusive agreement the Japanese broadcasters are closely connected with and rely on their affiliated sources for what they perceive as 'reliable information'. The availability of material and professional connections with these suppliers means that when possible the Japanese networks use material from their affiliates. Thus, from a globalisation perspective this is potentially a strong factor of Western influence on international news production.

It was found that differing strategies at the management level concerning international news presentation left content very varied both in news presentation styles and itinerary. A regional focus and moves of resources from West to the East were expressed as strategic measures at higher management levels.

Thus, the political character (pro- and anti-establishment), the dual broadcast system (public service and several private news suppliers), the differentiated affiliation to international news suppliers and finally regionalisation strategies were factors supporting the 'domestication' hypothesis. The vested interest in US affairs and the strong reliance on international agencies were factors supporting the global (Western) influence thesis.

The organisational level

The study at this level provides evidence that organisational factors including decision-making processes, newsroom practices and general institutionalised strategies behind news production affect 'global' news presentation. The practices at the public service and the commercial station differ greatly (as is also observed in the analysis of news presentations at the global level), and consequently 'global' news, processed by differing *formula*, is 'domesticated' differently. The following resumes the main observations at the organisational level.

The Public interest versus commercial business strategies were the prime factors of influence on production procedures at the organisational level. The fact that NHK is financed by public fees turns the focus of NHK news mediation on to political processes and public interest concerns. *News Station* in the original set up was conceptualised as a money-generating program based on commercial income, which influences the overall strategies of the program and the responsibility and focus on individuals. Whereas NHK news producers are regular NHK employees, *News Station* staff includes personalities from the TV Asahi Broadcasting Company as well as independent production companies. The NHK news producers are specialists within their field and the production process is negotiated between professional experts, while generalists are employed in most key positions at *News Station*.

The observed organisational difference between the flagship programs is partly due to the fact that the news producers at NHK are responsible for several news programs, while *News Station* has its own production crew. The role authority in the production hierarchy differs according to the organisational structure at the two stations. The hierarchical 'production line' or teamwork at NHK differs from the focus on a few individuals and strong personalities in the preparation and arrangement of *News Station*.

Further, the 'news' and 'views' strategies observed at the national level were reflected in production practices and strategic considerations at this level. The non-partisan view and adherence to traditional news reading at the public station was in contrast to the partisan new(s) epistemology focus on individual opinion at the private station. The fact that the members of the international newsroom at NHK are educated as journalists within the company as opposed the news producers at the commercial station that come from a variety of backgrounds, has important consequences for the framing of issues. The mediation process at NHK is influenced by the priority of traditional journalistic news values and expert knowledge. News values at NHK may, in short, be characterised as traditional, conventional and reliable. The production practices involve preparation to present 'objective' news from a system perspective. TV Asahi is crucially aware of the audience attraction and attention to issues and the *News Station* criteria following are proximate, interesting and instantly gratifying. The production practices of *News Station* are guided by strategies to prepare subjective, people-oriented and anti-establishment news.

The world-views of the journalists at NHK are connected to their area of expertise. Many news producers acquire a general overview and flair for news production over time, but the level of the international news coverage at NHK requires in-depth knowledge of an area. The NHK news producers have high levels of expertise. Although an audience perspective is supposedly incorporated into the journalistic 'sense' of what makes information fit as news, the final news presentations are products of high professional standards with a focus on the description of political processes. The diversity and general background of production staff at *News Station*, the mix of straight news and longer feature stories, although based on the same journalistic standards, results in more popular presentations and choice of issues. The models for news production as reflected in the production practices witness different mental strategies of the staff at the two stations. The mental models and scripts for news production differed concerning newsroom practices, editorial decision-making news values and audience aims.

Conclusively, the difference in production practices and models for news framing differed greatly at the two stations. Against the notion of homogenisation of information through 'global' news mediation, the processes of information at the two stations show that news even within the same country is 'domesticated' in different ways regarding differing political content, appeals and audience aims.

In sum, the study at the *organisational* level highlights differences and similarities in communication strategies at NHK and TV Asahi as a public and a private station. The organisational 'formula' for news production includes a political ethos of the stations as *pro government and anti-establishment* (which were more noticeable than their Danish counterparts). The analysis at this level provides a basis for shared production strategies or *formula* for news production based on general procedures in the news organisations.

The professional level

The study at this level explores and confirms the production *formulae* as observed at the organisational (and national) level. In other words, the study of professional strategies at this level provides insights about the implementation and emergence of production strategies (including factors from the above levels) in individual action in the production of specific news. The analysis at the professional level supports the notion that news is 'domesticated'. Firstly, 'domestication' is exemplified through intentional efforts to make information familiar to national audiences. Secondly, 'domestication' strategies at the two stations follow their specific production *formulae* (objective/subjective, news/views, pro/anti-establishment), which make the outcome differ. Thirdly, the expert as opposed to generalist schemes of knowledge of the news producers guides the choice of themes in different directions. Finally, the importance assigned to the international news agencies on location provides evidence of different ideas of framing through affiliated and trusted international news sources.

Specific house norms negotiated by NHK news producers included 'objective' news production and factual commentary, which was carefully considered in the production process. 'Domestication' policies were affected in the coverage of the consequences of the UN agenda on domestic policy-making. NHK news producers were strategically framing news in the capacity of a government spokes-channel and consequently sought to make little criticism of government action and less of international political partners of interest to Japan. In case of criticism (as in the US criticism of China), they would be less critical than the international news agencies and at the most make indirect criticism through use of agency material. The NHK journalists expressed knowledge about Chinese-Japanese political and economic relations, and their spectacles in metaphorical terms were focussed on political processes from a non-partisan point of view.

The Asahi news producers, by contrast, were not guided by elaborate schemes of knowledge about the economic and political implications of the conference. Their frame of mind was to cover the events of the conference though observation and interviews about popular issues. Entertaining, informative, and *critical* reportage about unfolding events describes their efforts to frame the atmosphere on location with national audiences in mind. The house norms reflected in the TV Asahi news producers' strategies were a) the eagerness to cover gender issues in Japan measured against foreign advances, and b) the effort to cover the comfort women affair, a recurrent public concern. The house norms most carefully followed by *News Station* staff were to express *critical* views. The coverage of the 'comfort women' with a critical commentary on the Japanese government's irresponsibility in war crimes and the human rights implementation and nuclear testing in China fulfilled the norms. The critical approach was similarly exemplified in the attitude towards the 'superficial non-confrontational appearance of the Japanese NGOs' and the only *male* government representative, who was Japanese. The participating Japanese female politicians were criticised for using the event mainly as a 'photo opportunity' without political engagement in women's issues. These were all critical views behind critical reports.

In sum, the strategies of NHK were to make 'objective' news in the traditional journalistic sense of appealing to rationality with statistical corroboration and political economic commentary. The emotional appeal of TV Asahi is a more 'subjectivist' approach to news coverage. The subjectivity can be constructed through a variety of textual means, including prominent use of visual, popular language and interviews designed to elicit emotive and experiential accounts. It is worth mentioning that the Japanese public service and the commercial station analysed were more factual and information intensive in their approach to international news coverage than their Danish counterparts (see news presentation Chapter Four and production practices Chapter Six).

On a final note, the strategies and factors of influence listed at each level serve to illustrate news 'domestication'. Two main factors support the notion of domestication across levels were: firstly, an intentional effort to make information familiar to national audiences incorporated into professional mental scripts and secondly contextual differences at the national, organisation and professional level which made news content differ.

The communication of complex international information

Cognitive theory provides a means in this project to describe the mental models and perceptions of the world held by individual news producers and shared at the social level of their professional environment. Two concepts stand out in the analysis, namely *framing* and *priming* (Fairhurst and Sarr, 1996). The following recommends the employment of these concepts in the analysis of international news communication. The ensuing sections summarise international news frames and world-views as expressed by the news producers and discuss the embeddedness of national linguistic and visual expressions in relation to theories of '*audio-visual* imperialism'.

Framing and priming

The research unfolds the complex arrays of mental strategies that underlie the production and circulation of media discourse. The analysis of professional mental models and negotiation of information between news workers reveal the multiple decisions made. Although intentional strategies may be at work, decisions may end up being arbitrary, while others emerge as visuals and texts are combined as news. *Framing* is the essential tool employed to describe newsmakers as managers of meaning. The ingredients in the framing process include the perception of and making sense of events, the ability to judge their character and significance, and finally the ability to mediate their content as news. The project relies on the concept of framing to explain the textual strategies in international news production.

The study of textual strategies in news production at several analytical levels brought forth insights about the use of agencies, audience considerations and knowledge about international affairs across contextual levels. The insights gained in the study of the specific news (the UN Conference on Women) concerned gender issues and equal rights. Specifically, the analysis made schemes of knowledge explicit about the notions of women's issues in UN policies; gender in media discourse and in society in general; gender in relation to work conditions in media organisations, and finally gender issues as individual knowledge and working strategies of the news producers.

The concept of framing was initially inspired by the empirical conceptualisation of the term as described in the methodological chapter. The concept of framing has been employed in previous research as listed in the theoretical chapter. It is referred to in the classic newsroom studies as the 'deep structures' (Schlesinger, 1978) of news producers, based on professionals' reference to a 'sense of news'. The 'sense of news' (*kan*) was likewise referred to in the Japanese newsrooms. It encompassed every aspect of the production from news values and newsworthiness to the concern with time, to political spins on stories, to the actual wording, fore-grounding and back-grounding of information in script writing and the choice of visuals.

Framing, in this study, is defined as professional communication strategies encompassing the 'sense of news', the acquisition of organisational values and knowledge about international events. Framing includes professionally learned models and intuitive abilities to grasp what was referred to in the newsrooms as the *atmosphere* of events. These intuitive abilities assume, as elaborated in the theoretical chapter, *synaesthetic* effects or cross-modal sensory modelling by which people perceive sensory equivalencies between colour and sound, or sound and smell. The present analysis assumes this synergy between senses but the analysis is limited to a focus on *audio-visual* mediation.

Priming, a subcategory of framing, is applicable to the study of news communication as it includes an awareness of *time, priority* and *context* in information processing. Priming refers to the preparation of one's unconscious mind before thoughts are expressed through language. It is a necessary state of readiness that is critical for effective 'spontaneous' communication as presented in news. The use of language in the process of priming and communicating news information may be both unconscious and conscious.

236

The concern with time is paramount in news reporting; deadlines and limited time on air make news producers develop certain skills for prioritising information, choosing headlines, metaphors, narrative forms, roles and actors familiar to audiences. The activity of priming occurs already in the initial negotiations between news producers in the field and the Tokyo office about the composition of visuals and text. For the reporter on location, anchors and commentators priming is an ability to prioritise and present information in the immediate situation. It requires vast reservoirs of world knowledge to make inferences (Van Dijk, 1991) and to prioritise information about political events.

In sum, the time factor and priority of information included in the concept of *priming* served well to analyse communication strategies in news production. News reporting may be well prepared but often circumstances allow little time for carefully scripted speeches. Priming serves to explain the prioritising of information in mind and making it explicit within the context of the situation. The anchor at the Japanese commercial station was exceptionally skilled in priming and framing. His ability to 'translate' international news and comment on complex information into everyday common sense terminology was a core reason for the success of *News Station*. The anchor was exceptionally skilled because (a) his messages although well prepared seemed spontaneous (b) commentary on air is irrevocable and the ability to make comments better than could later be thought up characterised his style of communication.

Conclusively, influenced by the myriad of contextual combinations of factors described in this study, the skilled framers 'read' a context and prepare accordingly. All other things being equal (such as the amount of information that they possess about a subject), news producers prime not only by reflecting consciously, but also and not least by communicating events to co-workers who may be gate-keepers or advocates of their story proposals. Negotiation of meaning occurs through discussion with co-workers on location or in the newsrooms (*ba*), which enhances awareness of the story content. The awareness through communication with co-workers primes the unconscious as reflection does. Whether reflections are communicated or not, mental models are brought to the surface and conscious recall leaves an unconscious imprint. The more communication draws from the state of mental readiness that priming creates, the more successful communication becomes. The artfulness of communication lies within the ability to frame and make comments on-the-spot "as good as the one that could be later thought up" (Goffman, 1986:50). This indeed was found to be an ability of the anchor at the commercial station.

Against this backdrop, it deserves emphasis that the present study does not contribute with cognitive theoretical findings. It merely employs analytical concepts based on a cognitive framework. Although not observed 'real time', the retrospective accounts of production processes and study of news presentations do provide examples of framing and priming strategies in action.

At the societal level the priming of public consciousness is one of the most important and powerful tasks of the mass media. Priming at this level has a dual function. On one hand national news discourse represents knowledge and public sentiment, on the other it constitutes it by bringing certain issues on to the agenda. While priming influences what to think about framing influences how to think about it.

The following reiterates observations concerning international news frames in the international newsrooms in relation to previous research on news criteria and newsworthiness.

International news frames

The news mix in Japan differed from the rest of the world as described in the previous chapter, and the degree of 'domestication' was high (see quantitative and qualitative analysis of three 'global' news stories in appendix 1). The difference in news mix was mainly due to the global position of Japan and its differing interest in international news due to national political and historical background. The ability to 'domesticate' was influenced by the national media organisations' economic ability to place Japanese held cameras and highly qualified staff around the world. It was a concern in the newsrooms that new models for political commentary had not yet replaced the overarching frames of interpretation of international news in the Cold War era. Concerning professional criteria for international news framing, the values referred to in Japanese newsrooms most resemble the criteria listed in research on international news agencies, as elaborated upon below.

It was a major concern in the international newsrooms that the Cold War news frames that had dominated international news production and political commentary in Japan since the Second World War had not been replaced by new frames of reference through which international events could be explained to national audiences. The US-Russian shadows have been used as *international frames for political commentary* in news reporting and new ones have not been able to replace this 'political consequences' frame since the fall of the Berlin Wall. With the end of the Cold War polarisation between the East and West, the central organising frame of international news was lost and many new ones emerged instead to guide reporters in their coverage of international news (see Chapter Four).

US-related events including US international involvement have been the focus of world events and an overarching theme and a strong point of identification for the Japanese national media. The result of this media focus is that the Japanese general knowledge of the US far overshadows that of other parts of the world. The cognitive map of the world as a result of excessive US-related media coverage occupies a disproportionate amount of space in the mind of the Japanese (Krauss, 1995). This cognitive map was congruent with observations in the newsrooms where knowledge about US affairs was considered general, whilst knowledge from other parts of the world was held by special experts.

In sum, the selection of issues and geographical areas was influenced greatly by Japanese diplomacy and foreign policy. This, in turn, was based on historical relations and economic ties. There is a strong awareness in the NHK newsroom that the Asian countries follow NHK news in order to be on top of political developments in Japan. It was expressed in interview statements that International news production is changing focus towards Asia.

News values that sum up studies of domestic and international news production and resemble most of those mentioned in the *international* newsrooms of the present study have derived from research on the international news agencies (Paterson 1998: 93). The list includes *timeliness, proximity, consequence, human interest* (emotional value), *prominence, conflict,* and importantly *visual quality* and finally *topicality*. Timeliness was connected to the judgement of whether a story was up to date in relation to recent Japanese media and political discourse. *Proximity* was, as mentioned above, the estimated sense of closeness felt by the Japanese audiences. *Consequences* of international events were judged against the relation of the news item to Japanese socio-political circumstances. It deserves mention that an 'economic consequences' frame was employed in order to mediate complex (*fukusatsu*) information about political and economic news. The specific example referred to economic affairs in the European Union. This finding supports the research of De Vreese (1999), who found the 'economic consequence' frame to dominate news presentations and reception of the introduction of the common coin into the European market.

Human interest issues were raging highly as news values in Japan, especially at the commercial stations. The presentation of stories concerning the fate of individuals with an emotional appeal was considered successful reporting at the private stations. *Prominence* concerned how well known stories and actors were. Current international political issues, government officials or representatives of nations were considered prominent. *Conflict* (from wars to political disagreements) was one of the most prominent values. This was because critical situations often demarcated clear views of pros and cons, which were easy to mediate as news. The visual quality was a major factor in news selection. Although the main part of the news presentation consists of professional newsreading and commentary in still (static) positions, visuals are paramount in the choice of themes. *Topicality* (*topics* or *wadaisei*) was mainly mentioned in the commercial newsrooms. The value of topicality was more prominent in the 'infotainment' and 'tabloid' styles of broadcast news. *Topicality* (which included accidents, disasters and social stories) was an incorporated news value replacing political economic commentary at some commercial stations. This bore witnesses to the market orientation of news production, mentioned above. *Topicality* was not mentioned as a news criterion at the public service station.

To sum up, the news values derived from production studies at the international news agencies as listed above (Paterson, 1998) resemble those expressed in the Japanese international newsrooms. The models of international news production, whether at the agencies or in international newsrooms, are similar. However, one important difference between their approaches is their audience considerations. The key target of the agency coverage is a few favoured Western broadcasters, namely the BBC, CNN and ABC (Paterson, 1998: 94), while the Japanese broadcasters, as observed in the present project, aim at a national audience guided by a different (non-Western) socio-political and economic agenda.

The following describes the observed embeddedness of language and visuals in the framing of international news. The observations support the 'domestication' hypothesis against theories of '*audio-visual* imperialism'.

Linguistic embeddedness

As was observed in the newsrooms, the process of making news scripts and framing events was based on linguistic considerations. The translation process may be described as a 'cultural translation' in which terminology, headlines, fore-grounding and back-grounding of information were means of 'domesticating' international events sentence by sentence. The process of translating international events thus involves an application and matching of Japanese expressions and ideas against the English interpretations while striving to make local and global coherence within audio-visual texts.

A considerable part of international news production concerns the translation of incoming information into Japanese. In the process, there were different steps of negotiation between scriptwriters, sub-desk, desk and producer in order to *shape* news and target the viewers in mind. These considerations included (a) the arrangement of information b) the selection or rejection of particular parts of agency scripts and (c) the choice of vocabulary. The negotiations about information and suitable vocabulary were extended from the newsroom to the foreign correspondents and occasionally to staff from the agencies, who were approached in order get more accurate information about the initial processes of making the event discursive. What were the experiences, ideas and considerations (motives) behind the initial 'framing' of the event? These questions were asked in order to estimate how the editorial interface at the agency had affected the story. In the Japanese newsroom a different angle more suitable for the Japanese audience was desired and it was important to acquire as much information about the original happening as possible. In the field, journalists were face to face with their sources; at the desk in the Tokyo newsroom it required years of experience and professional knowledge in order to make inferences about the occurrence of events. The ability to make inferences is learned over years of accumulated knowledge through experience.

It has been argued by the advertising scholars, Kramer and Ikeda (2000), that due to global media domination, Western tastes are becoming world tastes. The 'linguistic imperialism' (Phillipson, 1996) hypothesis implied in this argument is partly falsified in the present project. The public service and the commercial stations employed different strategies in their use of language. The public service very conservatively adhered to Japanese expressions, whereas the private stations included several foreign loan words. The language policy of NHK was conservative and no loan words were found in its news. The amount of loan words (English words imported and written in *katakana*) was considerable at the commercial station. Although the imported loan words and expressions were used by senior politicians and news professionals in the news presentations, the fact that they were not deleted in the editing process, as they may have been at NHK, witnesses a liberal language policy. This liberal language policy may be driven by an aim to address younger audiences, who are fascinated with English expressions. Although imported and appropriated with the English pronunciation, loan words in Japanese remain distinct as they are written in *katakana*, a phonetic syllabus for loan words.

Against the view of homogenisation and consensual communication around the globe as the 'global' news and 'linguistic imperialist' theories imply, the fact that international news is translated into different languages according to national frameworks of reference or webs of shared meaning (Geertz, 1973) makes content differ. The fact that 'global' news is translated into multiple languages world-wide according to different cultural (linguistic) and national political backgrounds supports the 'domestication' argument.

It is worth noting that the Japanese language has been claimed to be one of the most complicated and 'unique' languages in the world because of its 'situated meaning' (Bachnik and Quinn, 1994) and enigmatic expressions. It is claimed by a professor of Japanese Cultural Studies at the University of California that: 'There is no language better suited to obfuscation than Japanese' (Nathan, 1999). According to the 'theories of Japaneseness' (that have not been scientifically proven) one has to be Japanese to understand Japanese communication. Against these claims, there were no apparent problems in the translation of news discourse nor in interpersonal communication with news producers. Linguistic differences (such as omission of nouns as described in the methodological chapter) made Japanese communication no more 'contextual' and 'enigmatic' than professional communication would have been in the US or Europe. In conclusion, it deserves mention that although the theories of Japanese 'uniqueness' have not been scientifically proven the interview transcripts included many statements about the Japanese sense of self as influenced by these theories. (See discussion of *Nihonjinron* in Clausen 2000 Chapter Three).

Visual embeddedness

Related to the issue of 'linguistic imperialism' discussed above, Kramer and Ikeda (2000) claim that the present times are essentially *visio-centric* (as opposed to *phono-centric*). The world, in their view, is saturated with surface images in what they describe as 'a world of screens and tele-colonial powers'. They contend (like the premise in media agenda studies) that media not only influence *what* to think about, but also *how* to think about it. Kramer and Ikeda argue that as a result of technological development and Western influence on media conglomerates 'a single aesthetic body image is emerging globally and that is Caucasoid' (Kramer and Ikeda, 2000:83). They further argue that a Caucasian standard ideal is being promoted with intense force via the power of global media, which in their view confers status onto the 'surgically and computationally enhanced Caucasian phenotype and aesthetics' (ibid.). The findings in this project challenge the Western cultural imperialist thesis of Kramer and Ikeda. See also Ito Youichi 'Western Narcissism' (forthcoming) for a critical discussion of the one-sided 'Western cultural pre-eminence' globalisation perspective of Kramer and Ikeda.

In their critical assessment of the influence of Western tastes, Kramer and Ikeda argue that, according to the fundamental logical comparison and identity formation, non-western people inevitably find themselves to be different, and this difference is often cast in the light of being inferior. The result is that the more the non-Westerners attempts to "adapt" and fit the ideal mould, 'the more they are likely to come to see themselves a hopelessly inadequate, if not ugly' (Kramer and Ikeda, 2000:83).

Against this argument, although the formats of television news were found in this study to be modelled after Western formats, the content was 'domesticated'. The 'domestication' of content included the choice of actors, which included a mix of Asians, Hispanic and Caucasian. The professional TV staff was Japanese (except for one foreign news producer at the commercial station), while the focus on social actors appearing on the screen was on Asians as well as Caucasians with emphasis on Asian. There was no perceived preference for Caucasian actors.

In perspective, it should be noted that, while global formats (modelled after Western networks) were found to be characteristic of news programs, much other Japanese programming was 'local'. Japanese game shows, entertainment programs and dramas are characterised by their own formats, content and aesthetics. *Dallas* and other American dramas that have achieved world-wide success did not become popular in Japan.

As part of the 'domestication' strategy, the commercial station broadcast news about how foreigners perceived Japanese participation in the UN Conference on Women in Beijing. In this news, Asian and Japanese actors were interviewed more frequently than Caucasian. The inferiority complex mentioned by Kramer and Ikeda was not expressed in the interviews of the present project nor sensed in the newsrooms. Rather, comments were made about the US as a 'elder brother' in a family relationship at the public station, while critical attitudes towards the US were made clear at the commercial station.

The fact that Hillary Clinton was prioritised above the Japanese government spokesman on the second day of the conference was not a Japanese phenomena, but a world wide media reaction, which allowed the US first lady to highjack the media scene everywhere (but China). The massive coverage by the media around the world was based on the tense US-Sino relations concerning human rights. Although Clinton addressed various problems of the world's women in her speech, the main theme covered by the media was her criticism of Chinese human rights with the result that the most impressive messages and media discourse out of Beijing became international politics between the US and China. This international political agenda also affected the Japanese broadcast stations that allocated airtime to Clinton's speech (see appendix 2), with visual excerpts concerning this issue. In this case, the classic international news criteria put forth by Galtung and Ruge (1965) in which *elite nations, elite actors, individual action and negative events* are fore-grounded (see Chapter Two) were influencing strategic choice rather than a 'visual imperialism' due to a sense of Caucasian inferiority, as argued by Ikeda and Kramer.

The UN Conference coverage exemplifies the mechanisms of agenda-setting and coverage of international political events a chain reaction of coverage guided by big politics. The following is a discussion of remaining coverage, which although covering the same opening of government meetings on the first day of the remaining coverage followed a diversified agenda based on 'domestic' interests and interpretations of the conference. It is worth mentioning that although the Clinton speech was covered by the Danish and Japanese media under the headline of 'US Criticism of Chinese human rights' the remaining report was 'domesticated' according to the specific political and business strategies of the broadcast organisations.

Conclusion

Although recent research shows a decline in the politically and nationally integrative role of national news broadcasting, the present analysis argues that national broadcasters in spite of growing international and national competition maintain a competitive edge through their 'domestication' competencies.

At the global level (as described in the introductory chapter), the large international mediators of political and cultural information CNN International and MTV employ market strategies of diversification and *segmentation*. At the regional and national level, new concepts of diversity are found especially within the field of political communication in response to a 'growing social and political pluralism that corresponds to the diversity of the information environment' (Neuman, 1991: 38). In the US, the established networks of ABC, CBS NBC and PBS are decreasing their shares in a highly fragmented market. The original goal of domestic programming for government-regulated or public service broadcasters was social integration, a political 'unification' through the use of a domestic 'news' framework. (Dahlgren, 1991). The concepts of unification are, according to Dahlgren, in decline. This is also observed in the fall of public-service-broadcasting market shares in Western and Southern European countries. The services are losing their 'cultural' function in many countries, and are facing increasing competition with other national and international broadcasters. This trend includes the 'news' sector.

In the light of these changes, the present study found that Japanese national news producers, in spite of concerns regarding growing international and national competition (enhanced by 400 satellite channels), envision a continued need for national broadcasting. In spite of future strategies of segmentation in order to cater for individual needs in the development of new channels, executive managers envisioned no crises for their national flagship programs. Rather, the increasing international competition and growing availability of new channels according to their predictions make Japanese national broadcasts in the Japanese language as pertinent as ever. The financial and human resources of the national broadcasters are seen as enhancing the ability to frame information to national audiences. The interpretations of Japanese political processes and the translation of news into Japanese are perceived as being a competitive edge and *raison d'etre* of the national flagship programs.

The observations in this study are summed up as a discussion about particular and universal elements in production strategies. In the final analysis, the production of international news may be "characterised by a tension between the particularistic and the common; the shared world and the divided one; the effort to defend cultural borders and, at the same time, the effort to blur them" (Cohen, 1996: 154). The challenges in the international newsrooms, in other words, were twofold. On one hand, efforts were made to make international news 'a mirror on the world'; on the other hand, efforts were made to 'domesticate' international information for national audiences.

Appendix 1: Local appropriation of 3 'global' news

In the qualitative part of the 'International News Flow in the 1990s' study, three news events were considered 'global' news. Quantitative and qualitative exploration found these stories to be presented differently in Denmark and Japan. The news programs analysed were (and still are) flagship programs at the Danish and Japanese stations public and commercial stations with the highest viewer ratings[167] in the two countries. The study thus captures, as argued in the dissertation, some of the fundamental characteristics and nationally integrative character of mainstream news programmes.

The international news items were prioritised by the Japanese stations in the order: The UN involvement in Bosnia, The UN Women's Conference, The French Nuclear Testing. By comparison the Danish stations prioritised as follows: The UN involvement in Bosnia, the UN Women's Conference and the French Nuclear Tests. The newsworthyness and degrees of 'domestication' will be described in turn.

Figure 17: News Priority in Denmark and Japan

Priority	Denmark	Japan
First	UN involvement in Bosnia	French Nuclear Tests
Second	UN Women's Conference	UN women's Conference
Third	French Nuclear Tests	UN involvement in Bosnia

French Nuclear Testing

In the Japanese case, the news about the French Nuclear Testing in Mururoa contained information about the actual event. But even more so, it provided insight into the *particular* complex and emotional issue of international diplomacy and domestic policy of Japan as an antinuclear weapon country protected by the US 'nuclear umbrella'. The event was prioritised and received much airing time. On September 5th, the day of the testings, NHK extended its News Seven program with more than an hour of live reporting[168].

The French nuclear testing was a global political event. Consumer boycotts spread from Australia , New Zealand and Japan to Germany, Austria, Britain and Scandinavia. China had made tests over the past 14 months, but this met only pro forma criticism. The regional resentment from Tahiti lead by independence leader Oscar Temaru and the condemnation of the tests by Australian Prime Minister Keating therefore seemed like an economical attack by the countries in the Pacific region who wanted France out. In Denmark the Prime Minister on a trip to India condemned the tests "It is regrettable" and the Danish Minister of foreign affairs raised the issue in the EU parliament. The Japanese Prime Minister likewise in front of the cameras declared that the indident "was regrettable" (*sore wa ikan*). However, here rhetorical resemblances stopped. While both coutries are directly or indirectly protected by the US nuclear umbrella (Denmark through its Nato membership and Japan through after Second World War military

---

[167] NHK and TV Asahi 18 %, Video Research. DR1 17% TV2 21%, Gallup.

[168] The extended hour programme about the Nuclear tests is not included in the quantitative study of the News Flow Project. It was not recorded in the original material.

agreements) this was made clear in the broadcast news while the the Japanese spokesman did not address the issue further. Another Japanese Minister from the Sakigake Party protested against the testings through participation in peach marches in Australia. His activities were followed by the commercial station who made lenghty interview and coverage with him indirectly in support of his anti-nuclear views. The Danish Stations covered their own politicians filing complaints with French diplomats and venturing to Mururoa to condemn the tests.

The themes and actors in the account of the event thus featured national elite actors representing national and media organisational political interest. In Denmark, the EU nuclear policies and official stand on this issue within its members, 'our friends' became a topic. The 50th year anniversary of Hiroshima and Nagasaki, almost coincided with the first Nuclear tests on the Mururua Islands stirred revulsion against incidence. Sentiments and empathy with the Hiroshima and Nagasaki victims became the overarching themes of the Japanese public and its media coverage. Hour-long presentations of the events were presented in the national news as an urgent matter. The issue was emotional. Although France is geographically far from Japan the Japanese people felt that nuclear tests ought to be stopped immediately. Most Japanese shared this feeling and this emotional criterion carried much weight at both stations. The news was recognised as a priority at both stations, however, the approach and content of the news presentations differed. The journalistic practices and political stand of the stations influenced the news output according to the formulae described in Chapters Six and Seven.

Un Conference on Women

The coverage of the UN Women's Conference in Beijing took its point of departure in the conference and conditions in China, however, it provided coverage differed according to social political factors as described in detail in Chapters Five and Eight.

Bosnia

The news from Bosnia (which was considered big news in the Western Hemisphere), was covered in Japan for 30 seconds by the commercial stations on the day of the Nato bombings. A few days later, it was covered for 1.38 minutes by the public service station, with the headline "Three Bosnian leaders in peace negotiations". The Bosnia news in the Japanese case may be characterised as 'foreign news abroad' with no specific Japanese angle. Visuals and texts were chosen from the news agencies, translated, edited and broadcast. On the day of the Nato bombings of Bosnia, TV-Asahi covers the news from Bosnia (30 sec). This 'world' event entered the news scene in Japan only after the involvement of the global players UN and Nato[169]. The Balcan matter was seemingly very far from the matters of interest in Japan. Its news value and newsworthyness differed greatly according to socio-poltical differences in the regions of belonging. In Denmark the Bosnian war had first priority as news (It was a continuing story into the new millennium). In Japan it was barely presented as a short straight news spot.

---

[169] Interview with News Station, producer, September, 1997)

246

The three news stories considered 'global' news in the international News Flow Study included both global and local elements. Specifically, the news about the French Nuclear Testing in Mururoa presents information about the French action in Mururoa, but even more so, it provided insight into the complex and emotional issue of international diplomacy and domestic policy of Japan as an antinuclear weapon country and victims of the atomic bombings of Hiroshima and Nagasaki. The Women's conference in Beijing concerning the United Nation's policies on Equal rights, provided insights about happenings at the event with focus on the Chinese organisers. The topic and foci of framing differed greatly between Denmark and Japan following different strategies of domestication as argued in Chapter Five. The UN involvement in Bosnia was only fragmentarily represented. It serves as an example of 'straight' news based on feed from the international news agencies with no special Japanese angle. Although this news may be considered 'global' based on its content (see definition in chapters of Introduction and Conclusion). The quantitative difference and the dis-synchrone coverage do not support theories of 'global' news and homogenisation of 'global' consciousness through news.

Figure 18: 'Global' news in Japan

Station	News Theme	No.	Minutes
Monday, September 4th, 1995			
NHK	French nuclear testing continues –protesting	4	2.41
NHK	French Priests hunger strike as protest against French nuclear testing	5	0.55
NHK[170]	Women's conference – Government meetings opening – Equal rights demand	17	1.53
Asahi	Protest against nuclear testing – Diet members leave for Murora	4	6.46
Asahi	Women's conference opening – Government meetings begin	5	5.34

Station	News Theme	No.	Minutes
Tuesday, September 5th			
NHK	UN World Women's Conference – Hillary Clinton	13	1.39
Asahi	Nuclear testing – President Giraq	1-3	11.53
Asahi	Women's conference – Hillary Clinton – Spokesman Nosaka	6	5.21
Asahi	French nuclear testing - US nuclear testing at Marshall Islands	12	9.33
Asahi	Nato starts bombings in Bosnia	16	0.30

Station	News Theme	No.	Minutes
Wednsday, September 6th, 1995			
NHK[171]	French nuclear testing – Protest are spreading around the world	23-32	(20.33)[172]
TV Asahi	French nuclear testing –Murora		39.16
TV Asahi	NGO forum against testing		2.20

Station	News Theme	No.	Minutes
Thursday, September 7th, 1995			
NHK	French nuclear testing – demonstrations	9-11	5.37
Asahi	French nuclear test – French territories in Polynesia		13.22
Asahi	Women's conference – women's reaction to participating men		2.52

Station	News Theme	No.	Minutes
Friday, September 8th			
NHK	Tahiti protesting against nuclear testing	12	2.37
NHK	Nuclear protest in Hiroshima	13	1.00
NHK	Bosnia – 3 foreign ministers of fighting countries meet for peace negotiation	29	1.38
Asahi	French nuclear testing – violent action in Papeete	-	4.o5
Asahi	NGO – Final forum – feminism in Japan, general impression	-	5.57

---

[170] NHK educational channel broadcast three special programs in a series:" The United Nation's Women's Conference in Beijing – what are the world's women fighting with?" September 25th (8:00-8:45); II September 26th (20:00-20:45); III September 27th (20:00-20:45).

[171] The lawyer of the Aum trial -- Moto and family were found murdered. This issues covered the entire New Seven program. News Seven was extended for one hour and 15 minutes in order to cover the French Nuclear testing in depth. This extension was not tape recorded or coded in the original News Flow Data set. 8

[172] One hour extension

Figure 19: 'Global' news in Denmark

	Monday, September 4th		
DR 18.30	UN Women's Conference Opening – with song and drama	7	1.50
DR 21.00	Bosnia – quiet before the storm. Croatia – peace	55	6.7
DR 21.00	UN Women's Conference Opening – Chinese authorities cause trouble	9	1.37
TV2 [173] 19.00	UN/Nato ultimatum – last chance for the Serbs to withdraw	1	4.33
TV2 19.00	Women's conference – security control overdone by the Chinese hosts	3	2.47
TV2 19.00	French Nuclear testing – world delegations demonstrating in Tahiti (3 Danish delegates)	7	0.35
	Tuesday, September 5th		
DR 18.30	Bosnia – Nato bombings	1	2.40
DR 18.30	French Nuclear Testing – Protesting from Crook Islands – Chirac defends	10	1.30
DR 18.30	Hillary Clinton criticising host country for not admitting NGO's	11	1.25
DR 21.00	Bosnia – Nato continues bombing	1	5.5
DR 21.00	Protest French Nuclear testing – Girac reasons in technical term to save political face	9	0.30
DR 21.00	US Hillary Clinton sharp criticism of Chinese hosts	10	0.58
TV2 19.00	Bosnia – UN bombing – USS Roosevelt, Adriatic Sea (live)	1	7.35
TV2 19.00	UN Women's Conference – Hillary Clinton criticises China[174]	5	1.15
TT2 22.00	Nato - Serbia is bombed routinely – USS Roosevelt, Adriatic sea	1	5.19
TV2 22.00	US Hillary Clinton criticises Chinese hosts – Advocates freedom of speech	4	0.32
TV2 22.00	Nuclear testing – Mururoa Islands - Green Peace members detained by French military	5	1.07

	Wednesday, September 6th		
DR 21.00	The capital of Papete on Haiti half in ruins after anti nuclear demonstrations	1	4.07
DR 21.00	On the Tiananmen Square Danish politicians demonstrated against nuclear tests	2	-
DR 21.00	Russia's President Yeltsin condemns UN bombings	11	
TV2 19.00	France against the rest of the world – protests from the entire globe	1	11.51
TV2 19.00	The bombings will last for days – UN sees no Serbian withdrawal	3	2.17
TV2 19.00	Women's conference – Adoption of chinese orphanages – criticism against China	4	4.17

	Thursday, September 7th		
DR 21.00			
DR 21.00			
DR 21.00			
TV2 19.00	Violent Demonstration in Haiti[175]	2	2.10
TV2 19.00	Drama in Beijing – Danes protest against Chinese nuclear testing	5	2.51
TV2 19.00	Nato increases bombings in Bosnia – Golf war intensity	8	2.06

---

[173] TV2 nyhederne daily news reports (including week-ends) at 18.00; 19.00; 22.00

[174] Following the Women's conference information, a 4.45 minute piece of news about Chinese orphanages (mainly female) who are left to die in childrens homes. It is an advertisement for the English reportage "Death Rooms", which is broadcast later in the evening.

[175] TV 2 First news: 7 year old girl found sexually abused

	Friday, September 8th		
DR1 21.00			
DR1 21.00			
DR1 21.00			
TV2 19.00	Nato still bombing – Russia demands immediate stop of bombing	1	2.41
TV2 19.00	Tibetian women harasse by Chinese security – Danish delegates take action	2	2.11
TV2 19.00	Two Danish politicains protesting in Tahiti	3	1.42
TV2 19.00	EU security policy – Denmark leads criticism of French nuclear testing	5	6.12

Appendix 2: Global news visuals

DR   TV 2   NHK   TV Asahi

DR   TV 2   NHK   TV Asahi

Appendix 3: Information-processing model for schema theory.

(From "Schema Theory: An Information Processing Model of Perception and Cognition" by Robert Axelrod in the American Political Science Review, vol. 67, Spring 1973:1251. Printed with permission from Cambridge University Press 11.12.2002)

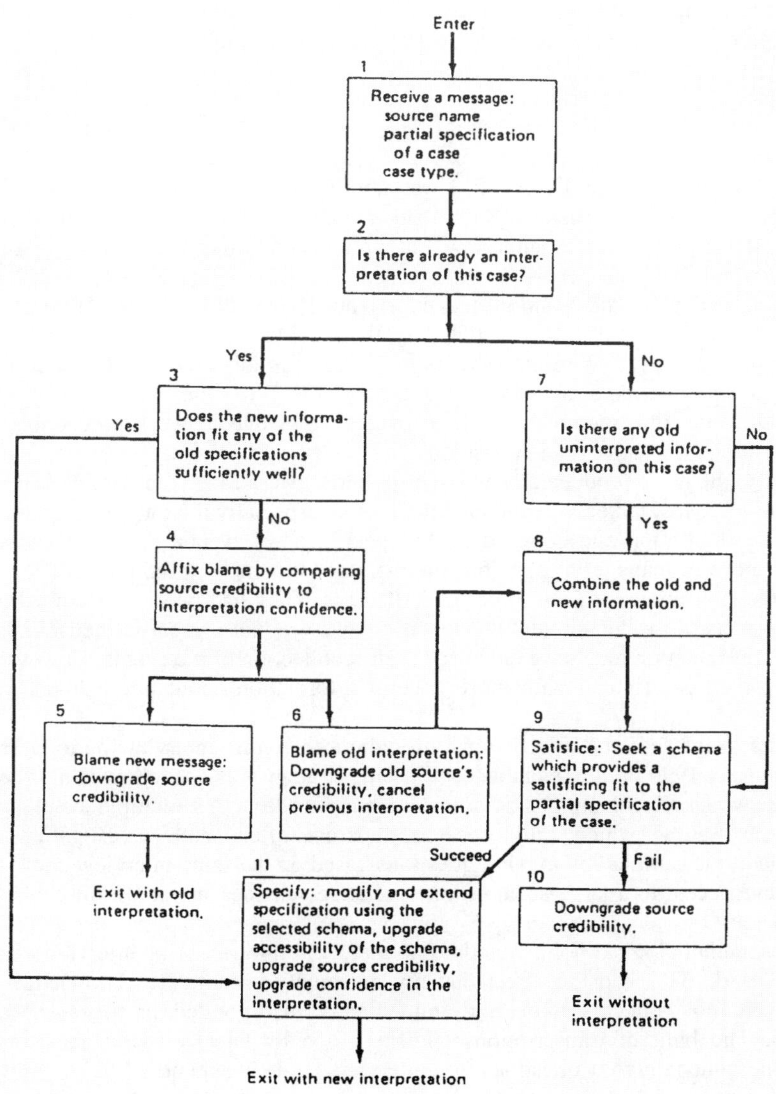

Appendix 4: Fieldwork description

Observation and interviews in newsrooms are by nature a confidential matter as they concern company strategy, production policy, political matters and in the case of international news is closely connected to domestic and foreign policy. Additionally, news is one of the programs that have the highest viewer ratings of any station. News broadcasters therefore are constantly aware of viewer ratings while trying to protect the originality of their own program. Thus, the trust in the researcher and the legitimacy of the project was important in getting access. The initial preparations, observation and the interview process lasted from the spring of 1996 until the end of 1997.

The set up

Through three months of regular observation at NHK, and the more occasional observation opportunities at TV Asahi, I was familiar and had talked with most of my interviewees on several occasions. Some had already explained part of their working experiences before the actual interview but volunteered information again with no hesitation when the tape-recorder was turned on. The interviews took different directions according to the position and experience of the interviewee. Trainees and scriptwriters were generally very detailed in their explanation of procedures, where highly ranging executives with many years in the news production business were more apt to explain production strategies as 'a sense of news'. In other words socialisation and internalisation of structures over time made knowledge of work procedures and production strategies (values) less conscious.

Generally, the news producers were eager to participate in the study and talked with no reservations. Most talked at length about an issue, especially the journalists, who had been active on location and engaged in the specific news events. Some interviewees especially those in managerial positions and some of the anchors did not recollect the actual production process of the three 'global' news. They had been preoccupied with different aspects of production and the specific news was not present in their minds. A short news presentation may have enhanced their recollection of the events. However, in most cases they contributed with more general information about international news production.

I adhered to the same basic questions throughout the entire interview period (which lasted from May 1996 until November 1997). This strategy was not followed in order to quantify answers i.e. generate positivist results, but in order to get multiple insights into the research issues (which only became apparent after some investigation and observation at the stations) by making questions based on the same interview cues. This strategy gave access to a large scale of 'interpretative schemes' about a limited number of phenomena.

Another methodological point was the fact that I did not transcribe interviews while doing fieldwork. This had the effect that my personally accumulated knowledge and insights were not reflected upon and immediately incorporated in the subsequent interviews. The bulk of transcriptions (finished 2 years later) provided answers to basically the same interview questions (see interview guide in appendix 5):

When introduced to the general research aim some talked at length. Others were more concise in their answers. Common for all interviews was the positive attitude and easiness with which conversation flowed. Many of the foreign correspondents seemingly enjoy being on the other side of the microphone. The interviews resulted in many 'selfcontaining stories' about news production. These individual stories were later 'torn apart' and reassembled in sections of generalised themes.

Interviews

Although the initial interviews and visits to the newsrooms were *explorative*, I soon decided to concentrate on the production of the specific news events, which made the interviews more focused although still semi-structured. The interviewees' statements are seen as discussed above as co-authored by the interviewer in a process of interaction.

The interviews were conducted with personnel from all levels of the companies as practised by several scholars in news production (Warner, 1970, Epstein, 1974, Schlesinger, 1987, Paterson, 1996) but did not include executives at the boardroom level. Interpersonal communication through computers and the use of technology was not part of the study (Paterson, 1999, Cottle, 1999). The interviews were semi structured with the 'cultural ignorance' approach (Spradley, 1979) empowering interviewees through active listening and encouragement to elaborate. All the while the interviewees were made understood that they were the experts their perceptions valid.

Transcription of interviews

Most of the formal interviews were conducted in Japanese. Although most of the international news producers were fluent in English (through stationing abroad and scriptwriting training) they seemed more at ease talking about their work in Japanese. The use of Japanese during interviews turned out to be an advantage in the transcription process. It was possible to transcribe and translate Japanese sentences because clarification of terminology was in many instances made during the interviews. In the English interviews on the other hand, I had relied on the English expressions without asking for clarification. The English interviews mixed with Japanese words made sense in the interview situation but away from the newsrooms or coffee-houses (*kisaten*) where the interviews took place, I had forgot the original understanding and meaning of the arguments. The coherence and situational understanding was lost and too many alternative interpretations possible in retrospect. Long passages of the English interviews were therefore not included in the analysis.

The interviews, which lasted between 40 minutes and two hours, were translated in the process of transcription. A native Japanese academic, who is fluent in English, has transcribed ten interviews. Over time, she became familiar with the material and able to translate even incomplete sentences with meanings implicit to immediate situation of the interview (newsroom descriptions, colleagues mentioned and on location facts concerning the specific news). I have translated and transcribed the remaining 30 tapes in full. Keio University students have written out the three hours of broadcast news into Japanese characters. Of the broadcast news material only a few exemplary news items are chosen for analysis and presentation.

In order to make the interviews coherent we have omitted repetitions and the frequent verbal acknowledgement (*aitsuchi*) of the listener.

As the material will not be analysed in linguistic detail some choices have been made in the transcription process. The subject (who does what) is often omitted in the Japanese language. In the transcription and translation of news texts and interviews, the subjects (personal pronouns) have been inserted. In some cases personal pronouns were made explicit in the interview. This was a special treat to the foreign researcher. The elaborate use of pronouns was further due to the theme of the interviews (the production of international news), which revolves around a continuous process of defining 'self' and 'other' in the space between global and national. At the global level 'we' (*wareware*), 'the Japanese' (*nihonjin*) and 'Japan' (*nihon*) express ideas about Japan in comparison with other nations or regions. At the organisational level 'we' (expressed by organisation name) represents the institutional identity of news producers. Finally, at the professional level, 'we/I' (profession, position within company, or implicit 'I') represents information about the news worker's professional and personal perceptions.

Newsroom Access

The access to any field depends on personal connections. Personal introductions to prominent members of the broadcasting world and to 'arteries' of human relations (*jinmayku*) within the media institutions were of importance. On several occasions, I learned that would *not* have been able to receive even the most general information on my own. One such occasion was a visit to the National Assembly of Private Broadcasters (NAB), where I was not permitted access to the library until my identity had been verified in form of a written introduction. Another was at Sofia University, where I needed the personal reinforcement by a Professor in order to even visit the library. The strategy of making initial interviews with media experts and top executives at the Japanese broadcasting stations gave the project scope and the affiliation with Keio University opened many doors. Finally, the fact that the project was part of an international academic study published in a foreign language added credibility (minimised anxiety) and was a convincing point. I will elaborate on these factors in
Through introductions at the NHK research centre, I first visited the directors of the international news department at TBS, Fuji Television, Nihon Television and the English CBS (the American affiliate of TBS). Interviews and visits to the newsrooms of these commercial stations provided me with broad perspective on international news production. In addition, I met and interviewed some members of the Japanese Press Club.

Doing observation and the main bulk of research at two competing stations was a difficult set up to start with. After meetings and interviews with the competing commercial TV stations, I was introduced to management staff at NHK and TV Asahi in order to establish an agreement. The executive manager at NHK had strong alliances. He was very open to the research idea and initially introduced me to the director (chief desk) of the international news department who again introduced me to all relevant staff. I spent more than three months at NHK and was free to join editorial meetings, news production events and to conduct interviews. Access to *News Station* was more complicated.

News Station is the flagship program at TV Asahi and the executive manager and the producer in charge at the time did not wish the production strategies to be analysed or publicised in any form. I was allowed to interview one of the program directors and yet another but then my path of introductions stopped. I went back to my contact at the

NHK Research Centre who tried to open news paths. However, formal access was not granted.

For months, I was pondering. What were the hindrances to gaining access to *News Station*? Was this failure personal (being a woman, an academic, a non-Japanese)? Or did it have something to do with the nature of connections (i.e. the key connection were not the 'right' person) Or was it in fact connected to organisational politics (in the sense that no commercial station is going to let someone attached to NHK study it)?

The answers to these questions depended on a combination of circumstances. It aspired that the producer of *News Station* did not have positive experiences with academics. Obviously he was not the 'right' person to ask to invest personal energy in the project or to secure meaningful research activity. Secondly, although the study did not have a comparative focus, the *News Station* management understandably was hesitant to grant access to production practices and business tactics for competitive reasons.

Eventually, after several months, I was introduced (through a personal connection) to the chief director of 'Super J. Channel', a newly started news program at TV Asahi. This director was well connected in TV Asahi, dynamic and open to the idea of academic analysis, which he saw as a possibility for new perspectives on news production. The Chief Director introduced me to staff at *News Station* involved with the three global news stories in 1995: the producer, the reporters, the program directors, the anchor and commentator. Introduction to others went from there. The chief director arranged access to the international newsroom (*gaihoobu*) of TV Asahi, where I watched the satellite staff, international correspondents and international 'desks' make the *straight news* circulated to all programs at TV Asahi including *News Station*. Further, the Chief Director let me observe the production of 'Super J. Channel' unlimited. Although 'Super J. Channel' was quite different in concept from *News Station* the opportunity to follow the meetings and decision making around this news programme gave an impression of the working procedures, the staff connections and company atmosphere of TV Asahi. Finally, the Chief Director arranged a one-time observation possibility of the production of *News Station*, which was too short for a detailed description but nevertheless gave an impression of the 'on air' procedures. The chief director took time on several occasions to talk (from one to four hours) about issues related to the production of international news (the history of News Station, the challenges of foreign correspondents, production procedures and co-working). One of these sessions is tape recorded and included in the interview material.

As free observation was limited to NHK, a detailed comparative description of the ad hoc working procedures at the two stations was not possible. The results thus are based partly on experience at NHK, some observation experience at TV Asahi combined with interviews. Further, it deserves mention again that the interviews are made in retrospect approximately two years after the actual production of the world news. The individual considerations therefore are made in retrospect.

The challenges of newsroom access, reseacher identity and advice for doing fieldwork in Japan are presented in the article 'Challenges in Japanese Newsroom Studies' submitted to the European journal 'Journalism' by Sage Publications.

Appendix 5: Interview guide

Introduction to interview: The purpose of this study is to describe Japanese television broadcasting policy and production processes of international news. The study is part of an international news flow research program.

What is the production policy of international news?

By which criteria/ values are international news items chosen?

What are the sources of international news?

Which considerations are made when choosing news items from the mentioned sources?

What is the political orientation of the station?

Which audience is addressed and what are consideration concerning the audience?

What were the strategies concerning the news from September 1995:

-   The French Nuclear Testing?
-   The UN Women's conference in Beijing?
-   The NATO bombing in Bosnia?

Please describe the planning, the decision-making, the production considerations and the final outcome of each piece of news.

What are some characteristics of Japanese international news production?

Appendix 6: Interview list.

Position	Date of interview
Senior researcher	December 1st, 1996 *(July 25th, 1997) (November 26th, 1997)

Position	Date of interview
Vice Director, Staff correspondent	(June 13th, 1997) July 10th, 1997
European Correspondent (General Manager)	August 21st, 1997
News 7 producer in 1995 (Executive manager)	October 10th, 1997
Chief Desk	July 17th, 1997
News Desk (French Nuclear Testing)	September 1st, 1997
News Desk	(August 21st, 1997) September 8th, 1997
Subdesk (French Nuclear Testing)	(August 22nd, 1997) August 26th, 1997
Subdesk	September 17th, 1997
Asian Desk	August 19th, 1997
Senior Commentator	July 23rd
Foreign correspondent	September 11th, 1997
Reporter on location	August 20th, 1997
Correspondent in Beijing	August 20th, 1997
Producer	August 23rd, 1997
Reporter/Scriptwriter A	August 19th, 1997
Reporter/Scriptwriter B	August 19th, 1997
Satellite Section Manager	September 11th, 1997
Trainee	September 17th, 1997
NHK International Radio	June 26th, 1997

Chief Director	(June 16th, 1997)
	November, 25th, 1997
Commentator	August 21st, 1997
Anchor	November 25th, 1997
International Department manager	June 27th, 1997
Reporter on location	July 16th, 1997
European correspondent	June 27th, 1997
Foreign Correspondent A	July 8th, 1997
Foreign Correspondent B	July 8th, 1997
Producer	June 11th, 1997
	(June 16th, 1997)
	(November 18th, 1997)
Program Director A	**) June 12th, 1997
Program Director B	October 27th, 1997
Program Director C	June 26th, 1997

TBS Director of Political News	July 11st, 1997
CBS Foreign Correspondent	July 14th, 1997
Fuji Director of Foreign News Department	July 2nd, 1997
NTV Editor of Foreign news	July 4th, 1997
Anchor	September 7th, 1997

Press Club Member	August 11th, 1997
Press Club Member	August 13th, 1997
Scholar	August 14th, 1997

Newsroom visit and interviews at Fuji TV, NTV, TBS/CBS July-September 1997.

Observation at NHK June – November 1997

Observation at TV Asahi July-August, 1997

Upon agreement with top executive news managers and media expert, they are quoted by their name in the report. News producers in other positions are quoted by their position.

*) Some news producers have been interviewed several times. The interview dates in brackets are considered general information interviews. The interviews without brackets have been transcribed for analysis.
**) This interview was not tape-recorded but written down immediately following the interview.

Appendix 7: Global news visuals

DR 1
TV avisen 21.00
September 4th
News number 9, 1.37 minuttes

Headline: The Chinese authorities create problems again

Jens Nauntofte:
The Chinese authorities created trouble today at the opening of the UN Women's Conference. The trouble occurred when the South African delegation was denied entrance. The reason was late arrival.

Bodil Kofoed:
With the Chinese sense of pomp and circumstance, colourful flowergirls, brass bands, prominent speakers and big words

- the Worlds Fourth UN Women's Conference was declared open this morning here in the People's Hall in Peking (Beijing)

[Niels Frid Nielsen]

Niels Fried Nielsen voice over:
While the Conference declared Women's liberations the last big issues of the millennium, one of the worlds most prominent female politicians South African Winnie Mandela

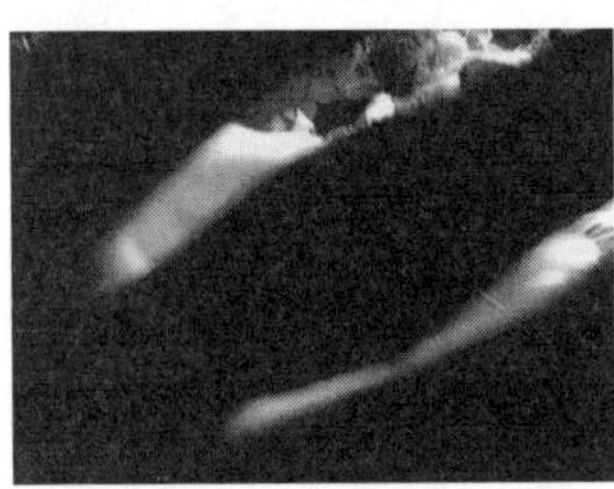

- was firmly (håndfast) denied participation in the opening ceremony.

Bodil Kofoed:
Yes, the Chinese security guards have problems with the press and the freedom of speech. Nertheless, this afternoon it was finally the UN's turn to officially open the conference

- here in the great Conference Center in the middle of Peking (Beijing).

Bodil Kofoed:
The day after tomorrow you have the chance to addres all the world's women. You have 7 minuttes. What will your message be?

Karen Jespersen, Minister of social affairs:
My message is that nice words are not sufficient - that the governments have to go home and act. They have to ensure that little girls get the same upbringing as boys - that they get food and education equally with boys.

- and they have to make sure that grown up women are not treated like the property of men, but that they have rights in equal terms and that they have the opportunity economically and in other ways to live their own lives.

Jens Nauntofte:
The alternative NGO grassroots conference continues side by side with the official UN conference until the eight of October.

TV2 Nyheder
September 4th 1995
New s no. 3
2.47 minuttes

Today was the UN Women's Conference opened in Beijing. A conference, which risks drowning in protests and conflicts because the Chinese security police has put women under constant observation and surveillance. Here is a report from our correspondent.

Eva Marie Møller voice over:
Today the opening of the Fourth UN's Women's Conference took place

Under surveillance by the Chinese security police.

[No stopping sign]

While delegates from 180 countries arrived

The Chinese had placed thousands of security guards

with walkie-talkies and videocameras.

Eva Marie Møller:
Everything looks festive here in front of the Great Hall of the People on Tiananmen Square. But behind flowers and brass band music an enormous arrangement of surveillance of each participant is hiding. This has caused a lot of irritaion among the participant already on the opening day .

Under great drama the security guards prevented Winnie Mandela from the South African delegation

[Protesters yelling]

in getting into the Peoples Great Hall when she arrived late.

Winnie Mandela was officially invited, and a group of delegates from the USA and South Afrika, were yelling in order to open the doors

The Chinese perceived it as a demonstration and pulled out the cords of the TV cameras

and hit the photograpers who tried to film the panic anyway.

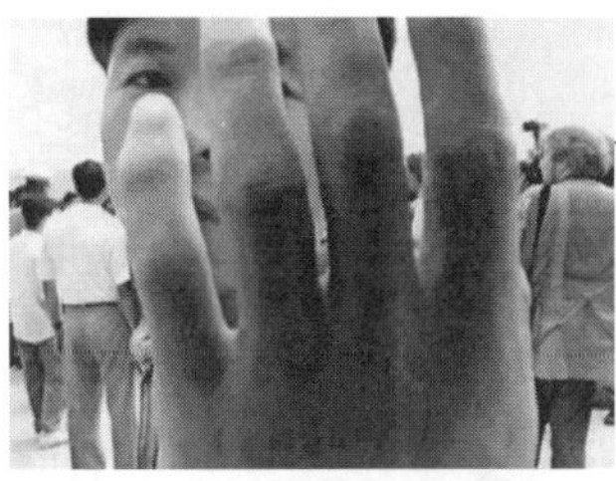

It is incredible, this uh treatment (vehemento)

Luz Gonzales
NGO deltager, Mexico

- because we come here for work together and for the dialogue inter [between] the nations.

It is not possible to work here.

The surveillance is very provocative, especially at a conference

where the headlines are equality, development and peace

Helle Degn, Member of the Danish delegation:
You cannot be a host this way. When you take on the host responsibility certain UN rules count. This is a UN country - the Chinese
security police has to play by the rules - and it is totally unacceptable and not according to the agreement
.

Eva Marie Møller: Does the strong security control lead to a boy-
cot?
Helle Degn: No, I don't think so. We have an agenda, which is so
central. Those things we have to protest against. And I feel like the
women in the NGO Forum are doing that. And we did it too before
we came and while we are here. Of course it will have consequences in the UN.

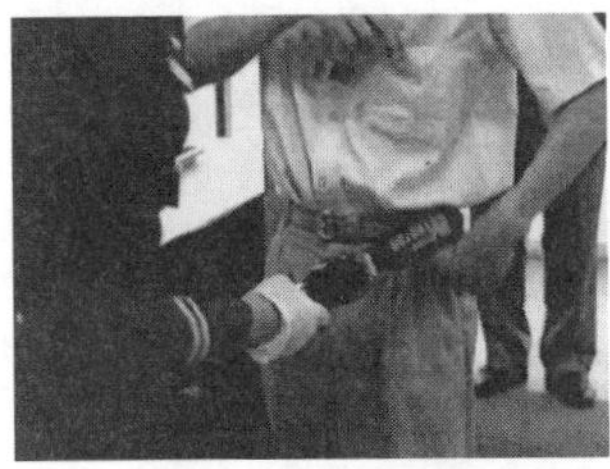

All participants at the Conferencen experience

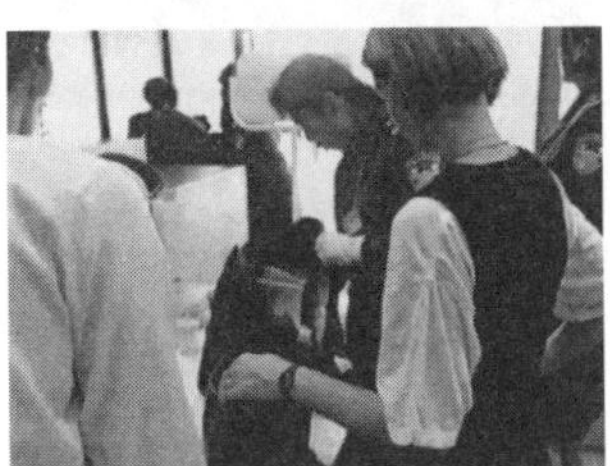

security checks several times a day

Even though the Chinese have promised

the UN to stop the constant surveillance, the participants cannot move around freely

without being filmed and shadowed by Chinese in hats and blue glasses.

UN General Secretary Boutros-Boutros Ghali was sick and had to cancel his speech today at the opening. Instead his opening speech was read aloud for the 4.000 participants.

Newsreader, Ms Morita:
At the United Nations Fourth World Conference on Women a ceremony was held in Beijing today to welcome government delegations.

The aim of the conference is to improve women's social position and achieve equality between men and women

The slogan of the equality development has been the focus of discussions since the first UN conference.

[Report. Tajima Naruyuki. Beijing]

The fourth conference is attempting to come up with specific action and implementing the slogan. Our correspondent is Naruyuki Tajima.

[Report. Tajima Naruyuki. Beijing]

Naruyuki Tajima voice over:
The UN World Conference on Women has drawn government representatives from 180 countries

Over the next 12 days the conference will address the various obstacles preventing women from having eqult opportunities

The UN Deputy Secretary General Izmad Kitani declared the conference open on behalf of the UN General Secretary Boutros
Boutros- Ghali, who could not attend the ceremony due to bad
health.

The opening ceremony was held at the International Conference
Hall in Beijing this afternoon.

Izmad Kitani:
They (the children) will look for concrete signs that Beijing in 1995 was followed by real action. Let's not disappoint them. Let's not disappoint ourselves. Together we will follow our words with our deeds.

Naryuki Tajima voice over:
Chief Cabinet Secretary Koken Osaka is leading the Japanese delegation.

At the conference Japan will make it clear that it will actively contribute to the improvement of women's status in society - and to promoting their greater participation in society.

US First Lady Hillary Rodham Clinton will take part in the conference tomorrow.

Many people are waiting to hear what she has to say about human rights issues at the conference.

The conference is expected to adopt a Platform for Action.

- which will spell out actions to be taken by the participating countries by the year 2.000.

the draft documents will address 12 mayor issues

[Platform of action]

- including poverty, violence and human rights.

[Platform for Action]

However, agreement is not likely to be easy on the issues of poverty and human rights. Many countries have different traditional values. And developing countries face situations very different from those in industrialised nations.

[Naruyuki Tajima, Beijing]

278

Komiya Tetsuko:
Yesterday we broadcast the opening of the NGO forum of the
Women's Conference in Beijing. Today the time came for the
opening of the Government meetings. The government opening
started out with a plan of action to improve equal rights.

Watanabe:
Today was the opening ceremony for the Government Forum of the
UN Women's Conference in Beijing. It was the fourth UN Wom-
ens' conference.

[World Women's Conference
Government Opening Ceremony]

Voice over:
The colorful festivities of the opening ceremony took place this
morning on the 4th of September in the People's Hall in Beijing.

[Music.. Welcome ceremony. Peoples Hall in Beijing. Today]

Following the greetings of Jiang Zemin

[Greetings by Prime Minister Jiang Zemin]

The General Secretary of the Women's Conference Mongella firmly expressed that

[Gertrude Mongella, General Secretary of the Women's Conference]

Mongella:
We are facing an historical moment. We have to change the injustice of equal rights.

Voice over:
This afternoon at four o'clock after the meeting opened

After the address of the ceremony President

[Opening ceremony. Beijing]

After the speech of the Pakistanian Benazir Butto

[Opening Ceremony. Beijing]

The state officials of each country proceeded to make their speeches receiving great applauses

Benazir Bhutto:
We are not alone in our search for empowerment - that women across continents are together.

[Prime Minister Benazir Bhutto].

[Audience clapping]

25.000 people including government representatives from 178 countries and UN delegates were gathered for the opening ceremony.

From the US Hillary Clinton arrived yesterday in order to participate and make a speech tomorrow

[Leaving from Washinton First Lady Hillary Clinton. The 3rd.]

The Cabinet Secretary Nosaka is representing the Japanese government

[Cabinet Secretary Nosaka meeting with Chinese Department of state official]

This afternoon Nosaka met with Chinese Department of State official upon arrival

- in order to suggest an end to nuclear testing

This is the schedule. From today the government meetings started. The NGO forum will run side by side with the government meetings until the 8th. The NGOs are working actively to lobby and influence the government meetings.
The plan is that the problem of women in civil war areas is included in the final discussions. The problem of the army's use of 'Comfort Women' is not on the agenda. Let's see how this is treated in the NGO forum. Hanamura Keiko is reporting from Beijing.

This is the daily paper, which is circulated from the NGO office free of charge. 2/3 of the front paper is convered with an article about the problem of the Comfort Women. The headlines says 'We need Reparations not Comfort.

[Hanamura Keiko. NGO forum in Huairou]

The Comfort Women urge the Japanese government to compensate for its war crimes and more demonstrations are planned according to the article.

[Forum '95: Reparations, Not comfort]

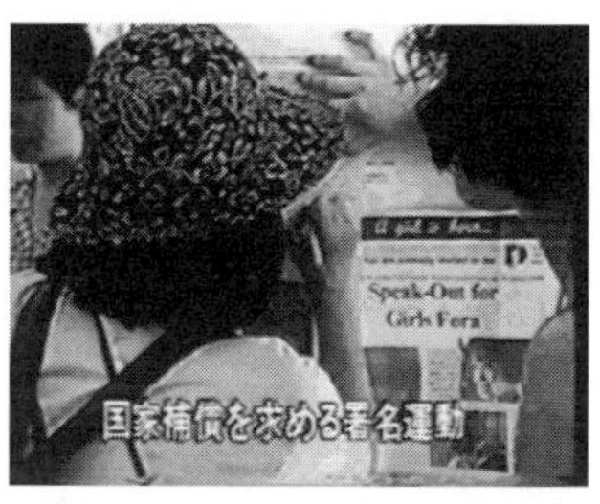

The participants from Japan are engaged in this problem.

[Petition for government compensation]

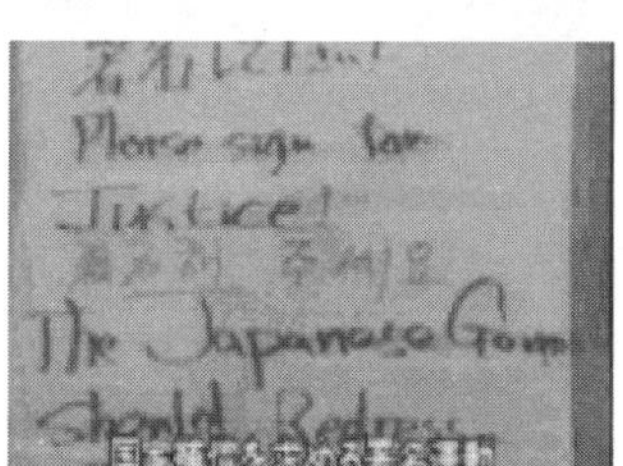

They feel that the issue concerns them

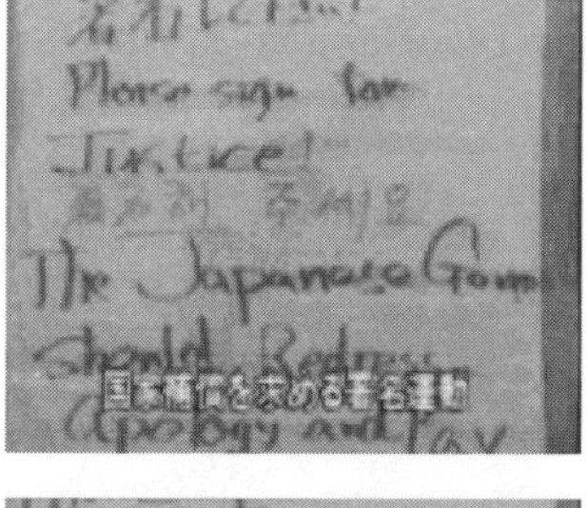

they are actively engaged in the problem

[Please sign for Justice! The Japanese Government Should Redness, Apology and Pay Individual Compensation for the Wartime Military's Sexual Slavery]

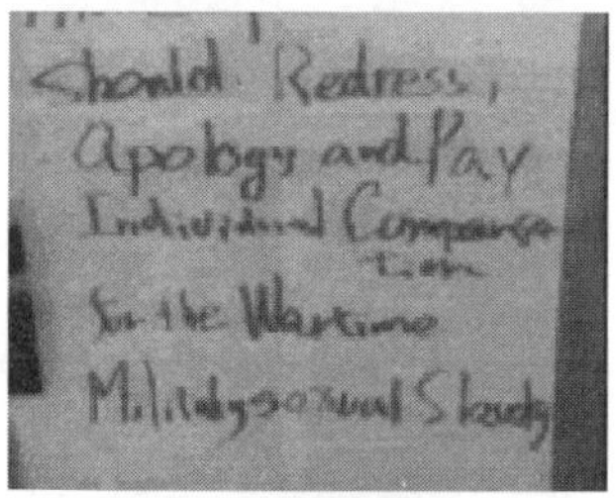

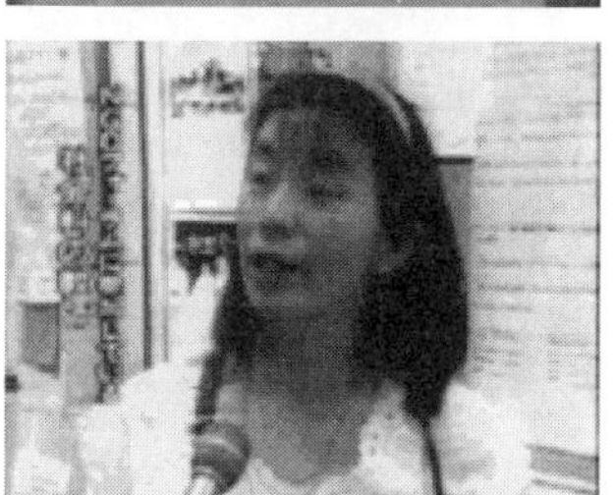

The problem is not only that the Japanese government does not apologize and take on responsiblility. The people at this conference need to know that there are many people at home in Japan, who are concerned with the problem.

[NGO Forum participant]

Movements from different countries have started working together

Korea, Japan and the Phillippines have organised a symposium

[International Symposium: Violence against women in war]

together under the theme 'violence against women in times of war'

Today about 1.000 people took part in this symposium. Among the participants were ex-'comfort women' from the Phillippines and Korea.

The Statement - that the Japanese government should make compensations and solve the problem at state level and not through its citizens - received great applause.

Participant:
It's unbelieveable. It's unbelieveable to know that situations like this happened with your women.

[Participant from Jamaica: I can't believe it. That such terrible things were done to women]

Participant:
I don't understand why it is so difficult for Japan to apologize for something that happened so long ago. It is very, very important to the Comfort Women and their family.

[Participant from Canada: I don't understand why the Japanese Government can't apologize for what was done in the past]

Participant:
I think the attitude of the Japanese government is extremely unacceptable.

[The attitude of the Japanese government is extremely difficult to accept].

Chairman of Lawyers Union:
For the individual this experience is a significant problem. It therefore raises the question whether Japan is behaving responsibly?

[Japanese Lawyers' Union: Chairman Tsuchiya]

Voice over:
At the govenment meetings starting today

One of the big themes was the prevention of violence against women.

In some countries these specific problem are not subject of discussion. A country like Japan with its specific memories cannot allow itself to ignore this motion.

[Opening ceremony. Beijing]

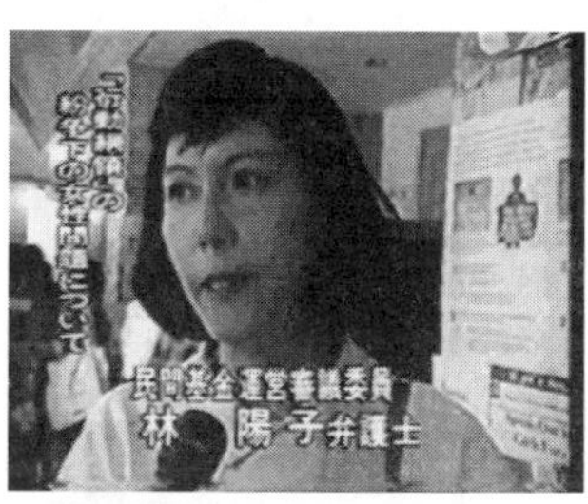

NGO Org. Lawyer:
I can't imagine that the Japanese govenment will be against the adoption of this motion. In my opinion it is not important whether the comfort Women's issue is adopted in the text or not. It is much more important how the adopted plan is implemented in Japan.

Anchor Komiya:
Certainly, the Japanese Government's thought that the Comfort Women issue is a problem of the past does not hold true.

[Sponsors: KDD, Noberu. Co. Ltd]

Commentator Wada:
That's right The problem of servicing an Army is one of the problems connected to war. Do you know the Greek play "The Peace of Women?" by Aristofanes. While the men are fighting back and forth, the women go on strike.

[Sponsors: Yonex, Sony, Suntory]

It is not the usual food strike. It's a sex strike. They strike in a group. Soon the men are in trouble and peace comes.

[Sponsors: American Express, Dai-ichi Seiyaku]

In other words, the servicing of an army is essential in war. Let's imagine that war was not possible without this service. It would be interesting to see, if future wars may be prevented by learning to master this evil.

Uh. Huh.
Hai.
Huh.
Is that so.
Hai
And now to commercials

Appendix 8: Competing new channels

Multimedia (new media) is seen as a challenge to the existing traditional broadcast stations. Along with cable TV, satellite multi-channel broadcasting is expected to have a major impact on the media scene. NHK and the commercial networks are hesitant, but the regulatory authorities are pushing to have everything, terrestrial, satellite, and cable TV, digital by year 2010. If all the planned systems go on-line, Japan will have over 400 digital channels available. The question remains whether the Japanese audiences are able to consume that much television and whether or not the programming is there?

Model: Satellite channels and ownership in Japan. (*Foreign Press Center*, 1997)

Company	PerfecTV	Space communi- cations	Japan sky Broadcasting	DirecTV
Ownership	Itochu*, Mitsui & co., Sumitomo** Corp., Nissho-Iwai		Robert Murdoch Son Masayoshi	Hughes Mitsubishi Group
Channels	97	100	150	-
Satellite	JCSAT-3	Superbird-C	J-SKY B (Japan Sky Broadcasting). JCSAT-4	Sky D?
On-line		June '97		

*** Itochu, U.S. West and Time-Warner form the multiple system operator Times Communication.**
**** Sumitomo Corporation and TCI form Jupiter Telecommunications.**

The Japanese broadcast regulations were drafted according to an American model. Until 1996 the Ministry of Post and Telegraph regulations were more restrictive than the U.S. system. The Minister of Post and Telegraph interpreted Article 59 of the broadcast law as prohibiting cable operators from providing overseas programming unless the companies delivering were either entirely or primarily Japanese. NHK's 2 satellite channels and the subscriber channel WOWOW were the main satellite programs from 1989. Until 1993, the Japanese were not able to watch BBC-Asia, STAR TV from Hong Kong, MTV or CNN International. In April the MPT further permission to STAR TV, Ted Turner's TNT and Cartoon Network to begin satellite broadcasts. (Cooper-Chen, 1997:180).

In 1996 the Ministry of Post and Telegraph further gave permission for 34 companies providing 57 television channels to participate in PerfecTV to conduct digitalised multi-channel broadcasting on consignment using communications satellites. PerfecTV is a joint venture by the four big trading companies Itochu, Misui & Co., Sumitomo Corp., and Nissho-Iwai. Australia's News Cop. President Robert Murdoch and Softbank President Son Masayoshi plan J-Sky B (Japan Sky Broadcasting). This will the JCSAT-4 launched in early 1997 and will broadcast 150 television channels in the spring of

1998. Space Communications, another Japanese satellite communications firm, wants to use its SuperBird-C satellite to be launched in June 1997 to start a 100-channel DirecTV. (Japanese Mass Media (1997), Foreign Press Center). Japan may have been slower than the rest of Asia to admit foreign competition. However, once opened, the market is exploding with channels.

Although the competitive challenge of 400 new channels, worry management at the terrestrial channels, some look forward to the new possibilities. The terrestrial stations have an advantage through their present role in society. News is an institutional medium of information catering to the need of viewers (as citizens and consumers alike) to be in tune with the beat of mass society. The ability to select and arrange international stories within a Japanese framework is the strength of the national broadcasters. "Japanese prefer to watch mass media that everyone else is watching/reading/hearing rather than to make choices. It gives them a sense of security and control." (Cooper-Chen, 1997:224) This, I believe, is not merely a Japanese trait. News viewing in both 'individualistic' and 'group-oriented' societies satisfy needs of identification. Watching domestic and international news is a means of measuring oneself within or against society at multiple levels.

It is forecast that the many new channels will cause a segmentation of society. However, the old channels will continue to broadcast for a 'society united' and offer solid competition to some 400 newcomers. NHK will still maintain its obligations to cover election campaigns, social issues and natural disasters in the public's interest.

References

Adorno and Horcheimer (1972/1979) *Dialectic of Enlightenment*, London: Verso.

Altheide D. L. (1976) *Creating Reality: How TV News Distorts Events*. Beverly Hills: Sage.

Altheide D. L. (1985) *Media Power* London: Sage

Altheide, D. L. (1987) "Reflections: Ethnographic content Analysis" *Qualitative Sociology* 10 (1) Spring. 65-77

Altheide, D. L. & Snow, R.P. (1979) *Media Logic*, London: Sage.

Altman, K. Kyoko (1996) "Television and political turmoil" in Krauss, S. Ellis, Susan J. Pharr (eds.) *Media and Politics in Japan* Hawaii: University of Hawaii Press.

Anderson, Benedict (1983) *Imagined Communities: Reflections of the Origin and Spread of Nationalism*. London: Verso.

Ang, Ien (1985) *Watching Dallas* London: Methuen.

Axelrod, Robert (1973) "Schema Theory: An Information Processing Model of Perception and Cognition" *American Political Science Review*, vol. 67, Spring

Bachnik Jane M., Quinn Charles, J., (Eds.) (1994) *Situated Meaning. Inside and Outside in Japanese Self, Society and Language*. Princeton University Press, New Jersey

Bagdikian, B. H. (1996) 'Brave New Minus 400' in G. Gerbner, H. Mowlana, and H. Schiller (eds.), Invisible Crises: What Conglomerate Control of Media Means for America and the World, Boulder, CO: Westview Press, 7-14.

Bagdikian, Ben H. (1982) *The Media Monopoly* Boston: Beacon Press.

Bantz, C. R. (1990) Organisational communication, media industries, and mass communication. In J. Anderson (Ed.), *Communication Yearbook*. Vol. 13, pp. 502-510. Newbury Park, CA.: Sage

Bantz, C. R. (1985) "News organizations: conflict as crafted cultural norm". *Communication, 8*, 225-244.

Bantz, C. R. McCorkle, S., Baade, R.C. (1981) The news factory. In G.C. Wilhoit & H. deBodk (Eds.) *Mass Communication Review Yearbook*. Vol. 2, pp. 366-389. Newbury Park: Sage

Beck, Ulrick (1992/1997) *Risk Society. Towards a news Modernity*. London: Sage.

Befu Harumi (1980) *The Group Model of Japanese Society and an Alternative*. Rice University Studies (66). Houston, Texas.

Bell, A. (1991) *The language of news media*, Blackwell

Berger, Peter L., and Thomas Luckmann (1995) *Modernity, Pluralism and the Crises of Meaning. The Orientation of Modern Man*. Güters: Bertelsmann Foundation Publishers.

Bourdieu, Pierre (1984) *The Distinction: A social critique of the judgement of taste*. London: Routledge and Kegan.

Bourdieu, Pierre (1998a) *Om TV – og journalistikkens magt*. (Sur la Television) (1996), Tiderne Skifter: Danmark.

Bourdieu, Pierre (1998b) *On Television and Journalism*, UK: The New Press.

Bourdieu, Pierre and Loïc J. D. Wacquant (1992) *An Invitation to Reflexive Sociology*. Polity Press: UK.

Boyd-Barrett, O. (1998) "Global New Agencies". In O. Boyd-Barett and T. Rantanen (Eds.) *The Globalization of News*. London: Sage.

Buckalew, J. K. (1969) A Q-analysis of television news editor's decisions. *Journalism Quarterly*, 46, 135-137

Budner, Stanley (1993) "United States and Japanese Media Coverage of Frictions between the Two countries," in *Communication across the Pacific* Missoula, Montana: Mansfield Centre for Pacific Affairs, 1993, By the Media] Tokyo: Keibunsha

Carey, J. (1989) *Communication as Cuture*. London: Unwin Hyman.

Chipnall, S. (1981) "The production of knowledge by crime reports". In S. Cohen & J. Young (Eds.) *The manufacture of news: Deviance, social problems and the mass media*. (p.p 75-97) Beverly Hills.

Clausen, Lisbeth (1996) *International News on Japanese TV – A reception Analysis*. Master's Thesis. Department of Asian Studies. Copenhagen University.

Clausen, Lisbeth (1997) "International news in Japan. A reception analysis" *Keio Communication Review*. No. 19: 39-67.

Clausen, Lisbeth (2001) *The 'Domestication of International News. A Study of Japanese TV production*. Ph.D. Dissertation Series no 21. Copenhagen: Samfundslitteratur

Clausen, Lisbeth and Thelle, Mikkel (1994) "Japanese and American Audiences – A discourse analysis of News Week Texts". Department of Film and Media Studies. Copenhagen University. Report.

Cohen, A., Gurevitch M., Levy, M., Roeh, I, (1996*)* *Global Newsrooms, Local Audiences: A Study of the Eurovision News Exchange*, London: John Libbey.

Cooper-Chen, Anne (1992) "A week of World News: TV Gate Keeping in Japan, the United States, Jamaica, Sri Lanka and Colombia" *Keio Communication Review* No. 14 March.

Cooper-Chen, Anne (1997) *Mass Communication in Japan*. Ames: Iowa State University Press.

Cooper-Chen, Anne (1998) "Trends in Japan's Foreign News: What's in, what's out". Paper presented at the International Association for Mass Communication Research (IAMCR) Glasgow.

Cooper-Chen, Anne and Kanayama Tsutomu (1998) "The Pacific Distortion: Mutual TV Coverage by Japan and The United States" *Keio Communication Review* No. 20 March.

Cottle, Simon. (1993) *TV news, Urban conflict and the Inner City.* Leichester: Leichester University Press

Cottle, Simon. (1995) "The production of news formats: Determinants of mediated public contestation" *Media, Culture and Society*, 17 (2): 275-291

Cottle, Simon. (1999a) "New(s) Times. Towards a 'Second Wave' of News Ethnography". A paper prepared for presentation at the News Panel of IAMCR conference at Leipzig 28.7.99.

Cottle, Simon. (1999b) From BBC Newsroom to BBC News Centre: On Changing Technology and Journalist Practices'. *Convergence: Journals of New Information and Communication Technologies* 5 (3): 22-43

Cottle, Simon. (2000a) "New(s) Times. Towards a 'Second Wave' of News Ethnography". *The European Journal of Communications Research* 25 (1) P. 19-41

Cottle, Simon. (2000b) "Rethinking News Access" *Journalism Studies*. (Forthcoming)

Cottle, Simon. (forthcoming) "Contingency, Blunders and Serendipity in News Research. Tales from the Field" *Communications*.

Crigler A. N. and Jensen, K. B. (1991) "Discourses of politics: talking about public issues in the United States and Denmark," in P. and C. Sparks (eds.*)* *Communication and Citizenship*. London: Routledge.

Dahlgren, Peter and Sparks, Colin (1991) *Communication and Citizenship*. London: Routledge

Dahlgren, Peter (1992) "What's the meaning of this. Viewer's plural sense-making of TV news" in Culture and Power, Scannell Paddy, Schlesinger, Philip and Sparks, Colin (Eds.) Sage publications: London, Newbury, New Delhi. (P. 201-218).

Dahlgren, Peter (1995) *Television and the Public Sphere - Citizenship, democracy and the media*. Sage: London.

Dale, Peter (1986) *The Myth of Japanese Uniqueness*. Croom Helm

Dayan, D., & Katz, E. (1992) *Media event: The live Broadcasting of History*. Cambridge, Massachusetts: Harvard University Press.

Denzin, Norman K. (1997) *Interpretive Ethnography. Ethnographic Practices for the 21st Century*, Thousand Oaks: Sage.

DeVreese, Claes (1999) "Framing the Euro in the News and in Public Opinion". Paper presented to the Political Communication Division of the International Association for Mass Communication Research (IAMCR) at the Annual Conference in Leipzig, Germany, July 27-31, 1999.

DeVreese, Claes (2001) "Frames in Television news. British, Danish and Dutch Television News Coverage of the Introduction of the Euro". *News in a Globalised Society*. Stig Hjarvard (ed.) Sweden: Nordicom.

Dimaggio, Paul and Powell, Walter W. (eds.) (1991) *The new Institutionalism in Organizational Analysis*, Chicago: The University of Chicago Press

Doi Takeo (1973) *The Anatomy of Dependence*. Tokyo: Kudansha

Epstein E.J (1973) *News From Nowhere: Television and the News*. New York: McGraw-Hill

Fairclough, Norman (1995) *Media Discourse*. Great Britain: Arnold.

Fairhurst, Gail.T. and Sarr, Robert.A (1996) *The Art of Framing: Managing the Language of Leadership*. San Francisco: Jossey-Bass.

Fausing, Bent (1994). "Glosuppe og Kigboller – om syn, køn og levende billeder". In Hoejbjerg Lennard *Reception af levende billeder* [The Reception of Moving Pictures] Copenhagen: Akademisk Forlag. 106-129

Featherstone, M. (1991) *Consumer Culture and Postmodernism*. London: Sage.

Featherstone, M. (1992) 'Postmodenization and the aestheticization of everyday life' in S. Lash and J. Friedman (eds.) *Modernity and Identity*. Oxford: Blackwell.

Featherstone, M. (1995) *Undoing Culture: Globalisation, Postmodernism and Identity*. London: Sage.

Featherstone, M. and Lash, Urry (1995) *Spaces of Culture: City Nation World* London: Sage.

Feldman, Ofer (1991) "Political Parties, Politics and the Japanese Media*", Keio Communication Review*. No 13. March.

Feldman, Ofer (1993) *Politics and the News Media in Japan* Ann Arbor: University of Michigan Press.

Fishman, M. (1980) *Manufactuing the News*. Austin: University of Texas Press.

Fiske, John (1986) "Television: Polysemy and Popularity" *Critical Studies in Mass Communication*: 395-408

Fiske, John. (1994) *Media Matters: Everyday Culture and Political Change*. Minneapolis: University of Minnesota Press.

Fiske, John (1987/1997a) "British Cultural Studies and Television" in Robert C. Allan (ed) *Channels of Discourse Reassembled* London: Routledge.

Fiske, John (1996/1997b) "Postmodernism and Television" in Curran, James and Gurevitch, Michael (eds.) *Mass Media and Society* London: Arnold.

Foreign Press Center (1997) *Japan's Mass Media*. No 7.

Franklin, B. (1997) *Newszak and the News Media* London: Edward Arnold.

Freud, Sigmund (1973) *Tre afhandlinger om seksualteorien*. 3rd Edition. Translated from German by Mogens Boisen. Copenhagen: Hans Reitzel

Friedman, Johathan (1994) *Cultural Identity and Global Process*. London:Sage.

Friedman, Jonathan (1999) 'The Hybridization of Roots and the Abhorrence of the Bush' In Mike Featherstone & Scott Lash. *Spaces of Culture: City, Nation, World*. London: Sage

Furo Hiroko (2002) "Frames in American and Japanese Political Discourse" in *Exploring Japaneseness: On Japanese Enactment of Culture and Consciousness*. Ray T. Donahue (ed.)

Galtung, Johan and Ruge Mari Holmboe (1965) "The structure of Foreign News" *Journal of Peace Research* 2:64-91.

Gans, Herbert J. (1979/1980) *Deciding what's news: A study of CBS Evening News, NBC Nightly News, Newsweek, and Time*. New York: Vintage Books.

Geertz, Clifford (1973) *The Interpretation of Cultures* New York: Basic Books.

Giddens, A. (1984) *The Constitution of Society: Outline of the Theory of Structuration* Cambridge: Polity Press

Giddens, A. (1987) *Social Theory and Modern Sociology*, Cambridge: Polity Press

Giddens, A. (1989) *Sociology*, Cambridge: Polity Press

Giddens, A. (1990/1991a) *The Consequences of Modernity*. Cambridge: Polity Press.

Giddens, A. (1991b) *Modernity and Self-Identity: Self and Society in the Late Modern Age*. Standford, CA: Stanford University Press.

Gieber, W. (1963 December) "I" am the news. In W. A. Danielson (Ed.), Paul J. Deutschmann memorial papers in mass communication research (pp. 9-17). Cincinnati: Scripps-Howard Research.

Gitlin, Tod (1980*)* *The Whole World is Watching: Mass media in the Making and Unmaking of the New Left*. Berkeley: University of California Press.

Glaser and Strauss (1967) *The discovery of grounded theory. Strategies for qualitative research*. New York: Aldine de Gruyter.

Golding P. (1981) "The Missing Dimensions: News Media and the Management of Social Change". In E. Katz & T. Szecskö (Eds). *Mass media and social change*. Beverly Hills, CA: Sage. P 63-82.

Golding, P. and Elliott, P. (1979) *Making the News*. London: Longman

Goffman (1974/ 1986) *Frame analysis. An Essay on the Organisation of Experience*. New York: Harper and Row.

Graber, Dorris (1984/1990) *Processing the News. How People Tame the Information Tide*. New York: Longman

Grey, D. L. (1966) "Decision-making by a reporter under deadline pressure" *Journalism Quarterly*, 43, 419-428.

Gurevitch M. *et al* (1991a) *Global News Rooms. Local Audiences. A study of the Eurovision News Exchange*. Academia Research Monograph 12. London: John Libbey

Gurevitch M., Levy, M., Roeh, I, (1991b) "The Global Newsroom: Convergences and diversities in the globalisation of television news", in P. and C. Sparks (eds*)* *Communications and Citizenship: Journalism and the Public Sphere in the New Media Age*, London: Routledge

Gudykunst W.B. (Ed.) *Communication in Japan and the United States*, Albany: State University of New York Press

Gydekunst, William B., Nishida Tsukasa (1994) *Bridging Japanese/North American differences* London:Sage

Habermas J. (1989a) *On Society and Politics*: A Reader. S. Seidman (eds.) Boston: Beacon Press.

Habermas, J. (1989b) *The structural transformation of the Public Sphere*. Cambridge: Polity Press.

Hall, Edward (1966) *The Hidden Dimension*. Garden City, N.Y.: Double Day

Hall, E. T. (1976) *Beyond Culture* New York: Doubleday

Hall, S. (1973) 'The Determination of News Photographs', in S. Cohen and J. Young (eds.) *The Manufacture of News*. Page 176-90. London: Constable

Hall, S. (1980) Encoding and Decoding the television discourse. In S. Hall et al. (eds.) *Culture, Media, Language*. London: Hutchinson

Hammersley, M. (1992) *What is wrong with ethnography?* London: Routledge.

Hammersley, M. and Atkinson, P. (1995) *Ethnography: Principles in Practice.* London: Routledge.

Hannertz, Ulf (1990/1997) "Cosmopolitans and Locals in World Culture" *Global culture: Nationalism, globalisation and modernity*. Featherstone Mike (ed.) London: Sage.

Hannerz, Ulf (1992) *Cultural Complexity. Studies in the Social Organization of Meaning*. New York: Columbia University Press.

Hannerz, Ulf (1996/1998) *Transnational Connections*. London Routledge

Harvey, D. (1989) *The Condition of Postmodernity.* Oxford: Blackwell.

Hastrup, Kirsten (1992) *Det Antropologiske projekt - om forbløffelse,* [The Anthropological Project and Astonishment]. Copenhagen: Gyldendal.

Hatch, Mary Jo and Sanford B. Erlich (1993) "Spontaneous Humour as an Indicator of Paradox and Ambiguity in Organizations" *Organisation Studies* 14/ 4: 505-526

Hattori Hiroshi, Moriguchi, Zaito Kensaku (1995) "Tokuhain ga mita nichibeihodo" [US-Japan coverage from the perspective of Foreign Correspondents] NHK Broadcasting Culture Research Institute. Broadcasts Research Report, 11

Horton, D. and Wohl R. R. (1956/1997) "Massekommunikation og parasocial interaction: Et indlæg om intimitet på afstand" in *Mediekultur*. No. 26. April.

Helland, K. (1993) *Public Service and commercial News: Contexts of Production, Genre conventions and Textual Claims in Television*, Report No. 18 Bergen, Norway: University of Bergen.

Helland, Knut (1999) "News Production Research, Textual claims and the Negative Reference System of Television News". Paper presented at the Internationa Association of Mass communication Research, Leipzig 28th of July.

Henningham, John (1979) "Kyodo gate-keepers: a study of Japanese news flow". *Gazette* 25 (1): 23-30.

Herman, E. S. and Chomsky, N. (1988) Manufacturing Consent, New York: Pantheon

Hicks, Georg (1995) *The comfort Women: Japan's Brutal Regime of Enforced Prostitution in the Second world War*, New York: W.W. Norton & Company.

Hjarvard, Stig (1994) "Intimitet, autenticitet og kvindelighed", in Dahlgren, P. (ed) *Den Maangtydiga Ruten*, Stockholm: JMK, Stockholms Universitet

Hjarvard, Stig (1995a) *Internationale TV-nyheder*, [International Broadcast News] Copenhagen: Akademisk Forlag

Hjarvard, Stig (1995b) 'TV news flow studies revisited', *Electronic Journal of Communication*, 5 (2,3): 24-38

Hjarvard, Stig (1999) *TV-nyheder i konkurrence* [Television news in Competition] Copenhagen: Samfundslitteratur

Hjarvard, Stig (2001*) News in a Globalised Society*, Göteborg: Nordicom

Hobart, Mark (2000) "The end of world news: Television and a problem of articulation in Bali" *International Journal of Cultural Studies*. Sage: Publication.

Höijer Birgitta and Anita Werner (eds.) (1998) *Cultural Cognition. New perspectives in audience theory*. Göteborg: Nordicom.

Ishida, Takeshi (1984) "conflict and Its Accomodation: *Omote-ura* and *Uchi-soto* Relation," in E. Krauss, T. P. Rohlen, and P. G. Steinhoff, eds., *Conflict in Japan*, 16-38. Honolulu: University of Hawaii Press.

Ito Youichi (1990) "Mass communication theories from a Japanese perspective" *Media, Culture and Society*. London: Sage Vol. 12.

Ito Youichi (1991) "Birth of *Johoka shakai* and *johoka* concepts in Japan and their diffusion outside Japan." *Keio Communication Review*. 13: 3-12.

Ito Youichi (1993) "Mass Communication Theory in Japan and the United States" in *Communication in Japan and the United States*. William Gudykunst (ed.) Albany, New York: State University of New York Press.

Ito Youichi (1994) "An application of the tri-polar *kuuki* model to the withdrawal of the United Nations peace cooperation bill in Japan." Paper presented to the International Association for Mass Communication Research, Seoul.

Ito, Youichi (1996a) "Determinant factors of foreign news in Japanese mass media" paper presented in to the IAMCR, Sydney.

Ito Youichi (1996b) "Influence of mass media on government's decision-making: A case study on the withdrawal of the United Nations Peace Cooperation Bill". In D.L. Paletz (Ed), *Political Communication in Action*, Cresskil, NJ: Hampton Press.

Ito Youichi (1998) "The pattern and determinant factors of international news". Paper presented to the IAMCR, Glasgow.

Ito Youichi (1999) "Theories on the Mass Media and Ethnicity: How do the Mass Media Affect Ethnicity and Related Problems?" in Goonasekera, Anura and Ito Youichi (eds.) *Mass Media and Cultural Identity: Ethnic Reporting in Asia*. London: Pluto.

Ito Youichi (2000a) "Historical Comparison of the Degrees of "Johoka" ("Informization"): Implications for Modernization" *Keio Communication Review* No 22.

Ito Youichi (forthcoming) "Globalisaiton and Western Narcissism" in *Faces of Global Communication* Naren Chitty (ed.) GPKH: India

Ito Youichi (2000b) "What Causes the Similarities and Differences among the Social Sciences in Different Cultures? Focusing on Japan and the West." *Asian Journal of Communication*, Volume 10 (2).

Iwabuchi Koichi, (1999) "Return to Asia? Japan in Asian Audio Visual Markets" in

Iwao Sumiko (1993) *The Japanese Traditional Image. Woman and changing reality*. New York: MacMillan.

Iyengar, Shanto (1991) *Is Anyone Responsible*. Chicago: The University of Chicago Press.

Jensen, Klaus Bruhn (ed.) (1986) *Making Sense of the News* Aarhus, Denmark: Aarhus University Press

Jensen, Klaus Bruhn and Jankowski N.W. (eds.) (1991) *A Handbook of Qualitative Methodologies For Mass Communication Research*. London: Routledge.

Jensen, Klaus Bruhn (ed.) (1998) *News of the World: World cultures look at television news*. London: Routledge.

Kawabata Miki (1999) "How TV News Matters?: TV news viewing and the environmental awareness in Japan". Paper presented at the Sociology and Social

Psychology section of The International Association for Media and Communication Research Conference in Leipzig, Germany, July.

Kim Young C. (1981) *Japanese Reporters and Their World.* Charlottesville: University Press of Virginia.

Kinsella, Sharon (1995) "The Cute Culture". *Women and Consumption in Japan* Moeran Brian, Skov Lise (Eds.) London: Curzon Press.

Kramer, Erik M. and Ikeda Richiko (2000) "The Changing Faces of Reality" *Keio Communication Review.* March. No 22.

Krauss, Ellis S. (1984) *Conflict in Japan* Honolulu: Hawaii University Press

Kraus, Ellis S. (1995) "Varieties of Television News Explaining Japanese and American Coverage of the Other". Reprinted from *Studies of Broadcasting* No. 31. Japan: NHK. Japan Broadcasting Corporation.

Krauss, Ellis S. (1996) *Media and Politics in Japan* with Pharr, Susan J. (eds.) Hawaii: University of Hawaii Press

Krauss, Ellis S. (2000) *Broadcasting Politics in Japan. NHK and Television News.* Ithaca and London: Cornell University Press

Kvale, Steiner (1996) *InterViews.* UK: Sage.

Lash, S and Urry, J. (1989) *The End of Organised Capitalism.* Cambridge: Polity Press

Lash, S. and Urry, J. (1994) *Economies of Signs and Space.* London: Sage

Lebra, Takie (1976) *Japanese Patterns of Behaviour.* Honolulu: University of Hawaii Press.

Lebra, Takie-Sugiyama (1993) "Culture, Self, and Communication in Japan and the United States". In Gudykunst William B. (ed.), *Communication in Japan and the United States.* Albany, NY: State University of New York Press: 51-87

Lewin, Kurt (1947) Frontiers in Group Dynamics II: Channels of Group Life; Social Planning and Action Research. *Human Relations*, Vol. 1, No. 2, p. 145.

Lippmann, W. (1922) *Public Opinion* NewYork: McMillan.

Lull, J. (ed.) (1988) *World Families Watch Television*, California: Sage Publications.

Maaløe, Erik Case-Studier. (1996) *Af og om Mennesker i Organisationer.* Copenhagen: Akademisk Forlag

MacDonald Keith M. (1995) *The Sociology of Professions* London: Sage.

Malik (1992) 'The global news agenda' *Intermedia* 20 (1).

Markova I. E. and Foppa K. (eds.) *The Dynamics of Dialogue*, New York: Harvester Wheatsheaf.

Martin, Joanne; Martha . S, Feldman, Mary Jo Hatch, and Sim B. Sitkin (1983) "The Uniqueness Paradox in Organizational Stories" *Administrative Science Quarterly*, 28. P. 438-453

Maslow, Abraham (1962) *Towards a Psychology of Being*, D. Van Nostrand

Matsuyama Yukio (1993) "Mass Media and Democracy" Paper presented at Hjarvard Business School. March 30th.

Masterman, L. (1985) *Teaching the Media* London: Comedia.

Mattelart, Armand (1994) *Mapping World Communication* Minneapolis: University of Minnesota.

Maula, Marjatta (2000) Three parallel Knowledge Processes *Knowledge and Process Management.* Volume 7. Number 1. Pp 55-59

McLuhan, M. (1960) *Understanding Media: The Extensions of Man*, New York: McGraw-Hill.

McQuail, D. (1983/1992) *Mass Communication Theory: An Introduction* 2.ed. London: Sage

Mead, G. H. (1934) Mind. Self, and Society. Chicago: University of Chicago Press

Meirowitz, J. (1985) No *Sense of Place. The impact of electronic Media on Social Behavior* New York: Oxford University Press

Miller, Jay K. (1994) "Broadcast News in Japan. NHK and NTV" *Keio Communication Review* No 16: 77-105

Mintzberg, Henry (1987) "The strategy concept I: Five p's for strategy" *Management Review*, Berkeley. Fall 1987; Vol. 30.

Mizuno Setsuo (1997) "On some Characteristics of Contemporary Japanese Society". In Anselm Strauss and Juliet Corbin. *Grounded theory in Practice*, London: Sage

Moeran, Brian (1996) *A Japanese Advertising Agency*, Curzon Press: UK

Moeran, Brian (1999) "Hierarchies, Networks, Markets and Frames: Reconsidering Japanese social Organisations". Unpublished paper presented at the Department for Intercultural Communication and Management, Copenhagen Business School.

Morley, David (1980) *The 'Nationwide' Audience*, London: British film Institute

Morley, David (1986) *Family Television: Cultural Power and Domestic Leisure*, London: Comedia

Mouer, Ross and Sugimoto Yoshio (1986) *Images of Japanese Society: a study in the social construction of reality*, London and New York: Kegan Paul International.

Nakane Chie (1970/1994 ninth edition) *Japanese Society* Japan: Charles E. Tuttle

Nakane Chie (1972) *Human Relations in Japan* Tokyo: Ministry of Foreign Affairs

Nathan, J. (1999) Sony. The private life. London: HarperCollins (p.xiii)

Neuman, R.W. , Just M.R. & Crigler, A.N. (1992) *Common Knowledge, News and the Construction of Political Meaning*. Chicago: The University of Chicago Press.

Nishida Kitaro (1990) An inquiry into the good, trans. M Abe and C. Ives, 1921. Reprint. New Haven, Conn.: Yale University Press

Nishida Kitaro (1970) *Fundamental problems of philosophy*. The world of action and the dialectical world. Tokyo: Sophia University

Noelle, Neumann, Elisabeth (1984) *The Spiral of Silence: Public Opinion – Our Social Skin*. Chicago: University of Chicago Press.

Nonaka Ikujiro (1995) "Managing innovation as an organizational knowledge creation process". Technology Management and Corporate Strategies: 73-109.

Nonaka Ikujiro and Takeuchi H. (1995) *The Knowledge-Creating company: How Japanese Companies Create the Dynamics of Innovation*. Oxford: Oxford University Press

Nonaka Ikujiro and Konno Noboru (1998) "The concept of "Ba" Building a Foundation for Knowledge Creation" *California Management Review* vol. 40. No 3. Spring.

Nordenstreng, K. with Sreberny-Mohammadi, A. Stevenson, R. and Ugboajah F. (eds.) (1985) *Foreign News in the Media: International Reporting in 29 Countries*, Paris: UNESCO.

Ogasawara, Yoko (1998) *Office Ladies and Salaried Men: Power, Gender, and Work in Japanese companies*. Berkeley: University of California Press

Ohnuki-Tierney, Emiko (1984) *Illness and Culture in Contemporary Japan: An Anthropological View*. Cambridge: Cambridge University Press

Parker, R. (1994) 'The Myth of Global News.' New Perspectives Quarterly 11, 39-45

Paterson, Christopher (1998) *Global Battlefields* in Oliver Boyed-Barett and Terhi Rantanen (eds.) The Globalisation of News. London: Sage

Paterson, Christopher (1996) New Production at Worldwide Television News (WTN): An analysis of Television News Agency coverage of Developing Countries, PH.D. Dissertation

Pharr, Susan (1996) *Media and Politics in Japan* with Krauss, S. Ellis (eds.) Hawaii: University of Hawaii Press

Phillipson, Robert (1992) *Linguistic Imperialism.* London: Oxford University Press

Piaget, J. (1960) The psychology of intelligence. Totowa, N.J.: Littlefield, Adams, & CO.

Pittelkow, R (1985), "Seernes TV-Avis" *in Antologi til undervisning i billedanalyse og audiovisuel kommunikation* bind 6, Copenhagen University, Department of Film and media studies. (1991)

Polanyi, M. (1966) *The Tacit Dimension.* London: Routledge and Kegan Paul

Postman (1985, 1987) *Amusing ourselves to death* London: Methuen

Potter Jonathan and Wetherell Margaret (1987) *Discourse and Social Psychology: Beyond attitudes and behaviour* London: Sage

Prime Minister's Office Japan (1995) "Japanese Women Today." Report.

Prime Minister's Office Japan (1997) "The present Status of Gender Equality and Measure." Report on the Plan for Gender Equality 2.000 (The first revision) June

Putnis, Peter: (1999) "A quantitative analysis of the Australian coverage of the French Nuclear Tests in Mururoa". Paper presented at the International Association for Mass Communication Research (IAMCR) at the Annual Conference in Leipzig, Germany, July 27-31, 1999.

Reed, Steven (1993) *Making Common Sense of Japan* Pittsburgh: University of Pittsburgh Press,

Renshaw, Jean R. (1999) *Kimono in the Boardroom: the Invisible Revolution of Japanese Women* Oxford University Press, Inc.

Robertson, Roland (1992) *Globalisation, Social Theory and Global Culture.* London: Sage

Rohlen, Thomas P. (1983) *Japan's High Schools,* Stanford: Stanford University Press

Ryle, G. (1949) *The Concept of Mind* London: Hutchinson

Said, Edward (1978) *Orientalism: Western conceptions of the Orient* Harmondsworth: Penguin

Schlesinger, P. (1978) *Putting Reality Together*. London: Methuen.

Schudson, Michael (1996/1997) "The sociology of news production revisited". In J. Curran & M. Gurevitch (Eds.), *Mass media and Society*. London: Edward Arnold. P. 141-159.

Schutz, Alfred (1962) "Symbol, reality, and society", *Collected papers* 1, The Hague: Martinus Nijhoff

Schutz, A. (1970) On Phenomenology and Social Relations. Chicago: University of Chicago Press

Schaberg, Linda (forthcoming) *Gender role expectations, dissent and perceptions of feminism: A study of multiple cultures and generations*. Doctoral Dissertation. University of Michigan. Department of Social Phychology.

Shiramizu Shigeko (1987) Nichibei Terebi Nyusu Hikaku Kenkyu [A contemporary Study of Television News] Takachiho Ronso, 62 (1):215-29

Shoemaker, Pamela J. (1991) *Gatekeeping*. Communication Concepts 3. Newbury Park: Sage

Shoemaker, Pamela. and Reese, S (1996*) Mediating the message: Theories of Influence on Mass Media Content*, New York: Longman

Shore, Brad (1998) "Models theory as a Framework for media Studies" in *Cultural Cognition*. Birgitta Höijer and Anita Werner (eds.) Göteborg: Nordicom

Shunji Mikami (1994), *The Role of Mass Media in the 1993 National election in Japan* Tokyo: Toyo Daigaku Shakaibu

Signal, L. V. (1973) *Reporters and officials: The organization and politics of news-making*. Lexington, MA: D.C. Heath

Silverman, David (1993) *Interpreting QualitativeData* Thousand Oaks, CA.: Sage

Soloski, J. (1989) "News reporting and professionalism: some constraints on the reporting of news". *Media, Culture and Society*. 11: 207-228

Spradley, James P. (1979) *The Ethnographic Interview* New York: Holt Rinehart Winson

Sreberny-Mohammadi, A., K. Nordenstreng, R. Stevenson, and F. Ugboajah (eds.) (1985) *Foreign News in the Media: International Reporting in 29 countries*, Paris: UNESCO

Sreberny-Mohammadi, Annabelle (1996) "The global and the local in International Communications " in *Mass Media and Society*. Curran J. and Gurevitch M. (eds). London: Arnold

Stempel, G.H. III (1962) "Content patterns of small and metropolitan dailies" *Journalism Quarterly*. 39, 88-91

Stevenson, Robert (1995) Project Proposal. Corporate Study of Foreign News and International News Flow in the 1990s. Http//sunsite.unc.edu/newsflow/

Surlin, Stuart H., Romanow, Walter I. and Sonderlund Walter, C. (1988) "TV Network News: A Canadian-American Comparison" *American Review of Canadian Studies* 18 (4): 465-475.
Takeshi Tamiya (1990) *Telebi Hosoo o Kangaeru* [Considerations about Television Broadcasting] Kyoto: Mineruvia

Tanaka Junko (1995) "Joseikaigihodonogenbakara" [From the reporting on location at the Women's Conference] The fourth UN Conference on Women. NGO Forum (7) Second Special Edition. NHK annual Reports.

The Beijing Platform: UN Women's Conference press releases: www: arcc.or.ke/gln./platform.html

Thompson, John B. (1990) *Ideology and Modern Culture* Cambridge: Polity Press.

Thompson, John B. (1995) *The Media and Modernity. A Social Theory of the Media*. Cambridge: Polity Press.

Tomlinson, J. (1991) *Cultural Imperialism – A critical Introduction*, London: Pinter.

Tomlinson, J. (1994) "A Phenomenology of Globalisation? Giddens on global Modernity" *European Journal of Communication*) (2): 149-72

Tokyo Women's Foundation (1995) "Research on the Formation of Political and Social Awareness in Women". Tokyo.

Tuchman, G. (1972) "Objectivity as strategic ritual: an examination of newsmen's notions of objectivity" *American Journal of Sociology*. No 77: 660-679.

Tuchman, G. (1973) "Making news by doing work: Routinising the unexpected" *American Journal of sociology*, 79 (1):110-31.

Tuchman, G. (1974) *Making News: The social construction of reality*. New York: Free Press

Tuchman, Gaye (1976) "Telling Stories" *Journal of Communication* 26, Fall: 93-7.

Tuchman. G (1978) *Making news: A study in the Social Construction of Reality*. New York: Free Press.

Tuchman, G., Kaplan Daniels A. and Benèt J. (1978) Hearth and Home: Images of Women in the Mass Media. New York: Oxford University Press

Tuchman, Gaye (1991) "Qualitative methods in the study of news" in *A Handbook of Qualitative Methodologies For Mass Communication Research*. Klaus Bruhn Jensen and N.W. Jankowski (eds.) London: Routledge.

Tveiten, O. (1993) *Just say no – Ideology and Opinion in the news: A case analysis of US media coverage of the General Elections in Nicaragua,* (1990) P.H.D. thesis. University of Minnesota.

United Nations. Commission on Human Rights. Fifty-first session . Agenda item 11. (E/CN.41995/42)

UN Press Release (1995) Prepared at the Fourth World Conference on Women by the United Nations Development Program. Statement by H.C. M. Koken Nosaka. Head of delegation of the Government of Japan at the fourth world conference on women. Equality, Development and Peace, 5. Sept.

Van Dijk T.A (1977) Text and Context: *Explorations in the Semantics and Pragmatics of Discourse*. London: Longman

Van Dijk T.A (1980) *Macrostructures: an Interdisciplinary Study of Global structures in Discourse, Interaction, and Cognition* Hillsdale, NJ: Erlbaum.

Van Dijk, T.A (1988) *News as Discourse* Hillsdale, NJ: Erlbaum

Van Dijk T.A. (1991) "News as discourse" Jensen, Klaus Bruhn and Jankowski, Nicholas W. (eds.) *A Handbook of Qualitative Methodologies for Mass Communication Research* London: Routledge

Van Wolferen, Karel (1991, 1993) *The Enigma of Japanese Power: people and politics in a stateless nation,* London: MacMillan

Varela, F.J., Thompson, E. and Rosch, E., (1991) Embodied mind: Cognitive Science and Human Experience, Cambridge, MA: MIT Press

Volkmer, (1999) *CNN News in the Global Sphere. A study of CNN and its Impact on Global Communication*. Bedfordshire: University of Luton Press.

Von Krogh, Georg, Katsuo Ichijo, Nonaka Ikujiro (2000) *Enabling Knowledge Creation. How to unlock the Mystery of Tacit Knowledge and Release the Power of Innovation.* Oxford: Oxford University Press

Wagatsuma Hiroshi (1984) "Some Cultural Assumptions among the Japanese" *Japanese Quarterly*, 31: 371-379

Warner, M. (1971) "Organisational context and control of policy in the television newsroom: a participant observation study" *British Journal of Sociology*, 22:283-94

Waters, Malcolm (1995) *Globalisation* London: Routledge

Westney, D. Eleanor, D. (1996) "Mass Media as Business Organizations: A U.S.-Japanese Comparison" in Krauss, S. Ellis, Susan J. Pharr (eds.) *Media and Politics in Japan* Hawaii: University of Hawaii Press.

Westney, D. Eleanor (1987) *Imitation and innovation: The transfer of Western Organisation Patterns to Meiji Japan*. Cambridge: Harvard University Press.

White, D. M. (1950) "'The Gate keeper': A case study in the selection of news" *Journalism Quarterly* 27, 383-390.

Whitney, D. C. (1981) "Information overload in the newsroom" *Journalism Quarterly*, 58, 69-76

Wilkens, Lesley (1981) "The process of selection" in *The manufacture of news* Stanley. Cohen and Jock Young (Eds). Sage Publications, Constable London.

Yin, Robert (1992) *Case Study Research, Design and Methods* London: Sage.

Yoshino Kosaku (1992) Cultural Nationalism in Contemporary Japan – a Sociological Enquiry. Routledge, London.

Yoshino Kosaku (1999) *Consuming Ethnicity and Nationalism: Asian Experiences* Richmond: Curzon